Stella Benson

Stella Benson

a biography

Joy Grant

MACMILLAN LONDON

First published 1987 by
MACMILLAN LONDON LIMITED
4 Little Essex Street London WC2R 3LF
and Basingstoke

Associated companies in Auckland, Delhi, Dublin, Gaborone,
Hamburg, Harare, Hong Kong, Johannesburg, Kuala Lumpur,
Lagos, Manzini, Melbourne, Mexico City, Nairobi, New York,
Singapore and Tokyo

British Library Cataloguing in Publication Data

Grant, Joy
Stella Benson: a biography.
1. Benson, Stella – Biography 2. Novelists,
English – 20th century – Biography
823'.912 PR6003.E72Z/
ISBN 0-333-39317-1

Filmset in Linotron Aldus by
Rowland Phototypesetting Limited
Bury St Edmunds, Suffolk
Made and printed in Great Britain by
Adlard & Son Ltd The Garden City Press,
Letchworth, Herts. SG6 1JS

For Lucy

Contents

List of Illustrations

Acknowledgements

I wish in the first place to thank the Syndics of the University of Cambridge Library for allowing me unrestricted use of the Diary of Stella Benson, of which they own the copyright.

A number of individuals have been kind enough to help me in different ways. I should like to mention in particular Mrs Georgina Berkeley, Stella Benson's niece and literary executor, who, along with other valuable assistance, allowed me to quote from Stella Benson's letters; Mr Riou Benson, Stella Benson's nephew, who gave me much valuable information, lent me letters and photographs in his possession and gave permission to reproduce the painting of Stella by Cuthbert Orde; Mrs Veronica Anderson, who allowed me to use photographs in her possession and gave me information about her late husband external to the diaries; Mrs Ann Watson, who gave me information about Laura Hutton and permission to reproduce the photograph of Laura; the late Lord David Cecil; Mr Cecil Clarabut; Mrs E. E. Duncan-Jones; Mr Roger Florio; Mrs Victoria Ginger; Professor H. J. Lethbridge; Mr Michael Luke; Mr John Mercer; Miss Naomi Mitchison; Mr John Monckton; Mr Nigel Nicolson; Mrs Patricia Pitman and Professor Kathleen Tillotson. Lord Stockton generously shared with me his memories of Stella Benson the Macmillan author.

I am grateful to the staffs of the following libraries for access to material in their possession and for their assistance: Cambridge University Library, and in particular Mr A. E. B. Owen, Keeper of Manuscripts, and his staff; the British Library and the Colindale Newspaper Library; the University of London Library; the Fawcett Library; the Imperial War Museum Library; the University of Sussex Library; the Berg Collection, New York Public Library; the Humanities Research Center, the University of Texas at Austin.

For permission to quote from unpublished letters of Virginia Woolf I am indebted to the Author's Estate, and for extracts from her published letters and diaries to them and the Hogarth Press; for 'Stella Benson' by Naomi Mitchison, to the author and Jonathan Cape, and for an extract from the same author's *You May Well Ask*, to her and Victor Gollancz; for a passage from A. S. Jasper's *A Hoxton Childhood* to the Author's Estate and Centerprise Publications; for a letter from Rebecca West to the Author's Estate and A. D. Peters; for a letter from James Anderson to Veronica Anderson and Chatto & Windus.

The drawing of Stella Benson by Wyndham Lewis, copyright © the Estate of Mrs G. A. Wyndham Lewis, is reproduced by kind permission of the Estate and the National Portrait Gallery. I am grateful to the *Illustrated London News* Picture Library for permission to reproduce the photograph of Cuthbert and Lady Eileen Orde.

My editors at Macmillan, and especially Brenda Stephenson who saw the book through the press, have given me valuable support and guidance.

Last but by no means least, I am deeply grateful to Elizabeth Ziman for reading the typescript at various stages on its road to completion and passing encouraging interim verdicts upon it.

Stella was quite happy about her writing, was sure of herself there, and had no thought of not being sufficiently appreciated. Her only real grievance was her health, which made so many things she wanted to do an exhausting effort. But she could never resist making the effort. I expect she was a remarkable writer, but I am certain she was a remarkable woman. Such wonderful courage and honesty. . . . I think she counted on her diary enormously as a friend and as a way to a little fame. (*J. C. O'G. Anderson, Stella Benson's husband, shortly after her death, to Marie Belloc Lowndes*)

Preface

I was walking through Leicester Squre – how far from China – just now when I read 'Death of Noted Novelist' on the poster [Virginia Woolf wrote in her diary on 7 December 1933]. And I thought of Hugh Walpole. But it is Stella Benson. . . . How mournful the afternoon seems. . . . A very fine steady mind: much suffering; suppressed. . . . A curious feeling: when a writer like S.B. dies, that one's response is diminished; Here and Now won't be lit up by her: it's life lessened.[1]

Virginia Woolf knew Stella Benson, had entertained her in her home, corresponded with her in China, hoped to know her better on her return: hers was a personal sense of loss. It was shared, however, by thousands who had not met her, readers of the serious novel to whom Stella Benson's voice was among the most interesting of their time, a highly idiosyncratic voice, odd even, yet with a tortured modernity that spoke directly to them.

Since 1915 she had published seven novels. All were well received, and the last, *Tobit Transplanted*, had met with notable success: it won the French *Fémina–Vie Heureuse* prize, brought its author the A. C. Benson silver medal of the Royal Society of Literature, and was chosen book of the month by the English Book Society. 'I'll think about jealousy,' Virginia Woolf had responded with an exemplary show of meekness when Ethel Smyth wrote rebuking her for not having read the novel of the moment.[2] In 1935 an unfinished Benson novel appeared to good reviews, and in 1939 came *Portrait of Stella Benson* a biography-cum-memoir by R. Ellis Roberts, a literary journalist who was one of her friends. The book was over-laudatory, almost fulsome, and prompted a critic in that captious organ *Scrutiny* to exclaim in wonder at how the literary pundits of the 1920s and 1930s had accepted Stella Benson as 'an accomplished artist' and 'an author of major contemporary importance'.[3]

Literary reputations stand on slippery ground: Stella's scarcely survived the changes in style and taste that accompanied the Second World War.

Now, some fifty years after her death, it is rare indeed to meet anyone under the age of seventy-five who has so much as heard of, let alone read, this 'author of major contemporary importance'. She still has champions, to be sure, but they date from her own time and are necessarily a dwindling breed. Some have spoken up loyally for her in print. When Naomi Mitchison and Steven Runciman, both octogenarians who had read her in their youth, were asked in 1985 to name some unjustly neglected fiction, they mentioned books of hers with praise,[4] and a comparative youngster, D. J. Enright, who was only thirteen when Stella died, named *Tobit Transplanted* in a similar survey.[5]

That was in fact the survey which drew attention to Barbara Pym's work after years of neglect, and won her a second wave of devotees. No such miracle of rediscovery has yet occurred in Stella Benson's case. But for her it was perhaps not so urgently necessary: she had a pot of treasure hidden away, which time would reveal. From childhood she had kept, and carefully preserved, a diary. She told her friends (tantalisingly, for they were not allowed to see it) that it was possibly of greater value than all her published work put together. How to bestow it after her death was the problem, a problem resolved when, at the age of thirty-two, she met the Cambridge biologist J. B. S. Haldane, Naomi Mitchison's brother: he suggested that his university would be a suitable depository, and that a fifty-years embargo should be placed up its opening. At first she hesitated – Cambridge seemed altogether too august and learned a location for her 'day-to-day jottings'. Haldane, she feared, was under the impression that the diary was 'an everyday story' of the times in which she had lived:

> But it isn't such a story at all – to begin with it isn't a writer's diary at all – nothing of my professional writing seems to belong to the Stella Benson who writes this diary at all. And there is no real story of the times – nothing special about the war and no echo of the political thunders that have raged all through my lifetime. . . . It seems a little doubtful whether the gropings of this desperate me would be of real interest to Cambridge University as the ages roll on.

But after all there was a certain rightness in their going to Cambridge, for in Magdalene College was housed the diary of her remote collateral ancestor Samuel Pepys; she could think of nowhere more suitable for her own diary, and so it was arranged. Accordingly, while half a century ticked away, the diary reposed, unknown to all but a very few, in a black enamelled tin box in the University Library awaiting the day, 6 December 1983, when it might be exposed to the public gaze.

The volumes are in fine condition, and they are a joy to read. Stella Benson wrote a delightfully clear. free-flowing hand, and wielded her pencil with a sort of prescient courtesy, as though she had in mind the comfort and convenience of a future reader: there are very few squashed or squeezed words, or words carelessly corrected, or ugly abbreviations. Her biographer has every reason to feel grateful for this.

The diaries run, with a gap of one year only, from the year she was ten to the year she died, thirty-one years and forty volumes in all (sometimes a twelvemonth occupies two books). Until 1918 she used printed diaries of the kind one buys at the stationer's; afterwards she opted for lined exercise books which imposed no restriction on the amount she could write each day. Between pages she kept memorabilia of all kinds, letters, photographs, theatre programmes, dinner menus, dance cards, newspaper cuttings, flowers – the poignant and evocative rubbish of a lifetime. Someone – her widower probably – placed between the two final pages a lock of her hair.

If the diary is neither a writer's journal nor a record of its time, what then is it? On the day in 1925 that she discussed its future with Haldane, Stella asked herself that question, and came up with a rather dusty answer:

What have these twenty years of everyday scribbling set down? Nothing at all of any interest to outsiders – simply because my diary is exclusively a self-encouragement. To set down a record of my contact with people – disastrous or happy contact – is most necessary to me. Because my most continuous sensation is a feeling of terrifying slipping-away from people – a most devastating loneliness – I have to place on record the fact that I was human and that *even I* had my human adventures.

Stella was never quite convinced that what flowed in her veins was warm red blood, and not some thinner, colder fluid, some tasteless ichor which signified that she was not in fact human, but a 'fairy', a 'snake-soul'. More particularly, she grew up feeling somehow less than a woman, different *in kind* from the cheerful, accepting, nubile throng of middle-class English females whom she labelled 'oh my dear girls', or – more significantly – 'real girls'. It was not for nothing, she was certain, that people likened her to Peter Pan!

Her mind was sceptical, questioning, her imagination active and vivid to a degree; shut away in sickrooms a great deal in her early years, she had too much leisure to think and to imagine. Partial deafness sharpened her eyesight, and she grew into an acute observer, of people as well as of places and things. People were to her rather like onions. She was impatient of their concealing skins and, when the skin was off, impatient of each transparent layer beneath: she wanted to get through them all to some quintessence of personality lodged in the very centre. She was just as impatient with her own make-up, with the poses, vanities, subterfuges, delusions that stood between herself and other people, between herself and herself. The central character in her novels is often someone, like herself, wavering between that which they are, that which they aspire to be, that which they think they are, that which the presence of others makes them (and each person affects them in a different way). From the frustrations and perplexities of human relationships she turned with relief to animals, and especially to her favourites, dogs. To watch a dog, totally absorbed in its simple animal consciousness, getting on with its own thing in its frank and free way, blessedly without *self*-consciousness, gave her true joy.

Like many of her Victorian–Edwardian generation she came to reject Christianity; indeed she rejected all religion, evolving over the years a private faith in the sacredness of the individual: every individual, whether man, woman, dog or caterpillar, had the right to live freely according to its lights (with the difficult proviso, of course, that it did not intrude upon the rights of others). To violate or tamper with another creature's integrity was the only sin. It was a belief which grew naturally out of her deep, desolate sense of the separateness, the loneliness of all sentient beings.

But – and this is only one of the paradoxes of Stella's complicated character – she was far from being a nature-loving solitary. While she found it extremely painful, it is true to say that she was mesmerised by human society. A great part of her life was spent in places where people make it their business to be sociable – in hotels, on board ship, among groups of expatriates in out-of-the-way corners of the globe – and more often than not Stella was to be found in the thick of the company, talking quietly but with wit, and with intense engagement if that was at all possible, or singing to her guitar, dancing, playing silly games. She met innumerable people, and large numbers of them make their appearance in her diary. She became expert at the verbal thumbnail sketch – honest in intent, if hasty – which strips a layer or two off the onion of personality.

Basing a biography upon a diary, I have learned, is like trying to sail a course in a cockleshell across a wild and stormy sea: there is altogether too much water, and it seems to be going in every direction at once. The best that the poor mariner–biographer can hope to do is hang on and pray that the tide will bring her in.

Being a day-by-day record of events, non-events, moods and opinions, a diary is full of inconsistencies. It is full of contradictions. A day's entry, one might say (borrowing a phrase), is less 'a day in the life' than 'a life in a day'. James Lees-Milne, in editing his own diary, has wittily pointed this out. On Sunday, he says, the diarist may be 'wildly in love with life, and on Monday he may be suicidal. On Tuesday he may go to three cocktail parties, and on Wednesday prepare to enter a Trappist monastery. On Thursday he may adore someone whom on Friday he may abhor. On Saturday morning he may rob a church box, and the same evening give the proceeds to his favourite charity.'[6] With her acute, twentieth-century awareness of the fluidity of life and consciousness, Stella would have readily agreed.

In addition to the diaries, I have read a large number of Stella Benson's letters. There again, a fascinating aspect is the variation in her tone when addressing different correspondents: guarded to a mother, butter-wouldn't-melt-in-the-mouth to an aunt, frank – more or less – to an intimate friend, passionate, demanding, in a letter – not sent – to a lover.

All that said, one has to confess that a sense of personality, strong, living, growing, continuous, emerges from these two or three million written words. In her later years Stella spoke and wrote of the inalienable essence of a person, their 'me-ness', the intrinsic something with which, 'while this muddy vesture of decay doth grossly close it in', we can scarcely hope to make contact, as 'bone'. Where from the shifting evidence of her diaries and letters I have misjudged, misrepresented or even – though I sincerely hope I have not – traduced Stella, may her 'bone' forgive me.

One last word. With respect to individuals, whether famous or unknown, whom Stella met or who played a part in her life, the diaries speak for themselves. I have not modified or attempted to verify or correct the picture she gives.

Joy Grant
Thames Ditton
September 1986

Part I

The Sick Child

Chapter One

Stella Benson was born at 2.20 a.m. on 6 January 1892 at Lutwyche Hall, a mansion built in Elizabethan times on the south slope of Wenlock Edge in south Shropshire. She joined a nursery population consisting of George Reginald, the Bensons' son and heir, who was almost four, and Catherine Maia, not yet two (four years later appeared a second son Stephen). She arrived on Epiphany, and her parents had the happy idea of commemorating the fact by bestowing on her the Christian name, then fashionable, that means a star.

Almost certainly she made her first appearance in her mother's bedroom, one of the large south-facing rooms that enjoy fine views over the gardens and park and on towards a broad stretch of undulating countryside, streaked with dark woodland and patched with red-brown soil. Nearly all this land, and most of the nearby village of Easthope, belonged to Stella's father and formed a small part of a large estate built up during the nineteenth century by five successive generations of Bensons. In Victorian England nothing short of ancient lineage was so likely to gain for a family the acceptance in county society that the Bensons sought. For a certain taint attached to the Benson wealth of which some of its beneficiaries, and Stella's father in particular, were uncomfortably aware. Moses Benson, 1738–1806, the founder of the fortune, had been a man of larger ambition than his forebears, who were Lancashire 'statesmen', plain freehold farmers. Early in life he sailed to the West Indies, where he acquired highly profitable slave plantations and rose to be Justice of the Peace and Colonel of Militia. Among the handful of dry facts ascertainable about Moses are a couple that seem to draw him closer as a human being: the name of his Jamaican residence, Harmony Hall, implying as it does a certain robust whimsicality of mind; and the personal coat of arms he assumed which, with its elaborate set of allusions (perhaps not in the best of armorial taste) to his career and achievements, seems to betoken the same merry bent – 'argent, a ship in full sail, Union ensign flying, all proper; and, on a chief wavy, azure, a military officer's dexter hand, holding a sword erect, argent, hilt or, bearing the Scales of Justice, between two pineapples erect of the second, leaved, vert'. Returning in middle age to Liverpool with his pile, he set up in business very prosperously as a ship owner and slave trader, rose to prominence among the rich merchants of the city, bought a grand house, and founded a school for the poor. In 1806, planning to end his days as a country gentleman, he bought Lutwyche, but died before living in the house, which passed to his heir.

His son, Ralph Benson, 1773–1845, followed a course not infrequently taken by the children of the *nouveaux riches*: he bought his way into high society. Known with startling directness simply as 'Wicked' Benson, he was a friend of the Prince of Wales (later George IV), generous enough, the tale went, to share with Prinny the favours of his wife, the former Barbara Lewin of County Mayo, leaving subsequent Bensons in tantalising uncertainty whether or not rogue royal blood flowed in their veins. He took his London morals back with him to the provinces, being sued by a neighbour for 'criminal conversation' (adultery) with his wife, the plaintiff alleging in addition that the shock of his wife's misconduct had sent him out of his mind. *Parr* v. *Benson*, tried in the King's Bench Division before the Lord Chief Justice, was a *cause célèbre* in 1808. Evidence of the juiciest kind was adduced on both sides, but Ralph Benson, while admitting adultery, was able to show that the husband had acted the complaisant cuckold throughout and that his mad fits predated his wife's infidelity. Instead of the immense damages hoped for – £33,000 – the plaintiff was awarded a mere £1000. Even when he was long under ground, Wicked was up to no good: during the Second World War the nuns of the Sacred Heart used Lutwyche as a boarding school, choosing as their chapel the room in which his portrait hung; on feast days, at a particular point in the mass, the cloth which covered the painting invariably fell down to reveal Wicked's surprisingly harmless-looking face.

The next two generations set out to achieve what the earlier had lacked, respectability. Moses George, son of Wicked, was MP for Stafford, Justice of the Peace and Deputy Lieutenant of Shropshire. He made extensive alterations to Lutwyche parish church, no doubt simultaneously dipping deep into his pocket; he it was who ordered fashionable improvements to Lutwyche ('a Victorian–Jacobean trim of a nature to outdo all the old Elizabethan work', remarks Nikolaus Pevsner tartly)[1] completed by his son Ralph, 1828–86, who was a barrister-at-law and Recorder of Shrewsbury. Ralph's wife, Henrietta Cockerell, added a few illustrious drops to the family blood: she was descended from Samuel Pepys's nephew and heir John Jackson – as a diarist herself, Stella cherished the connection. The couple had five children, and the eldest, Ralph Beaumont Benson, born in 1862, was Stella's father.

By the standards of the ancient landed families of England, who could trace their line back to the Conquest and beyond – families like the Cholmondeleys to which Stella's mother belonged – the Bensons had no ancestry worth mentioning. They were *arrivistes* whose not distant past was darkened by the shadow of trade – while if there was anything discreditable in the way the Cholmondeleys had acquired land and fortune it was safely hidden in the mists of time. In its more illustrious ramifications the family boasted marquesses and earls; Stella's mother belonged to the Condover branch which had owned lands on the Welsh borders for centuries, and from which sprang the Barons Delamere. However, the proud name descended to her via younger sons who, while they had the breeding, lacked the fortune to match it. Her father, the Reverend Richard Hugh Cholmondeley, like his father and grandfather before him, was Rector of Hodnet in north Shropshire.

Caroline Essex Cholmondeley (known as 'Essex', a name traditional in the family for girls), Stella's mother, was one of a brood of eight, three boys and five girls. The former went away to school, the latter stayed at home, picking up what knowledge they could from governesses; Stella wrote of her mother's having 'little education'. Two of the girls were literary. The youngest, Hester (who died at twenty-two in 1892, the year Stella was born), was a compulsive writer, leaving a 222,000 word diary commenced at eighteen, stories and essays galore, and a biographical survey (incomplete) of the 'Great Names' of the nineteenth century. She was no mere flaccid, young-ladyish scribbler, as is proved by a scrap of her verse that survives. It was used by her sister Mary to head a chapter in one of her novels, *Diana Tempest*, and thereafter, according to Mary, was 'frequently quoted in religious works':[2]

> Still as of old
> Man by himself is priced;
> For thirty pieces Judas sold
> Himself, not Christ.

Perhaps Hester inherited her gift for religious verse from Bishop Reginald Heber of Calcutta, the famous hymn-writer, a great-uncle on her father's side.

Hester was a pious girl, as were all the sisters, more or less. However, Mary Cholmondeley, the eldest, caused quite a flutter at the turn of the century with a novel, *Red Pottage*, containing a satirical sketch of a parish clergyman which some thought rather *risqué*, coming from the pen of a rector's daughter; it included, moreover, a spirited attack on *nouveau riche* vulgarity that was considered faintly unbecoming in a lady who was herself of irreproachable breeding. In 1899 it was the book of the moment, with waggish novel-readers enquiring of each other *ad nauseam*: 'Have you read pottage?' Between 1887 and 1921 Mary Cholmondeley published eleven novels, of which *Red Pottage* enjoyed the greatest popular success. All are characterised by a sharpness of moral perception and a causticity of tone that raise them above the mass of novels of the time.

On her father's death in 1910, Mary moved with her younger sister Victoria (Stella's 'Aunt V') to 2 Leonard Place, an early Victorian terrace (since demolished) opposite Holland Park and forming part of Kensington High Street, and there reigned over a discreet little literary coterie.

Aunt Mary was a major force in the family. To her nephews and nieces she set a formidable example of aristocratic dignity and superior moral tone; what was more, she took a keen interest in their development. Loving nothing more than a cosy feminine chat on a serious, searching level, she was adept at drawing Stella out – in order to administer sound advice at the close – and by the time her niece was in her teens she had learned to be on her guard against Aunt Mary's blandishments.

As soon as she was old enough to be aware of such things, Stella realised that she was the fruit of a union between very disparate families. In her mind, Cholmondeleys came to stand for tradition, acceptance of responsibility, dutifulness, prudence; no Cholmondeley, the joke had it, ever took a step in life, even a small one, without endless 'plans and messages' flying back and forth between family members. By contrast, Bensons were pragmatic, impulsive, 'egotistical', 'coldhearted' (both Stella's words); some of them had brilliance, but not always, alas, the good gifts of industry and application that are needed to make the best of it. They tended to eccentricity – a present-day Benson says (with a strong hint of pride) 'Bensons are all mad!' When Stella acted on impulse, one might say, she was a Benson; when she abode by the consequences, she was a Cholmondeley. She respected Cholmondeleys, as none could fail to do, but she found the atmosphere they created oppressive. She identified far more closely with Bensons: they were not, of course, so utterly worthy, but that – as she recognised – was partly why she preferred their society.

Moving as they did in the same county circles, it was inevitable that Ralph Benson and Essex Cholmondeley should meet, but Shropshire may well have raised an eyebrow when in 1886 they wed. Heir to the Benson property, good-looking, clever (a product of Harrow School, he went to Balliol College, Oxford, on an open scholarship) – at twenty-four Ralph Benson was a very good catch. Essex, on the other hand, though at twenty-five a pleasing-looking, amiable girl enough and with a lively turn of wit, had no claim to distinction but her name.

Essex was in love when she married, and perhaps in the early days she enjoyed some happiness. If so, it did not last. Many years later, when Stella was eighteen, Essex told her that the years when her children were little were so dreadful that, looking back, she wondered how she had kept her sanity. Marriage, and the early inheritance of a large fortune (his father died in 1886, the year of the marriage) seem to have changed Ralph, or at least to have brought out in him characteristics that his adoring fiancée had not even guessed at.

It is not easy to form a consistent picture of Ralph. There is not much to go on; Ellis Roberts's discreetly glossed remarks in his book on Stella, a few crumbs of innocent comment in her own early diaries, some pained, bewildered accounts in those of her teens, family legend (he is remembered as a 'womaniser'), a couple of early photographs. 'He was an impulsive man who feared his impulses,' Roberts writes '. . . he had a certain Spartan streak in him.' He had an extreme physical fastidiousness, a dislike of being touched. 'He was a solitary man,' adds Roberts, 'intent on intellectual and religious problems which he did not share with his family.'[3]

One presumes that he spent a good deal of time in his library, and it was to that sanctum that Stella, around New Year 1900, when she was almost eight, sent her first surviving letter, inscribed in pencil on some of her new Christmas gift stationery:

My dear Father,
    I hope you will like my letter. I have never written to you since I remember. This is my own writing paper out of the little box that Aunt Lucy gave me there is envolopes – this is my own envolope. Did you think that this was from me before you opened the envolope? Please, answer and tell me. Hasn't this letter come a long way, from Nurseryland to Libraryland. I hope you will have a happy New Year. Goodbye
    Your loving
        Stella.[4]

Going through her husband's papers after his death, Essex Benson found the letter carefully preserved, with attached to it a remarkable note. Couched in imagery of genuine poetic power, it brims over with passionate, possessive love for a delicate small daughter:

This is the first bloom of my *winter* rose. Born in the *coldest* winter, on Jan 6th Epiphany, so I christen my rose *Stella*. I planted my rose tree and have got no bloom till now. Now it seems to me as gardener that the east winds have caught her, like autumn and winter roses, and already make her outside petals crumple up and look brown. But the heart of my rose is warm, because it looks west and south.[5]

Were it not for the fact that the odd intensity of feeling in Ralph's effusion (those curious underlinings) suggests a mind slightly off balance, one might conclude that the soil was right for a relationship of perhaps unusual intimacy between father and daughter, and it may be that in Stella's earliest years they *were* close.

However, by the time Stella began keeping a diary her father was absent a great deal: he went to Sierra Leone on what seems to have been a kind of pilgrimage of reparation for the sins of his slave-trading great-great-grandfather, adopting some black children there, and bringing them back to Lutwyche with unhappy results. Later he was living and doing charitable work in the East End of London.

From the children's point of view, perhaps his absences were no bad thing, for in adult life they retained alarming memories of him. There was the incident of the family magazine. Entitled *The Holiday Magazine*, it was planned that it should appear thrice yearly, in the school holidays, and the proceeds were to go to charity. The children grew tired of producing it, but Father took the line that a hobby should be stuck at just like work: grimly he demanded further issues, insisting that they be submitted for his inspection. Stephen recalled reciting a poem in the Scots dialect – and being struck violently across the face by his father for mispronouncing it. Stella had an unhappy memory of a country walk she took with him when she was little. They came to a stream spanned by a slippery tree trunk. 'Are you afraid of crossing?' asked Father. 'Yes,' she replied. 'Then you must cross,' uttered the voice of doom. And heart in mouth she crossed.

Stella's few teenage meetings with her father were all rendered hurtful, terrifying even, by his strange behaviour. But as this enigmatic father had noticed, the heart of his Stella-rose was warm. As she grew up, she retained an urgent need to relate, somehow, to her extraordinary parent, and was most reluctant to dispose of him once and for all on some lunatic rubbish dump. Prepared to overlook any number of slights and rebuffs, she longed for some excuse to explain them, but it was not until 1910, when she was eighteen, that her mother saw fit to proffer one, taking her daughter completely by surprise, as the diary makes clear:

> I am sure it never occurred to me. Of course, he drinks. . . . when I was younger I used to think it was gentlemanly to be so irritable and eccentric. I used rather to despise people who had ordinary fathers who played with them, and were more or less like a masculine Mother to them. My own Father was quite unapproachable and unaccountable, and I used to admire him for it. Ever since I have grown older, it has never struck me that there must be something behind the fact of Father not being able to bear the sight of us.

Chapter Two

At eight years old, Stella disconcerted a new governess by greeting her with the grave words, 'I am young, but I have had a great deal of sorrow in my life.' Only the previous year she had suffered a blow in the death of her nine-year-old sister Catherine – of whom it is recorded that she was a 'gifted' child. How much the girls meant to each other we cannot know, but Stella must have keenly felt her loss, and quickly understood what it meant to herself as a family member. At lessons she was now the solitary pupil, at play a difficult gap of four years separated her from each of her brothers – and in any case George, her favourite, was already away at preparatory school, destined for Eton. She was condemned to a new loneliness. And she would have been aware of a heightening of anxiety on the part of her mother for the one sickly little daughter who remained. Ten years later, on the day that Catherine, had she lived, would have been twenty, Stella was to exclaim with the violence of eighteen, 'If she had lived I couldn't have been the spoilt little brute I am!'

Stella was delicate. In the silent years before the diaries begin, no doubt she ran the gamut of childhood ailments usual in her day, enduring the long cossetings in bed that were standard in Victorian sickrooms. But her health was a matter of special concern. The colds that she caught at Lutwyche, a bitterly cold house six hundred feet above sea level in a county notorious for sharp winters, tended to linger, to settle on her chest and turn to bronchitis. The spectre of tuberculosis lurked frighteningly in the wings. So she was taken to live in places which were reckoned to be salubrious. Some of the time her mother was with her, her daughter's delicacy giving her a socially acceptable excuse for living apart from her husband. At five or six Stella was in France; between ten and eleven one finds her living with her mother and brothers in Norfolk Square, a somewhat forbidding rectangle of houses in the then unfashionable region north of Hyde Park, where the Bensons had their town house.

It was a Norfolk Square neighbour, mother of a small girl with whom

Stella shared her lessons, who did Stella the important service of presenting her with her first diary, a matchbox-size pocket book for 1902 bound in turquoise leather; a step in the right direction certainly, though as the tiny pages afforded only one square inch of space for each day's entry, her natural flow of words was woefully circumscribed. Her next year's diary was a gift from George, and offered twenty times the space; she began to expand, though even now (and again in 1904), childlike, she commits to paper only the barest record of events, with no hint of her feelings or reactions.

Except that her father's visits were occasions of note – 'Father came home to-day, so as Mademoiselle is sleeping in his room she had to sleep in mine, and I went down to share the big bed with Mother'; 'Father came to tea with us, and afterwards had games with us. Then he had to go back to Poplar' – the picture of life that Stella drew in her early diaries is typical of the upper-class town child at the turn of the century. In the morning the governess called; in the afternoon a resident Mademoiselle took her on a French-speaking perambulation of Hyde Park or Kensington Gardens; once a week she attended dancing class (on one occasion noting with pride and condescension of a younger brother, 'Stephen nearly did the polka'). A visit to the pantomime or a trip to Kew Gardens was a rare treat; she was twelve when she made her first visit to the theatre proper to see Shakespeare's *The Tempest*, which she found 'awfully decent'. Polite tea parties supervised by Nurse were exchanged with a few neighbouring children. It is not surprising to find her carefully noting each time what was played, for throughout her life Stella enjoyed games; she was fond of cards and never lost her relish for disconcertingly childish romps and recreations. Some of the games they played – Hide and Seek, Blind Man's Buff, Up Jenkins – survive to this day; but Jildie Jildie, Dolly Dumps, Spoof, Bumblepuppy, Piladex and Agricultural Show are now locked secrets.

Books, the weighty 'children's classics' that remained staple children's reading right up to the end of the Second World War (Scott, Ballantyne, Kingsley, with Rider Haggard for light relief) helped while away wet days indoors, as – in Stella's case – did her pen; her diary for 1904 lists carefully in order of composition all the poems and stories she has written to date. A good deal of time is passed 'out in the square', a safely railed-in area of grass and trees, paths and benches, overlooked by a myriad windows; after a week of baking hot June weather it is exciting and rather daring to be allowed in the square 'with bare legs and sandals on'. On most Sundays church service is attended, Nurse withdrawing the children 'before the sermon'.

Summer 1903 saw some of the household (which included an African kitchenmaid, perhaps a relic of Ralph's Sierra Leone adventure, and, more strange, a Japanese butler, servant of a deceased Cholmondeley relation) remove to a rented house in Felixstowe, a Suffolk resort popular at that time with families of the Bensons' class. Once installed, Mrs Benson toyed with the idea of hiring the latest extravagance, a chauffeur-driven motor – but she decided that at four guineas a day she couldn't afford it. On the beach she had her hut moved to be near her friend Lady Emily Lutyens,[1] who was there with her mother Lady Lytton; juvenile Bensons and Lutyenses combed the sands together looking for pieces of cornelian and amber, while less agreeable flotsam came drifting in: 'a dead body was brought up to our part of the shore. We were all shut up so that we should not see him.' Father, even, came some of the time.

But Benson holidays were never such fun as times spent with one particular set of Cholmondeley cousins: Regie, Mary, Essex, Hester, Hugh and baby Joan, the children of her mother's eldest brother Reginald, a robust father-figure of whom Stella stood in some awe, and his wife Florence, whom she thought quite perfect, at their big, rambling house, Preshaw, near Winchester in Hampshire. Slipping naturally into the life of schoolroom and nursery, with a role to play in all her cousins' entertainments – the charades, puppet shows and theatricals of the age – giving solo performances on her zither, playing on the long lawns or among the great 'crinolined' beech trees, watching with sharp eyes a husband and wife fundamentally happy together, Stella absorbed a lesson of the greatest importance: what it is to be a member of a united family.

It was perhaps because she was disturbed by her own father's habitual absence that Stella kept such a close eye on her mother, noting her appointments, marking her comings and goings. Essex Benson's enjoyment of things social had survived the disaster of her marriage, and she could be good company. There were frequent visits to relations and little trips abroad; in Norfolk Square she was At Home to tea on Thursdays, when her little daughter might be asked to 'help' by making conversation and handing round cakes. Like many an upper-class woman of the day, Essex Benson dabbled in social work, which again could involve her daughter: 'Mother had a headache, so she wants me to be the Old English Lady instead of her. So I sold sweets and flowers instead of her at the Bermondsey May Day Festival.' And we find Stella helping to raise funds for a subsection of society not the least of whose misfortunes was to be branded Bermondsey's 'Brave Poor Things'.[2]

Stella was a quiet, serious child; 'ill used', her mother said, meaning by this that other children were aware of oddity in her, and resented it. It was not that she was unfriendly or morose – she seems to have been almost pathetically eager to meet other children half way – but she was possessed of a probing eye with a power to disconcert. There was a strange and significant incident in the garden of Norfolk Square when she was only six or seven years old. Her elder brother George was involved in some sort of serious boys' play with friends. An admiring group of little girls looked on. Stella joined them, but she said nothing. She just watched, and smiled. George saw, and knew at once that his little sister was not admiring him. The game continued, and still, in a detached, unbearable way, she stood and smiled. George strode up to her and told her to stop smiling, and when she did not or could not, hit the smile off her face. The friend – unnamed – who related this anecdote to Ellis Roberts remembered her own terror at Stella's immobility, her curious, sensitive, aloof refusal to get excited by the game, and remembered that when Stella burst into tears at the blow, she cried 'beautifully', letting the tears run down her stinging cheek without rubbing a clenched hand into her eyes.

The year 1905 was the one year when Stella failed to keep a diary, but its outstanding melancholy features can be ascertained from a catalogue that she drew up as a tailpiece to the previous year's volume: Stella got appendicitis and Stephen rheumatic fever, Mother had an operation, Father was run over, and Fly the dog went mad and had to be shot. 'Did any family ever have such an unfortunate year?' Stella asked, a hint of satisfaction in her tone. 'Poor Mother, I wish I had kept a diary because it would have been so full of events.'

From 1906 on, the stormy emotions of adolescence began to wash over the diaries. At the same time Stella's health declined. Having abandoned any pretence of sharing a home with her husband, in 1906 Essex Benson was living with her children, modestly by the standards of her class, in a rented house in Hindhead, Surrey. (From here one morning she was summoned post haste to her husband's bedside: he was seriously ill. 'I think we shall not have a Father long,' wrote his daughter sadly. But he survived.)

For the spring term of 1906 the experiment was made of sending Stella to a local private school. At fourteen, for the first time in her life, she found herself in a crowd of her contemporaries. That she was shy, and very much at sea at first, comes across plainly: 'I wish I could be a little more sociable and decent with the other girls, but it does not seem my nature. I should like the other girls to like me.' However she was not overwhelmed, began to make friends, developed a healthy crush on an older girl, 'a person I almost worship'. True, she was made a little unhappy when her mother told her that she did not consider 'anyone in the school are [*sic*] quite ladies . . . as I certainly think two people are' – and it was horribly galling to have to admit in her secret heart that the goddess herself did not quite make the grade. But when after lunch at home and a little lie-down on account of her delicate health, she was picked up by the school crocodile for the statutory afternoon walk, she joined it without serious misgiving. She was even schoolgirl enough to begin to be naughty, confessing proudly, 'I got into my first scrape about drawing on the blackboard'; adding, with the modesty proper to a novice at sin, 'I was rather unhappy about it, but I suppose people are in their first.'

The Easter holidays saw her at Preshaw, tending her pet lizards, formulating plans for what sounds like a very ambitious effort of historical reconstruction: 'I am thinking of writing a novel just for practice. I think I have the plot, which is Egyptian in the time of the tenth plague.' The previous term's schooling must have been considered at least a qualified success, for when Mrs Benson moved house (to Fleet, still in Hampshire), she consulted the family doctor about sending Stella to the select boarding school in Eastbourne that her cousin Mary Cholmondeley attended. Approval being given, one May afternoon, feeling 'very unhappy', Stella was abandoned by her parent in the midst of a milling, if ladylike, throng.

Though eventually she was to win a silver photograph frame for third place in the tennis tournament, and to end up 'top of the class in some things' (quite a creditable performance in a girl whose education had been so desultory), these were paltry successes as far as Stella was concerned. What she craved was to be accepted as ordinary, to be one of the crowd. It was humiliating to be singled out as a weakling and have to lie down after lunch every day. It was appalling to find herself fainting in the middle of the singing lesson – she was swept into a vortex of painful emotion, afraid the others would think she was shamming, furious with self-reproach. It was cruel to have the insight to perceive, as she did early in the term, that 'the reason why people do not like me is because I have not been much with other girls and do not know how to behave with them'. It may well have been among the pushy, pubescent girls at Eastbourne that the sense of her being in some way innately different from other young females took conscious hold of Stella, the feeling that she was not a 'real girl' at all.

Illness supervened. A perceptive school doctor sat by her bed and got her to talk: 'I told him all sorts of things. He draws your troubles out of you.' In a couple of days he had her on her feet, but now she had fresh reason to be miserable: 'I have made a discovery. I have found I am treated differently from the other girls. They are all very patronising and soft to me. I hate it. I am a softie myself. No other girl would nearly cry when they got their lessons wrong.' She saw the term out – her father's daughter, she was not the child to beg to be taken away – but the Eastbourne experience told her mother that for the time being at least she was too delicate, too highly strung to stand up to the rough and tumble of school life. A new, living-in governess, young, cheerful, modern-minded Miss Puick, was engaged to take up the threads of her education, while, in vain, Mrs Benson tried to discover some suitable girl to share her classes.

'Same old lonely lessons again,' sighed Stella when Miss Puick arrived to start her second term. It was January 1907, and Stella was just fifteen. Few sufferings of later life equal the despair of the adolescent who sees life passing her by, just when it seems to be opening out delightfully for the rest of her generation. Her Cholmondeley cousins, she told her Aunt Mary in the course of a confidential chat on a visit to her rural retreat at Ufford in Suffolk, had everything she longed for. Hitting each nail squarely on the head, she named 'companionship, good looks, health, money – motoring, nice house, plays, getting away'. When it came to looks, few indeed could vie with Mary, the eldest Cholmondeley girl, who was so beautiful that Stella was to marvel that every man she met did not fall in love with her. Essex was extremely good-looking too. Her own looks Stella regarded with something approaching contempt – they were, she would have said, so ordinary. Small grey eyes, sunken, with a hooded look, mouse-coloured hair that was straight and fine and irritatingly difficult to keep tidy; a profile that she would prefer not to contemplate – jaw of idiosyncratic line, nose with a bump at the end. As often as not she was wiping that nose, or coughing, or had half her voice gone; and it was husky at best. Her height, which was to reach five foot four,[3] was unexceptionable certainly, but that was no great consolation when the *tout ensemble* gave an impression of thinness, pallor, delicacy. What, she must have breathed to her pillow, had she, in relation to other girls, to be confident about? If we are to take her daughter's word for it, Mrs Benson was worse than useless in bolstering her self-esteem in this regard: on the Victorian principle that vanity and false hopes must be discouraged in a girl, she made a point of reminding her that she was rather plain.

For Stella 1907 had opened with a bout of influenza, then she damaged an ankle and progressed slowly from bed to sofa to wheelchair; a tiresome course of styes followed, and at the back of all an operation loomed. A specialist, investigating a new affliction, deafness in her right ear, had been inept enough to let her know (or perhaps the news came through her mother) that in adult life she might well be stone deaf; meanwhile certain fluid must be drained. Familiarity with the business of operations (this would be her third, she says) had not rendered them any less terrifying to her; as usual she inhaled the ether bravely, but 'hung on to Mother as long as I had my senses'.

About this time what later she called 'Eve's pain' would have begun to add to her physical distresses. She took to marking the start of a period with a cross in her diary, followed often by a dismal account of going back to bed for an hour or so 'with the pillow stuffed into my mouth and all the sheets and blankets grasped furiously in one fist', until the pain died away. 'Sometimes I think I should believe in things more', she wrote at eighteen, 'if Christ had been a woman so that he could have understood the constant pain and discomfort that make up so much of a woman's life.' Later she commented snidely, 'if men had this periodical pain, the world could never have kept it a secret. It would have been talked of by the dear fellows at their clubs, and compared with friends' pains, and discussed in the family circle for days before it was expected. Also doctors would have found a cure.'

Among women who experience menstrual pain, those of poor constitution and sensitive temperament are said by doctors to fare worst, so it is not surprising to find Stella enduring monthly agony. The psychologists have views on the subject too. Dr Laura Hutton, a specialist in feminine psychology (and coincidentally, Stella's closest and longest-standing friend), in her *The Single Woman: Her Adjustment to Life and Love*[4] sees period pain in adolescence as 'more often than not an unconscious expression of a passionate rejection of femininity'. Stella's acute attacks could, then, be connected by underground links with the uneasy consciousness of not being a 'real' girl.

For good or ill, a girl's attitude to sexuality is generally grounded in that of her mother. Even if in later life she rebels against what reason and observation tell her is false doctrine, it is from the basis of her mother's attitude, voiced or implied, that rebellion has to start. Reading between the lines of Mary Cholmondeley's somewhat bleached account, in *Under One Roof*, of life as lived in the rectory at Hodnet, it is easy to discern certain more colourful truths. 'Upright', 'rigid', 'austere' were all words that Mary used of her mother, whose dreadful maxim was: 'Duty is the only thing there is.' Would it be improper to suppose that it was solely on the principle of duty that this grimly repressed woman allowed the good rector to beget upon her eight children? Or presumptuous to think that from the sofa where, long before they were grown up, she lay 'paralysed and severely depressed', she instilled in her daughters an attitude less than positive towards their biological role? Only one of them, Stella's mother, married, and that fact may help provide an answer.

In 1922, when Stella was herself a young wife trying to come to terms with the physical intimacies of marriage, she knew that it was no use talking to her mother. She remembered only too vividly how, braced to the disagreeable task and 'full of domestic dutifulness', her mother had 'shed hysterical tears when telling me the "facts of life", and saying "It's a thing women have to bear, to please men – it's their duty – they must learn to bear it."'

Though nothing is of more urgent, palpitating interest to the young girl, Stella in her teenage diaries makes no reference to sex. By the cruellest of ironies, the portion of humanity that was expected to find fulfilment in love and marriage was permitted to give only shy, half-averted glances at its physical realities, and certainly not to commit its thoughts on the subject to paper.

Stella was a conscientious child. Pitying her mother's forlorn, husbandless condition, she made serious efforts to be considerate to her. When George arrived from London full of the joys of *Peter Pan*, 'my great wish is to see that too', she wrote, 'but I am trying to rule my thoughts as it is selfish to wish it as Mother cannot take me'. A few days later conscience took a fall: 'I asked Mother straight out about *Peter Pan*. She gave a decided refusal.' George, out of Eton and cramming for the Royal Military Academy at Woolwich, was throwing his weight about when he came home. It was not long before he was talking airily of having 'caught an heiress, not half a bad girl', and playing meaningly on the piano a ballad that went 'The finest lassies in the land cannot compare with Mary'. Female versus male, Stella wrote of her beloved brother after one of his lapses, 'George was beastly to Mother, Father has gone away from Mother, and I do not see why George should try and make her unhappy too.' (Father in fact made one of his peculiar incursions into their lives in June 1907, first summoning them to meet him in London, and then wiring to say he was off to Scotland on the night mail; they went all the same, and met him in the Great Northern Hotel. Stella had not set eyes on him for two years: 'he was very much smaller and thinner than I expected, and his hair was rather white'.)

Mother was much to be pitied; all the same, how infuriating she was, going 'waxy and injured-martyrish' at the least thing, yet feeling she had a perfect right to criticise her daughter on her looks, facial expressions and manners towards the governess, and taking unfair advantage of her position to complain of Stella to other people, with remarks like 'There, you see, she is never sorry for what she does!' Pointing out that Stella was not affectionate, didn't run and kiss her as Stephen did – when in actual fact 'I sometimes wish to do this, but when it comes to the point somehow I can't. So I don't, and Mother never knows I want to.' Likewise 'always saying she wants little changes and galloping off somewhere, though she gives us a fortnight at Preshaw and thinks that ample once a year'.

As for Stephen, it was a strain to come down to his level now, the gap between them seemed suddenly so much wider. Who *was* there to be friends with? Her social life seemed to consist of teas with 'Suffragy old maids and toddling babies', and when she did find herself in company with her contemporaries she felt painfully shy and awkward. 'When I grow up,' she decided, 'unless I grow very different I shall live apart rather from other people because directly I get with them I always seem to make mistakes . . . other people don't seem to.' On the theme of woman's suffrage, she heard more than enough at home, with her mother and Miss Puick talking of nothing else at mealtimes, 'both violently for it, as I think most women are, more or less . . . it seems curious, however, that people think it necessary to make these undignified female riots to bring it about'. And then the ridiculous Open Air Cure she was supposed to be on: if Mother really wanted her to be out of doors so much, why didn't she let her join the tennis or golf club? – 'I should have thought with teaching I might have been strong enough to swing a club.' She was sick and tired of bicycling for the sake of bicycling: 'It is a pity that Miss Puick gloats upon going for rides so, especially as she always bags the free-wheel.' As far as she could see the Open Air Cure was simply an excuse for her mother to deny her the concerts and plays she so passionately yearned for. Even the vicar, who was preparing her for confirmation, irritated her by suggesting that keeping a diary was not good for a girl: 'I wish he would keep more to the subject in hand. This diary is going on just the same.' Essex Benson, struggling in difficult circumstances to do what seemed best for her children, no doubt deserves more credit for kindness and good sense than a fractious teenage Stella was disposed to give her. But she does seem to have erred on the side of wrapping her in cottonwool.

To Stella, in her tragic discontent, it seemed that Pepper alone, 'my sweet Pepper', the Aberdeen terrier that Aunt Mary gave her as a consolation after her appendix operation, truly understood. To the best of his doggy ability he seemed to try to make up for the bosom friend she longed for and failed to find among the 'second-rate Fleetites', whom she at once feared and despised. Happily, the Highland breed is clamorously affectionate and transparently single-hearted. When in 1915 Pepper died, her heart went back to those miserable Fleet days, when he was her sole confidant, indeed her mirror image:

> You felt the same. You understood.
> You too, defensive and morose,
> Encloaked your secret puppyhood –
> Your secret heart – and hid them close. . . .
>
> When filthy pain did wrap me round
> Your upright ears I always saw,
> And on my outflung hand I found
> The blessing of your horny paw.[5]

Pepper made her conscious of dogs in general. She started a 'dog notebook' in which were entered the good points of neighbouring dogs and doggy quotations; she studied canine anatomy in order to improve her sketches of dogs; she was thrilled when a doggy sitter was produced at an art class she attended. Fascinating and consoling (though in a very different way) were her pair of literary lizards, Pride and Prejudice, whom she kept in a cage. 'Lizards and snakes love music,' she observed when her pets showed their appreciation of a tune on the piano (one longs to know how). Prejudice she took about on her shoulder 'much to the terror of the servants, who might be excused, as she is rather large and snakey, though she is such a darling'.

In her isolation she fell back on the dangerous comfort of imagining herself superior to other people; after an unsuccessful encounter with some of the despised young Fleetites, she wrote, 'I know I have something infinitely more important which these giggling girls have not.' She had in mind first of all her writing, and more particularly a something-in-progress that even her diary was not permitted to know about; she calls it 'The Secret', and it was probably a long-since-vanished attempt at a novel. Three amateur magazines received her poetic efforts and once, greatly daring, she submitted a poem to a 'real grown-up magazine', *Pearson's* – and promptly had it back.

The pinnacle of her literary career to date, and a pretty sublime one at that, had come two years before in 1905, when her poem won the award for extreme merit offered by the *St. Nicholas Magazine*, an admirably whole-some and high-minded children's periodical issuing from New York in the early years of this century. It had enthusiastic subscribers the world over, none keener than a group of boys and girls who flourished in its back pages, and were known as the St Nicholas League. They wore a badge displaying the Stars and Stripes and, as the American writer E. B. White, who was one of their number, explains, 'wrote poems and prose, took snapshots with box cameras, drew pictures at random, and solved puzzles'.[6] League members who later made names for themselves as writers were Edna St Vincent Millay, Babette Deutsch, William Faulkner, Victoria Sackville-West and Margaret Kennedy. 'They submitted the results of their fervor to the League,' White affectionately recalls, 'and the lucky ones pocketed the Gold or the Silver Badge. . . . We were an industrious and fiendishly competitive band of tots, and if some of us, in the intervening years of careless living, have lost or mislaid our silver badge, we still remember the day it came in the mail; the intensity of victory, the sweetness of young fame.' Stella's award-winning effort, on a prescribed theme, was as follows. No doubt the judges thought it a *tour de force* as coming from the pen of a thirteen-year-old, with its lines of cunningly varied length, and a rhyme scheme that in the fifth line of each stanza arrests the flow of water, and in the lines that follow lets it go again:

> The little brook went winding down the hill,
> Ran rippling down the hill,
> The frowning, gloomy hill,
> When all the world was dark and gray and still,
> Preparing for the tempest that was nigh;
> But still the brook went rippling, dancing by,
> Laughing, all heedless of the stormy sky.
>
> Unceasing ran the brook – a silver thread,
> A narrow, winding thread,
> A dancing, shining thread,

> A little spark of life amongst the dead;
> And when the sunbeams drove away the rain,
> Still happier was the brooklet's merry strain
> Because the world was gay and bright again.

A couple of years later, in 'The Heart of Youth' – hardly a subject that would occur spontaneously to a fifteen-year-old – she obligingly took up her lyre and struck a more portentous note:

> Borne upwards on its gold and silver wings
> Rises the Heart of Youth,
> With its fond hopes and sweet imaginings
> It wanders through this sordid world, nor brings
> To mind the hard, undecorated truth;
> And future cares and sorrows left behind
> Are spurned, because the Heart of Youth is blind.

At this stage of her life Stella was happy to force her muse, as long as there was a chance of seeing the result in print. Yet at about the same time, in her diary, she was recording in delightful, unaffected diction the intense pleasure that came to her by way of her eyes: at Fleet Pond, for example, where she espied 'a heron standing thoughtfully in the water and the sun went down in pink making the island a black silhouette against a pink water, while the reeds and docks which grow so thick in places . . . became a russety browny pink. It was gorgeous, and a kind of poetry without words rose in me which I often wish I could put into words.'

She was reading a good deal – Carlyle's *French Revolution*, lives of General Monk and Gustavus Adolphus of Sweden ('three rather stiff books but I like them awfully'), Austen, Gaskell, Kipling, Mrs Craik – some of the novels being read to her by her mother 'downstairs'. But Stella never made literature a substitute for life in the way some lonely children have done, for, since the age of five, deep inside she had a different resource, one so profoundly secret that she resisted disclosing it even to her diary, until on 7 June 1907 it slipped out:

When I say in this diary that I read, it very often means, I'm afraid, that I get out a book, but do not think of it again. I don't know whether other people are the same as me in having an imaginary world filled with imaginary people to whom at every spare moment of the day one's thoughts return. I daresay it is childish, but it has grown absolutely indispensable to me. When things happen in my thoughts I feel them almost as much as if they were really happening.

In September she was writing:

> I wonder if I shall grow out of the way of imagining. It seems to be getting
> stronger and stronger, except when I have a lot of people with me which
> seems to prevent me. I always somehow imagine I have someone with
> me. Of course, I know there is nobody, but I sometimes find myself acting
> as if there was, and also I suddenly discover sometimes that I am talking
> out loud. These thought people are not exactly with me, but I somehow
> see them together, they make up a kind of different world from which I
> am apart. I only look.

By April 1908 she was noting, almost with alarm, that:

> my dream people are getting so real that they are mixing up with real
> people in an extraordinary way. . . . I don't think I or anybody would have
> believed what company thought people are, and how they drive away
> loneliness. . . . I have never met a real person who could give me half as
> much comfort.

Real people could be terribly disconcerting. Summer 1908 brought
another painful meeting with her father, who was golfing at Felixstowe
within visiting distance of her mother and herself at Southwold. Things
looked normal and hopeful when he asked them to lunch, and offered them
the use of his motor. But no sooner were they arrived than he 'seemed
annoyed to see us . . . made faces to show me what I looked like, and said I
had old clothes on, and did things to make us uncomfortable'. On leaving
they managed to miss their train and Father positively refused to drive them
the 'twenty minutes'' journey to their hotel (an instance, this, of hurt
feelings overriding hard facts: in 1908 no car could have done well over
thirty miles on country roads in that time). They had to wait a good hour
and a half at Felixstowe station for the next train: 'Poor old Father',
commiserated Stella, studiously forebearing as ever. Next summer they
were to see him once again, for a few moments, when they passed through
Shrewsbury station (he was living in the neighbourhood of Lutwyche,
which was let): 'I always feel almost annoyed with him for being so
peculiar,' Stella admitted on this occasion. 'He gnawed his hands and kept
saying "Maiden, maiden-a-grown-up-maiden" on and on and then got out.
Poor darling.' Whatever explanation Essex saw fit to give Stella for her
husband's strange behaviour (the eccentricity of genius, perhaps), she must
have realised that he was moving towards mental collapse, and any sign of
morbidity in Stella must have come with doubly worrying force. Perhaps
this was why she arranged for her, during the winter and spring of 1908–9,
to escape to Preshaw. To Stella it seemed almost too good to be true, and
when kind Aunt Florie extended the invitation to Pepper, she was ecstatic.

The half year at Preshaw passed agreeably. Though her hearing after surgery was still erratic, and there was talk of another painful operation, she was able perfectly to appreciate the peculiarities of her aunt's guests, from the woman dismissed as 'a person who says would-be smart things which you feel have been said before and will be again if the same subject be brought up', to the young wife, 'a little shy round-shouldered thing evidently newly married. She always stops what she is saying to listen with obvious admiration to anything he says, however trivial.' Under her cousins' influence a new interest in her appearance budded. Shortly before her seventeenth birthday (having of course sought her mother's permission) she said goodbye to 'flapperdom' as defined in 1908, and let Mary put her hair up. It gave her an 'awfully joyful, optimistic feeling. . . . I don't know why, but it struck me that my hair suited me, and that I am nearly grown up now, and that I may be able to squeeze a bit of fun out of life yet.' With the adult hairstyle crowning a new outfit in fashionable purple, what she saw in the mirror pleased and excited her so much that she tried on for size a readymade idea to go with it: 'Brains were not meant for women. They often misuse them, and to please with looks is the only thing a woman can do better than a man.' Two years later we find her still denigrating the female brain, this time opposing woman's suffrage on the grounds that '*women are and always must be inferior to men in mental power*', emphasising her view with one of her rare underlinings. 'The mess that dear Asquith is making', she went on, 'is – must be – incomparable to the mess that women would make if they were in Parliament.'

In the normal course of things she could expect to 'come out' at eighteen, and while agreeing with her mother that Fleet was not 'the best kind of neighbourhood' for this to happen in, was looking forward to it. In the meantime, pent up together in their house, The Beacon, mother and daughter were not finding life at all easy. To judge by the diary entry for 3 April 1909, things were said that would have been better left unsaid:

Mother says that as I am neither pretty nor clever it will be no good me going to dances when I come out, and she says I am not strong enough to go abroad. So I might as well be a kid of two and there is nothing to look forward to in coming out after all. And she had promised me since I can first remember that I should have such fun one way or the other – I have had so little yet – and now we shall stick at this beastly little cottage with half a servant and no gardener as if we were paupers, and I shall be expected to sit alone and watch Mother dig potatoes until I die, which I jolly well hope will be soon.

The disloyal thought passed through her mind that her father, who could afford *himself* a motor and other extravagances, could possibly let *them* have a little more money to play with. By June Mrs Benson was getting desperate about the tension between herself and Stella, and secretly began making plans to send her abroad. It strikes one as extraordinary today that parental high-handedness of this kind could be taken absolutely for granted by a high-spirited youngster, and apparently not resented; but so it was in 1909: 'I am sure there is something afoot . . . when I observe a Cook's schedule on the price of fares to Munich and elsewhere appear on the writing table – what do I infer? Nothing, of course!' It was over the dinner table of her mother's friend Lady Battersea that the truth casually popped out: 'Mother is thinking of sending me to Munich to stay with a family before the winter.' However, this particular scheme came to nought, and Stella spent the summer trailing her mother to garden parties and teas in her 'best hat' with nothing immediate to look forward to.

Then a fresh plan emerged, far more exciting than the first: she was to go to Freiburg in the Black Forest, with a party of English girls, to study music and German. 'I sleep with the thought of it,' she wrote, entranced, 'and dream of it and wake saying "one day nearer".' On 23 September, the eve of departure, she breathed, 'This and to-morrow was [sic] the most exciting day of my life.'

The party of twelve girls, escorted by their mistress Mrs Denne, departed from Victoria Station at 8.30 in the evening for Queenborough in Kent, where they joined the night ferry for Flushing. Barely were their heads down, so it seemed, than the stewardess was rousing them. Dawn was breaking, and as their train crossed Holland the sun rose. In the fields Stella saw peasants early at work, wearing 'white flappy caps and sabots', just like their pictures. At the German frontier, customs officers – thrillingly – entered their compartment, and soon the River Rhine and its fairy-tale castles were rolling, incredibly, past the windows. For Stella, however, the greatest wonder by far on this day of wonders was to be sharing it all with a crowd of girls of her own age: Nora, Betty, Gracie, Ruth, Nancy, Annie – she was quickly getting their names. Because they were all equally strangers to each other, all eager to establish relationships, she found herself not in the least shy; on the contrary she was being rather particularly talkative. If it went on like this there was surely a good chance (delirious thought!) of her being accepted as a 'real' girl at last.

At Freiburg next day there were voice trials, piano trials, and then the fun of exploring the market and looking at the peasants in their quaint, decorative costumes. Afterwards there was delicious near-riot in the bed-rooms, Mrs Denne being no great disciplinarian: 'Heaven defend us from another night such as last night,' Stella joyously cried, 'in which I never closed an eyelid.' Next day being Sunday, two services at the little Anglican church somewhat chastened the mood, but on Monday the girls were at it again with tugs o'war, dancing, fighting, buckets of laughter. Stella brought out her sketchbook and drew caricatures, and everyone was 'pulpy' with laughter, especially over her sketch of poor Vera, 'a great fat ass' as Stella rather cruelly described her, who had been quickly seized upon as the laughing-stock (someone persuaded her to put her weight down on a concealed balloon and someone else crept up behind and popped it). 'Thank God for giving me this taste of Heaven,' wrote Stella, enraptured. With a girl called Nora she visited a certain favoured *Konditorei*, 'as everybody does who is not prigs whenever they go out', and sampled a Freiburg speciality, a Sarah Bernhardt cake – 'nyum!' One evening there was a 'ripping' dance (with girls for partners, of course); another night they went to the opera. In the light of events, one detects a note of hysteria in Stella's response to *Lohengrin*: 'four hours of heaven. . . . one cried when one wanted and laughed and soared and almost screamed over the more rapturous parts'. During the interval she did another thing obligatory for anyone who did not want to be thought a prig: in the passages of the opera-house she 'chose a German officer, an awfully nice-looking one', adding daringly, 'officers are lovely things in Germany, but I wish they wouldn't wear stays!'

Retribution followed. On the second Sunday, after church, Stella felt an 'awful' pain in her side. For the next six days she was in bed. Everyone was tremendously kind, made an immense fuss of her, tried to persuade her that she would not have enjoyed *Orpheus* as the hero was sung by a woman and so there was no one to fall in love with. At this stage, though she commented bitterly, 'I always have to pay for being happy,' it did not occur to her that the setback was other than temporary. A fortnight passed before she learned the devastating truth:

> It is a rotten world, I wish I had never been born. The doctors say I am not to stay here. . . . I am to live by myself with Mother on the top of some nasty chilly Swiss mountain. . . . They all went to a concert to-day. And I am never to go again. I hope I shall die in the night.

Her mother's arrival spelt her instant departure. She 'howled' as she entered the cab. 'I can't bear going back to living alone with Mother as always, and all the thought people will come trooping back.' At Freiburg they had not come once.

Part II

'I Won't Stop Kicking'

Chapter Three

Stella was suffering a severe attack of pleurisy, a disease with whose symptoms she was to become all too familiar in the years ahead: the sharp, shooting pain in the side caused by the rubbing together of the inflamed pleura, the double layer of membrane enclosing the lung; the dry cough deliberately held back to avoid agonising movement in the chest; the rapid, shallow, guarded breathing; the raised temperature. As she was to put it in a bad bout a few years later, 'one just screws oneself up to bear a pain at the top of each breath, and then one has to cough and that is about the limit of human endurance'. Pleurisy has links with tuberculosis, and that, no doubt, was why the Freiburg doctors recommended a mountain top so urgently for Stella.

Essex Benson intended to take her daughter to the prettily named resort of Arosa, six thousand feet above sea level in the most easterly canton of Switzerland, but on the way, at Chur, Stella had a relapse – 'the pain in my side came back like billy-o in the night' – so they stayed there a few days and then made a quick dash for Arosa in a hired carriage. After a steady climb through scenery that Stella was too ill and depressed to notice, they were set down before a large hotel in the Swiss style, multi-storeyed, multi-balconied, and reassuringly named the Alexandra, in honour of England's Queen. The proprietor, Herr Grube (who, the stationery indicated, had perfected his craft in a railway hotel in Southampton), welcomed guests of all nations, but specialised in the British. He offered them 'Every Modern Comfort, Electric Light, Lift, Billiards', but over and above he offered distinct *cachet*: there could be no shadow of doubt that for the British visitor to Arosa the Alexandra, if he could afford it, was the place to stay.

In this fortunate haven Stella kept to her bed, visited and condoled with by various invalid residents (one woman called her 'a poor little mite', reminding her of cheese), but after a fortnight Mrs Benson decided that the place was too expensive and they transferred to the Châlet Soldanella, by contrast a depressingly humble establishment. It was kept by two English spinsters (one an invalid and said to be dying), and a full-time nurse was employed. Stella was carried upstairs by two perspiring men and deposited in a room that looked straight down the main street, with a distant view of mountain, forest, glacier and lake. Like all bedrooms in such establishments it was complete with balcony on which guests could 'cure', and there, well wrapped up and nourishing resentful thoughts, she sat watching tobogganing, and reading and re-reading letters jam-packed with giddy news from Freiburg. 'Heavens! What a miserable set of people!' she exclaimed on meeting the three English spinsters who comprised dining-room society; they had 'boarding house' stamped all over them. Excellent ladies such as they were hardly fit company for a fun-loving seventeen-year-old, and the thought people throve, getting 'so frightfully vivid that they seem to take something out of me'. Worst of all, when she happened to meet some girls of her own age, she found that her new-won confidence had flown, and that she felt a 'solemn kind of invalid stick again'.

Towards Christmas Stella's doctor allowed her to start skating, which she enjoyed; but her reaction when she got up early one morning to watch some bobsleigh races seems to typify her fate: half way there her hands began to feel cold, she sat down on a camp stool to rest, and promptly fainted away. However, her verdict on 1909, a year that had offered the kind of fun she craved only to snatch it cruelly away, was touchingly cheerful, and remarkably philosophic for a girl of her age – but then Stella had caught the invalid's trick of making the most of trifles:

> When one thinks one has the dullest of dull times before one, one cannot foresee the countless insignificant little pleasures which generally make the present bearable. Why even a little jokelet, a good meal, a nice hot bath, are for the moment tiny pleasures which one cannot take into account when looking forward.

The 'fussy Dickensian ways' of the Châlet Soldanella fairly quickly proved intolerable. One Sunday in February 1910 Stella and her mother moved a section of their belongings back to the Alexandra. For some reason of decorum now obscure, they did it furtively: 'Most of the day was spent in packing and in taking suspicious-looking underclothes round to the Alexandra while people were in church.' With the presentable part of their luggage they moved in next day.

Once in younger, livelier society Stella plunged with surprising aptitude into mild flirtation: 'It is awfully interesting that these men like me,' she confided; and it was not only pale, delicate young men looking for a sympathetic ear in which to pour their blighted ambitions and lost hopes who sought her out; she was equally successful with the middle-aged, and with such unlikely subjects as 'an awfully jolly, red, loud young man, just the sort I should have thought would hate me, and I should hate'. A couple of months and she was something of an addict: 'I am impatient when night comes that there should have to be twelve hours' check in this new and enthralling game of mine.' What, she wondered, could be the secret of her apparent charm? Was she pretty, after all? 'I am rather pretty. Just a tiny bit. I put a red ribbon in my hair yesterday night and corals round my neck,' and one stout Dutchman murmured in the ear of another, '"from dis side she ees a leetle like an angel. But not quite," he added with a sigh.'

Even without the advantage of much beauty she had discovered by the time autumn came that 'if I like, not that I do like, I can make most very young men much unhappier than they can make me', and by the end of her second winter 'season' at Arosa she was writing, 'I have not been entirely unpopular. . . . I don't get on so very well with girls. To be quite frank, in fact, I always feel most at home among men, old or young. That is an appalling thing to say, but somehow they seem so much simpler to get around and please.'

In spite of its inauspicious beginnings, Stella was to pronounce her seventeen-month sojourn at Arosa 'the happiest time in my life', and the little resort 'the loveliest place in the world', a place where 'you can't go a step without finding something that startles you with its beauty'. The winter season lasted from the beginning of December, when the diligences dropped off the first invalids – many of them accompanied by healthy friends or relations – to the end of March when they departed; only a handful stayed on – as she stayed – for the whole year. Dutifully dividing their time between consumptive husband and baby at home, anxious young wives would arrive on visits. Occasional deaths 'of whatever anyone who dies here, dies of' (tuberculosis) were taken for granted; semi-invalids indulged in surprisingly energetic pastimes – skating, tobogganing, bob-sleighing. Doctors permitting, Stella threw herself into whatever fun was going, but what with influenza (a temperature for her often meant hallu-cinations, and this time the tea-things made faces at her), tonsillitis, a throat abscess, rheumatism (which kept her in bed for nine days in, of all months, July), period pain, anaemia, general lassitude and a tendency to faint, her enjoyment was continually interrupted. In October she was restricted to half an hour of skating a day, a few minutes only on her new enthusiasm, the guitar, and absolutely *no* whistling: 'Siffling', declared Dr Roemisch (nicknamed 'Sunbeam' by Stella because he always brought bad news), 'is *not* a lovely thing for the lungs.' Frustrated as she was by her body in so many ways, she turned for consolation and compensation to fantasy: 'My thought people are everything that I long to be and am not. They are beautiful and strong, above all strong.'

From time to time Mrs Benson went home. (On one occasion an anxious relative wrote to say that her husband was out of his mind, and people would say that she was neglecting him; from England Mrs Benson wrote that he was 'mazed and silly'.) When she was away, Stella was under the chaperon-age of various mature ladies – whether the arrangement was discreetly financial is not clear – one of whom taught her the rudiments of the guitar. It was this lady who, on being confined to bed, plunged Stella into a dilemma: was it or was it not 'shocking' of her to be at table alone with two men? – 'She would say if it was. Whatever it is, it is ripping fun.' For some of the time, Susan McLeod, a snappy, shabby, warm-hearted spinster 'character' who had attached herself to them at Fleet, came out to chaperone. Essex Cholmondeley and George paid a visit.

Stella was learning bridge, and joining in Shakespeare readings – which could be embarrassing, especially in a mixed group. The part of Lysander in *A Midsummer Night's Dream* was 'a little *risqué* at one point. Something about "one bed, one heart, two bosoms, and one troth", and just before and after this I read it in a purple sort of blushing voice.' A cinematograph display could be awkward too: 'in a mixed assembly some of the scenes were impossible, but there was nothing to be done. I wonder which feels the most uncomfortable on these occasions, men or girls?' But spectacles that would embarrass today for quite other reasons did not so much as raise an eyebrow: Stella and her mother, for instance, going to a fancy-dress ice carnival as little-girl twins, 'with a huge flob of hair tied at the side in a tremendous bow, and we carried Teddy bears and stuffed white rabbits'.

On 7 May 1910 rumour reached Arosa of the death of King Edward VII. 'If it is true what an awful thing for England,' wrote Stella, 'to be ruled by that little whippersnapper George, just after this tremendous political crisis [which had followed the veto by the House of Lords of Lloyd George's 'People's Budget' of 1909]. Poor dear Tedward, I don't suppose we could have had a much better king lately. He has been so splendid, forwarding Entente Cordiales always . . . he was no doll, as I am afraid, George will be. Why can't we get on to that sporting little Edward now Prince of Wales?' Stella was seriously out in her judgement of royals, for King George V was to prove a capable and conscientious monarch, while his sporting little son was to shake the very institution of monarchy. A fortnight later Stella was at a memorial service for the old King, finding it 'more laughable than impressive': it was managed entirely by ladies from the Châlet Soldanella, 'which accounts for everything'.

The English, with their own church, tea-rooms and newspaper (the *Arosa Chronicle*, featuring facetious verses by Stella) had gone some way towards colonising the village. How far the social distinctions of home could be preserved in the promiscuous atmosphere of hotel life was another matter. Stella herself remarked on the inferiority of 'Arosian gentlemen and ladies'. She found herself rubbing shoulders with a young woman who reeked of Parma violets, and a brassy flirt 'the vulgarest of the vulgar, who goes about with the worst and fastest set in Arosa', but who turned out, rather shamingly, to be nursing a dying brother with the utmost devotion; 'so that this squalling, barmaidy creature, tearing about dressed in screaming plaids, stout and almost repulsive to look at, is worth twenty times more in the scale of things than these pretty refined Miss Trenches and Miss Ravertys'.

On her feelings about class Stella was examining herself rather closely: 'One has quite a different liking', she found, 'for a person one feels is one's equal, and a person who one knows to be vulgar, though one may like them more.' It was all very puzzling, though at the same time most instructive. There were old women in Arosa who, by making use of the expression 'quite the lady', clearly indicated that they were not themselves in that category (yet oddly enough one notices that she and her mother, about whose good breeding there could be no shadow of doubt, could describe people as 'not quite ladies' and get away with it). Most of the visitors were in fact what Stella, using the term pejoratively, described as 'middle class . . . the sort of people who always notice if you have a new clo on, and talk about "itching" and love talking about the state of people's lungs' – the sort of people who could smell out a 'case' (a love affair) ten miles off, and then never stop talking about it. The Alexandra Hotel was, Stella reckoned, her 'university of human nature'. Early in 1911 she noted how 'passionately interested in and fond of people' she had become, and how her hobby was 'the collection of human characteristics'. People passed through in such numbers that she became enured to meetings and farewells, and lost a lot of her shyness. There is no doubt that for Stella as social creature and novelist the pleurisy attack at Freiburg was a blessing in disguise.

If her criticism of other people's motives and behaviour was at times severe, she was even harder on her own:

> I feel a cheat when somebody likes me. They wouldn't if they knew. There, for once I have been honest and told the truth about myself. My one redeeming point is that I want to be better, but that counts for nothing if no improvement ever results from it.

Even her apparent good deeds came under acid scrutiny. If she did something that in another she would think kind (like running up to the village in the June heat to get a person something), somehow, in herself, it did not seem very kind: 'It is only kind in the sense that it would be unkind not to do it . . . it is a cheap way to get gratitude . . . it makes me almost unhappy . . . as if I was pretending to be a more unselfish person than I am.'

Each morning she examined her conscience and resolved to be good. Her sins were chiefly social ones, hotel peccadilloes – exaggeration, insincerity, self-consciousness, talking scandal. As she saw it, vanity was her cardinal sin. It was a base craving for admiration that made her practise her guitar, perfect

the art of whistling, polish her caricatures and indulge in argument and
repartee, especially with men. Worse, vanity ruled her likings and dislik-
ings, the people she liked most invariably being the people who liked her.
Alone of her occupations, her writing seemed innocent of vanity, because
she never showed it to anyone (between August 1910 and March 1911 she
was busy with a novel, now long dust; with a certain sense of relief she
found that writing drove away the thought people – 'they seem to have gone
into the book'). Friction with her mother was another rich source of
self-reproach. Storms seemed to blow up out of clear skies, and Mrs
Benson's high-bred inhibitions, her inability either to demonstrate her own
warmer feelings or to enable her daughter to demonstrate hers, were often
the root of the trouble.

After receiving a casual caress from a girl of her acquaintance, Stella wrote
in July 1910,

> I suppose it shows a very cheap taste in me to love touch, friendly touch,
> so much. One takes for granted people love one or like one more or less.
> But when one belongs to strenuously undemonstrative people like mine,
> it is such heaven to be shown that somebody likes one now and then.
> Mother always seems to be dissatisfied. Ever since she arrived here she
> hasn't given any sign of being pleased with anything I have said or done or
> tried to do. She can hardly expect demonstrativeness because she can
> never give it herself. But if I ever have girls dependent on me, I shall try
> and be just as keen on showing them where they have been right as where
> they have been wrong.

When her mother was expected back from England, Stella keyed herself to
give her a warm welcome, but it was no good: 'I get stiff and a little shy, and I
don't suppose she will ever know how much I want her always.'

She prayed to God to help her overcome her faults, she prayed for faith,
and it was the apparent failure of the deity to respond that made her lose
patience with religion:

> How can I believe in a God that does not answer my prayer for faith? It is
> not logical [at this time Stella had a high regard for logic, which she saw as
> an essentially male, and therefore superior, attribute of mind]. I shall not
> pray any more, because it is a mockery, and useless. I will see whether I
> can improve my life without any Deity's help by just trying to think of
> other people. But I wish I knew someone well enough to ask about these
> things.

Some time later she gave God another chance. She asked Him to help her
to be good for just one day. It didn't seem to work. At some point in the day

her mother had occasion to ask her why she was being sulky, and she was 'so furious that this God of theirs could let me down like that, that I ran out of the room and banged the door', leaving God to the true believers. When her mother was away she rarely went to church, and, when she did, made a point of not saying the creed.

'Sometimes a sort of strong-minded feeling wells up in me. I grit my teeth and know that nothing can prevent me from doing what I wish to do. . . . I feel that if you won't admit defeat, there is nothing left for defeat to do except to turn into victory.' This was the young woman of nineteen whom her anxious and careful mother escorted home to England in the early summer of 1911. Home was not Hampshire now, but Kent. Mrs Benson had rented an old house at Glassenbury near Cranbrook, 'all uneven passages and great black beams. . . . the panes in the windows are for the most part the original 16th century panes with funny old names scribbled and dates'. Stella had a rapturous reunion with Pepper and then she succumbed to flu. As usual, it hit her hard: this time huge faces seemed to peer in at her through the window. Flu over, her mother insisted that the Swiss 'cure' continue, even while admitting that it did not seem to have done much good; for her part Stella thought that she would be better dead than lying in a summerhouse all day and occasionally taking the dog for a walk round two or three 'beastly old fields'. To occupy what was in fact a fairly quiet summer, she rewrote her novel, and had Laura Hutton to stay. Two and a half years her senior, Laura had been a friend since Lutwyche days, when her father was the incumbent of Easthope. She had grown into an unusual young woman – 'saintly', 'sweet', 'delicate of heart', wrote Stella, who felt protective towards Laura, despite her friend's superiority in age. When Stella revealed her taste for flirtation, Laura confessed that she never flirted, and could not even if she wanted to. In spare moments, Stella pencilled in her diary sharp critical comments on the hundred and one members of Cranbrook society who passed before her eye, read Emerson, and, as an alternative to the Christian God, was attracted by his idea of an 'Oversoul': 'God is merely the collective name for all the good in us.' In August she had what was to be her penultimate meeting with her father. At forty-nine he was quite white, seemed broken in mind and body, and had a nurse in attendance; she found him 'not in the least terrifying now, but very gentle'. To humour him she played her guitar and whistled while he, enjoying it very much, joined in with 'funny topsy-turvy accompaniments on the piano'. The meeting was strangely comforting, only going to show 'how happy it all would have been' if he had not let himself get into the power of 'that dreadful thing'.

In October she and her mother set off abroad, their destination Chernex, a village near Montreux which they had seen and liked the previous spring.

'Blinking to keep himself from crying', Father had waved them off from Folkestone. After three days came news that he was dead of haemorrhage of the brain.

While her mother hurried back for the funeral, Stella got her clothes dyed to mourning and awaited the arrival of a temporary chaperone. She felt closer to her father than ever before, which scarcely seemed 'logical'. But, faced with the ultimate mystery, she was prepared to concede: 'what could be more illogical than Life, and Nature, and Death?'

The hotel at Chernex was run by the Dutch largely for the Dutch: 'I am so bored, I am so bored,' cried Stella, and after a month she and Susan McLeod, who had come out to relieve the temporary chaperone, moved to Corbeyrier, a resort near the eastern tip of Lake Geneva, where things began to look up: 'How I love being liked! How I revel in being a little bit pretty! And how beastly it is of me to write that!' She threw herself into the familiar pleasures of an alpine resort in wintertime, until in February her mother came to take her away to the Pyrenees, where at Vernet the Cholmondeleys were living the life of luxury and ease always associated in Stella's mind with that fortunate family. She had a day 'in heaven' motoring with them to the Mediterranean: 'all the time the delight of it was running in my head – motoring in the South of France, motoring in the South of France. How perfect it sounds and how perfect it is!' There were endless picnics, tennis tournaments, charades, sketching parties, concerts and dances; the visiting English community staged Gilbert and Sullivan's *Trial by Jury* and bridesmaid Stella was obliged to flirt before the public gaze. In April she shared the world's horror at the *Titanic* disaster: 'It is the struggle and choke that make me cry, and the incredibly brave way in which most of the men met it. There were only three who forgot themselves, and they were Italians. They were shot down at once.' (As we now know, early reports of the tragedy were highly inaccurate.)

Vernet abounded in young men. 'I have never flirted or been flirted with so strongly,' she confessed, after a reckless evening spent with a 'bounder'. It taught her what may well have been among the unwritten ten commandments of the young lady of that age: 'Never begin in flirtation [*sic*] sort of strain at the beginning of dinner. It gets out of hand. Begin mildly, and if you must flirt arrive there at dessert, not before.' But none of the young men touched her heart, and after three seasons of vigorous socialising with no more than a few transient *tendresses* to show for them, an undercurrent of anxiety, almost of panic, underlay the admission: 'I have seldom been in the least hard hit by a man, but I don't care how hard hit he is by me!' In her imagination an ideal of manhood existed, certainly: cultured, gentlemanly, brilliant, but – alas! – tragically flawed: 'If I could meet a man like Father must have been I would love him at once, but I don't think such men exist now. . . . Besides Mother thought him perfect, and look what he became.'

*

Back in England for the summer of 1912 she seemed in better health than she had been for years, so well in fact that her mother let her embark alone (after all she was twenty and old enough to travel unaccompanied on trains) on a strenuous series of visits to friends and relations dotted about England and Wales: Cholmondeleys at Preshaw, Pinfields at Bishops Stortford, Lloyds at Reading, Prescotts at Bockleton, near Tenbury (her father's sister Frederica, 'Aunt Freddie', had married into the landed gentry of Herefordshire).

The Prescotts drove her to see Lutwyche, more than sixty miles there and back. It was years since she had been there, and the first sight of the old house, along the wide walled drive of portugal yews, was 'heaven'; the tenants were away and the butler let them see round: 'I didn't remember the inside of the house much, only the picture over the drawingroom fireplace, and the hall, and the little panel in the diningroom that opens into an "unknown vault".'

On to Uncle Tom Cholmondeley, her mother's elder brother, and Aunt Margaret, at Pant-y-Ochin near Wrexham (Uncle Tom gave her pause for thought when he took her aside and told her that when she came of age in six months' time she would have £178 a year), then to Custs at Fleet, Drummonds in London, to Aunt Mary Cholmondeley at Ufford, 'constantly on the watch for the first signs of inner things to come bubbling out', to Gibsons at Newbury and Pennimans near York. She saw the season through in apparent health, and when in October a cough and sore throat developed, for the first time in her life she was surprised: she had been thinking that her 'idiotic delicacy' was a thing of the past. It made the expressions of sympathy of kind relations doubly unbearable: 'I hate my body – can't they listen to me, and not my cough? Can't they guess that I've had my health to bear all my life and don't want to hear any more about it?'

With the prospect before her of another Swiss winter, during her last weeks she made a point of sampling what London had to offer. There was the newsreel of the Delhi durbar, showing 'our poor puny little George' receiving humble obeisance from 'magnificent Indian princes'; she came out from that feeling 'about three inches taller, very proud to be English'. There was the Post-Impressionist Exhibition at the Grafton Galleries. She stood with furrowed brow before Picasso's *Tête d'homme*, 'a collection of drab-coloured angles and lines of different sizes and with no regularity clinging together. I might draw this and exhibit it.' Her period of mourning now being nearly over, she bought herself a coloured two-piece suit, and sketched it in her diary: tight-fitting jacket with high upstanding collar, narrow ankle-length skirt, close-set buttons from top to toe; to go with it she bought a wide, floppy, beefeater-style hat with plume. She hoped the ensemble would boost her confidence and keep her warm during the coming season at Corbeyrier.

After a considerable search, Mrs Benson had lit upon a suitable girl of Stella's own age to act as 'companion' (we learn nothing of the financial side of the arrangement), and in October they set off together. It interested Stella that Barbara Drummond – no relation of the family she had stayed with in the summer – insisted on having two hours a day free 'for writing', but any hopes she had of finding a kindred spirit were soon dashed: Barbara's *forte* was turning out the most saccharine of romantic verse, and when Stella asked her why she did it, she replied – in surprise that anyone could ask such a silly question – 'to get a little money out of the magazines'. It was not a happy relationship, and when eventually Barbara packed her bags and went, relief was no doubt mutual. 'I don't think I have ever met a genuine prig before,' Stella wrote.

The alarming deterioration in Stella's health that autumn had made her difficult to live with. Her 'dear old acquaintance' pain was back in full force. Her right ear was hurting, she had a cough that seemed to 'explode in my brain', and a very severe pain beneath her ribs which made a worried doctor fetched from afar think that she was on the verge of congestion of the lungs. Also, she was getting bad headaches, which she had never had before. She spent her twenty-first birthday in bed, and when, shortly after, her mother arrived ('very sweet' and bearing Aunt Florie's coming-of-age present, a pendant opal set in diamonds) she at once set about 'invaliding' her. For once, her daughter did not mind, as 'deep down in the truthful regions beyond self-deception I know that I feel particularly bad at times'.

Chapter Four

In March Stella had flu, in April the pain in her side was still 'bubbling and booming away' and a doctor, with more candour than tact, told her to consider herself 'a cracked tea-cup'. The corollary – that henceforth she must exist on a shelf – she rejected with utter scorn. Her hearing was deteriorating, and a specialist consulted in Lausanne warned that total deafness was not far off; 'very kind and most impressive in manner' as Dr Barraud was, he hurt. On the third of a series of visits he had her 'screaming and beating his hands away from my poor head'. Between visits Mrs Benson improvised little treats, and on that occasion they went out and bought Stella a 'bright gold dress'. But what would be the use of pretty clothes, she asked herself, once she became stone deaf and could no more 'talk and retort and be amused'? Suddenly, all sounds were precious: 'I listened hard to silly little homely sounds like a distant dog barking, or the wind in the trees, or people crunching biscuits.' When at the end of April they started for England, Barraud's treatment was by no means finished: he expected her back in the autumn to tackle what he suspected was the root of the trouble, blocked and infected sinuses. It was a dreadful prospect, and, when they passed through Paris, as a tiny sop she was treated to some 'golden shoes and stockings' to go with the dress.

That spring and summer England was a-buzz with talk of the militant suffragettes. Faced with what they considered to be repeated betrayal by Asquith's government, Emmeline Pankhurst's Women's Social and Political Union had stepped up its campaign of violence. Suffragette arson was at its height and suffragettes were actually seeking arrest, and continuing their protest in prison by means of hunger-strike. The resulting outcry had prompted parliament to pass the Temporary Discharge for Ill-Health Act (the notorious 'Cat and Mouse Act'), which gave the authorities power to release in mid-sentence hunger-strikers whose health was in danger, and when they were partially recovered to rearrest them.

Up to this time Stella, in so far as she had any view at all, sided with the moderates – men and women who deplored the use of violence, and put their faith in constitutional methods of protest; thousands such were banded together in Millicent Fawcett's National Union of Suffrage Societies. It was the death of the militant suffragette Emily Wilding Davison, the so-called 'Derby Martyr', who flung herself in the path of the king's horse at that year's race, that made her think again. She did not doubt that Emily Davison had made a deliberate sacrifice of her life. The tragic gesture fired her imagination, and – rather confusedly – she felt that because of its extreme nature it deserved support. Characteristically, she talked herself round in the course of debate with various friends and relations. 'It is a revelation', she wrote indignantly after one such exchange, 'to hear well-educated and clever men argue so fatuously. The discussion left me a Militant in theory. The practice is yet to come!'

Defying 'bad deafness', 'violent headaches', 'intermittent blindness' (no doubt associated with the head pain), plus the consciousness that she was speaking in a husky voice, she set about her own 'private Stellarian Suffrage Campaign' of argument and persuasion, carrying the gospel into a number of peaceful drawing rooms. A charming family of Bengoughs, landowners in Worcestershire temporarily resident in Cranbrook, were particularly appreciative of what she had to say on that, or indeed on any subject, even if they did not always share her point of view. In spite of her keen appetite for praise, Stella found the innocent blandishments of this warm-hearted family somewhat excessive; Gwenda and Evelyn, the two elder daughters, were often censured in her diary for being 'sugary'. As to Nigel, the second son, he was most flatteringly ubiquitous at all the social events in and around Cranbrook that she attended. In fact it was obvious that he was falling ever more deeply in love with her. The year before she had singled him out as 'an attractive youth' (he was two years her junior), adding airily, 'I should have said by his face he was a genius, but I believe it belies him'; now she was saying, 'if he were three years older I should propose to him', not meaning it for an instant.

For alongside her new-found militancy, a resolve was growing in her to leave home and take up some kind of work. Paradoxically and typically, it was the recent shocking collapse in her health that decided her. If she was never going to be strong enough to marry, as increasingly she feared, then certainly she was not going to spend the rest of her life at home being pampered and protected by her mother: 'I don't want to die,' was how she put it, 'but I won't stop kicking.'

Though the male sex interested her enormously, and in weak moments she very much wished that she were more sexually attractive – 'I am a beastly inward flirt without the outward means of flirting,' she wrote, characteristically undervaluing her successes in that field – she was not at all sure that she wanted marriage: 'I want to be great in ways that marriage would prevent. If it was impressed upon me that I was perfectly ordinary and my future ordinary marriage and consequent silly dependence, I should have no more illusions left to live on. I should flare up and die a burnt-out cinder.' Meanwhile, a great deal depended on the result of the coming sinus treatment.

In October Stella was back in Lausanne. There was a series of painful sessions with Barraud, culminating in the extraction of a piece of bone under local anaesthetic (because of the state of her lungs doctors were unwilling to give her total anaesthesia). Stella was prepared to admit that her sufferings were 'to a great extent nervous', but that did not make them one whit less real or terrifying. There was the feeling that 'with such tremendous pressure as he uses, leaning all his strength', he might let the instrument slip 'and go right through my skull, pinning it to the wall at the back'. There was:

> the terrible feeling of a bone splintering before it breaks off. I can't get rid of the fearful pain of it. After it I became altogether immovable and couldn't stand up, and couldn't stop screaming. The doctor carried me about and patted me and for a long time I lay on the operating table. I think I fainted. It seemed hours and hours. Every time I felt better I remembered the splintering and lost my hold on myself again.

He was not done yet, for he wanted to approach the obstruction in her maxillary sinus by way of an incision in the roof of the mouth. Before the operation had even begun her brain had 'gone to water' with sheer fright. She was partially anaesthetised with morphia, and cocained in the immediate area of the incision, but she was conscious throughout the hour-long ordeal. What was desperately needed was a drug to numb her imagination. 'I was on that terrible table to be vivisected. The breaking of the bone above my teeth was fearful. At one time there was loud screaming, but I did not realise it was myself for some time, when I put a stop to it.' If Stella is accurate in her account, Madame Barraud, who was assisting, almost fainted, Monsieur swore loudly and now and again seemed to be weeping – but possibly the moisture that she observed on his cheek was only perspiration.

The convalescence was painful. She spoke of 'great pain all day and a waking nightmare of a night'. Then the stitches in the 'great wound' began to come out, and that was 'no less disgusting than interesting. It seems to give my tongue access to my brain, which is most shocking and hardly bearable.' Six days after the operation they let her see her face; it was 'pale grey–green on one side deepening to a rich indigo tinged with gamboge round the eye'. Four days later – and weighing only seven stone – she

was taking a walk in the hospital garden. Five days after that she was
gone.

Anxious to indulge Stella after her ordeal, and aware of the therapeutic
effects of the Jamaican air, Mrs Benson had booked their passage on a ship
bound for the West Indies. Stella chose a 'Blick' typewriter before she left,
'as the first step to getting my book published', and it formed an important
part of her cabin luggage when, on 19 November, she embarked on the SS
Magdalena, though it is doubtful whether she touched it on the voyage. Her
spirits had bobbed up corklike from the sufferings of Lausanne, and she was
agog for all the fun that was going. Indeed so full of events were her days
that she found it necessary to supplement her diary with separate sheets,
densely covered and attached with pins.

What made social success comparatively easy was the fact that the ship
was filled with unattached males, with no more than a trio of unmarried girls
to occupy their time and attention. Having only days in which to get to
know each other, there was no risk of awkward entanglements, and Stella
found herself circumambulating the decks in uninhibited fashion with a
whole string of young men in turn, 'saying what I like and indulging in
cigarettes in public'. The atmosphere was one of 'great and all-embracing
friendliness', but even so Stella's fragile self-confidence could easily be
shattered. A small setback, like finding that her dance card had not filled up
as fast as the other girls', could plunge her into deepest despair: 'Of course, I
am not a real girl. There is no game like playing with men, but I must give it
up.'

At Kingston they were invited to spend the first night at Government
House. The Governor, Sir William Manning, terrified Stella, and under his
'cold eye' she dared neither smoke nor trot out her more outrageous
theories; she was not a bit surprised to hear that his wife had run off with the
aide-de-camp. Next day they proceeded inland to the pleasant village of
Mandeville, famed for its salubrious climate, its oranges and its superficially
English appearance, installing themselves in a 'shocking' and 'dirty' hotel
which had its bathroom and other necessaries at the bottom of the garden: 'I
like roughing it a little,' claimed Stella, but this was altogether too much.
After a week they moved to a suitably civilised hotel, the Newleigh, where
Stella set about typing her novel in earnest, in the intervals of pursuing an
agreeable social life: 'I am very seldom shy now,' she noticed, 'as the shyer I
am, the more I talk.' The climate provided the only exotic note at Christmas.
Then, on a note of ease after pain, the old year faded out.

Stella set about the preamble to her diary for 1914 in a spirit of qualified
optimism: 'I am expecting a good deal from 1914, but what exactly, or even
approximately, I don't know. Every year I think I am on the brink of a great
adventure, but only minor – though at times splendid – adventures come.'

She hoped to become more settled in her beliefs during the year: 'I have honestly tried to believe in the things I have been taught, but now I will be more honest still and admit that I can't. I am not a Christian, at any rate till I find something more in Christianity than I have noticed up to the present.' Discarding religious faith, she was actively searching for an alternative form of belief: 'I have worked one out,' she explained with earnest naivety, 'but am at present not thoroughly convinced by it.' She expected to be lonely (the Bengoughs would be abroad during the summer, George was in India), and since loneliness made her difficult to live with, there might be ructions at home. But the great consolation was that her health – her comparative outward health, as she guardedly put it – seemed better than ever before: 'At least it does not now become immediately known that I am an unhealthy woman, when I meet anyone new. My voice at least is normal, and though I cough all the time, still a cough is more tolerable than an inadequate voice. This improvement I owe to the tortures at Lausanne.' She ended on a note of cheerful defiance: 'Now, 1914, do your worst.' Nine months later, with half Europe locked in bloody conflict, she was to add the bitter rider: 'And it did.'

Meanwhile the Jamaican idyll continued. As the only 'civilised English girl' at the Newleigh, Stella was the recipient of a good deal of male attention, holding court on the verandah in a swaying three-seater 'hammock-sofa'. One youngish parson was seriously smitten, and less young men seem to have found her blend of pert argumentativeness and youthful vulnerability piquant and appealing; the way in which, each evening, they conspired to rustle up a bridge four, simply in order to indulge her known passion for the game, seemed to her almost embarrassingly attentive. Two men, both a good deal older than she, occupied a lot of her time and thought. An American in his mid-thirties, Arthur Bullard, a professional journalist-cum-novelist, was interestingly different from any man she had met before. Plebeian, and ugly into the bargain, he was intensely sympathetic, candid and kind, giving her hardheaded advice on how to write fiction and 'place it on the market'. After reading her newly completed novel he advised her quite frankly to rewrite it, pointing out that, while there were excellent things in it, they were nearly all in the wrong places, and a lot of them in the wrong book altogether. At one stage she was afraid of losing her heart to Bullard, which she knew would not do: 'I find that though I am not conventional, I am not far gone enough to wish to introduce A.B. to my haughty relations as the man I had decided on.'

Mr Duncan, at forty-two, was quite a different kettle of fish: he was that tragi-comic figure, the remittance man. Boasting of having run through thirty thousand pounds in his twenties and three minor fortunes since, he was exiled to the Colonies on a modest pension pending signs of amendment. From periodic drinking bouts he would emerge haggard and baleful, to mesmerise Stella with his sado-masochistic style of flirtation: if she paid what he considered too much attention to another man he sulked tragically for days on end, and did his best to make her suffer too. On one occasion he brought a guest under the lee of her sofa and talked loudly about 'the awful life he had been living, with only fools (damn fools) to talk to, and no pretty girls'. (The laugh, it transpired, was on Stella, as the unfortunate Duncan had paraded his guest, one Lord Henry Carr, before the other residents as a peer, whereas in fact he was the son of a local storekeeper, and 'Lord' was his Christian name.) But even as poor a creature as Mr Duncan, given the appropriate setting, could trigger novelettishly romantic thoughts. Alone with him one evening Stella 'knew for the first time in my life how exciting it was to sit in the moonlight with a man who cares for you. Somehow it didn't seem to matter that the man was a waster and impossible. . . . It was just so glorious to be a girl, and to know that you and the moon shared all the power in the world.'

Apart from enjoying tributes to her feminine charm, there were excursions to be made in motor cars to recognised beauty-spots, and to view in production the local manufactures – sugar, rum and cigars. The hotel residents were on easy terms with the local whites. One Jamaican gentleman presented Stella with a couple of boxes of lizards which she set about taming, with some damage to Mr Duncan's fingers and hers. And the visitors made their own amusements: the Benson ladies introduced to the West Indies the institution of the Tango Tea, which had been all the rage in England for a year past. Stella's daring home-made tango dress reappeared in tableaux successfully put on by her and another girl:

We heard as we stood the sighs of real approval, or the unpretended laughter of the audience as the case might be. I had my Tango pose violently encored, and kept my transfixed eyes glued on the expression of young Clarke at the back, who had probably never seen anyone with so little skirt on in his life.

Nowhere in the diary does Stella refer to her family's former slave-owning interests in the West Indies; and certainly she shared neither her father's guilt-feelings towards the negro race, nor his sympathy with it. Her attitude – of scorn, even disgust – is marked, and not unfairly represented by her behaviour towards a black boy who followed her and her mother on a walk, 'smelling horrid, and commenting on our remarks to each other. Twice I told him in my lordly way to desist and he would not. I then hit him with my parasol, and he recoiled slightly, but continued the impertinence at a safer distance. We then met a neighbouring nigger, and wormed from him the name and address of our aggressor, which frightened him off. I regret very much that I did not hit him harder.' She was more tolerant of mulattos, while being vividly aware of their lowly social status. To her mother's

distress she even sat down at the card table with an 'altogether unpreten-
tious and nice' half-caste man; he played a good hand at bridge, yet 'it felt
rather like playing with one's butler, one spoke to him in a cooing lordly
way, and took care not to hurt his feelings. It is incredible what a difference
black blood makes in one's attitude. Before I came here I couldn't have
understood it.' With a large female contingent from the hotel she went to
see a smart mulatto wedding, afterwards reflecting: 'I hope these people
don't feel as inferior as we instinctively think them. It would be an almost
killing feeling to be born the other side of that cruel barrier.'

While piquing herself on being 'modern', Stella was in many ways a
typical product of her class and time. She was appalled to hear of any
mingling of the social layers:

'You ought to have come out by the Direct Line [said one young woman
archly]. There is only one class and all the servants were with us. It is
much more fun.' I broke my rule and asked why. Miss Joint replied in a
voice of surprise at my inanity that it was such fun dancing and flirting
with the chauffeurs and valets. Some of my Socialism fell from me with a
crash.

On the woman question she had genuinely up-to-date views, and was on
the lookout for opportunities to air them – or even to give them practical
demonstration: 'That was a fine moment for Woman's Suffrage and
woman's independence and woman's claim to equality,' she triumphed,
after climbing a lichi tree that Mr Duncan dared not attempt.

Many a painful discussion about her future must have taken place
between Stella and her mother, but in her diaries she chooses not to go into
them: we map Stella's determined advance, her mother's watery-eyed
retreat only from hints. However, it is clear that by this time Mrs Benson
had resigned herself to the fact that when they got back to England her
daughter was to leave home and live on her own, the better to devote herself
in some as yet undefined way to the suffrage cause. Feeling that it was her
duty to do so, Mrs Benson did not fail to point out that in that way Stella
would 'drop out of her class', and find herself mixing with 'terrible men and
exasperating women'. But Stella was unmoved:

This would matter if I intended to marry, but for the present I am firmly
determined not to, so it doesn't matter to me if for a few years I never
meet any eligible men. I don't intend to stay at the bottom of the ladder,
and when one gets to the higher rungs on any ladder one can always
follow one's bent socially speaking. Beyond this and the important
objection of my health, Mother does not raise any obstacle in the way of
my independence. She is extremely kind and unselfish about it.

This being so, it was all the more infuriating when Mother chose to side with an old gentleman who expressed the ridiculous view that women should all stay at home until they married, even if their relatives did not depend on them in any way:

> It is a long time since I have been so angry. The interfering old brute with his ideas for the slow murdering of women's hard-won souls. Ideas that date from Adam. Even Eve was allowed her own views about the apple. . . . I wish I had been ruder, and I wish I had not cried. . . . I don't think it is very generous of Mother to collect old fossils to snub me about my plans. . . . with Sir Anthony there she mourned and said she depended on me at home, which is directly untrue. Nobody could be less needed at home than I am, I don't even arrange the flowers.

The voyage home, aboard RMS *Danube*, started on 18 March, and on the third day out passengers had the opportunity to view a tourist attraction of the first magnitude. The Panama Canal, after a long series of setbacks, was verging on completion, and would have its formal opening in August. Stella was duly impressed. 'Culebra Cut[1] is a marvel. On one side the great wall of natural rock rises up sere and safe and solid. On the other it is just a string of old tragedies. Slide after slide breaks the outline of this poor stupendous effort of man. . . . But the Americans will carry it through because they are beaten, and they won't admit they are beaten, and that is a quite invincible spirit.'

On board, she was discontented. After being the recipient of so much flattering attention in Jamaica it was galling to find herself, on the *Danube*, simply one of a crowd – especially when that crowd was made up of such tiresomely typical representatives of 'The Generation'. 'I absolutely refuse', she protested, 'to compete with these other wriggling, giggling girls for the attention of conceited youths'. *Faute de mieux*, with passionate intensity she played bridge with her seniors, 'while the young people danced'.

For all her sense of exclusion from the younger set, she led an intensely social life, and – vital to her self-esteem – was not short of male attention. There was a certain Sir John Smiley of whom she had to confess:

> He behaves very oddly, and it is my fault. He touches me too much. I think he is a bad man, and not one for a woman who hopes soon to be unprotected to have for a friend. He wants to take me to dinner at the Savoy when I am alone in town. Of course, I said I would be too busy, and that what I wanted was isolated independence, and he clutched my arm and said, 'Don't you see I can't stand this!'

Eventually she got his measure, and found to her amusement that two could play at his game: 'Of course, he thinks he is breaking my heart, and believes he is fooling me. I do not attempt to undeceive him, and enjoy fooling one so sophisticated.' More seemly (indeed in the best drawing-room style) were the attentions of a Mr Russack, who humbly asked permission to instruct her in the uses and advantages of her own eyes: 'I have gazed at them since in the glass,' Stella wrote in all seriousness, 'and I can't see anything in them very special. . . . Everything about my looks is as ordinary as possible.'

Three days before docking at Southampton, Stella went down with pleurisy, and was confined to bed; fellow passengers visited, one young man sitting outside her open door talking for hours, until her mother caught him at it and sent him packing.

To convalesce, she went to Dorton, the Cholmondeley's new place in Oxfordshire. She found the house 'unnecessarily solid and overpoweringly large', and was never to take it to her heart like Preshaw. On her first evening the old nanny gave her a bath, calling back childhood memories – not all of them welcome:

> It was rather nice making such an entire lapse into infancy again and being sponged and rubbed, and talking breathlessly through the towel, and Nana saying 'Yes, dear,' without paying the least attention. Talk about childhood being impossible to recall, one can seize it like everything else, if one sets about it in the right way. Only one doesn't want to get it back much as a rule, unless it comes spontaneously. Personally I have no wish at all for the return of my childhood. I hope never to be so unhappy again, or so unlovable, or so morbid, as I was up to the age of seventeen.

Sitting at her bedside next day, her privileged friend Aunt Florie spoke her mind about the unwisdom of her seeking 'independence', and for good measure gave her a talking-to about her mother: 'she says that I have formed the habit of mistrusting anything that Mother sets her heart on, and of choosing always to set my heart on the things that Mother distrusts'. In reply – armoured with the ruthlessness so necessary to youth's survival – Stella said in effect that she was very sorry, but there was nothing she could do about it. To her aunt's objection that she was careless of her health she opposed her current philosophy of positive thinking, what she called her 'Christian Science methods':

> I am so lucky that the dice fall right for me nine times out of ten, and the freedom gained by trusting to luck is quite worth the catastrophe that befalls me on the tenth throw. I am quite sure that my ill-health will pass away and is passing away. If I decide to become healthy, and behave like a healthy woman, I must become healthy.

On their way through London she and her mother called on Aunts Mary and V, and after lunch 'as I knew they would' the two younger sisters 'melted away', leaving Stella to have her plans talked over with Aunt Mary: 'However, I tried gently to imply that they were all settled as firm as a rock, and that any discussion must be altogether posthumous. After this ordeal I went and bought myself a hat, and looked rather a cherub in it.'

At Cranbrook she broke her plans to Susan McLeod, who was 'rather upset'; however, she agreed to accept as a gift Stella's aged dog Tupman, the former Pepper, who somewhere along the road of life had undergone a change of name. 'The Adorable Nigel', far from having matured during 'this immense six months that has passed', seemed younger than ever. Sitting on top of a haystack together, they merrily 'talked tosh': 'he is such a boy that the kind of tosh I talk to him and he talks to me is perfectly unconscious, and has none of the tiresome element of tosh with a grown-up man'. Clearly his immaturity and the absence from their relationship of sexual tension were, to her, major attractions.

One presumes that the Rodney Club, Emperor's Gate, South Kensington, had been personally recommended as a safe haven for Stella. On Monday 27 April she went to London and closed with a room there, 'the best room in the house'. However, she did not escape a brush with the secretary, Miss James, a woman 'brisk and bright and overflowing with commonsense':

> She found fault with me on the ground of my youth, my look of delicacy, and my professed Militancy. The youth objection I treated with silent scorn, the health objection I argued away, and as for the protest against Militancy, I merely promised not to use that address if in trouble.

As the day of the great move – Saturday 2 May – drew yet nearer, Stella showed signs of strain. On the Wednesday, with all the polite society of Cranbrook and neighbourhood, she went to a matinée recital given by 'THE Percy Grainger, England's Percy', the Australian-born pianist and composer celebrated for his dedication to English folk music. After the concert things went badly wrong at home, 'entirely owing to my miserable temper. . . . I am at once ruffled by Mother's inconsequence and inconsistency, but of course ought not to be, as they are only the echo of the first approaching steps of old age' (Mrs Benson was then fifty-three). On the Thursday she packed all day in a fury of nerves, as though Kenya not Kensington were her destination: 'Everything I ever loved I could not find, and all the bugbears of my childhood appeared in forgotten receptacles.' It was scarcely an auspicious moment for a first lesson in driving, and sure enough, on the Friday, in Nigel's dashing Martini car – Gwenda at her side – she ran full tilt into some railings.

Afterwards over tea Gwenda 'burbled with flatteries' (not about the driving), but as Stella remarked to her diary that evening, cryptically, 'luckily for my soul, I shall soon be beyond the reach of flattery'. It was as though she were entering a religious order – or even going to her execution.

Part III

'Independence' 1914–1918

Chapter Five

Saturday 2 May 1914

To-day ended the old life and began the new. Mother was very much grieved at my going away, and just at the point of departure dreadfully distressed, but whether because she thinks it unkind of me to go, or because she is afraid it will end disastrously for me I don't know. . . . I think it is only because she feels in a vague way painfully left alone and unloved, and because her children are no comfort to her middle age, and because she has few friends and nobody always there to be happy with. It is her nature to be happy in company, I can't imagine her alone. Still if she would only realise it, I was never in sympathy with her, to all appearances, and she never was at her ease with me. . . . We none of us seem to draw her out at all, it seems a long time since I heard her whistle and sing. I have distressed and hurt her by going away. It would have been nobler and finer to have stayed at home, but it would be almost super-fine, as my presence gives her no pleasure. . . .

Anyway I came up to my Rodney Club, and was there pressed under the wing of Miss James, who appears to think me too young and thin to be without a wing. I had dinner with about a dozen other Working Women. My neighbours were a typist and an artist, we talked dully about the weather in spasms . . .

Two days later, on the Monday, Stella called on a woman met on the *Danube*, who was hopeful of finding her work for the suffrage cause ('steer clear of the Pankhursts', she advised). She now produced two ladies prominent in the Women Writers' Suffrage League.[1]

Little did those self-important persons suspect what was proceeding in the mind of the modest-seeming young woman before them: one lady 'seemed chiefly notable on account of her fluent acquaintanceship with all the big actresses and the big authoresses', the other was 'an ugly hardworked smart woman who talked politics, insisting all the while that she was non-party, an impossibly Utopian pose'. However, the upshot was the offer of a job in the impressive sounding 'Literary Department' of the League; a glimpse of the headquarters in Henrietta Street, Covent Garden, a few days later told Stella that the office she was to work in was a 'very small and dingy spot', and that her future chief was 'fat, smart and loud in talking'. As things turned out, it was some time before she could take a closer look.

She had spent her first week in London pleasantly enough in the company of old friends. The faithful Nigel was in town, studying at the Royal School of Mines, Imperial College, South Kensington; on the first Sunday he tickled her vanity by crossing Emperor's Gate in all his 'superbness' under the admiring eyes of several of her fellow 'working women' while they were at lunch. He took her to the zoo, where they looked at snakes and stags, her favourites and his (she had a theory, which Nigel was happy to go along with, that everyone had a soul-affinity with a particular animal; hers was with snakes, because of their cold blood, and ability to propel themselves with only minimal contact with the earth). They went to the Coliseum Theatre to see Lily Langtry, and had tea in the Piccadilly Hotel afterwards. Nigel was all eagerness to take her out again, but she refused, being of the opinion that he was 'spending too much of his poor little dress allowance' on her. Her cousin Essex was in town, Gwenda came up for the day, the three girls lunched and 'tead' together at a ladies' club, the Women's Athenaeum. 'Finding that Gwenda was not yet considered an independent woman enough to be allowed on the Underground alone,' Stella noted with half-playful scorn, 'I chaperoned her back, and packed her safely off to her homely little Cranbrook again.' Nora Pinfield of Freiburg days had asked her to be a bridesmaid at her June wedding; she had a fitting for her dress – in her opinion very dear – but 'sniffed at' by the dressmaker as being ridiculously cheap, and after its brief moment of glory fit only for 'every night at small hotels abroad'. (Stella considered she looked 'quite inoffensive' in the dress, which, with 'quite harmless', was the current London locution for unexpectedly pretty: 'our verbal enthusiasms in this generation are becoming so faint that presently we shall have none left us'.) She went to see the cinematograph pictures of R. F. Scott's Antarctic expedition of 1911–12: 'It was incredible to be able to wave goodbye to Scott and his four companions, to watch them wave so jokily and yet to know that they never came back.' She spent a couple of tiring days helping her Aunt Phyllis[2] with Labour Exchange Committee work. But none of these doings seem to account for the dramatic decline in her health – the feverishness that ruined her enjoyment of Shaw's new, much talked about play *Pygmalion* (to which, 'chaperoned by Essex', she took Nigel), the coughing up of blood that brought the aunts' physician Dr Robert Monckton rushing round from his residence close by at 1 Emperor's Gate, and on the following day the outpouring of blood from her mouth: 'I lay down, but it would not stop. I knocked on the walls and floor and shouted for help, but nobody came. . . . I got very much frightened. So I got up, which made it worse, and made the most terrible journey up the stairs to get help. I am so weak, I had to sort of say a prayer on every step.'

This time she was sure it was tuberculosis: 'I only hope it will be quick . . . and not let me linger on. I don't feel frightened of dying, and don't want to cry about it. I should be much more frightened of loving a "lunger".' Cousin Essex came and wept at her bedside, a queer, moving experience; her mother arrived, fairly calm, saying that it might have been only a bronchial haemorrhage. Stella was deeply depressed: 'I hate the world, and I loathe myself, and I am disappointed that there is no immediate chance of dying. Except that dying', she added with a faint return of spirits, 'would savour of "Now I'm dead, an angel passed away, so there, I guess you're sorry now." A terrible pose, the dead pose.'

A lung specialist confirmed the diagnosis of bronchial haemorrhage and thought the stairs at the Rodney Club were to blame; there was no present risk of tuberculosis, and she might work in moderation in London until the end of the summer, when he advised her to set sail for the southern hemisphere. 'It is evident', she reflected bitterly, 'that Providence is trying to bully me into being a gentle anti-militant, and an ordinary soft and pretty girl with flirtation for a hobby. But', she went on through rising tears, 'I will not be bullied. And though I may cry a little the heart of me doesn't mind,' proceeding to quote in its entirety W. E. Henley's 'Invictus':

> Out of the night that covers me,
> Black as the pit from pole to pole,
> I thank whatever gods may be
> For my unconquerable soul. . . .

– without in the least perceiving what a monstrously posing poem it is!

Her mother took her home, where absorbedly she began work on a new book (it was to occupy spare moments during the next nine months, and emerge as her first published novel, the oddly but unsurprisingly titled *I Pose*). She decided to accept an invitation from George to spend the winter with him in India; it promised another blissful sea-trip, and some pleasant touring in a colony with 'quite a coat-and-skirty kind of climate in the cold weather'. After a week or so's convalescence she returned to London – no doubt to her mother's dismay – to stay in a Bayswater boarding house named, extraordinarily, Abaadeen House, which furnished material for the budding novel. Nigel came to dine, to listen, and to be dazzled: 'I talked a lot of perfectly apparent lies to Nigel, and one or two truths. I bullied him a lot and posed some, and he left surprised and gratified.'

*

The Literary Department at Henrietta Street seemed, even to Stella's inexperienced eyes, to be in a somewhat confused state. While trying to make head or tail of the business side of the operation, she sorted and catalogued books and toiled in the heat of that eve-of-war summer from one suffrage headquarters to another with samples of the League's publications – a task not made easier by the fact that she was in process of having a 'swelling' in her foot (a verruca?), which had been troubling her since Jamaica days, expensively 'burnt out'.

One afternoon she crossed the Strand to Adam Street, took a deep breath, and offered her services at the offices of the United Suffragists, where both men and women worked, and at first glance things looked better organised. A new 'party of the centre', the United Suffragists (now some five months old), was attracting members in large numbers. It had been formed by several of the leading male intellectuals and politicians associated with Emmeline Pankhurst's WSPU, together with some of the more gifted women, all of them alarmed by Mrs Pankhurst's growing commitment to law-breaking, and unhappy with her autocratic rule; they saw themselves as standing somewhere between her and Millicent Fawcett. Frederick Pethick-Lawrence and his wife Emmeline (known among United Suffragists as '*Our Emmeline*'), who had been leaders in the WSPU but were summarily expelled in 1912 for holding very similar views, had offered to conduct their organ *Votes for Women* on behalf of the new organisation.

A day spent examining the wealth of suffrage literature and memorabilia in the Fawcett Library makes one realise what an enormous amount of propaganda work and fund-raising activity went on in branches of a bewildering number of suffrage societies all over Britain, chiefly among middle-class women, but also among sections of the working class. Marches, which varied from the highly organised symbolic procession that accompanied the hearse of the 'Derby Martyr' to cheerful assemblages, were a well-established means of protest. A People's March from Bow to the House of Commons, organised and led by Sylvia Pankhurst (who six months before had a break with her mother and sister, and now was running her own autonomous East London Federation of Suffragettes) was scheduled for 10 June. Its purpose was to demand the vote for every woman over twenty-one. Stella, despite her bad foot and the fact that only a month before she had given herself up for dead, was determined to be on it. Her Christian Science methods – 'faith pitted against facts', as she put it – would, she was convinced, see her through. It turned out to be:

An eventful day. My foot was so terribly painful all the morning that I did my work, going to the offices and toshing about with pamphlets, as if I were a sort of noisy blank, shot with great pain. I collapsed in the lift in Henrietta Street this morning much to the surprise and sympathy of the lift man, who let me sit on his little chair till I was better. I came back, and I am sorry to say shed one tear on the top of a bus, but hid it successfully. I felt absolutely sick with the fierceness of the pain, so I had a small scratch lunch at 12.30 and then dressed up to be Nora's bridesmaid. Essex came to dress me. I looked quite harmless, and my foot, though the new shoes hardly improved it at first, became better later owing to furious bathing. It was a nice wedding, Nora looked a perfect darling, and Vincent extremely courageous. At the reception at Claridge's I knew very few people. . . . •

I then rushed home, tore off my finery, had another very scratch meal, put on immense old shoes, tho' my foot was better, and went to the United Suffragist Office. After a long pause there, picked up a Mrs Gedd, and we went to Ford Road, Bow, to join the working women's procession. We were addressed by Sylvia Pankhurst from a window. She looked in a dying condition and said she was out of prison on licence under the 'Cat and Mouse Act', and expecting rearrest. She implored us to keep the agitation up. [Her actual words on this occasion, as reported in *Votes for Women*, were 'If I am arrested to-night and come out of prison, I shall take the first available cab, and go to the House of Commons and there continue the hunger and thirst strike. But I am weak, and do not know what may happen. So my last appeal to you is to "fight on".'[3]] She seemed adored by the entire enormous crowd, men and women alike. She was cheered to extinction without audible exceptions, and I saw one extremely dirty man cry. Then she was carried before us in a chair and, with a band egging us on, we started, a procession as long as I have ever seen [it was five miles long], quite as many men as women, but no respectable-looking men except half a dozen or so from our office.

The temper of the procession was delightful. One youth who looked like a super-hooligan trod on my heel once and hoped repeatedly that he had not hurt me, and patted my hand. Of course we were cheered madly through Sylvia's own district. In Whitechapel, however, about halfway through it, there was a sudden terrible collective shriek of angry men, and an army of youths, very rough-looking and very young, attacked us. It felt like being a bit of bomb. As is my wont, because of my absence of weight, I shot corklike into the air in the fighting, and was then ground against a wall, but not much bruised. Sylvia's chair was upset, but I did not see what happened to her. We heard that she was arrested. The police did their best to protect us, and having lost my party I squeezed to the weather side of a policeman and held his cuff. Presently the roughs were quelled, and we marched on again, the dear dirty ladies with us, most of whom carried babies, shrieking 'Murderers, murderers' at the world in general, as word was rife that Sylvia had been killed. I should certainly think someone had been killed, I saw several women lying on the ground, and a policeman on a horse knocked prostrate under the horse. We then walked and walked, Whitechapel seemed interminable. We were immensely cheered in Fleet Street, and contrary to my expectations, none of the men in the crowd seemed to mind expressing sympathy, although booers were booing next them. I could tell off the fingers of one hand the number of concerted boos we heard. The cheering was incessant, and men and women equally shouted 'God bless you' from the tops of 'buses. At St. Paul's, which was glorious by moonlight, I began to feel as if I could not walk one step further, but I did because it was so exciting. . . .

Halfway down the Strand we were dispersed peaceably by the police who were most amiable throughout, and by our own leaders, and ordered to go separately to Parliament Square. So we went, it seemed a tremendous way, without the band. In the Square we didn't do much good. We were chivvied by the police to keep us moving, and later when the crowd got very big the mounted police rode into us with some violence, and I was almost pressed to a wafer. An infantry policeman took me and put me inside the Underground gate, the railway men there received me as tho' I were a parcel and shut the gate. So I went home nearly dead, and fairly bruised.

Stella evidently regarded this march of almost seven miles as a baptism of fire, out of which she had come rather well, and she had to caution herself severely against striking a 'warrior pose', and going and kicking a policeman simply for the honour and glory of serving a term in Holloway Prison.

Her immediate aim was, rather, to find a niche for herself at the United Suffragists' office, if possible using her pen. She was granted an interview with the great Emmeline Pethick-Lawrence herself, 'rather the strong-minded type that men believe all Suffragists belong to . . . untidy and firm, with scratched, clever hair', who in the kindest possible way told her that there was no longer any scope in the movement for the amateur, and advised her to get some training; she asked to see a specimen of her writing, however. Stella sent her a copy of a suffragette poem she had written, and in reply Mrs Pethick-Lawrence voiced a doubt whether 'so fine-edged a blade' would be serviceable in the rough and tumble of campaigning.

However, despite discouragement, Stella edged herself into the US office as stamp-licker and addresser of envelopes, and, once in, quickly rose to penning routine notices for the press and acting as treasurer for the entire US when the regular officer went on holiday. More prosaic duties included officiating at speakers' training sessions (putting the lights on and the chairs out, wringing pupils' hands as they arrived and wringing sixpences out of them as they left, with an exhilarating, unchaperoned journey home afterwards: 'I came back happily on the top of a bus very late in the hot and glary night. All the other girls had a man, and I felt very fine and superior without one'). She gave out handbills at street meetings; waved a flag with vigour from Victoria Embankment to Trafalgar Square (where she tackled a 'rough' in argument, and was taken aback by his 'brutal' manners); dressed in 'more or less white' stewarded a meeting at the Kingsway Hall; attended a Suffrage Costume Dinner attired as an Egyptian queen; presided over a display of prison licences issued to heroes and heroines of the cause; was even asked to dress up hotly herself, and languish in a model cell.

On orders from the US, early in the morning of 19 June she went to Holloway Prison to watch for the release of Sylvia Pankhurst (who had been rearrested on the People's March), and then to trace her movements. It was an experience of nightmarish horror for Stella: 'The policemen laughed at me, and pointed me out to their friends, the wardresses came out to shriek with laughter too. I got fainter and fainter. . . . at last I began actually collapsing on the doorstep of a sort of church. The police, thinking it was a ruse, were more and more amused. I felt I should never see a friendly face again.' When she got back to her boarding house in a taxi, between paroxysms of weeping she was dosed with brandy by an anxious man-ageress. Her direst thought was that she might indeed not be strong enough for the life she longed to lead – and it was deeply distressing, on top of that, to read in the newspaper that Miss Pankhurst had been released the night before, and her society had not taken the trouble to let her know.

On 26 June Stella fled from Abaadeen House. She went back to the Rodney Club, to a room four flights up – never a woman to take doctors' advice over-seriously. Nigel, with a lover's eyes watching her becoming ever thinner and more strained, chose his moment with care and made a 'desperate appeal' to her to give up suffrage work before it was too late. The next time he mentioned her 'delicacy' he was not so lucky, offering tender sympathy on a day when already she had been infuriated by chance-met strangers wanting to know what was the matter with her chest, and recommending her to Dr So-and-So. Scorched by her anger, poor Nigel 'put his foot in the door, and looked as if he was going to cry'. By way of apology for his kindness and concern, next day he sent her quantities of her favourite flowers, salmon-pink sweet peas, and quite melted her heart: 'I made the masses of sweet peas into an altar, and before it I beat my breast and reproached myself for having been so petty and wrong in my attitude to such a pure, simple soul. My poor little dark green stag!' Outings with Nigel had resumed, but as often as not Stella paid her own way; supper at the Coventry Street Hotel, she decided, had been too expensive for both of them, and besides it had been very late, 'and of course I should not have gone there; there were painted ladies there, and gentlemen who waltzed with the waiters'; a weekend visit to Charterhouse to see Stephen was heaven (they hired a punt and a gramophone and went on the river) until at the end of the day Stella discovered they had only a few pence left between them, and was guilt-stricken on Nigel's account.

During that last summer of peace – so poignant in retrospect – Society was going through its usual paces, as confident as the rest of the population that any unpleasant 'incidents' that might arise between the nations of Europe could be settled by diplomatic means; not until 30 July, six days before the declaration, did Stella (in connection with her projected voyage to India) so much as remotely refer in her diary to the possibility of war.

With most of her Cholmondeley relations (she had a tiff with Cousin Regie which, before a year was out, she had bitter cause to regret) she foregathered at Lord's for the Eton and Harrow match: 'It was hot and giddy and full of beautiful clothes,' she wrote, adding judicially, 'but I am not born to be a Society woman, and I look forward to the time when I can smother this wish to attend such brainless and undemocratic gatherings.' In the evening she went with a large party to Earl's Court, where they all 'shrieked E-ton and Har-row with the best' (Eton had won by four wickets), and gave themselves 'heart-thrills' on the switchbacks. In the company of girl cousins – Nigel being on the continent – she went to the Russian Opera and Ballet at Drury Lane. Between the acts of *Boris Godunov* (Chaliapin was 'near perfection'), there were two suffragette demonstrations, one universally clapped, the other partly hissed. On each occasion Stella 'screamed' approval, reflecting on how a few years earlier demonstrators would have been roughly handled, and supporters afraid to clap: 'As it is, the most irritating attitude is that of the fool-women who sit in the boxes and follow the King's thoroughly weak lead of not apparently noticing what is taking place. They have no grievances themselves, and think it most unladylike to have grievances and put words to them.' Stella's comments on the public reaction to the suffragettes tend to confirm the now widely held opinion that the tide was running strongly in favour of woman's suffrage before the outbreak of war, and that it would have come inevitably and quite soon without the added impetus of the feminine contribution to the national effort.

On the last day of July she went down to Glassenbury to spend part of her summer holiday with her mother; since she had left home, relations between them had been strained. Her mother, deeply hurt, had retreated into buttoned-up resentment, and for her part Stella felt that any overture of goodwill that she made was met with distrust. Early on the morning of 2 August Stephen came in with the news that Germany had declared war on Russia, and fighting had broken out: 'So now all our hopes of sitting out and looking on are over. . . . I was *distraite* and saw that I was apt to give Suffrage too large a place in my sphere. It is awful not to know what is happening, and yet to feel that somewhere heroic stupid men are dying, as dumb as brutes, for reasons beyond their fathoming.' On Bank Holiday Monday reliable news was hard to get: 'There are sickening rumours that our Government means to refuse to fight, but I am sure the country wouldn't stand it'; Stella went to the Cranbrook Horse Show and 'talked a lot of tosh to various people, but the War forced itself incessantly into words, and there was a sort of visible hunger in every mind for news.' On 5 August Britain was at war: 'We heard what sounded like guns very far off all the morning. The trains and railway lines are commandeered, and we shall all have to remain *planté là* exactly where we are planted for some time to come. I felt very bad in health, with wretched little Stellarian guns roaring in my head all day.' By 9 August Nigel and his brother John had enlisted, and Stephen, just out of school and worried that no military unit would want him on account of his weak heart, a legacy of rheumatic fever, was rushing about the country interviewing recruiting officers.

In London, Stella went to a bureau of the Women's Emergency Corps, one of the first agencies to recruit women for war work, and enrolled her name as clerk, typist or French interpreter, liable to be called anywhere at a moment's notice. The capital was full of troops, cocksure little booklets entitled *In Doleful Memory of Poor Germany* were on sale in the streets, the US office was 'in a doubtful state', and Thomas Cook informed her that her sailing was cancelled.

The atmosphere of tension told on her nerves. The secretary of the US got a sharp reply to his letter summoning her to sell *Votes for Women* at street corners: 'I know I can write,' she protested in her diary, adding irritably, 'old Pethick-Lawrence herself has admitted I can write. Why therefore does she depute me to street-moping?' One day she awoke with thought people 'shouting' at her, 'explosions' happened in her head, she was half deaf with internal crashings and splittings. Staying with her Prescott relations in Herefordshire, she reached a crescendo of misery:

> I remember coming back and talking to Aunt Freddie about drowning myself. She said 'I shouldn't do that.' I then came up to my room and cried with earthquake fury for some minutes, very cowardly, and then went to bed and refused supper, in a sort of access of temper against this fearful body of mine. . . . It seemed incredible that the others should not hear those awful noises that were filling up my world. I thought Stephen must be pretending there was no shrieking outside until there was a lull, and I heard what a still, starry night it was.

Early in September she went back to the Rodney Club, with vague ideas of war work in mind, but only the perilous cold and fogs of winter to look forward to with certainty. (A couple of months later, on the day she was to have sailed for warm, sunny India, she sat in her room in the evening in her 'boat coat' and 'deck shoes', pretending she was on her P & O liner crossing the Bay of Biscay on a fine, windy night 'with little blinking lights on a rocking horizon'.) In the meantime she had presented herself once again at the Women's Emergency Corps, 'made a stand', and been promised some hard work to do in the East End. *En route* for Shoreditch Town Hall, the headquarters of War Relief in the borough, she passed a long troop of young men, led by a band, on their way to the recruiting station; to her sentimentalising upper-class eyes they looked 'so vulgar and so splendid', and seemed to be proclaiming 'we are mediocrities, born of a mediocre class in a mediocre age, and yet we can give our lives with the best . . . and we can go to our death singing about "Mibel" and "the dysies". I cheered till I nearly choked.'[4] The director of War Relief, Mr Edwin Konstam, 'rather a bewildered-looking man with a good smile', put her to work sorting applications for relief; she was shocked by what she learned that first day of the distress which poor families were already suffering on account of the war. Next day, owing to some administrative muddle, she was summoned into the presence of one Lady St Davids, an *outré* specimen of the upper-class females who enjoyed devoting some of their leisure to raising the working class – or to directing others to do so:

> She wanted me to go down to Bow with my typewriter and *let my soul flow* into factory girls. At first she said that I might be given a commission as Ensign in her army of intense factory girls, who learn to be angels, and bring every art to perfection, but afterwards she said that I looked so modest that I might be one of the common privates, and let my soul flow from the same level as the girls themselves. . . . She did not ring true, but I really believe she thought she did. Anyway, she was excellent copy. La, how she spat out the underlinings, the sofa quaked!

In the event, Mr Konstam despatched her to Hoxton to work with the Charity Organisation Society[5] at their office in New North Road. Among East End districts, Hoxton had a very bad name. In 1898, when Charles Booth was gathering material for his monumental social survey *Life and Labour of the Poor of London*, he singled it out as 'the leading criminal area of London', abounding in thieves and fences of every kind, though he conceded that 'decent and worthy people' lived there too. He found chronic unemployment, overcrowding, drunkenness and malnutrition; yet for the 'pleasures of the moment' – the pub, music hall, funeral, wedding, jaunt to Epping Forest – there always seemed to be money in plenty. Poor children, he noted, were never without money for sweets. 'More than mine have,' said a member of the clergy. 'More than I had when I was young,' echoed a schoolmaster. One hears the same complaint today.

That many in Hoxton were living the same feckless, hand-to-mouth existence when, sixteen years later, Stella arrived is clear from the artless but racy memoirs of A. S. Jasper, as set down in his autobiographical *A*

Hoxton Childhood; he takes up the story in 1910. Counting the parents, the Jaspers were a family of eight, and their life was a constant struggle to survive, mainly because the father was a chronic drunkard. It was the mother who kept them together. What she could earn with her sewing machine was vital to the family income, and on Saturdays during the war she set up her stall and sold her wares in Hoxton Market, where her son, seated on a box, watched the women shopping. These were the women whom Stella would be meeting and learning how to deal with:

> they were treated by their menfolk like serfs. Most of them were dressed in a long skirt and a coarse canvas apron, with an old coat or shawl over their shoulders and a man's cap with a big hatpin on their heads. All their shopping was put in their aprons. Usually there were two or three children tagging along. Somehow they didn't seem to know anything different. Most of them came from poverty-stricken homes, and drink was a common cause for misery as well as an escape from it.[6]

Such families teetered on the edge of catastrophe, and prolonged illness or unemployment could easily push them over. Many of them teetered back and forth across the line that divided the legal from the illegal. Such errancy, if detected, would, as far as Stella's organisation was concerned, put them outside the ranks of the 'deserving'.

By the time Stella joined it, the COS was probably as well known to Londoners as the Salvation Army, though perhaps not so widely esteemed. Founded in late Victorian times with the object of co-ordinating the efforts of the thousand and one small charities then striving to assist the London poor, it was cast in the Victorian mould, and not concerned to change. At a time when political parties of all colours were beginning to recognise the need for social welfare legislation, the COS was doggedly as ever opposed to state aid, firm as ever in the principle that only the 'deserving' should be helped. Thus it incurred the wrath both of the socialistically inclined and of philanthropists with soft hearts in all the parties.

For the 'relief of distress', the COS considered that private philanthropy sufficed – except in cases of utter destitution, when the Poor Law guardians would be invoked – and its work largely consisted in registering applicants for relief, then channelling them to the appropriate sources. Selection was a vital part of the process: before recommending an applicant or 'case', the COS regarded it as essential to enquire into his life. A lady or gentleman volunteer worker would be detailed to call upon the case; one dodge was to arrive an hour or two earlier than specified, so as to catch the victim unawares with, say, beds unmade, dishes unwashed or, worse, a bottle of spirits on the table. After taking a shrewd look round and making detailed enquiries, the visitor would withdraw and make up a report to be considered at the next district committee meeting.

There was much to be said for the system, which was the seedground of social casework as practised today, but too often the COS administered it in a stone-cold, self-righteous way. Stella, when once she was let loose on the streets of Hoxton, reacted strongly against its methods: 'The C.O.S. motto', she wrote indignantly in her diary, 'is, hasten to drown the man who can't swim, directly pride begins to weaken, kill it. . . . I hardly think Christ would have worked through the C.O.S.' In *Living Alone* she satirises a 'Charity Society' which is nothing more nor less than a thinly disguised COS – imagining that it keeps two separate lists of crimes, 'a short one for the registrars and workers, and a very long one for the registered'. High on the list of crimes possible to registrars and workers comes 'sentimentality': 'It is sentimental to feel personal affection for a "case" . . . or to acknowl-edge the right of a "case" to ask questions . . . or to disapprove of spying and talebearing, or to believe any statement made by anyone without an assured income . . . or in fact to confuse in any way the ideas of charity and love.' She was writing out of experience, for more than once she had been rapped over the knuckles by her COS superiors for following the dictates of a very tender heart and dispensing what was disapprovingly termed 'promiscuous charity'.

But her immediate task, in that first week of September 1914, was to master the cipher in which all COS records, necessarily confidential, were kept, and then to help register the tidal wave of applications for relief that were coming in from dependants of enlisted men, and from people who had lost their jobs on account of the war. Her mentor was the registrar, kind, efficient, pious Mary Marker – 'rather a dear, but almost too brisk' – who lived in a nearby social settlement, St Hilda's. After a month, she invited Stella to dine there. Stella was impressed: 'I talked to several of the Saints Hilda, and they all seemed much more intelligent and thoughtful and less childish and petty than the girls I meet on my ordinary way. I suppose only the more sterling girls give their lives to this sort of thing.' (The official title of St Hilda's was the Incorporated Cheltenham Ladies' College Settlement, and the 'sort of thing' these girls were doing was district visiting, charity organisation, Board School, country holiday and club management, and running classes for invalid children and pupil teachers, in close association with nearby parish churches.) Mary Marker, a typical 'Saint Hilda' of maturer age, was to earn Stella's respect, not least for the manner in which she bore the death in action of her only brother, whom she had mothered all her life and who alone made her feel that she lived to some purpose: 'Just exactly as usual, no forced courage, or heroism. Same old timeworn mockeries about the index.'

In theory Stella worked a five-and-a-half-day week, though in practice she sometimes took a half day off. Lunch was taken humbly and economically in a grubby teashop of the Aerated Bread Co., one of the 'ABCs' found all over London in those days; 'there were potato chips at the dirty lunch shop', she notes on 10 September, 'which were a tremendous treat, although they necessitated my lunch costing 11d instead of 9d which was extravagant of me'. The pressure of work was such that quite often she stayed late – until her head 'span' and she had what she called 'a brain lapse', a kind of mental paralysis brought on by strain. Then came the journey home to Kensington by bus and underground.

Dreary as it sounds, it was what, passionately, she wanted to be doing. For to many middle-class young women of her generation 'work' – even the most prosaic work – stood for 'independence', and held a glamour and excitement that it takes an effort of imagination today to understand. All the same there were times when being 'an austere suffragette threading the fogs alone' told very hard. Unpaid, she was attempting to survive independent of her mother on an investment income that in 1912 had amounted to £178 per annum, but which had suffered a sharp reduction with the outbreak of war. It was not going to be easy, she suddenly realised, to find the cash to pay for the warm clothes she needed in order to face the onset of cold weather – and it would be her first trial since childhood of the foggy, dangerous London winter.

During that autumn, the capital was waiting apprehensively for the Germans to take advantage of the first foggy nights to send their Zeppelins over. A solitary British airship prowled the dark sky; Stella watched as a gun and searchlight were mounted on the arch at Hyde Park Corner, and one night saw the combined mass of London searchlights come on simultaneously: 'The tall shafts of blue light sprang up from all sides, and inclined one to the other like tall angels saluting each other. It was a sight to make one pant, and be glad to be alive in these terrible and exciting times.' The blacked-out streets were nearly pitch dark, buses crawled 'with one eye shut', cars with bright headlights were stopped by the police, while in strange contrast Hyde Park was ingeniously lit up with brilliant winding 'streets' of lamps, in hopes of deceiving an airborne foe. From her perch aloft a bus Stella saw a group of refugee Belgian monks embussing at Charing Cross, each with his sad little bundle; and the twenty-four-year-old Prince of Wales marching with a troop of Grenadier Guards along Kensington High Street. He was tiny and wistful looking. She thought he looked honest and true, but 'sadly childish'.

In various ways the horror of war was coming home to Stella. George, in a series of letters from the Western Front (he was in command of Gurkhas), told how he had been seriously ill, was expecting to go into action any day, had got his company (in order to fill a fresh, tragic gap, Stella guessed), had experienced battle. One regiment of Gurkhas had been practically wiped out, he reported:

> What remained had been actually trampled in their own trenches by victorious Germans who trod the wounded, killed and unhurt alike down into the mud. Fifty men survived, and George said they were just 'pillars of mud with two holes for eyes'. Nothing in the way of clothes for George's gunners have been provided and they are all in their thinnest Indian things. Ammunition is getting very short, and they are forbidden to fire more than an absurdly inadequate number of rounds a day.

Regie Cholmondeley, revolver at the ready, was piloting reconnaissance planes behind the German lines. He had had a fight, single-handed in his biplane, with two Germans in a Taube. Stella gave a second-hand report based on a letter to his mother:

> He fired thirty shots at them from such close range that at one point the machines very nearly collided. They replied with interest, and his machine was much perforated, though he was not touched. He has luck. Finally he brought them down, and turned very sick, because he was so close that not a detail was spared him. They were all so high up that he could see England sitting watching on the other side of the sea. He has not been able to sleep since for thinking of it. It will be a miracle if we get our Regie home. I wish I had not been irritating at the Eton and Harrow.

Captain Reginald Cholmondeley, mentioned in despatches in February 1915, was killed a month later with all his crew, when the bombs in his aircraft exploded as he was about to take off on a raid.

From a fellow Rodneyite whose sister was an army nurse, Stella heard terrible details of the efforts made, during the Channel crossing, to keep the wounded alive long enough for them to glimpse the white cliffs of England. 'I sat in my room in the dark,' Stella wrote after hearing this, 'and mourned violently [wept, she means; with Stella tears flowed readily and freely] for the pain there is in the world these days. And for the incredible sin of several millions of men paid to inflict these things upon each other.' Nigel, meanwhile, was making tremendous efforts to get himself attached to a fighting unit, and doubted if he would live to see the New Year. It was against a background of news like this – when, as Ellis Roberts writes, 'it was extraordinarily hard for girls to resist the ardours of young men trying to marry them'[7] – that Stella entered into an engagement to marry Nigel.

Nigel had suddenly reappeared, bristling with a new moustache, fired with fresh determination to bring their relationship to a head, and swept her off in the family Sunbeam in the direction of Newbury, Berkshire, where he had hopes that a yeomanry regiment would take him on. Before they set off, Stella sounded his mother's feelings about the whole affair by asking, in unexpected phrase, 'whether she minded my playing with Nigel, but far from it, she pressed rugs and fur coats upon me and advised me to go as far with him as possible, and blow Hoxton out of my head'. Since Stella loved motor-cars, and did not in the least mind how fast they went – 'my heart runs ahead calling "quicker, quicker"', she had once confessed – all was fine as long as the Sunbeam purred: 'Nigel is a really adventurous driver, though a most skilled one. I love that Sunbeam, she goes like a velvet cat on soft paws.' But things were not so much to her taste when it stopped:

> Nigel completely lost his head as regards me, which I hated, and thought rather mean of him because he is so strong, and I was alone with him. . . . In theory I am awfully fond of Nigel, and thrill a little when I touch him by mistake, but when he touches me on purpose, I hate it, my hand still feels as if blushing furiously where he kissed it. Obviously I am born to be a lone literary woman as close proximity horrifies me so.

Four years earlier a girl's passing caress had given her keen pleasure; what she shrank from now was the sexuality implicit in Nigel's touch. Though Nigel was in some disgrace and not to be allowed to forget it, she could enjoy the rest of the drive:

> It was a ripping night, fantastic with a high moon and a flat mist. We were stopped by the fortifications of London, which appear to be built of tubs across the roads, with a large special constable fitted into the space in the middle. As there was nothing to suggest that we were alien enemies we were allowed through [enemy nationals had to keep to within five miles of where they lived]. It was a lovely drive, but when I said goodbye to Nigel on Reading Station, I was glad to be an independent suffragette, and ate a joyous poached egg at Paddington with more pleasure than I should have taken in a dinner à deux with Nigel at Reading.

No doubt it was entirely owing to the temper of the times that on 9 October, just a week later, she was writing:

> I have done very wrong. I went to the play with Nigel, and to supper at the Cri [the Criterion Restaurant in Piccadilly Circus]. On the way back in the taxi he persuaded me and persuaded me, so at last I said yes. . . . Part of me grieves that I didn't show him what I felt, apart from that curt yes, and part of me that I have tied up my fickle heart (not that I have any) in this way. He is too young to have bound his poor hands.' . . . My dear

little big clumsy Nigel, but it is a feverish thought. What have I done?

. . . I only gave myself away that once and the rest of the time was very suffragetty, but of course that was enough. On the doorstep I patted him and he kissed me and the blot was that Miss Butler [a fellow-resident] appeared just then. How much she saw I don't know, but evidently something, for after I got in she stood an appreciable time in the hall wondering what to say. Whereas there was nothing to be said.

But evidently Miss Butler thought that there was something to be said, for 'on first rising I discovered that Miss James seemed very angry with me, and called me Miss Benson for the first time for three months. However in the evening when I rang her up, she called me "Baby" again. Otherwise I was sure that Miss Butler had reported faithfully on what she may have seen last night.'

In spite of her initial misgivings, for a few days Stella lived in a state of heady rapture: 'I have my Nigel all around my horizon, and I can feel him thinking of me, the Adorable. I feel frightfully happy and thrilled about the place where my heart would be if I had one. Everything reminded me of him, even the point on Brompton Road where he used to begin to swear great oaths because we were getting so near home.' Then a sense of reality came creeping back. She must have told herself again – what she admitted to her diary weeks before – that his chief attraction lay in his touching devotion to herself. She did not find his company enthralling: 'he is so young and rather commonplace, and does not see the salient points of me at all'. Whereas she could entertain him for as long as she pleased with her theories and her poses, when he managed to get a word in she found to her dismay that she was bored.

In letters, she tried to take back her consent, but when he re-emerged 'looking adorable in his uniform', and saying that all he wanted was to be happy when his time came to be shot, she settled for an engagement of one year: 'The extraordinary thing is I do love him, but I just hate it when he gets violent and kisses me. This must be a sign of heartlessness. . . . I wish it were possible to love and be loved without touching.' Nigel, if he thought about it at all, probably reckoned he had enough physical passion for the two of them.

At work, she was appointed organising secretary of a workroom set up under the Queen Mary's Work for Women scheme, a project funded by charitable donation which aimed to provide employment for women who had lost their jobs on account of the war. In securing the appointment for her, Mr Konstam, who evidently had a high opinion of her potential, had gratifyingly swung a committee in her favour:

Mr Konstam trusts me, and takes for granted that I can do anything that is necessary. I think, though as a Suffragette I am loth to say it, that men often judge less by appearances than women, and whereas the women on these petty little boards take one's measure at once as a fool-babe impossible to trust with anything grown-up, the men look twice and then come and find out if one really is so guileless and childish as one appears.

The job meant a chilly daily trudge along the Regent's Canal to rather cold workrooms, where the women, some eighty of them, sewed plain, service-able articles destined for hospital and army use, in contrast to the luxury goods that most of them were producing before the war. Though so young, Stella possessed a certain patrician self-confidence in dealing with working-class people, not to be confused with the air of condescension she noticed and disliked in the 'queenly souls' who came down from HQ on tours of inspection: 'They were "chatty", which is a pose I cannot bear in connection with poor people, because they seem so defenceless against it. Why should a sensible elderly woman be chatted to by patronising hypocrites?'

Things only became difficult for her when Central Office decreed that a kitchen be set up in conjunction with the workrooms, with the dual purpose of feeding the workers and teaching them how to cook – for the ignorance of East End women of even the simplest processes could be astonishing. Since no funds for equipment appeared to be forthcoming, Stella set to and begged, circulating the local shopkeepers, who, on the whole, 'scintillated with generosity' – though a certain Mr Peggs of Hopkins and Peggs got so worried because he could not find a pair of kitchen cloths inferior enough to give her that she implored him to content himself with his other gifts, at which suggestion he jumped. Other deficiencies she supplied from her own purse to the tune of eighteen shillings a week, until Mr Konstam found out and put a stop to it. Opening day in the dining room was stormy, but she weathered it with exemplary calm: 'There was a horrifying stampede, and an aggrieved roar, and a dozen women rushed in to pour their cocoa down my throat, on the grounds that it was undrinkable. I must say it was beastly, the meat also was tough. It is disappointing, our hon. lady cook appears not worthy of us.' Next day, with cockney good nature, the women came to say that the meal was entirely satisfactory and they felt 'reg'lar blowed out'.

She was still involved with the United Suffragists. The outbreak of war had put suffragists in a dilemma: how far were they bound to support a conflict prosecuted by a government that denied women the vote? Mrs Pankhurst swung the weight of her militants behind the war effort, and herself toured the country making speeches urging men to join up. The Women Writers were bitterly divided. Evelyn Sharp, novelist and promi-nent suffragist, declared that she would resign if the League did anything to help its country, and ex-president and novelist Flora Annie Steel threatened to quit if it did not; Stella, staunch patriot, enthusiastically backed Mrs Steel.

Stella gave two evenings a week to a club that the US had set up to spread the word among young factory girls in Southwark. Playing Peter her guitar, whistling, organising games, dancing with 'hot, dirty girls in thick boots', to her surprise she was a great success. 'Now, gals, 'oo d'you think's come?' called out the caretaker as Stella climbed the stairs. 'Miss Benson!' a gleeful chorus yelled in reply. It was 'cocklewarming' to be so popular: 'Perhaps this is my vocation,' she speculated, 'rather an exhausting one, but not so bad, and fine and busy.' What particularly appealed to her in her dealings with the girls, and with her social inferiors in general, was that they never told her that she had a bad cough, or was looking white, or was doing too much, as her 'politer' acquaintances did. And she freely admitted that she preferred doing things for people who had nothing but thanks to offer in return: 'This is my domineering spirit, I love feeling motherly, but not daughterly.' At the Rodney Club among middle-class women, she tended to sit silent, invaded by thought people; or she succumbed to the temptation to strike attitudes: a certain Miss Buckland seemed positively to insist that she pretend to be a romantic novel heroine of the untamed, eccentric kind: 'For her benefit I have to pose as myself accentuated,' she complained. 'She always seems to understand a little bit more than I meant, and her eyes always say "Ah yes, just as I thought, quite Mrs Humphrey-Ward-like!"' (The heroines of Mrs Humphrey Ward's novels often combined beauty with brains and independence of mind.)

Meanwhile her mother was predicting that if she continued to work as hard as she was doing, she was unlikely to survive the winter; indeed, in early December Stella herself was alarmed by an ominous-seeming pain in her 'topmost lung'. On 17 December it flared up, and she found herself late at night ringing the doorbell of 1 Emperor's Gate, and moments later facing a startled Dr Monckton in his dressing-gown. He diagnosed muscular rheumatism, an opinion which, while she distrusted it, delighted Stella, since it meant that she would not have to stay in bed. Naturally she had failed to disclose what had probably brought on the attack: the fact that only a few hours earlier she had met Nigel and – reneging on her promise to let it run a full year – had broken off their engagement. Her conviction that for both of them it was the right thing to do had not made wounding Nigel any less upsetting.

Before the engagement, the difference in their ages had enabled her to view him with a touch of elder-sisterly condescension, as a promising youth who one day might develop into a worthy if not distinguished man; and the age difference had acted as a barrier, keeping him where she wanted him, at arm's length in more senses than one. But war had brought him leaping over. His ardour had touched and flattered her and her judgement had been shaken. But very quickly she had seen that marriage with him, marriage with anyone at this point in her life when she had just sipped freedom, was absurd. When she told him this, clutching at straws he said that he thought married people could be 'independent together'. The idea struck Stella as new and 'quite startling', but she was in no frame of mind to be convinced.

What of her hope that 1914 would find her more settled in her beliefs? It was not altogether disappointed. In November Laura Hutton took her to the Ethical Church in Queen's Road, Bayswater. Where methodists had once praised the Lord, now members of the West London Ethical Society raised their voices in tribute to human benevolence and secular wisdom.[9] The congregation, in the body of the church, gazed upon a sort of ethical Holy Trinity ranged around an imposing central pulpit (all the church's fittings were in expensive good taste) – above the speaker's head was Minerva, Roman goddess of wisdom, on her either side, Buddha and Christ; busts of such luminaries as Plato and Galileo adorned the walls.

The church was a curious halfway house, attracting people who were in some way alienated from traditional religion, yet reluctant to abandon communal spiritual exercises. Stella was impressed:

> I was very much more moved than I mentioned. I believe I have in this discovered a doctrine in which I can conscientiously believe. I suppose that the Human Brain is the core of this belief, and faith is not paramount. We sing and read and consider the inspired words of our brother man, rather than the cryptic and ambiguous utterances of saints and super-naturals. The words that greeted us as we came in, very beautifully sung, touched me hard: 'Though I have faith so that I could remove mountains, and have not love, I am nothing. . . .'

She could equally well hear those words, of course, at her former place of worship in Norfolk Square, but there the ambience would have been quite different. A serious discourse, tailor-made to the times, was a feature of the proceedings; Stella heard denunciations of militarism, and a prophecy, in the manner of that yet undisillusioned age, that moral evolution would one day lead to the control of arms manufacture and the ending of wars. Dr C. W. Saleeby, a follower of Francis Galton the eugenist (his initials, appropriately enough, stood for Caleb Williams, eponymous hero of William Godwin's freethinking novel), spoke of the price the nation would have to pay for the war in terms of 'racial degeneration', his theme being 'the racial poisons'. To judge from his published writings, he would have cloaked his references to the most virulent of them, syphilis, in delicate language that made it difficult for the uninitiated to know what he was talking about; however, Stella seemed satisfied that she had taken his message. A 'dear little pessimistic hymn by Shakespeare' followed.

Chapter Six

At Bockleton, where she spent Christmas with her Prescott relations (which perhaps tells us something of how strained things were with her mother), as well as a streaming cold Stella developed a philosophy for 1915: 'To discard as far as possible everything comfortable or easy. To despise peace and love loneliness.' When her Aunt Freddie – speaking, as she said, 'impersonally' – suggested that such a philosophy could conduce to a sense of moral superiority, Stella neatly ducked the issue: she was determined to don her 'hairshirt', in all its prickliness. Taxis, superfluous clothes and food had gone by the board with the outbreak of war; now sweets must voluntarily be added to the list. Two remaining comforts, however, she considered herself as not yet strong enough to forego: being very warm in bed, and smoking – though cigarettes were restricted to one or two a day, and there was to be a grim week when, as a gesture of solidarity with one of her protégées who was trying to give up liquor, she smoked none at all. 'The hairshirt was something more than self-discipline,' Laura Hutton has written, 'it was a kind of expiation. . . . Not that that meant it wasn't also a joke. We used absurdly to vie with one another as to who spent less on our Express Dairy meals together.'[1] For someone as physically frail as Stella to attempt to get through a hard-working winter's day on the menu of 2 September – grapenuts and cream at 8.0, a poached egg at 1.0 and tripe and onions at 6.30 – seems to be asking for trouble; it is as though, behind the acknowledged motives, there was a need to defy her body, even a need to punish it for all the pain and humiliation it had brought her.

Stella was still on terms of friendship with Nigel, and before going to Scotland with his new regiment, the Fife and Forfar Yeomanry, he had chosen her a Christmas present. It could hardly have been more unfortunate: it was a sumptuous edition of *Omar Khayyam*. 'The spirit of this unholy thing is loathsome to me,' she exclaimed in no uncertain terms on examining that lush celebration of oriental sensuality. 'If I did anything thoroughly I should be an ascetic. I would like to tie a millstone round my body's neck and drown it in the sea.' Her puritanism received quite frequent affronts in the increasingly permissive climate of wartime Britain. She was hot with indignation at the stage revues that were just becoming the rage, with their lines of sinuous chorus girls, scantily clad by the day's standards: 'pink and golden young ladies with neat calves make me furious', she exclaimed. May Sinclair's novel *The Three Sisters*,[2] appearing two months after the outbreak of war, showed the influence of Freud in its frank acknowledgement of female sexuality; 'the virginal figure on the Victorian sofa is also shown to be a woman of strong desires', writes Jean Radford in her introduction to a recent edition.[3] It disturbed Stella, and she found it 'dirty'. It stirred dim virginal misgivings about the role that 'sensuality' (which in this context meant sexuality) might conceivably play in her own psyche:

> Of all things in the world I most loathe sensuality. It would be an eternal shame to me to discover that my incurable restlessness and always looking through what should be sufficient to something vague and more satisfying, was the result of some undercurrent of sensuality.

However closely she looked, she could scarcely suspect anything sensual in the feeling that she had for her chief Edwin Konstam, a gentlemanly and somewhat ethereal-seeming bachelor of forty-five. It was as bodiless as a passion for one of King Arthur's knights, or for some ideal figure in a dream – indeed, as she said, 'he makes me have a high romantic feeling at the top of my head exactly as thought people do'. Its seat was clearly as far away as possible from the organs of generation. Konstam, a barrister with a career in the Indian Civil Service behind him (and, as it happened, a friend of her Cholmondeley aunts), hid brains and determination behind a shy, conciliatory manner; it was a combination with strong appeal to Stella, who could respect him as a father, yet at the same time 'feel so motherly that I have forcibly to keep down my suffragettism for fear of frightening him'. A one-sided fixation of this sort can linger on indefinitely, and her feeling for the 'Older and Wiser' as she called him persisted at least until the end of the war. It had its ebbs and flows, the ebbs invariably coming when she had been in immediate contact with the man, and found that the reality did not quite match up with her dream. As late as 1918 she was writing raptly:

> He is still there, and it is before him that all the reality of my work is spread forth. It isn't folly, it is just inevitable, and as it had to happen, it is very well that it should happen to me, and not to a real woman, who perhaps couldn't have borne it.

It evidently did not strike her that a 'real', emotionally mature woman would never have got herself into such a position in the first place. The announcement of Konstam's belated engagement to be married, at the age of forty-eight, left her unmoved by jealousy. This did not surprise her, as from the start she had never 'felt anything for him that should make me mind this news'. Neither betrothals, wedding bells nor physical consummations were for the likes of her, it seemed:

> For after all I am a sort of 'Natural' in mind, and have a negligible body, and I never looked for satisfaction out of life, only interest. And that I have found. To have an ideal is more than I deserved – disabled as I am – and I am lucky in not being tempted to put my ideal to any proof. Nobody shall be able truthfully to say that I have not got all that I was capable of receiving from life. I am not a real woman to need more.

The resigned pose? Perhaps. But in the final teasing words of her first novel: 'Yes, I pose of course. But the question is – how deep may a pose extend?' In her case, on this question of sex, only time would give the answer.

In the calendar at the front of her diaries Stella had the habit of marking, as they occurred, the good days. The year 1915 was to yield forty-seven, six of them enclosed in the double squares that indicate special happiness, and four with the rapturous, squiggley edges of extreme bliss. In the second category was 6 January, her birthday. Helped by her mother, Stephen, Laura Hutton, Evelyn Bengough, her forewomen, and last but not least Mr Konstam himself, she threw a party for seventy of the Queen's Fund workwomen. The 'Great Radiance' of the day was George's coming home on leave:

> but there were other radiances. Nothing went wrong, except that Mr Konstam fell downstairs to start with, which petrified me. The Assistant Forewoman sang, Stephen sang, played, and was generally facetious, Evelyn played such a footstirring melody *von Handel* that it made our wag Mrs McCullagh apparently drunk and she leapt upon the platform, tho' short, stout, and elderly, and danced high prancings. My dear women all got feverishly excited, and would have roared with delight had we played Old Maid or General Knowledge. Mr Konstam is a cherub, I believe he looks with an approving eye on my work, and warms the cockles of my vanity. I whistled by the way, without disgusting myself and got three encores.

'Coarse and grubby' as they were, a 'sort of fast love' was growing up in her for the women of Shoreditch. 'I don't feel I shall ever want a baby of my own so very much,' she wrote, 'while I have all these hungry, dirty, confiding grown-up babies to look after.' There was no end to the calls on her sublimated maternal instinct: Mrs Cribb with a terrible record of nine stillbirths behind her, who just possibly might produce her last baby live if only she knew that her husband was dying in hospital, and not in the dreaded workhouse infirmary (Stella tried but failed to secure the transfer); or Rebecca Walker, newly blind at seventy-three (it was to supplement her old age pension one week that Stella braved the pawnbroker for the first time in her life, popping her own earrings); Mrs Faiers, for whose sake she incurred the COS's rebuke for promiscuous charity (finding her pregnant and hungry she gave her a parcel of food on the spot; when thereafter the woman regarded her as a soft touch, Stella had to concede that the COS might just have a point). Then there was one-legged Mrs Mary Ann Smith, dismissed from the workroom on a technicality, who needed a job and somewhere to live. Stella found her convenient ground-floor premises, helped her to set up a paper-bag-making business, and went into partnership with her; in return, for the rest of Stella's life 'Mrs Oneleg' offered her her fierce protective loyalty. From the first it was more than a business partnership. Stella felt a warmer affection for this 'snappy little one-legged angel' than for any other of her protégées, 'rough little coster that she is, with a bad word for religion in any form, and for all the things that less independent people respect, furious and surly at being helped, and yet wonderfully faithful and refined above almost anyone I know'.

It was the pitifulness of Mrs Oneleg's plight that had initially moved her. One does not begin to understand Stella until one appreciates her capacity for pity. In the presence of suffering, human or animal, she felt, literally, such a quick, strong pain in her heart that her immediate reaction was to do something to stop the suffering – and her own pain. 'I can't bear anything from a friend down to a beetle to be sad or cry in vain,' she once said, at the same time – and paradoxically – reproaching herself for lack of heart: 'You see, I am *impersonally* tenderhearted. . . . there is only one thing everybody wants, to possess their friends, to fit their friends to them, to attach themselves the vitality of personal love.' Laura recalled an incident from those days which illustrates rather well the point that Stella was trying to make; Stella had burst into loud tears, 'like a child', because she had been unable to get the help for some invalid out-of-work that she had appealed for: 'she flung herself on the bed, and I on an impulse – utterly wrong – went to put my arms round her. She just froze within them.'[4] It was Laura's way to give her personal heart only too freely. On the other hand, Stella's brand of universal benevolence did well enough, and was welcome enough, in the Shoreditch of 1915.

If Stella planned to dedicate such heart as she possessed to Shoreditch, it seemed only logical for her to go and live there, and in January she found lodgings with a policeman's family at one of the more respectable local addresses, Nichols Square, Hackney Road, Haggerston. 'Pretty, pinchbeck, semi-detached, stuccoed Tudor cottages',[5] Nikolaus Pevsner calls the charming if humble houses that occupied the centre space in the broad early Victorian cul-de-sac, since demolished. At No. 84 Stella had a bed-sitting-room, clean, decently furnished but suitably austere, with a french window opening on to a tiny garden. The vision of herself sitting in contented solitude eating her modest supper (prepared by Mrs Smith, the policeman's wife) beside her humble grate was very beguiling, and rather guiltily she made it plain to Laura that she did not wish to share a flat with her. Truth to tell, she was worried about their relationship. It seemed to be all give on Laura's part, all take – and sometimes ungrateful take at that – on hers. No one, she uncomfortably felt, could hope for a truer friend. When she was sick Laura appeared almost at once to nurse, mourn, care, even to take over her work: 'It is astonishing to be cared for in this sombre and overwhelming manner. I must be heartless not to treat friendship more mutually.' The fact that at times she found Laura drab and depressing, some of her female friendships over-intense and distasteful, was not, as at lucid moments she realised, the whole of it. There was something 'morbid' in Laura's devotion against which instinctively she stood on guard:

> She talks to me as a lover would talk to any other woman, when she goes to sleep at night she always thinks of me also squidging up in bed, when she gets up she wonders if I am awake, she hardly ever passes a day without ringing me up, she almost cries if by mistake I show any solicitation [sic] about her. It puzzles me. . . . these things leak out as having been her habit since ever she and I met.

To the end of Stella's life, clever, intense, suffering, sensitive Laura was her closest, dearest friend; but it was not until the late 1920s, by which time Laura had qualified as a doctor and was specialising in psychiatry, that they were able to recognise and openly discuss the passional element in her attachments to women.

By March 1915 Laura's devoted services were on the point of being called in. Stella, working a five-and-a-half-day week in Hoxton, giving four evenings to the Southwark girls, another to a Soldiers' and Sailors' Wives' club in Bethnal Green, and still managing to squeeze in late-night calls on various 'babies' in need, was fast approaching collapse, and wondering indeed if duty was going to demand 'more of me than my help and my sympathy and my boot-soles' wear. . . . I don't mind dying at all, only I would love to get the Book finished.' (The book, I Pose, was claiming her attention between 11.00 p.m. and midnight each night.)

The moment an honourable excuse for a break came along, she jumped at it. George wired that he was due to be sent to Nice to convalesce, and could his mother or sister or both possibly be there to meet him in two days' time? It was ridiculously short notice, especially in wartime, but Mrs Benson had a string to pull: her brother-in-law Commodore Robert Benson – the head of the family, and Stella's 'Uncle Bob' – escorted the two ladies to the Foreign Office and, hey presto, 'we just talked to a great man, and a clerk brought us the complete passport'. But before she left the country Stella felt in duty bound to report personally to Mr Konstam, and ran him to earth in the Law Courts: 'Imagine the feelings of a suffragette in such a very Anti spot. . . . Mr Konstam did not look severe but rather stunned to see me rolling up even there.'

Two uncomfortable nights – one on a British ferry ('I didn't think half so much about the danger of being torpedoed as I thought I would, but I didn't sleep much'), one in a French train – and they were at Nice – only to be informed that George was delayed. He turned up on their fourth day, tightlipped about his experiences at the front, but guardedly admitting to having had a 'wearing time' on observation duty in his 'little barrel house', a shell-damaged villa the chimney of which had been replaced with a barrel painted to look like bricks and with a spyhole; he spoke confidently of having Stella to stay with him in India 'next winter'. In a car jam-packed with officers they drove to Monte Carlo to hear Caruso in *Aïda*; soldiers in uniform being forbidden to enter the casino, Stella ventured in alone and lost twenty francs. The return journey she undertook on her own, stopping overnight in Paris where – hairshirt temporarily forgotten – she bought herself 'an alarming little hat'. It was nearly midnight on 23 March when she got back to Nichols Square, having been away for two and a half weeks: 'I nearly cried with joy to be back alone again with the brown smells and sights of Shoreditch around, and humble bread and dripping to eat.'

It had not been a relaxing trip, and no sooner was she back in harness than she felt quite as exhausted as she had before she set out. A new set of 'babies' had fallen ill and demanded her attention; and at the Bethnal Green Wives' club on Maundy Thursday she found herself at the centre of events that were the talk of Hoxton over Easter; they left her badly shaken in body and mind. It had all begun quite innocuously. The Victoria League, an Empire-minded, middle-class organisation with which Laura had connections, had at her prompting despatched eastwards a West End actress to give a poetry recital as an Easter treat. The unfortunate sequel was described by Stella in a letter to Laura, who was on holiday that weekend:

I shall never be able to look you in the face again. Your Miss Lewis came last night. Twenty-five members attended and of these possibly four were sober. I don't think Miss Lewis was physically hurt, although we got to fighting almost immediately, but tho' she behaved splendidly, I'm afraid she must be annoyed. She recited one piece amid loud songs and caterwauls and then everybody rose and began blacking everybody's eyes. I dived into the fray, on one side I had a lady shouting over and over again 'You're a leddy, Miss Bezzon, every inch a leddy, every 'air of your 'ead's a leddy, but them as you work for is —,' on the other side was my rather beloved Mrs Wigston, a six footer, shouting to me to come along and she'd 'urt me. I did come along and she did hurt me, some splitter on the lower neck, I also seized her arm and was waved about like a flag. I then sent for the police and they came and removed the ringleaders, but on finding I didn't want them charged, unfortunately let them go again. Upon which to my horror the four sober ladies, who had been hanging desperately to my coat-tails, and watching me being thumped with incredulous horror, immediately charged into the street and began fighting the offenders. I left it at that, I really couldn't champion my champions in a Hoxton Street row, but I am afraid they all, righteous and unrighteous, spent the night in prison. I played the piano like the boy on the burning deck and managed to silence the singers and soothe the sleepers and revive those who had swooned, in time to have some excellent recitations from Miss Lewis. It was really heroic of her to see it through, a lot of people of her sort would have gone away, in fact I begged her to do so I was so afraid she would get one upon her powdered nose. . . .[6]

Stella's investigation into the origin of the affray disclosed wheels within wheels, but a lot of the responsibility seemed to rest with a backbiting club member. Two wearing weeks more in which (ever the frisky subordinate) she had a number of brushes with authority, and once again she was working herself towards breakdown. On 16 April, after a night of high fever – 'I ramped and roared' – she dragged herself across London to see Dr Monckton. He thought she had diphtheria, changed his mind to measles and arranged for her to enter a fever hospital, changed his mind again and sent her to a Kensington nursing home, no doubt opining that whatever her complaint she would be better off under medical supervision. She was there ten days. To convalesce she went to stay with the Bengoughs at their house in Worcestershire, part of which was turned over to a hospital for Belgian wounded. Cosseted by kind Bengoughs who pitied her 'green and thin' look, she felt 'rather treacherous', as well she might: Nigel – who was in process of transferring, partly on her advice, from the yeomanry to the Royal Flying Corps – had just received a very sharp letter telling him that never, if she could help it, would she be alone with him again.

Round a maypole in innocent pastoral fashion the three Bengough sisters leapt, but Stella was not considered strong enough to join in. The coming month, for her, was to be far from merry. On 12 May anti-German riots flared all over London. She saw shops attacked:

> a little knot of people, mostly women and boys, gathered round a suspect's door, and swelled into a compact silent crowd, all looking hard and saying little, while the unhappy suspect was hiding behind his curtains. Then someone, generally a child, would throw the first stone, and the window would fall to bits under a hail of bricks and fists. And then goods and stock would come flying into the street.

By evening things got wilder. In Hoxton the pubs closed early, and after eight o'clock only police ventured into the main street. Returning from Southwark, Stella saw the German confectioner's shop at the corner of her square with its window smashed in, and a crowd waiting in ominous silence for the owner's return. Next evening at the Wives' Club tales were told of a German butcher being killed and a German woman hauled by her hair up and down her shop. Wrecking bakers' shops was a fine lark and a paying lark too, the price of bread having gone up. One heroine boasted that she had led a raid on a hardware shop simply to get herself a new scrubbing brush, and had come away with several.

On 31 May came the first Zeppelin raid on London. At twenty minutes to midnight, having just changed into her pyjamas (the new nightwear for women), Stella heard bangs. She put on a coat and went outdoors to look:

> everybody was out, and everybody had a different story. There was an immense glare in the sky and dense smoke from the Hoxton direction. It seemed so calm in that still island silence of the square, with distant sounds of shouts and fire-engines and running crowds, and here in the square the cats were sitting washing their faces.

She dressed, and made her way to Hoxton, groping along streets thronged with people, and pitch dark but for the glimmer of men's pipes. At Bacchus Walk, where one of her old women had survived unhurt, a fire, 'high and passionately fierce', was raging – 'but they put it out in twenty minutes'. As experience was to show, there was nothing like a Zeppelin raid for boosting Kitchener's recruiting campaign: five incendiary bombs had brought the reality of war home to Shoreditch as nothing else could, and next day at the town hall Stella saw the young men queuing up to enlist under the shadow of the smoke from their burned-out houses.

There were four more Zeppelin raids on London in 1915. It is interesting to observe how Stella comported herself when the City was set ablaze on the night of 8 September. She went out to survey the damage in much the same spirit of concerned inquisitiveness as her ancestor Sam Pepys had displayed nearly two hundred and fifty years earlier, in another and far more devastating fire. Altogether it was:

Some day. I rose at 7 and breakfasted and was up at Islington by 8.15 to take my old Rebecca to the hospital. We spent three hours over this, although I bribed and corrupted and got in before anyone else. . . . I was rushed all day, I hardly had a bite of food that I didn't have to finish in the bus. I went to the Club. Coming back from it a lot of foghorns chorussed [sic] from everywhere, and I wondered at the time whether that was the sort of noise a 'maroon' would make, the signal to get back home before firing. I had hardly got in when I heard a singular loud and distinct pattering. I went into the garden and saw a Zeppelin not very high, exactly above me, with every searchlight in London looking at it. Then the guns began, a deafening row. I fetched Mr Smith to look at it. He said 'We're in for it now' and threw me downstairs into the basement. I helped to get the children down, 'Rene was in hysterics and I was more humorous than I ever am outside nightmares and said it would be over Holland by now. But I went up much to Mr Smith's annoyance and saw the beastly thing standing there. Mr Smith seemed to have the police regulations by heart – being a policeman – he shut all the windows and gave commands, though we couldn't hear each other speak through the firing. I was glad to have been born in time to appreciate these things. Presently I went up when Mr Smith wasn't looking, and saw it, with its back to us, much further away, the searchlights and guns still working hard, and a huge fire down in the City. I went out and before I knew how tired I was, had walked to the Guildhall. The fires were in Fetter Lane, Farringdon Road, St. Bartholomew's Close, and Smithfield, they said. But I only saw one off Basinghall St., an immense crowd. I nearly cried with glory when I saw the fire engines come by, and the word was passed along to clear the way, and the bell rang. Also when motors full of Flying Corps men passed, and we cheered them all along. I was very anxious about my dear St. Paul's, until I got to the City and saw it was safe. The streets were very brilliant – though lampless – the fires were so big, dancing over the roofs, and all the chimneys and high buildings were red even in Shoreditch – like a sunset. I talked to everybody, and didn't come home until I could find nothing more to look at. Up 'ackney Road, Shoreditchers, whose enthusiasm always takes a wrong turning, were roughly handling bicyclists who still had their lamps lit. I watched several skirmishes and then came in. I wonder if I should behave decently under fire. Certainly to-night though I looked up at the Zeppelin standing exactly above me, in a position to drop a pea into my mouth, I wasn't frightened, only brutally excited.

In June, purely for the sake of the one pound a week that it would bring in –
and rather shamefacedly – Stella had accepted a salaried post at the COS.
Laura remembered how, in telling her about it, 'pale Stella became rose-pink
with embarrassment . . . a mixture of exaltation and Victorian shame'.[7]
The job involved the meticulous kind of clerical work that she was not good
at, and the strain of it may account in part for her collapse at the end of July,
only two months after getting over her last illness. On this occasion Laura
'galloped' promptly across London to render aid, her mother arrived hotfoot
and stayed the night, hot fomentations rained on her chest, and the local
doctor, diagnosing pleurisy, murmured that 'the lung was affected'. She was
coughing up blood and continuing to cough it up and (exactly as a year
before, though this time without apparent bitterness) she decided that
she was about to embark prematurely on 'a further adventure'. Her
mother thought so too, and sadly urged her to devote what time remained
to her to her writing. She saw the illness out in Nichols Square, attended
(what would have been unthinkable in time of peace) by a prattling district
nurse, her mother wishing to give time to George, who was home on
leave, and no private nurse being obtainable as all were busy attending
war-wounded.

Convalescing at Cranbrook with Susan McLeod, she heard to her dismay
that Nigel was on leave (having taken part in 'that big raid on Germany'),
and might at any moment descend on Cranbrook in his aeroplane – 'almost
too characteristic of this century'. But when eventually he did turn up,
looking attractive in his new uniform, it was only prosaically in the Martini.
To Stella's relief he had two brother officers with him, and by dint of
pouring out a stream of frantic chat about munitions, she succeeded in
keeping the three of them together in Susan's drawing room, thus thwarting
any intention that Nigel's companions might have had of jumping to their
feet and proposing for themselves a stroll round the garden.

By the end of August *I Pose* was ready for the publisher. She chose
Macmillan, her Aunt Mary's publisher, being at pains not to mention the
connection until after the book had been accepted. In fact, the acceptance and
an offer to bring out the book 'at once', came in just over a week. Stella
soared:

> It was so glorious – it frightened me. I couldn't sleep. I allowed myself to
> look at the letter by candlelight every now and then, to see if it was still
> the same. . . . Perhaps it may be a stock letter that publishers always
> write to encourage the young. But of course it isn't – it's a good BOOK. I
> have done something worth doing.

Next morning she was up and across London in time to tell the family the
news before she went to work:

I gave them three guesses. They all of course guessed I was engaged to be married (oh no, much better than that) and secondly a fortune left me. Aunt Mary guessed right – she laughed and nearly cried and hugged me and ran about. It was better than my dream in the night, I dreamt Mother was snubby, but she wasn't.

To add to the drama of the moment, Nigel was in England again, this time on melancholy special duty. He was escorting home for burial the body of his friend Captain John Liddell, VC, one of eight members of the RFC to be honoured with the supreme award for gallantry in the war.

Elements of tragedy and euphoria met and mixed in Stella to produce a spasm of returning affection for Nigel – especially as in his present chastened mood he was 'most genially rational, and hardly ever employed the burning dark gaze stunt from behind a hand'. She promised to send him a copy of the book, due on 16 November, though she knew that he was bound to think:

a lot of false things out of it, I know he will squeeze himself in where there was never a place for him. But what does it matter what he thinks – the Childe Adorable of a hundred years ago when I was young, he who has done a man's work and grown into a man – let him get out of it what his heart chooses, my dear.

Pert, clever, original, irritating: adjectives that spring to mind at sight of the title *I Pose* hold good for the novel itself. What is one to make of a work of fiction whose hero and heroine have no personal names, but are referred to as 'the gardener' and 'the suffragette' throughout, while a plant in a pot has the fine old cognomen Hilda? Whatever is the author, patently so young, about?

Eyebrows quizzically raised at the self-pleasing roles people play, pen poised to catch whole flocks of epigrams on the wing (though her bag is of uneven quality), she is out to amuse and (a little) to shock, but she has a passionately serious purpose too, a number of points to make about woman's role in the society of her day, and about the perils awaiting the woman who chooses to think and act for herself.

Unusually for a first novel, the heroine is not a self-portrait of the author, though in some respects she is what the author would have liked to be. Twenty-six years old, solitary by choice, diminutive and 'quite plain', she is a militant suffragette, who gives Holloway Prison as her permanent address. She is first encountered striding along a country road, matches in pocket, intent on burning down the home of a 'scion of sweated industry', and last seen – dead – beside the chancel screen of a church in which she has just exploded a bomb. The desultory adventures that she encounters in between stem from her meeting on that Hampshire road with a young man three years her junior, a very young and downy individual indeed, who calls himself a gardener, and carries in his hand the aforementioned potted plant as if to prove it – to himself as much as to anyone else, for his knowledge of gardening is minimal and his experience nil.

On the face of it, two such disparate characters can have no meeting ground. But the insidious, impertinent power of sex to effect an unexpected transformation in things is seen when, on a second meeting, the suffragette explains to the gardener that she intends to destroy a building for which, as it happens, he has a special regard:

The gardener closed his hand about the suffragette's thin arm. 'You will force me to take advantage of my privilege,' he said, and looked at his own enormous hand.

The suffragette stood perfectly still, looking in the direction she wanted to go.

'Turn back,' said the gardener. But she made a sudden passionate effort to twist her arm out of his grasp. It was absurd, and very nearly successful, like several things that women do.

The gardener's heart grew black. There seemed nothing to be done. No end could be imagined to the incident. . . .

'Do you know why I want to stop you?' he said at last.

'Yes.'

'Why?'

'Because you are not a woman, and don't understand.'

'Because I am a man, and I understand.'

She was silent.

'Do you know what I mean?'

'Yes.'

'You don't. I mean that I am a man, and I am not going to let you go, because you must come with me to the uttermost ends of the earth.'

'Why?'

'Because I love the shape of your face, you dear little thing.'

Her heart, in defiance of nature, had gone to her head, and was thundering rhythmically there. She was despising herself passionately, and congratulating herself passionately. How grand – she thought: how contemptible – she thought. For she was a world's worker, a wronged unit seeking rights, a co-heritor of the splendour of the earth, a challenger, a warrior. And now, quite suddenly, she discovered a fact the existence of which she had seldom, even in weak moments, suspected. She found that – taken off her guard – she was a young woman of six-and-twenty.

For a while, but not for long, their lives run parallel. They embark on a voyage of 'mutual exploration' to the West Indies, living as friends – they have separate cabins – but for convenience calling themselves husband and wife. A clerical fellow passenger, the villain of the piece, the egregious Father Christopher, a self-righteous hypocrite posing as a man of God (he even succeeds in convincing himself), discovers that they are not married, presumes they are 'living in sin', and thinks it his duty to expose them. His machinations matter little, as by this time the suffragette has repented her moment of folly, and is in full flight from the lovesick gardener. From a West Indian isle, where they have quite separate adventures, she makes good her flight to England, resumes the 'hairshirt' she has so rashly cast off, goes to live in London's East End, and plunges into social work and suffragism. Her big mistake is to try to form a trade union branch among some underpaid factory girls who happen to be members of Father Christopher's church club.

Meanwhile the gardener, in hot pursuit, has crossed the Atlantic. After Father Christopher has succeeded in torpedoing the union branch it is to him that the suffragette turns in her distress. At the end of Chapter One (a single chapter of no less than 302 pages) she is sufficiently untrue to her convictions as to consent to marry him, on the understanding that they will be both 'lovers and friends' when wed. At this juncture it looks very much as though the suffragette has arrived, albeit by a very unusual route, at woman's common destination, and like the heroine of conventional romance, will shortly dwindle into a wife.

Chapter Two (only eight pages long) reverses all that: a visit to the East End, scene of her wrecked endeavours, reawakens her fury with male attitudes in general and Father Christopher in particular. On the way to the registry office she enters his church and – leaving the gardener in the safety of a rear pew – advances up the aisle, gazes defiantly at the altar and hurls her bomb.

Stella called *I Pose* a 'post-impressionist' novel, thereby licensing herself to distort reality in various surprising ways. Thus she telescopes time, and does extraordinary symbolic things with colour: there is a Mrs Rust (first of a series of large, overpowering windbags of women in her fiction), whose predominant feature is her hair, dyed a forcible crimson to match her personality. As a first novel it is endearing: 'Miss Benson's talent is beyond question,' thought the *Spectator*. Most of the critics who noticed it, finding it both clever and puzzling, were facetious at the expense of both it and its author, in a kindly way. Over the *Scotsman* she wept, but glowed when the editor of *Punch*, Sir Henry Lucy, in a private letter to Sir Frederick Macmillan, called it 'the most original, brightest, and best written book that he had read – or may read – for a long time.'

A year later, on 16 November 1916, the journalist and future novelist Rebecca West wrote to register her '*joy in I Pose*':

Having been in my day a suffragette, my feeling is that I want to pass a motion about it with no dissentients – you know the flushed, platform feeling. How superbly you've done the snake that was the soul of the suffrage movement. How lucky you are to have written the only novel of genius about the Suffrage. And how wonderful of you to know that 'succour is a pose word'. And how gorgeously you describe scenery. I have a suspicion that your visit to the West Indies has been your solitary treat. I feel just the same passion for Spain because it is the one loophole out of England I have ever looked at. I have often wondered whether one wouldn't lose that intense feeling if one had travelled more. Every page of your book is glorious, so I had to thank you.[8]

The letter might have been even more welcome a year earlier, for in November 1915 Stella had needed every scrap of comfort she could get. That familiar bugbear, her health, was troubling her again, threatening her very existence – so that on publication day, far from feeling like 'a new planet risen on the world', she saw herself as 'really just an old cast-off star sinking'. On 12 November her Shoreditch doctor had startled her by saying that he now considered her consumptive. He went on to advise her that she should, if she wanted to stay alive, do only the mildest of work henceforth, which made me smile some, secretly'. Mary Marker, told the news in strictest confidence, advised a second opinion, recommending a woman specialist of her acquaintance. A good, dependable, over-talkative sort the lady turned out to be, and it was her unenviable task to tell Stella that indeed she was consumptive – hopelessly so; however, if she were to give up work altogether, go to the seaside for three months and take every possible care, she might remain alive for a good while yet. A third consultation yielded the opinion that she might not be consumptive after all, but definitely had fibrosis of one lung, and should be living on a horse ranch in Texas.

Between various advices Stella found herself hopelessly confused: 'I don't seem to have much spunk to fix up any plan,' she sighed. Mary Marker took her courage in both hands and wrote offering to help her financially if she gave up work; from the Western Front a scared George – 'I am terribly afraid of you at times, and most of all now' – wrote promising her two pounds a week on the same condition. Stella was very much touched, and a tear 'wandered' into her eye. But there was no question of her giving up work, no question of her accepting: 'it worries me very much that anybody should bother about me at all, and above all bother *me*'.

I Pose in its pleasing cover – 'very ladylike, bound in suffragette grey, with gold lettering' – was selling well on the Christmas market; rumour reached her that 'Mac' (Sir Frederick Macmillan) was dining out on it, 'would talk of nothing but *I.P.* and me, the progress of whom satisfies him'. (After six months, 1044 copies of the English edition had been sold, 335 of the Empire edition; it was also published by Macmillan in the United States. When accounts were drawn Stella had made the not inconsiderable sum of sixty pounds.) On 21 December she and Laura took time off from West End shopping to call in at the Times Book Club and enquire after it: 'Oh – Benson's *I Pose*. It's sold out of stock,' they were told. '"Benson" it was that stunned me. Both Benson and Hutton got incredibly tired, the rush was such!'

George was in France for Christmas. Mrs Benson spent the holiday with her two younger children (Stephen still not in uniform) at 10 Leonard Place, Kensington High Street, where she had moved earlier in the year to be near her sisters.

New Year's Eve 1915 found Stella gazing back appalled over twelve months of horror; bloody stalemate on the Western Front; the fiasco of the Dardanelles; the first use of poison gas; the first bombing of civilians in their homes. Hope for the future seemed to be pretty much illusion, yet still one found oneself hoping against hope:

So it is nearly 1916. Curious how we cut time up, and yet he goes on whole, unaware of our limits and periods. To-morrow will be the same as to-day, and not a bit more hopeful really, yet somehow it seems if we can only cast this terrible stretch of time – 1915 – behind us, new things will be born, and new hopes rise. The malignant year finished badly, as might have been expected, a cruiser, the *Natal*, blown up, and three hundred lost.

Chapter Seven

Early in January 1916 Stella retired to a hotel in Margate to recuperate for six weeks. Despite the Kent resort's vulnerability to sea and air attack, throughout the war invalids continued to go there for the sake of the celebrated air. But January was a dead month and the Kingscliffe Hotel was nearly empty. Stella was very much on her own but she was not unhappy: she took the hotel dog for healthy walks, ate well, and was surprised to find, when she woke up in the morning, that she no longer felt 'wretchedly ill':

> It is a very long time since I have felt that there could be any physical happiness in life. I have got used to thinking of living as enduring, even when it is mentally exhilarating. But here the sun and the sea seem to bring back something to me which I suppose is youth, and anyway it is freedom from poor old body.

She caught up with some of the latest books – Chesterton, Wells, Compton Mackenzie, Hardy, Maurice Hewlett – and wrote an article (her first venture into commercial journalism) for the London evening paper the *Pall Mall Gazette*; it was a whimsical piece about London buses, and under the title was prominently emblazoned 'by Stella Benson, the author of *I Pose*'. Stella was delighted to see her work in print, but already she took a strictly practical view of journalism, ending her diary jubilation: 'Now I want my two pounds.'

Reminders of war were everywhere. Her first thought on waking was of 'death coming in the dark to strong young bodies that have never even known pain. I think the hearts of us all will be several degrees more dead before this is done.' Her visitors – her mother and Laura came down – learned to get used to the distant crashing roar of British warships firing on Belgian ports. To Stella's disappointment – for despite her horror of the war she longed to experience its dangerous excitement – there were no raids on

Margate while she was there: 'Five Taubes passed over here this morning, coming from Dover where they killed several people and did some damage [she wrote on 23 January]. They didn't drop any bombs here, and didn't even wake us up, so it wasn't a successful raid, as far as I was concerned.'

A year later, 'I would have loved to have been there,' she wrote, when she heard that Margate had been shelled by submarines. The most exciting event while she was there was the bombing 'to its death after putting up a fight with its guns', of a German submarine stranded on the Goodwin Sands, some seven miles out to sea:

> a solid oblong of black smoke stood in the mist to a great height, then it spurted out like the advertisement of Stephen's Ink. I had time to say 'look out there'll be a great bang' and then there was a great bang, of a most wicked sound, that seemed to dwell, like the smoke, on the air. . . . I heard the shriek of the bombs and shells before they exploded, which always fascinates me in a red sort of way. But it is about the nearest I have been to furious death, I think.

When the time came to leave Margate, Stella decided it would be a graceful act of reparation to her mother to go and stay with her, and so sink her 'poor beautiful brown loneliness and scarlet independence' in comfortable Kensington for a while. But a grave obstacle was her mother's refusal to give house-room to David, the hotel dog – and if Stella could not have him (the hotel proprietor no longer wanting him) he was to be destroyed. A passionate exchange of telegrams got them nowhere, and it fell to Aunt Mary to hit on a solution: the dog could be boarded in kennels convenient to Kensington Gardens, where Stella could walk him each afternoon.

Nigel came to stay at Leonard Place. He was as fervent and pressing as ever – and as firmly rejected: 'I shuddered and felt rather sick to think that he should think of marrying me.' It was bitter to think what a gap separated her dream hopes from this, her only actual offer of love:

> Curious that one should, in the back of one's mind, build all one's life on some vague foundation which one calls Romance, and then when it comes it should be an unmoving emptiness like this. It is difficult to get used to the presumption that my life does not include, and will never include, the hot feverishness of Romance. I guess I was born old, and certainly I was born cold. . . . I have a big heart for David, and a big heart for Hoxton, but it seems to dissolve when put to its normal uses.

Just before leaving London, she had given a party for her Hoxton 'babies'. The plight of one of them, 'my poor little Mrs Granville, wrung my heart. She seems on the point of death, and I don't know what to do with her beautiful boy, John.' The mother, who was tubercular, was found a bed in a sanatorium, but the problem remained of what to do with ten-year-old Johnnie: either, said the relieving officer, he must go to a Poor Law school to board, or Stella must formally adopt him. The former Stella could not bear to contemplate; she let her heart rule her head and – quixotically, impulsively, Bensonically, saddling her future with heaven alone knew what – she resolved to adopt.

She arranged an interim home for the boy with Mrs Oneleg, who was now ensconced at 50 Hoxton Square with her paper-bag business and her deceased sister's small daughter Rosie, Stella paying the rent. But alas, when Laura came down to Margate she had sad tidings to tell of young Johnnie. He was taking the spotless Rosie out thieving, and had asked Mrs Oneleg 'why she didn't bring a gentleman back o'nights, and earn ten shillings every time?' – a way of supplementing her income which his mother had turned to from time to time.

Regretfully, Stella decided that Johnnie must be put in a 'Home', and addressed herself to the problem the moment she got back to London. As he was a baptised Roman Catholic, she arranged for him to go to a convent near Horsham in Surrey, and (ignoring his last-minute protestation that he intended to give up his religion) escorted him there herself. On arrival it was embarrassing enough to have him taken for her son (she being in her respectable town clothes, and he in torn breeches with a silk rag round his neck by way of tie), doubly awkward when the Mother Prioress blushed bright pink on learning that she was unmarried.

Johnnie's actual mother, now in Hoxton Union workhouse, was being difficult. She was accusing Stella of child-stealing, and threatening to send her brother to 'show her what's what'. While in *her* care, Mrs Granville affirmed, Johnnie had been very well looked after, and had never been without 'his own little white bed'. With vivid recollections of the heap of rags that served as a couch in infamous Jerusalem Passage, Stella wheeled to the attack: what about the times Johnnie had had to sleep on the steps or in public WCs while his mother entertained half-quid gentlemen lodgers? 'Nah then, none o' that,' said Mrs Granville. In the end, Stella's good sense and kindness won through: when in June Mrs Granville died, she was fully reconciled to Stella, blessed her and said she would never have believed her Johnnie could turn in a few months into 'such a big, brown, handsome boy'.

Stella was back at work with the COS now, in theory mornings only, though in practice the pastoral ramifications of her work, and her private and personal Hoxton commitments, meant that most of her time was taken up – and what with 'adopted sons, and aunts, and grandmothers in increasing herds', a worrying amount of her money.

One particularly trying client was a certain Mary Moon. Appearing on the scene one evening roaring drunk, she had played havoc with Mrs

Oneleg's room and stock, and next morning, reappearing full of contrition, had begged Stella to get her into a Salvation Army home for inebriates. From this haven she eventually felt herself ready to sally forth, prematurely as events showed:

> When I called on Mrs Oneleg Smith she told me to 'run along the street and see a sight'. I ran and found Miss Moon, drunk, with a can of beer in her hand. I gazed at her silently for a long minute, and she burst into tears, much to the interest of Hoxton Market. I took the beer and poured it into the street. After long and confusing arguing, I decided to give her the benefit of a very big doubt, and look upon it as a slip that she herself deplored. She said her landlady had been tempting her. So I walked across with her to her lodging, paid a week's rent for notice, and helped Miss Moon to pack filthy effects, and carry them across to Mrs Smith's back room. We had some stirring, not to say ear-splitting scenes between Mrs Smith and Miss Moon. It is all bitterly disappointing. . . . she is so shameless and ungrateful, she doesn't seem to be on our side in trying to save her. . . .

Mrs Oneleg, with her long experience of East End ways, probably had a shrewd idea of what would be the outcome – but even she may not have expected it so soon. On the very next day, Stella darkly records, 'things happened' with Miss Moon, and she received notice to quit. In an article for the *Dial*, Stella related the end of the story:

> I called on the Salvation Army. A saint in navy blue told me that I was 'one of little faith', which indeed I was, in the circumstances. The saint received the sinner again, albeit with arms a shade less open than before. As Miss M. disappeared, she winked behind the saint's back. The latest news of her is not inspiring. She sent for me to visit her in a Workhouse Infirmary; she said that she was now saved, and was it true that the price of spirits had gone up again 'outside'?[1]

The premises at 50 Hoxton Square comprised two ground-floor rooms: a front room where the paper-bag business was carried on (and where possibly Mrs Oneleg and Rosie slept), and a small room behind, filthy and dilapidated when Stella took over the premises, but afterwards brought to a semblance of decency. This room she let to a series of tenants, not one of whom was respectable enough to have qualified for assistance from the COS. Take Dolly Dalley, for instance. Her home life, as Stella describes it in her article, could have come straight out of A. S. Jasper's *A Hoxton Childhood*:

> They lived six in one room, before Dolly left them. The father is never sober to my knowledge . . . the mother, though by incessant and

heartbreaking work she manages to support her family on fifteen shillings a week, the fruit of painting toys with more or less unhealthy paint, is not really in possession of her intellect. . . .

At sixteen Dolly 'got into trouble', and her virtuous father turned her into the street, whence Stella rescued her, providing her with necessities through the charity of her aunts. All that Dolly had brought with her from the parental home were 'two little framed seaside prints'. With her 'boy round the docks', she moved into Stella's back room, and when shortly afterwards Mrs Oneleg and the neighbours urged marriage upon them they complied, having no strong views on the matter:

The effort of getting married seems to have been too much for them. . . . Dolly cannot even muster up enough vitality to do up her hair or even dress herself except in two sacks and a little string. The local authorities have offered her free meals, but Dolly would rather starve than dress up in her shop-provided clothes and walk two blocks to a good meal. The boy brings home a bloater at night, when his earnings run to it.

When I said goodbye to Dolly, on leaving my shop, she looked like a cave-dweller, wrapped in shapeless things and with her matted hair about her eyes. But I doubt if the cave-dweller would appreciate the comparison; after all, he was progressive enough, in his own way.[2]

In her article Stella outlines her philosophy in relation to the 'undeserving' poor, breaking out – very unusually for her – into the language of rhetoric, and by a simple device identifying herself with their cause:

The march of civilisation is not a particularly well-organised procession; sometimes it almost seems as if the stragglers outnumber those who keep in step. At any rate, in the Brown Borough [her name for Shoreditch] most of us are content to linger on the long road, even though it be dark, and though there be no lights to lead us, and no flowers to make lingering worth while. In the van of the march music brays confidently, wearying the ears of heaven with brazen brayings of progress, but no echo of that music reaches or cheers us, strung out wearily as we are along the forgotten miles. Perhaps even Heaven only hears the boasting, perhaps Heaven has washed its hands of us, perhaps after all we are but dirt and deserve nothing better.

For Stella, wartime London held romance: 'Sometimes, on the way home just after the lamps are lit,' she wrote in her diary in March of this year, 'when everyone is streaming outwards from the City, and there is a little fog to paint the air and the further ends of the perspectives, I revel greatly in the gloriousness of the City. I love the crowds, and the crossing and recrossing of men and traffic, and the noise. . . . It is the race and the panting that I love. The feeling that I am part of the heart of England, beating with hopes and horrors on one tremendous subject.'

But for much of the next six months she was to be out of London. In April she was at Lutwyche Hall, guest of George's tenants. There were duty calls to pay on some of the villagers: 'Very hearty outwardly, I was, but coy within, not being a feudalist at heart'; many of them remembered her christening. In the churchyard, her father's and her sister Catherine's graves brought her up hard against a juxtaposition of ideas that was new to her, 'the rather incongruous forming of a connection between earth lumps and scratched stones and very living people who are, I am sure, extremely busy somewhere else.' (No room for doubt there, apparently; she had cast aside conventional faith, but her assurance of personal survival was such as a believer might envy.)

On 10 June she was in Reigate for the start of a three-day motor tour of Sussex and Kent with some friends, the Charringtons. Petrol was not officially rationed in the First World War, but citizens were called upon not to use it frivolously, and there is an element of guilt in Stella's comment that the trip was 'most unwarlike'. It was to cover 130 miles, without breakdown and without benefit of male superintendence.

In July Stella went on her own to Cornwall, passing an idyllic, escapist month there. She stayed near Tintagel, first on a farm where all the farm men whistled hymns – 'I woke to the tune of "Fight the Good Fight" mixed with larks, and the cows have just marched past to "How Sweet the Name",' she told Laura[3] – and the only other guests were a pair of 'superfluous young artist ladies with short hair (with bows on the top), pink smocks to the hips and riding breeches' (omitting the bows, precisely the emancipated style of hair and clothes that she herself would be sporting in a year's time); and then at a small hotel. Except when Laura and Essex came on visits, she was alone with her dog. In all winds and weathers they walked the clifftops, explored harbour villages, sat on rocks and watched the sea. Stella bathed, which at first David considered so peculiar and unnatural that he went bounding in to her rescue.

Sitting in the sun, Stella made progress with her new novel *This is the End*. Some of its scenario is pure Cornwall. The fact that thought people have a prominent role to play in the book explains why, in her own life, they were temporarily quiescent. They intruded powerfully only once, in a dream, and then they hung about all next day; it was as if she and David and the thought people all together 'bathed, and lay down among the fern on the cliff and did nothing at all, except be happy'.

War thoughts were never far away. There was a 'big push' in progress in France (an early stage in the Battle of the Somme): 'George and Billy [a

Prescott cousin] are in the hottest part of it; George is now in command of a battery, firing with great effect over Billy's head.'

The second half of 1916 was a tale of worsening health; she was back in London, and a London autumn was always unsafe for Stella. In September she left her mother's house and went to live in rented rooms in new, 'progressive' Hampstead Garden Suburb, at 20 Asmun's Place, fifteen minutes' walk, beside the hedges and ditches of the Finchley Road, from Golders Green Underground station. She was cooking for herself for the first time, and seems to have lived off tinned sardines and the occasional chop; 'I rather depend on a meal or more with the family on Sundays,' she admitted, relieved that her mother was prepared to waive the embargo on David at weekends.

She was still 'registrating' for Mary Marker at the COS, and had taken on two other jobs, both of which involved traipsing about Shoreditch knocking on doors: collecting war savings contributions and seeing discharged servicemen about pensions. As if all this were not enough, she let her Aunt V take her to see the place of her own more genteel war effort, the Wounded and Missing Officers' Bureau of the Red Cross in Carlton House Terrace. Though put off by the gilded splendours, and 'terrified' by the 'beautifully gowned' workers flitting about, she seems to have been unable to resist the offer of further part-time work there. However, the 'Mayfair' atmosphere soon wearied her – 'as Mother says, I have got out of my class, I hate the sleek and opulent pose', and in any case half her mind was on her book, which was now finished and being retyped. So when after a fortnight a series of blunders committed among the filing cabinets earned her 'the polite sack' she was not sorry.

Stella was out and about in the evenings a good deal. She was taken three times to *A Kiss for Cinderella*, the latest offering from James Barrie, 'the Adored One' (as she called him) of that day's stage. It was an embarrassingly sentimental piece, as Stella perfectly well appreciated – 'your heart curls up with sentimentality, and you almost blush for it the while'. But she could see the reason for its success at that time: 'He turns his back on the dreadful complicatedness of things. . . . There are a few childlike things, and a few quiet smiles, and a few sentimental tears mixed up in chaos after all. One is apt to open one's eyes too wide and see too much, but he can forget, and he can make you forget for a few blessed hours.'

Stephen took her to see *The Bing Boys* at the Alhambra Theatre in Leicester Square, a notorious pick-up place. Though she laughed and sang with much energy and enjoyed the show, she could not keep her mind off:

the gimlet eyes of the men in the promenade. I thought perhaps that there must be that side of life, and that there is something in that side that no other side has got, and that young men and young women ought to know everything they can. . . . Yet it is wrong that women should be so monopolised and that men should only show one side of themselves to it. Men can go one evening to meet their — and another to meet their mothers, but a woman, when once she has done that promenade to the full, can never do anything else. Can it be that even the number of souls is excessive, and that some must be lost?

With Laura she went to a poetry-reading at Harold Monro's[4] Poetry Bookshop, the well-known rendezvous for poets and poetry-lovers in Devonshire Street, Theobalds Road. She thought the proprietor a 'very commonplace looking young man', though with 'understanding eyes and voice'; the reader, Thomas Sturge Moore,[5] came off decidedly worse: 'he was a very shy, poor creature, and his voice was like the bleating of a boiled lamb, dreadfully affected and posed. You'd have to be like that – I guess – to stand up at a desk and read your own unpublished burblements.'

But Stella was not feeling well. Scarcely a day passed without mention in her diary of one kind of physical distress or another, and at the end of October she went to see Monckton. His strictures on her head, nerves, pleurisy attacks and pain 'on occasions which should be nameless' led to the depressing conclusion that she had the 'brain and body of a fifty year old, rather worn out' and very carefully to be nurtured; 'anyone but a Benson would have seen that long ago', he added. She was to cease work at once, go to the seaside or country and eat well for four to six weeks, after which 'a little operation' might be necessary; 'and when I was well after that I was to occupy myself entirely with writing book [sic], or basket making. Office work is apparently fatal to such a weak head as mine. I can't think what to do.' One thing that clearly she had no intention of doing was to take Dr Monckton's advice seriously; and indeed, when next day Mrs Oneleg saw fit to utter a sympathetic murmur, her inward comment was 'it is absurd, because I am quite well'.

However, in the weeks that led up to Christmas, while remaining in the Garden Suburb, she made some effort to rest, winding up her official duties in Hoxton (though retaining a bevy of unofficial ones), correcting the proofs of *This is the End*, which had been accepted by Macmillan in November, and taking healthy walks with David on the Heath. A heavy 'flue cold' did not prevent her hostessing a pre-Christmas party for some of her old ladies; most arrived in tears 'in the brisk and joyous way that Hoxton guests affect', and one poor soul, crying because she was lonely, refused to sit down, and went away again bearing a present and three buns; the remainder enjoyed themselves in their peculiar Hoxton fashion, with much damp discussion of 'dear departeds' and other 'dismalities'.

George – on long convalescent leave, 'eyes crocked up, not looking bad, very darling' – was home for Christmas, a major's crown on his shoulder. It was their first wartime Christmas all four together – but 'none could describe it as a merry one'. They were all more or less stricken with influenza, so that it took real effort to be 'hilarious' over the turkey. A few days later, Stella's epilogue to 1916 took the form of a kind of grim anthem to war:

I believe secretly one dreads Peace almost as much as one would have dreaded War had one known enough about it. We know War now, it is like a terrible chill in the air, we breathed it in, we grew upon it. And one of the things it has taught us is that Peace was also a terrible thing, how did we live without choking. It is pathetic to think of those fool Americans still proud and careful of their untested peace. . . . There is no getting back to peaceful peace. War has made drunkards of us all, we can never drink barley water with pleasure again. If peace comes we shall make something new and terrible out of it. We have grown up, we have put away childish things.

Chapter Eight

On 3 January 1917, 'my rest cure being now over, such as it was', Stella presented herself at Dr Monckton's – only to be peremptorily ordered to bed, to await his visit in a few days' time. There was a night of delirium when she fancied that she was a hamper 'the lid of which would not shut', and when 'Monckey' arrived, he despatched her to a Kensington nursing home and kept her there ten days. After toying with the idea of Switzerland or Naples for her convalescence, 'Monklet' plumped for Devon, where – as she put it – 'some fool friend of his' would 'coddle' her for a week. She could then go wherever she liked, provided it were by the sea, and in April she might risk the return to London. The sting of the prescription was in the tail: 'It was no longer a thing of my own choice whether I work or not, but just a thing my body would not do.'

By no possible stretch of the imagination could Stella be mistaken for a docile patient, and by this time Dr Monckton understood her well. So when in conclusion he appealed to her to behave thenceforward as an invalid, and live only with people who would look after her, he was no doubt prepared for her queenly retort, 'Not under any circumstances would I bind the happy if rare stretches of time when I am not ill.'

The winter of 1916–17 was bitterly cold. Stella kept warm indoors at 10 Leonard Place, reading, among other things, Mendel the eugenist and reacting strongly against the coldly scientific materialism of his theory of selective breeding. No woman, she thought, could write such a book, 'no woman would want to. Yet the physical point of view is a point of view, and oughtn't, I suppose, to be ignored. Are poetry and romance really to be sneered at, and left to women?' Already, she felt, her own writing was out of tune with the new harsh realism, and her future work would be more so: 'Probably I shall go on writing of unvital and unphysical things, and shall die the Mrs Braddon of the twentieth century – Readable but How Insipid.' (Mrs Braddon had died in 1915, pouring out almost to the last a flow of lurid tales with moral endings in the Victorian tradition.)

George and she were composing a masque together (he doing the music, she the words), and the house was full of 'constant unpremeditated singing'; it was really only an extension, she felt, of the time-honoured family practice of singing partsongs in taxis. Stephen indeed, who was also there, had something to sing about at last – in January he was gazetted second lieutenant 'after many years of really patient waiting and longing'.

In February public events took an ominous turn when the Germans unleashed their unrestricted blockade of Britain, attacking all shipping bound for British ports, regardless of flag. (It was to bring the Americans into the war, in Stella's opinion disgracefully late: 'Serve 'em right if we knuckle under now,' she had expostulated just before Christmas, 'it would be worth doing if we could guarantee that the Germans would be all over their Monroe Doctrine within five years.') Down in Cranbrook, staying with Susan McLeod, she was shocked to find some of the local ladies lightly brushing aside Food Controller Lord Devonport's proposals for 'voluntary restrictions' on food consumption; his suggested limit of two and a half pounds of meat per person per week seemed perfectly reasonable to her (and in the Second World War would have been beyond the dreams of gluttony).

Stella was still under doctor's orders to go to the seaside or country and eat well, so in late February, taking David, she went to stay at the Hare and Hounds, a comfortable, newly built inn at Cookham Dean near Maidenhead in Berkshire. It was typical of her overreaction to patriotic directives (earlier she had contributed self-sacrificially to War Savings), that when the landlady told her that she had 'not started rationing anybody yet', she begged her to start on herself; one hopes the suggestion was ignored. Braving the weather – it was still bitterly cold, 'cold enough to move a stone to tears', and she feared her old reaction, the faintness that came when her hands were chilled – she and David took daily walks in the Thames Valley, a bare, red landscape as yet untouched by motor roads and creeping suburbia.

On 28 February an advance copy of *This is the End* arrived, 'handsomely bound in bright blue', but next day, because it gave her so much pleasure – she had slept with it under her pillow, and run to peep at it at all hours of the day – for 'hairshirty' reasons she sent it away to her mother.

Back in London early in March for a 'dinner fight' hosted by George, Stella met for the first time the girl whom in less than a year he was to marry – ravishingly pretty Olive, formerly a dancer, now working in a government office. With Stephen and *his* girl they went on afterwards, a group of five, to the 'Troc', the popular, pacey, none-too-select Trocadero Restaurant in Shaftesbury Avenue. A few days later Stella was feeling 'hot-hearted and proud' at *Young England*, a light operatic hit set in the time of Elizabeth I, and unashamedly a morale-booster; on coming out, she glowed: 'there is no enemy can beat us while the salt sea blood runs in our veins'. They went on to the Café Royal, where again they were a party of five (of whom two were obviously in love), and Stella the odd one out. It was an occasion to test her 'independent' pose and, alas, reveal the bitter feeling of inferiority lying only a skin's depth beneath:

> Those springing and surpassing things that happen in one evening shared by two people, I must never expect. I never had any charm, and even my youth was very short. Of course I am lucky to be able to get romance indirectly through my Secret Friends, and through my writing, but still it is grievous to find how very far I am from the direct intoxication of being a woman. Any fool except me knows the art of being a woman. George and the two 'real girls' sailed away in a taxi. . . . I woke up remembering how comforting it is to write, so I came back hurriedly with a deep breath of relief to David and Cookham Dean.

The notion of staying on in the country beyond the period specified by Dr Monckton and looking for work on the land came to Stella quite suddenly, and if any doubts of its wisdom arose in her mind she did not confide them to her diary. Just as the weather worsened – people were saying it was the coldest late snap since the winter of 1077 as recorded in Domesday Book – she found a job:

> A severe yet amusing old farmer called Mash agreed to take me next week on approval, at vegetable work, 2/6 a day, on condition I would not carp at wearing no skirt, and would try and *love* vegetables, as they do not grow without honest love. . . . He says the country women workers are nearly always beastly to people like me, but I must keep my end up, and retort that indoors I could beat them hollow with the pen.

Women volunteers for landwork in the First World War stood out sartorially from the regular workers, who kept to the bunched-up skirts of yore: Stella was told to get herself sweater, breeches, men's boots and gaiters, or, if breeches were unobtainable at such short notice, a skirt 'cut up not lower than the knees'.

Her gameness and humour, her unusual blend of lady and boy, must have disarmed her fellow working women, for there was no persecution. Work began at 8 a.m. and continued, with a break for lunch, until 4 p.m., by which time it was dark. Picking Brussels sprouts was searching work for someone not used to it, especially bare-handed in a biting wind, and when lunch was consumed outdoors 'on the lee side of a barn in a snowstorm, with drifts forming on every sandwich'. Stella passionately enjoyed her food, and the hot, strong tea carried out to the field by Mrs Phoebe, the foreman's wife. As far as the actual picking was concerned, for Stella make-believe took away some of the monotony:

I pretend to myself that the sprout field is a city, and the sprouts families, living in rows. There are aristocratic districts where the sprouts are as beautiful as grapes, and green and crisp and generally perfect. . . . Then there are great slum areas, sprouts with their souls killed by cold circumstances, rarely worth picking, but sometimes in an ugly crust of brown dinginess there is a very stout green heart.

She and her co-picker scored record amounts, with the result that 'my hands are so cut and blistered it hurts me to write, and I ache three times in every limb'. In dreams at night 'terrible thought people' came, sure sign that she was over-tired. But when at the end of the week she was offered a permanency, 'having given satisfaction', she was pleased and proud to accept. Sadly, the next workday found her incapacitated for what she imagined to be 'normal reasons' (though in fact the menstrual stream failed to flow), and because of a painful hand. Mr Mash gave her time off until after Easter, and she went home.

The diary is strangely silent on Dr Monckton's reaction to her so flagrant flouting of his advice (he had recommended country air, but hardly in the quantities she was getting it), noting merely his diagnosis of 'thekilitis (!)' in relation to her hand, and calmness in face of 'certain phenomena'. Nature, Stella gathered, 'occasionally does take people at their word when they go on the land, being unaccustomed to the same, and they become temporarily Farmer's Boys within as well as without'.

She found *This is the End* on sale in the shops – but not every shop had a copy: 'it is selling rather well and has to be ordered'. Sir Frederick Macmillan (who had a very kindly feeling for Stella and her work) had predicted that it would do better than *I Pose*, but unfortunately the sales figures do not survive.

While it was still in the writing, Aunt Florie had been asked to look over the manuscript: Stella had wanted to know whether, in publishing it, she would be exposing too much of herself. Her aunt had advised her to go ahead, but one sees why Stella hesitated, for *This is the End* lifts the veil, part way at least, from her 'secret' fantasy life. With characteristically Stellarian bravado, it opens with the surprising assertion that the world of fantasy is an altogether more consistent and reliable place than the 'real' world:

There is no reason in tangible things, and no system in the ordinary ways of the world. . . . I should not be really surprised if the policeman across the way grew wings, or if the deep sea rose and washed out the chaos of the land. . . . But if the things which I know in spite of my education were false . . . if the faery adventures that happen in my heart fell flat, if the good friends my eyes have never seen failed me -- then indeed I should know emptiness and an astonishment that would kill.

It is wartime. Jay (very much a self-portrait) has run away from home and taken a job as a bus conductress; only her beloved brother knows where she is, and he is sworn not to tell. From time to time she sends letters home. They are cheats. They describe not her real whereabouts in East London, but her imaginary home, a 'House by the Sea', with in it a Secret Friend (male), and a host of happy children. Taking these clues for genuine, her family (which includes another preposterous female windbag) sets out to look for her; with them goes middle-aged, married Mr Russell, who, unawares, has in fact already met Jay in her role as bus conductress and been attracted to her, as she to him. (It scarcely needs saying that Mr Russell has a lot in common with Edwin Konstam.) In the dim and distant past before he degenerated into an Older and Wiser, Mr Russell was himself a denizen of the world of fantasy, and so it is through his agency that the family locates the spot (near Tintagel), where by rights the House by the Sea should be. It has been demolished! From the moment that Jay learns this, her Secret World starts to crumble. In the end – tragic and vastly inferior substitute for what she has lost – she accepts marriage with a pleasant, prosaic young man, long her suitor.

Though almost certainly Stella did not intend it, a chill atmosphere of menace pervades her House by the Sea. It derives from the fact that whenever Jay escapes there it is as a mere ghost – an onlooker, never a participant. Thus the entire phantasmagoria has been sucked out of her, as it were, and in its hallucinatory vividness seems to menace her very existence as a 'real' person in the 'real' world. Take the following passage about Jay, which gives a startling insight into Stella's imaginative life:

I can't tell you what countless miles away the 'bus-conductor was by now. A certain fraction of her, to be sure, was sitting in the dark room at Number Eighteen Mabel Place, Brown Borough, with fierce hands pinching the table-cloth, and a hot forehead on the table. All day long the thirst for a secret journey had been in her throat. All day long the elaborate tangle of London had made difficult her way, but she had kicked aside the snare now, and her free feet were on the step of the House by the Sea.

No voices met her at the door, the hall was empty. The fire-light pencilled in gold the edges of the wooden figure that presided over the stairs. I think I told you about that figure. I never knew whose it was – a saint's I think, but her virtuous expression was marred by her broken nose, and the finger with which she had once pointed to Heaven was also broken. Her figure was rather stiff, and so were her draperies, which fell in straight folds to her blocklike feet. Her right hand was raised high, and her left was held alertly away from her side and had unseparated fingers. She had seen a great procession of generations pass her pedestal, but she never saw Jay. Of course not, for Jay was not there. Only a column of thin watching air haunted the House.

Mr Konstam, 'slightly prosy but cherubic as ever', was 'nice' about the book, and Aunts Mary and V were eager to discuss it, obviously hoping for a nice explanatory 'burble' about Secret Friends. But Stella allowed herself to be only very slightly drawn – and, besides, she could not be 'as didactic about my dear thought people as Older and Wiser people are. I cannot bother about "lessons to be learned".' Evidently a puzzled older generation was searching avidly, in its Victorian way, for a useful moral message.

Considering its content, such reviews as it attracted were surprisingly favourable; perhaps the vogue for Barrie made critics more indulgent of waywardness and whimsy than they would otherwise have been: 'With her sympathy, her realism, her wit and ability, it would seem that Miss Benson's possibilities are limitless,' opined the *Bookman*. 'It is the second step in a very brilliant beginning. . . . You will be foolish if you miss this book,' avouched *Punch*. The *Times Literary Supplement*, while expressing a fear that 'her sentences are so uniformly clever that the reader will tire of her cleverness', found 'imaginative tenderness' in the novel, 'and when she is describing coast scenery she makes us see it with her own seeing eyes'.

Down on the farm snow blizzards persisted, improbably tumbling out of blue skies. But Stella was equipped to face them now: her new kit had arrived – wide-brimmed rustic felt hat, rustic smock, rustic gaiters and boots, with in between a pair of breeches which, far from being rustic, were 'Mesopotamia model (officers'), and err on the over-chic side' (a couple of lively sketches give an idea of what she looked like in them). Thus stoutly attired, she spent an entire day clearing fields of hard substances, mostly old traps, that threatened to damage the blades of cutters at harvest time. During the night she was feverish, and when – after four days off work – reluctantly she sent for a doctor, he diagnosed bronchial asthma and (preposterously in her view) 'burbled, as doctors will, about giving up work'. He even insisted on calling again: 'Is this why doctors are called leeches?' she asked. The setback was to cost her a total of ten days' work (of the 112 days that she might have worked while in the employ of Farmer Mash, she missed 48 through ill health).

While she was idle, thought people invaded her mind with unusual power and frequency. It was 'a happy double life' they brought her, but sometimes she wondered 'what will happen to my brain if the activity of Secret Friends goes on increasing at its recent speed, at the expense more or less of real friends. I would be awfully happy at this moment – in an unholy way – in a convent . . . but I would probably be mad within six months.' When she went back to work the thought people accompanied her: 'I had Secret Friends all day, mostly singing, which I always like. There are days when that House is full of singing, hour after hour.'

That was on 23 April, St George's Day, and she had been weeding a ploughed field, 'heartbreaking work, but lovely weather, an intermittent sun among silver clouds'. As April dissolved into warm May, despite the war her thoughts about life and death – especially about death – were vernally hopeful:

> I feel absolutely perfectly happy in my dinner hour in this sort of weather, just lying on my back against that bank with white violets near my head, looking over the almost goldenly green larch wood at the great view of the 'coloured counties'. . . . When I feel like this, I think 'Why are we so troubled?' . . . It shall be spring again, and we shall be young again. After all, we condemn Death unheard.

She was planting potatoes – 'I did feel I was doing National Work at last' – staggering along at speed with a heavy pailful, a team of horses pressing at her heels to cover in the furrow. Or uprooting some very queer weeds:

> Chooks, in fact. Some chooks are so long that I think they must go right through to New Zealand, especially as they are green at the nether tip; I suppose they are New Zealandish chooks at the other end. The whole field seems to quake as some of them come up, and then they often snap when one has got no more than two or three hundred yards out, which makes me think there may be somebody weeding simultaneously in New Zealand, occasionally hitting on the same chook as me, and pulling the other way.

She was sorry to leave orchards in bloom, woods full of bluebells, skies humming with aerobatic planes, to be in London for her mother's appendix operation.

While in town Stella went down to Hoxton and 'fawned upon' a Jewish dealer in order to get Mrs Oneleg some low-grade paper at seven times the peacetime price. It could have been the occasion described in one of her journalistic pieces when, after she had struggled back to Hoxton Square with the paper, 'three or four glorious reams of it flopping like jelly on a borrowed coster-barrow', Mrs Oneleg and the 'barrer chaps' could see in it nothing better than a joke, wittily sticking their fingers through the precious substance to demonstrate its inferior quality. But Rosie, aged seven, had upped and rebuked the circle for its levity: ' 'Ere, 'ere, ma, less of it. 'Pears to me it ain't no blasted joke. We got ter live on this giddy rubbish, an' bread gawn up another farden to-diy'[1] (in rendering dialect, Stella generally plays fortissimo). She went to see Ibsen's *Ghosts*: 'I do not like a play to be advertised BANNED FOR 7 YEARS. If I had seen this I wouldn't have gone.' The theme of inherited syphilis horrified her, and moved her to irreverent anger: 'I did not know that God had such appallingly filthy retorts to give to man's unspeakable impertinence.'

Back at work she was hoeing vegetables, and having her hair cut short in the modern, emancipated style by 'a rather darling young widow', a fellow resident at the Hare and Hounds, who thought the experiment 'fascinating fun'. 'I must say it looks quite successful but not so much under a hat of any sort, and ghastly under a tidy hat.' (The milliners' answer to this dilemma came in the cloche and bandeau styles associated with the 1920s.) Then in early June an attack of pleurisy, exceptionally severe and painful, struck her down, and she was off work for over a month. Fortunately, as temporary neighbours she had a Mrs Peggy Boulenger and a Captain Austen Allen, who initially had swum into her orbit as admirers of *This is the End*, and then decided to rent a nearby cottage; for the second half of her illness she went to them to be 'poulticed and otherwise fussed with'.

Peggy Boulenger had a husband at the front and a young child somewhere in the country. Captain Allen was a bachelor and had a position at the war office. For adults of opposite sexes, not related, to be sharing a house was hardly, as Stella put it 'convenable', even in the relatively relaxed atmosphere of wartime; and for this reason, when a third member of the party had cancelled at the last moment, the gentleman had considered backing out, or so he said. However, Stella seems to have seen nothing in their *ménage* to cause her to raise an eyebrow. Indeed, as time passed it was obvious that she herself, and not his cottage companion, was the focus of the Captain's attention. A big, gentle, childlike man of about thirty, he could enter with enthusiasm into the rumbustious romps that, at twenty-five, she still enjoyed. Between them they laid out 'a tiddleywink golf course' all over the house, and 'two specially loved tiddleys – his Willie, and my Bernard – jumped upstairs and down and into fireplaces, and on beds, into various laboriously difficult holes. I won.' She climbed a cherry tree and pelted him with the fruit, 'me being a Zeppelin and he an "Archie gun"'. Intermittent pillow fights took place all one evening, culminating in 'an explosion after baths, when practically all the furniture (including a teatray and the doorkeys) took the air'. It sounds more than a trifle bizarre, and one observes that Peggy Boulenger took no part in the fun and games.

For a while Stella fancied herself a little in love with Austen Allen – and he, she sensed, would gladly have given their relationship a different turn. Aunt Phyllis, when she came down for the afternoon, was quick to perceive this, making Stella 'tremble within by burbling of the heating conclusions at which she had arrived. . . . I wish I was a real girl and had experience, instead of pretending all the time to be young, and feeling so unsure, like a bad pupil at a dancing class with the corner of her eye fixed upon what everybody else is doing.' Peggy Boulenger later talked over the whole affair with Stella – what Allen had said about her, and how she (Peggy) had told him that Stella was 'not that kind':

> It is most odd, because the silly thing was – for the moment – I was that kind, and for some days felt most exalted and romantic. How is it that nothing of this ever leaks out in my manner? Why is it that I am always taken for a sort of boy–woman? What is it that real girls do to convey that they are prepared to be that kind?

Up in London for a few nights, she saw Dr Monckton again, when 'his seeking hands touched up Julia like anything' ('Julia' and 'Bill' were her wry pet-names for pleurisy and bronchitis). In Hoxton she found Mrs Oneleg 'weeping and raving in bottomless despair', partly for lack of paper, partly as an effect of a recent daylight raid – bombs had fallen in Hoxton Square itself, with dead and injured laid out at her door. On the spot Stella decided that she must get her and Rosie away to the country. It was a charitable thought, and on first arrival Mrs Oneleg seemed happy enough – pleased with the 'scenery' ('a word that makes me sick'), but three weeks of rural tranquillity were as much as she could stand, and she went back to the danger zone with relief, marvelling that country people 'isn't sick of being so safe'. Rosie stayed on, to be joined during August by a stream of ill-assorted East End women and children. The fact that Rosie's head was alive with vermin (in these troubled times Mrs Oneleg had been letting things go) was only one of the complications of Stella's scheme of philanthropy, and before the end she was 'brain-lapsed' with the worry of it. Johnnie Granville came on holiday from the convent orphanage. If Stella ever regretted deciding to adopt him she never admits it in her diary, though there are hints that 'my son John' was more an anxiety than a joy. He was not happy at the convent – it was not that anyone was unkind to him, he said, simply that he was always hungry. 'I think he is a little boy for private life rather than a school,' Stella confided, and began searching about in the Cookham Dean area for someone who would take him as a boarder. (A further complication was that the attention she gave Johnnie made Mrs Oneleg jealous.)

At work – picking beans and carting dung – she was learning about working-class village society, discovering that it was sharply divided into respectables and unrespectables – and that the latter were generally the more attractive and quick-witted. Unrespectable Carrie, who talked smut and had borne another man's child while her husband was away at the war, was a lamentable case certainly, yet after all 'dirt isn't half so dirty in beautiful surroundings. Carrie, who is determined to go further in the path she chose, is quite bearable and quite lovable even, on Winter Hill in the sun.' What bothered Stella in relation to Carrie was her influence over the as-yet-respectable Polly, a pretty seventeen-year-old of good intentions but 'no balance'. Stella badly wanted to put to her 'the other side – without confusing it with the Church, or the district visitors', but probably never did expound to Polly her arguments for chastity on enlightened modern principles, sensing as she did that to the girl she was only 'an interesting foreigner', someone infinitely remote.

The first week of August was cold, wet, depressing. Two more female volunteers – 'we are known as Young Women, as contrasted with the others who are just Women' – had joined Stella on the farm, and it was the three of them who, in classic revolutionary style, incited the rest to rebel for higher wages. (Their pay was fifteen shillings for a full six-day week; as some indication of value, Stella was paying precisely twice that sum for board and lodging.) As spokeswoman for the group, she bearded Mash in his bath-chair; his expression changed 'terrifyingly' as she put her request, and he proceeded to give the capitalist's time-honoured reply: he paid them what they were worth, and would not pay a penny more. Next day he took a regrettably mean revenge (for in many ways he was a decent man). Sitting with his strongbox open on his knee, he made her wait half an hour in the pouring rain for her wages. As far as she was concerned, enough was enough. She never went back. Sadly, history does not record whether, without her to inspire them, the rest of the women went ahead with their threatened strike for eighteen shillings a week.

Chapter Nine

In September 1917 London was thinly sprinkled with United States military. For all her crossness at America's attitude to the European war, Stella had to admit that it was 'somehow comfy' to see them. They were showing the same exuberant interest in English girls as they did in the Second World War, and Stella, part Cholmondeley though she was, was not above larking with a group of them – officers, but 'oddly plebeian looking' – who were 'chucking' tickets at her from atop a rival bus as they passed and repassed in the Strand. She had gone to live as paying guest, for 'forty shillings a week *tout compris*' – in Peggy Boulenger's flat at 190a Sloane Street above her dressmaker's showroom, which in its turn was over a teashop of Messrs Fuller. Sociable, easygoing Peggy was leading a somewhat harumscarum wartime existence; to add to its unconventionality, Austen Allen resided in the same building and took his meals with her. No mention is made of a servant; unless they went out to a restaurant, Peggy prepared dinner and washed up, with some help from Stella, who was no great cook. On one occasion, when admittedly she was not feeling well, she records that she 'buckled to and did dinner, rising no higher than two hardboiled eggs each, cold tongue, hot cheesestraws and coffee', adding with some pride, 'I was not muddley but on the contrary washed up to the last eggspoon.'

Rather to her relief, Stella found that Austen Allen did not improve on further acquaintance. She thought him self-centred and curmudgeonly, and did not at all like his views on women: 'he looks on them either as physical necessities or as sort of boys like me. . . . He is the only young man with brains that I know who has those ideas.' It was odd that, about women, he was so very 'Victorian', since (like the rest of Peggy's set) in most of his ideas he was consciously 'modern' and 'progressive'. Stella had to be careful not to introduce in Leonard Place many of the notions that were taken for granted in Sloane Street: 'Mother hasn't the remotest idea of the sort of views they take, and I am sure she would be grieved if she knew of what she would call "free thinking and free love ideas".' (Mrs Benson was firmly wedded to traditional values, perfectly content to dismiss the aims of socialism, for instance, in a single woolly-minded phrase: '*I* have no hankering to be a duchess.') But in Sloane Street Stella found herself discussing with real freedom 'the rightness and wrongness of things one had always been taught are certainly wrong' – prostitution, for instance, on its various levels:

I have long suspected that there are people set aside for the Gaby Deslys life[1] in a greater or lesser degree, just as there are people set apart to play with words, or lines, or notes of sound. Nevertheless, tho' I am fairly calm about the gay thorough successful prostitute, I still cannot feel the same about Johnnie's mother who died in a hell of beastliness, and her daughter and all the other women of Jerusalem Passage who will die the same. I suppose the lowest rung of a trade is always unworthy, yet I believe there is bitterness and disillusionment even on the higher rungs of this special trade, and although I concur in an annoyance with 'Rescue Work' as run on C.O.S. lines, I should wish that every girl who goes on the street should go deliberately after being shown the other things she might do, so that she can know really if she has no other vocation.

She was taken to Fabian Society lectures, where the audiences struck her as 'dry, cynical and dusty', and Bernard Shaw awed her with his 'monstrous cleverness' and the 'peculiarly bearable flavour of his insolence':

He talks with a sneer on his face and a charming Irishism in his voice. His theories were destructive, but afterwards unexpectedly fine and so spiritual and hopeful. He laughs at the man in the street, and yet loves him. At any rate the future seemed imaginable to him, which is more than it has been to me lately.

On a less earnest note, they went to see the latest Barrie play, *Dear Brutus*. 'Fat slow tears of slightly oversweet sentiment' crawled down on to their chocolate rations as they yielded to its specious charm. Almost against her will, Stella warmed to Barrie's world-beyond-our-ken whimsy – she was even inclined to think she was 'a rudimentary Barrie' herself. And the Boulengers were able to provide her with a long-desired thrill: in time of peace, Peggy's husband was Director of Reptiles at the London Zoo, and when he appeared on leave he took her behind the scenes at the reptile house. She passed with flying colours what must surely be the acid test of the animal lover, letting a boa constrictor wind itself about her body – 'an extraordinary iron feeling' – and lick her with its tongue – 'he could bite but hardly ever did'.

David must have his daily walk, so she could take on only part-time work. Peggy offered her a temporary job as 'showroom hand', but 'I am the last

person in the world I ever thought would go into the dressmaking and
millinery trade.' Instead, she went back to Shoreditch and was told to carry
on with her War Pensions visiting in the afternoons. It was rather pleasant:
'Each new soldier I track down to his lair I think to be the nicest man of his
kind I have ever met. Surely war never taught the hooligan manners, how
have these loud raucous youths been transformed? Perhaps hospitals have a
taming effect. Yet they are not ladylike to me, just nice and welcoming and
not shy.' And she gave some evenings to helping Aunt Phyllis at a West
London girls' club: 'I seem to have been given by mistake a certain facility
with young Shepherd's Bushy sort of girls.' A young American, Brooks
Henderson, a reader for Macmillan New York – he had read and approved
This is the End – presented himself. He was full of the eager-eyed
enthusiasm of the educated American abroad, and she 'at once begged the
job' of showing him London. She liked him and he amused her, 'such a very
nice gentle U.S.A. accent, and a U.S.A. way of completing every grammati-
cally perfect sentence even to the last stop, and of joining two sentences
together always with "furthermore".' His wire – 'Goodbye Jay' – coming
out of the blue on 25 October was saddening, for it meant that he had joined
up in the British army: 'So that's that.'

Stella was writing a good deal, managing to place the occasional article
with the *Pall Mall*, and on 26 October made 'I think a final start on a new
book'. Like *This is the End* it was set in the London of wartime, and was to be
called *Living Alone*.

Stella had come back to London in time to experience a mini-blitz, the only
concerted series of aeroplane attacks on the capital in the war, which –
though it pales in comparison with what Londoners underwent in Hitler's
war – was at the time felt as deadly menacing. There were five raids in eight
nights, and by the end some three hundred thousand people were flocking to
the Underground tunnels to sleep, and thousands more were fleeing London
to seek accommodation in the home counties or, failing that, sleeping in the
fields.

The occupants of 190a Sloane Street had been warned by police to shelter
in the basement of the nearby Hyde Park Hotel in the event of a raid, but
when it came to it they preferred their own basement. During the first raid,
on 24 September, Stella did not even take the trouble to go down. Instead
she:

> looked out of the Showroom window for a bit and saw shells bursting.
> Then the scene of action changed to the S. W. side, and I put one eye
> round the front door and saw more shells, but could see no enemy, though
> I heard an aeroplane very loud. The streets absolutely deserted, one
> soldier passed supporting a drooping young lady, the noble buses passed

empty but for the Casabianca-like conductors cheering on the roofs. . . . Then all seemed over and the basement contingent began to come up, when suddenly the Hyde Park gun began firing, the noise shook the house, and the shells went over us, incredibly slow-moving, with astonishing howls. Captain Allen came and told me the different kinds of shells, and how the slightly defective ones howled louder than the others. It was a row. There is silence now, but the All-Clear motor-bikes have not come by.

Five nights later, Stella and Peggy and 'Captain Allen' (Stella never refers to him on paper in any other way) were seated in the stalls at an operetta when rapidly approaching crashes and loud firing signalled the return of the Gothas, the dreaded German bombers. A soprano, caught in mid-solo, brought her aria to a graceful close. Only one member of the audience moved: a woman left one of the boxes, while her men, torn between the rival claims of gallantry and face, sat tight and let her go. At the end of the performance the cast rewarded the audience for their coolness with a round of applause. The raid was still in progress when, back at 190a, Stella sat down to discuss the operetta in her diary:

As for the show I thought it a good – (Another Take Cover warning has just gone by, am going to cellar). Nothing except very distant guns. As I was saying, I thought it a good show except that it seemed like comedy occasionally too heavily laden with moral suggestions and earnestness. . . . Still distant guns, but I can't keep out of bed any more.

Stella noticed that people tended to speak of Gothas as if they were canaries, with an entirely inappropriate suggestion of innocence. She read in the newspaper that fifteen had been destroyed 'in their nests', and a bus conductor told her that he would give twenty pounds to know where their various 'cages' were – 'I rather dally with the thought of a Gotha loud in song hopping from perch to perch.'

On 2 October she visited a Hoxton reeling from the effects of what was in fact the last of the so-called 'raids of the harvest moon'. Sal volatile and a sleeping draught were needed to quell the 'horrors' that she had afterwards. She had seen looting, very rough crowds, and queues of a length she had never seen before waiting to be let into the town hall, police station and public baths for the night, in search of safe cover: 'People staggering about vaguely with the newborn or the very aged in their arms looking for safety, a tremendous rush of people trying to get away by bus, tram and train.'

The autumn of 1917 brought terrible news: revolution in Russia with the possibility of a cessation of activity on the Eastern Front, the collapse of the

Italians at Caporetto, and, closest and most vivid, the mindless carnage of the Third Battle of Ypres – Passchendaele. Combined with her own petty, private stresses – an increasing dread of raids, the tensions of flat-sharing – they reduced Stella to a very low state indeed. Sometimes she fell on her bed too weary and depressed to undress, and then 'awful war horrors' would pounce, and she would wake next morning sick, shaken, unrested. The fact that her principal Secret Friend, Conrad by name, was a Russian, and that Russia was therefore her 'secret country', had the effect of bringing that nation's sufferings morbidly close:

> I had a violent brain lapse without any warning [she wrote on 8 November] and lay on my bed in the dark, and began going mad about the dreadful world and poor Russia in her agony, and I was actually visited by my Secret Friend for the first time in my life, generally I am nothing when I am with Secret Friends, but to-day I swear he came and sat on my bed in the dark and put his hand on my arm and I got the hope that the agony of the world and of Russia is not so bad individually, and that all over the world there are people exulting, as I do in my saner moments, that they have been born in these terrific times . . . and I am lucky to have a Secret Friend like that and yet not be really very mad with it.

Apart from all this, she had constant reminders of her sexual immaturity, administered quite unconsciously by the people she was mixing with. Allen was involved with a girl, but it was Peggy he chose to confide in, Peggy whom he whisked off on a mysterious errand one afternoon: 'one of the workgirls said (I was telephoning in the same room) "he's gone to get his engagement ring".' *She* had not been told. Then George and Olive walked about in a private aura of sexuality; after their marriage, when she went to stay with them in Camberley (George now had a good job as instructor at Sandhurst), she felt aloof, every inch the maiden sister.

Stella spent Christmas alone with her mother, and they got on together so unexpectedly well that she feared they were becoming like strangers. She was busy with *Living Alone*, and in addition she was getting together a collection of poems. Most of them had already been printed, either in periodicals or between-chapters in her two novels, and it was her hope that Macmillan would reissue them in the form of a slim volume. They did, and *Twenty* (which was the number of poems) came out to kindly notices in June 1918; it was to be Stella's one and only volume of verse.

As befits the young woman who wrote it, it is passionately defiant, bodiless, intense. In high-flying, allusive imagery, Stella sings of the 'ecstasy of loneliness', of how contemptible it is to travel on safe roads, of the preciousness of her secret, inner world, of one special 'secret day', alone in north Cornwall:

. . . I have built To-day, more precious than a dream;
And I have painted peace upon the sky above;
And I have made immense and misty seas, that seem
More kind to me than life, more fair to me than love –
More beautiful than love.

And I have built a house – a house upon the brink
Of high and twisted cliffs; the sea's low singing fills it;
And there my Secret Friend abides, and there I think
I'll hide my heart away before to-morrow kills it –
A cold to-morrow kills it.

Interestingly, the pattern of repetition in the first stanza is almost identical to that of her poem of 1905, when she was thirteen. A few of the poems deal with war. The sardonic 'True Promises' purports to speak in the voice of the fallen in battle, and is addressed to all those who bade the men march away:

You promised War and Thunder and Romance.
You promised true, but we were very blind
And very young, and in our ignorance
We never called to mind
That truth is seldom kind.

You promised friends and songs and festivals.
You promised true. Our friends, who still are young,
Assemble for their feasting in those halls
Where speaks no human tongue.
And thus our songs are sung.

Stella was ill at New Year and again in February, when she went to see Monckton. He spoke of 'much increased' lung disability, and told her to come back again after a week's rest – by which time she was laid up with severe pleurisy which was to last with little intermission for two months. Putting a good face on things in a letter to Laura, she wrote, 'he says I am practically inoculated now against being very ill with Julia. Anybody unaccustomed to same, with as much pleurisy as I have, would have a temp. of 104° and three nurses.[2] But even if the disease was likely to be restricted in its future impact, it was there to stay. Dr Monckton suspected that it was 'trying to become chronic', and recommended her going at once to South Africa. On 25 March even she was thinking in terms of nursing homes, always with her a last resort.

All the more astonishing then is her next move. On 7 April 1918, while staying at Cookham Dean, she sat down and wrote out 'a number of little papers offering my services as Outdoor and Indoor help at 6d an hour', and proceeded to distribute them among the larger houses round about. For all its cock-eyed air, her action was in the spirit of the time. At this stage of the war, with most male servants in the armed forces and many of the women in munitions, members of the middle class unfortunate enough to be encumbered with large properties were crying out for help. In particular, gardeners were in demand, not simply to tend the flowers but to assist with the great national effort to raise vegetables, which had caused the Archbishop of Canterbury to issue a pastoral letter sanctioning Sunday labour, and persuaded bishops to grant to zealous clergy permission to hold services in the allotments. Setting a fine lead, King George himself had attacked the grounds of Buckingham Palace with a spade, and directed that vegetables be planted in the flowerbeds surrounding the Victoria Monument, right opposite his own front door. Committees of lawn tennis clubs were even authorising the sacrifice of their courts.

Stella's advertisements met with a good response. Among others she heard from the vicar, and from an old lady who, with a 'straw hat dissolved by rain, wisps of grey hair, dirty hands and a violent cold', was trying to do her own gardening. People took it for granted that she could tackle the heavy work, in spite of her fragile look. The vicar, on her first day out, asked her to sharpen his scythe and then cut his grass. With the fatal blend of enthusiasm, pride and recklessness which made Stella accident-prone, she set to with a will and, missing the whetstone, slid the blade along her hand, 'cutting same to bone . . . instantly soaked two hankies and wrung them out, and soaked them again and could not stem the flood'. The vicar, 'though grieved', told her to try his mechanical mower, but the grass proved impossibly long. Finally he set her to rolling his lawn (which happened to run uphill), and this she did for three hours, coping as best she could with her bleeding hand by staunching the flow with one handkerchief while the other was spread out on a bush to dry in the rain. When at last, mackintosh 'carmine down one side', she stole away, she left the handle of the vicar's roller 'soaked with gore'. There is no record of his ever employing her again. That evening she could not bear so much as to think of the cut: it reminded her too vividly of other, altogether graver wounds of battle, 'terrible wounds that don't get so easily comforted'.

One allows for a degree of exaggeration in Stella's more dramatic accounts, but clearly the cut was serious, since for a fortnight – during which she was in London – she was unable to write her diary, making it up later from notes. By that time she was back at work – trenching potatoes, planting onions, digging marrow beds, and getting furiously tired, 'but I will be daily now'. In one place where a professional gardener was kept, she hoped in her innocence to have his help in clearing an orchard; but he 'wasn't going to dig no new ground for the likes of her'. So she did the job herself, getting stung by nettles from top to toe. Weeding a rose bank in the pouring rain left her with a badly scratched hand, and soaked 'to trickling point'. Next morning her chest felt 'very Julia-ish', and her hand offended her so much that she wondered if she should follow Christ's precept and cut it off. Her patriotic effort coincided with the severest food shortage of the war in Britain, and with the imposition of rationing. (The government's clamp-down on the manufacture of dog biscuits made her wonder momentarily whether she should have David – who was with her in Cookham Dean – put down.) Her landlady was not finding it easy to feed her adequately. 'One gets devilish hungry digging,' she had to admit, 'and I get very little at midday and only an egg for breakfast.' Keeping clean was a problem too, as her lodgings did not boast a bath; desperate, she approached the owner of one of the larger houses for permission to 'sneak in' and use her bathroom; 'great bones' were made, and at last a grudging consent given for her to come in once a week at such time as the 'companion' did not want the use of it.

Throughout the spring of 1918 the news from France was extremely grave. In a desperate last throw, the Germans were making spectacular advances, regaining with heavy losses territory already drenched in three years' blood. 'It is a constant fight to keep it at the back of one's mind,' Stella wrote on 22 March, when news came of the launching of the German offensive; and on 29 May – by which time the Germans were within fifty miles of Paris – she noted with grave concern: 'For the first time one begins to ask oneself not only when it will end, but how it will end.'

The application, which she had put forward in May, for a passport to go to America on the grounds that the Californian climate would benefit her lungs (she had had the idea somewhere at the back of her mind since 1914) began, in this time of national crisis, to look selfish, opportunistic: 'Is it beastly of me to want to go? There must be many who feel equally that they cannot bear England and this weariness any more, and yet they must. Does my health really justify my flight? Am I a secret hypochondriac?' Nevertheless, when her application foundered, she had no scruples in turning to her Uncle Bob for aid, as her mother had done with such good results in 1915. At the Foreign Office Uncle Bob worked another instant miracle; a passport materialised, and she booked her passage on the first available ship.

Having made her will, interviewed a self-congratulatory Sir Frederick Macmillan – 'I think he thinks he created me instead of God's doing so' – and astonished her stockbroker with the news that she was in fact the identical Stella Benson, the up-and-coming author – 'he puffed and blew' – she still had the more difficult goodbyes to face. From Mrs Oneleg, who had begged to be allowed to accompany her to California and set up another paper-bag business there for their mutual support, she had 'a harrowing farewell'. With a fine natural sense of drama, at the last moment Mrs Oneleg would not so much as turn round and wave. Saddest of all was the parting from her 'crumpled and pitiful' mother: 'She is alone now. . . . she has been so used to looking after me whenever I called her, her hands feel empty now.'

From the Hotel St George, Liverpool, she sent a last letter to Laura:

Dearest little Lowera [this was 'Laura' in dog-language, to be pronounced gruffly],

I just write to send a final goodbye and love before starting although I have nothing to say because I am stunned with so many difficult goodbyes. It will not be like being apart, everything I see I shall be pretending you are there and imagining what you would think of it, because I am so used to you being there and us talking together about everything that happens. I will write whenever I can, and you must write to me at every possible and impossible moment. You have been most good to me, it has gone far beyond the scope of any spoken gratitude from me, I always feel as if the people who haven't known friends up to your high standard don't know what friendship is. A thousand loves, my dear.

Your loving
Stella.[3]

Not even the best of friends, not even Laura, could ask more than that. She had already said goodbye to David, who was to be left in Laura's care, 'and now it is goodbye to my diary, the most comforting friend of all'. Tomorrow she would be starting a fresh volume.

Part IV

Voyager

Chapter Ten

Stella sailed from Liverpool on 10 July 1918 on the Cunarder *Orduna*, her Aunt Margaret and Uncle Tom Cholmondeley coming up from Wrexham to wave her off. Her quarters were rather lavish: 'a nobil room with a real bed and a wardrobe, none of your bunks and cubby holes', her Uncle Regie having dispensed £25 towards the purchase of a first-class ticket at £31 14s 0d. The wardrobe was, in fact, a luxury rather than a necessity, since all her clothes fitted into 'Humphrey', her solitary suitcase.

At this stage of the war the U-boat menace in the North Atlantic was much reduced, but sailing as they were alone, not in convoy, they were in real danger; and the sighting of a torpedoed ship, 'three forlorn masts, one broken, and on the crosstrees seagulls sitting', was a reminder to keep a lifebelt to hand at all times on the first days out. Life on board was very different from what Stella had known on the happy, hedonistic ships of pre-war days. Most of the passengers were Canadian or American service-men on various war missions, and their chief diversion seemed to be drinking. With some difficulty she drummed up a bridge four: 'I think "cut hair" must mean intense youth in America, for everybody was very fatherly to me and did not take my bridge aspirations seriously.' However, once started, bridge continued, and there was the extra diversion of a couple of concerts hastily thrown together by first and second class. Stella, who had been airing her views at the captain's table, was called upon to give an impromptu address on the woman question; instead, she recited some verses by Hilaire Belloc. On the tenth and final morning she got up at 5.30, hoping to see the approach to New York harbour, 'feeling, I admit, sick with excitement and fright at such an unknown day before me'. But it was too misty to see much, and when at last the fabled skyline appeared it was a trifle disappointing, 'stupendous, but not quite so overwhelming as I thought'.

'I never wish to pass a more wretched thirty hours than this last,' Stella wrote on the evening of 20 July, her first day in New York. She had been rushed by an officious fellow passenger through customs and into a taxi, with no chance to establish connections as she had meant; Macmillan had had no warning of her coming and had readdressed all her mail; last straw, the lift boy in her Washington Square hotel, true to type, had got 'so angry' on her omitting to tip him that ignominiously she had produced a belated quarter and then, overcome by loneliness, confusion and the great heat, had melted into tears in her bedroom. She awoke next morning from dreams of 'death and despair, so to speak, feeling incredibly far away from Mother'

A friendly woman at Macmillan, Rebecca Lowrie, came to her rescue. She whisked her out of the hotel and into the Women's University Club, 'cool and white and windy . . . and kind untippable ladies to look after you'. (After a few days, though physically she still found it excellent, 'mentally the presence of so many highly educated, highly specialised young women without imagination lies heavily on my soul. When first I came I thought I would send my daughter – if I had one – to Vassar, now I think I would rather see her a slacker.')

In Greenwich Village – 'the Chelsea of New York' – her new-found friend introduced her over lunch to 'a bewildering company of artistic young women', and on various roof gardens gave her iced eats and drinks; looking over the edge at the shivering skysigns, Stella felt as if she had 'fallen off my own world by mistake'. Rebecca escorted her to Sunday worship (not what Stella would have done if on her own) and then on to lunch in her 'dear little way up flat'. By Monday she had her on her feet again, fit and ready to make an assault on journalistic New York: she was resolved to earn with her pen at least some of the train fare to California. Despite an initial blow from 'a serious young man with blue eyes and a highly discouraging manner' at Curtis Brown the literary agents, who told her that Americans were just 'nut interested' in anything she had to offer (memories of wartime Britain), on this and other days she plodded to the offices of the *New Republic*, *Bookman*, *Vanity Fair*, *Good Housekeeping*, *McCalls* and other periodicals, getting if not precisely the polite brush-off, certainly no very positive encouragement. A different sort of girl would have capitalised on an introduction to an elderly Judge Cohen, who knew editors and was disposed to help. What if there *was* 'something wrong' in his manner with women? What if he had 'pudgy' hands, and sat 'too close' in taxis? A girl less squeamish than Stella might have thought his rather gross proximity a small price to pay for a 'luscious' dinner at the Lafayette, followed by a first-class seat at the theatre – and when he suggested a weekend at his 'little nook at New Canaan' to meet a leading editor would have leapt at the chance, instead of, as Stella did, wriggling out of it.

An invitation that she did accept, and which in its way was delightful, was from friends of Brooks Henderson at their home in upstate New York. She was impressed, even awed, by the lavish luxury of the place:

There could not be anything more perfect than a really carefully done American house like this, if anything perhaps it is all a little too expensive and faultless, but it would make an adequate alternative for heaven anyway. There are great beautiful rooms full of books with perhaps just one perfect whisper of a Japanese print on the wide walls. There are huge verandahs looking down into far valleys, and the most restful rocking chairs and hammocks in the world. There is a bathroom to every bedroom, and all sorts of little details like new toothbrushes and hair-brushes (ivory) etc. that most English houses don't provide.

But she was not quite at ease with such perfection. There seemed something 'unnatural' about it – as there did about the children's play area in the garden with its 'little teeny houses to sit in, and sandpits, and slides, and gymnastically inviting ropes':

I feel that if we had had these things all our lives we should have perversely refused to play with them as time wore on, we should have built something of our own, or played chessmen in the common hayloft, but every one of these perfections here is in daily use by Renée and Pierrôt [her hosts' children]. They don't seem to play imaginative games much, though she is a clever and perhaps imaginative child. She will develop into a Vassar young lady, I am afraid, she is a great and interesting talker and extremely selfconfident. I felt rather humble and inadequate, as I shall have to get used to feeling in this country.

She had fallen among highly cultured Americans. Her host read her his new verse-drama, a five-acter on a Greek mythological theme (which she enjoyed, 'especially the lyrics, I seem to have a cheap mind that looks upon the lyric as the line of least resistance'), one of his friends seized the opportunity of their dropping in to play a symphony in five movements for organ that he was composing, another showed them an open-air theatre under construction in his garden: 'Everyone seems to have a lot of money to be artistic with here,' Stella opined, slightly out of her depth. However at West Point, the crack military academy, she felt a resurgence of British self-confidence: while the cadets looked smart enough *en masse*, taken individually a lot of them were 'cropheaded and spectacled, and too fat and short . . . rather plebeian, like waiters, very far from possessing that grace and beauty that I have always noticed among English boys of the Eton and Regular Army class'.

Her base remained New York (a note in the money accounts that she kept at the end of her diaries, 'skyscraper – 55', indicates that for just over half a dollar she made the statutory elevator ascent of the Woolworth Building, still at that date the highest in the world); but contact once made with family friends, and she was off and away on a wave of hospitality. At Cotuit on Cape Cod she joined some of the Lowell clan, vacationing in a well-organised little colony of three cottages in a pine wood next the sea. 'I am having a very good time,' she wrote, the blend of outdoor exercise, culture and good conversation being exactly to her taste. Alongside boyish, humorous Mrs Lowell – 'such a darling, a socialist and a rebel in spite of being a Lowell' – she decorated chairbacks with tasteful designs in paint; with Mariana, fourteen, she went sailing for the first time in her life, and loved it; she swam, but the joys and humiliations of that were familiar – 'I love the look of the water from inside, and the happiness of swimming, but I always feel an ache of coldness round my heart when I am in, and a great giddiness and dazzled head when I come out. . . . I am a beastly and unhardy soul.' There was music-making – 'a lot of men and women, old and young, with I thought a pleasing naïveté and unselfconsciousness came to sing Bach chorales' – and Stella improved their repertoire with all the English rounds and partsongs that she could remember. Her singing voice was small, but clear and sweet, 'the perfect choirboy's voice', Susan Ertz, the American writer, once said, 'one would never think it was a woman singing'.[1] She had no objection to performing solo, but 'I most tremendously enjoy singing in parts, it gives me real ecstasy, so that I have almost a pain in my heart.' She had a hidden source of happiness as well: her fantasy world had crossed the ocean with her, and 'every crack in the day is filled with ecstatic Secret Friends'.

The free and easy yet thoroughly responsible way in which the Lowells were bringing up their family struck her as admirable:

> if ever I have a child I shall bring it to America until it is twelve, and then never let it revisit this country until it is thirty. I can't bear the adolescent American youth and youthess, but I love them before they begin to adolesce, and it is splendid to see such unspotted happiness. To keep children healthy and happy here is treated as a parent's only business, and the Lowells, noisy and friendly and brilliantly clever, and yet bursting with unstrained good manners, are a noble example of the results.

She went on to the Emersons, 'muddley, gentle, orthodox people' in comparison, and with noisy, bouncy children. At a smart beach used by well-dressed New Yorkers, she battled with great breakers and a powerful undertow, feeling 'rather coy' because her bathing dress was of the English kind, the only scanty one among the voluminous skirts and harem trousers which the cautious Americans wore. There was a blue sky and a faint sun, and they built a fire and toasted bacon and marshmallows, walking back in and out the waves to where the motor was; 'and we drove through the misty pinewoods to Riverhead, and there we alighted and went into a gay place, loud with soldiers and their young ladies, and had ice cream sodas, and then re-embarked again upon the dark road'. A perfect New England afternoon.

New York by contrast brought her up sharply against mainstream America. Nineteen-eighteen was a touchy time for a Britisher to be in the United States. Stella had found it hard, on first arrival, to sympathise with people basking in the '1914 phase of war, the romance and the chivalry of death and danger, the "glad to be alive" phase'; later she was furious with a nation a large part of it cock-a-hoop at its success in seemingly sorting out without too much trouble the mess that the tired old Europeans had got themselves in. Unbeknown to her hosts, Stella was ignoring American war reports, and 'going by despatches from London, diluted with those from Berlin'. At a movie of a crassly jingoistic kind – it showed a Hollywood King of the Belgians 'patting the head of the entire American army', and thanking them for being 'champions of the world' – she fumed inwardly, cooling her indignation with condescension of a lofty older-and-wiser kind: 'after all they are a nation of schoolchildren . . . poor lambs, coming fresh and cocky into somebody else's war, after the somebody else had used up most war enthusiasms and established a firm hell of their own, how could they be expected to understand? Just children, and children given work to do beyond their desserts.' But the rather intelligent New Yorkers with whom she was currently 'batting' around (their phrase), took a broader view. She was enjoying herself among them; and then it was time to depart, to stay with a Mrs Bertha Pope – another of Brooks's friends – at Cornish, a noted literary and artistic colony in New Hampshire.

Bertha Pope, at first meeting, struck her as a 'rather vivid, overflowing person' – fair comment, one feels, on a woman who, in the early hours of the morning and while driving a newly arrived and frozen guest up and down dark hills after an eight-hour train journey, could expatiate to the company at large on the 'styles and points of contact of various modern American poets.' Next day afforded a closer inspection of the lady: 'extraordinarily full of vitality, rather lovely to look at, with a deep voice and a slow accent which I suppose is western, and really witty and lucky in finding opportunities for the apt word'. While picking Lima beans they swapped philosophies, 'and she was downing the hairshirt theory as excluding the joy of life. . . . so many people are asked to wear grandma's shirt cut down, and then they naturally at the first opportunity peeled it off and cavorted naked'. It took Stella a day or two to get into the knack of life in the Pope *ménage*, where guests were expected to do all their own work and cook their own meals as the spirit moved them.

A bonus was the proximity of the Winston Churchills,[2] he a novelist of repute, 'interesting, interested, and kind'; at their house Stella met – and was not unimpressed by – a phenomenon strange to her, an apostle of the new age: 'a psycho-specialist, who apparently goes about the world study-ing people who don't fit, and not exactly trying to make them fit, because he thinks they are spiritually worth more than the people who do fit, often, but trying to find a standard in their dreams and their inadequacy' (Stella must have wondered where she belonged in this scheme of things). As a sort of pocket exemplar of what he could do, he carried about with him a disciple, 'a vulgar looking little, shortsighted, almost totally deaf Jew, with absolutely calm, happy eyes. . . . This man had been a businessman and successful, and had suddenly, in middle age, awoken to the fact that he was getting nothing joyful or splendid out of life at all, and he had abandoned his means of livelihood, and simply wandered off to find joy and truth' – and had found, or been guided to, the practitioner. Rather to Stella's surprise, although Bertha found him *sympathique*, neither of the Winston Churchills seemed much impressed by this saviour figure.

An air of mystery surrounded Bertha. To begin with, where was her husband? He seemed to be a forbidden topic, except behind her back. Stella was led to the tantalising edge of the mystery when a fellow guest let fall that it was 'worse than if he were dead.' 'I did not like to enquire further,' Stella added piously, 'I can see for myself Mrs Pope's state of mind, the reason for it is not of so much interest as the state of mind itself.' Indeed, Bertha's moods of profound depression, when she had recourse to the whiskey bottle, were only too apparent.

But indubitably the lady had the power to attract: 'She is always something new. . . . whatever she is, she is that wholeheartedly and sincerely, and yet with a sort of witty knowledge of herself.' Stella was pleased when (the other guests having left) Bertha suddenly upped from a sickbed and proposed a walking tour. It consisted of shortish spurts on foot to beauty spots and other ports of call, between lengthy train rides. As a finale, and as if to make up for the unenergeticness of the previous days, Bertha had so arranged it that at 5.30 on the following morning a train was to be picked up at a point eighteen miles away. There was nothing for it but to tramp through the night. Allowing precious little margin for error, they set off at 11.30 p.m. wrapped up Mexican-poncho-style in blankets borrowed from an empty house at which they had made an unauthorised stopover visit, and looking, Stella said, like two ambulant bolsters. 'We're safe anywhere,' said Bertha, reckoning that the ponchos would do away with any risk of sexual molestation.

At 4 a.m., having lost their way and been redirected by a postmaster awakened for the purpose, they still had six miles – six 'New England miles' – to cover in less than two hours. It was at this point that they ran up against backwoods unhelpfulness of a peculiarly infuriating kind:

When we had gone three miles by the signposts a man passed grandly in a buggy and said we had five miles yet, but we kept on, gasping. When we had only fifteen minutes before the train we met a milk cart, and offered the man a dollar to turn round and take us. He pondered for an exasperating minute and then refused. Then we met a man in an empty car, and we waved and shouted appealingly . . . he slowed up a little, laughed, and went on. At one mile from the station we heard the puffing of the train and saw smoke in the valley and gave up. We then walked slowly and realised how awful we felt. When we had walked slowly to within 100 yards of the station, we saw that the train had backed in again. We made one last absolutely torturing effort, and got on to the platform in time to see the train disappear round the bend. It was an extraordinarily complete disappointment, no suspense or additional annoyance was wanting.

We sat on the railway track in the very cold dawn and held our hearts in our bosoms, for they were like to leap out, and the man whose buggy we had passed came round and said that he had told his friends 'If them women had been anyone I noo I would sure go back and give them a lift when I've done with you, for they won't get their train lacking it.' Apparently women whom one does not know cannot be worth a helping hand.

'It was altogether a stupid thing to do from the standpoint of health,' Stella admitted, 'but still I am glad to have proved once more . . . that a person with one lung is not so very much worse than a person with two.'

At the inn where they rested while awaiting the next train, Stella could not sleep. The 'hot bath' they were offered was cold, and her garments were soaked in sweat, but worse — acutely disturbing, unbearable — was the proximity of free-and-easy Bertha in a double bed: 'Mrs Pope hugged me that we might get warm, and this, the closest physical contact I have ever known, made me feel sick, because I am deficient somehow and hate physical touch. . . . I rose up after an hour because I hated the bed.'

Back at Cornish an 'unsoothing' mail awaited her — two returned manuscripts, and two invitations from a poetess unknown to her, a Mrs Fiske Warren, who claimed to be an admirer of her work. They were couched in remarkable terms: 'She says there is something psychic between her and me, and she is quite certain she can cure me of all ills. . . . She had from the time she first read my book an overpowering feeling about me, and wants just five minutes' talk with me on the subject, no more.' To many it would have been an eminently resistible invitation, but Stella was young, inquisitive and flattered, and resolved to go. A snag was the location of the poetess, at Camp Devens, Massachusetts, some thirty miles out of Boston, in the heart of the Spanish influenza epidemic. Having entered the United States by way of the eastern seaboard, the disease was raging through New England, and at Camp Devens people were dying at the rate of ten a day. However, not to be put off, Stella reasoned away the risk on the dubious grounds that 'I am not so liable to catch it or die of it as strong people, who break like oaks where I should only bend'; in any case, she hazarded, there was no point in taking care of herself too assiduously, 'nothing can take from me a future full of adventure, whatever happens'. So, 'sodden in Listerine', off she went, the first sight to meet her eyes on arrival at the station being a platform stacked with coffins from Camp Devens, with the Stars and Stripes, 'for which, poor dears, they did not succeed in dying', perfunctorily nailed on each lid. Driven through Harvard, she saw houses ominously branded with the fateful word 'Influenza', and her Listerine use 'degenerated into practically an orgy'.

For Stella the weekend turned out to be intensely flattering, though at the same time, and typically, she was able to appreciate how comic it was. The poetess, 'a very lovely small person with a sweet English voice', had gathered together several admirers of her work, and 'the motto of the house seemed to be that as a group our talk might be general and lightsome, but that each got a tête-à-tête with me'. On being led away into the woods by her hostess, she found herself half mesmerised by her twitterings:

> She told me how long ago she and I had been on a journey together, and had deliberately chosen and surmounted great dangers from the sea of space and eternity, and had triumphed over that sea and come to a safe place . . . and that I ought to treat myself as a shell, a poor rather trivial shell, which had in it eternally the sound of that sea that she and I had once overcome. . . . she would, if I asked her, share everything she had with me, so as to keep my old vulnerable shell from harm, so that the sea sound might be heard by people who wanted to hear it. I got lost in a sort of dream. . . .

Coming down to earth in New York, she lunched and tea-ed with playwright Ridgely Torrence,[3] 'rather an adorable young man, so bodiless somehow', and at successive Liberty Bond nights touched a high and then a low in American culture. At the theatre, the leading actor, Norman Trevor (who happened to be English) collected ten thousand patriotic dollars in the interval 'by force of mere unaffected gentlemanliness'; at the movies, from an audience largely, according to Stella, 'intertwined and listening only between loud smacking Jewish kisses', two celebrities from Hollywood managed to rake in only a few paltry shekels after performing embarrassing monkey tricks for over an hour. The miasma of Stella's anti-semitic feeling (which is undoubted) drifts luridly over the scene:

William Fox, a very greasy Jew, there with his family, girls of about thirty dressed like twelve in short white costumes and oily ringlets over the left shoulder, threw all dignity to the winds, begged and begged, had doors locked, offered to – and did – kiss Farnum and dance with him on the stage [Fox was a millionaire film producer and theatre owner, William Farnum one of his star actors] . . . but all the audience went on kissing each other, and only a few hundred dollars came out of it.

It was only when the fund-raising was over that the show could begin – 'a film of such astonishing futility that I began to wonder whether it was allegorical or whether it was somehow so deep and clever that I was missing it being a foreigner, but no, all the Jews pealed with laughter, but there was no enlightenment for us.'

Next stop Radnor, just outside Philadelphia, where she had an invitation to stay in the congenial, ladylike surroundings of Miss Mott (an old friend of her mother's) and her sister. Here she found good servants, warmth and quiet, and on leaving was moved to say, 'I have been too comfortable here, too much at home.' But whether the staid society of her hostesses began to pall or – as she claimed – her conscience pricked her, after a few days, despite their protests, she betook herself to nearby Bryn Mawr, where flu was rife, to offer her services at the emergency hospital. To risk her own life was one thing; to expose her hostesses to infection quite another, and one sympathises with the annoyance they expressed. Stella reported for duty, and was sat upon a porch to type out lists, mostly of the dead, who even in so small a place averaged six a day, the majority, she noted, young males – 'providence seems terribly set on thinning out the ranks of the men of this generation'. Mysteriously, she never went again, and one can only assume that the timely illness of Miss Mott's elderly sister was the reason.

She was still in Pennsylvania when America celebrated the ending of the war – twice over. On 7 November the news came, erroneously, via the United Press Agency, that an armistice had been signed and hostilities had ceased. The nation took to the streets in a frenzy of jubilation, and Stella, determined not to miss the glorious moment – 'I was wanting to hear the loud joyful noises and the Mott household was too damned peaceful' – cadged a lift to the big city:

all the skyscrapers were showering down little scraps of paper so that one stood in a very gay looking paper snowstorm all the time and the streets were solid with paper to walk on. A lot of soldiers and sailors, and two English sailors, had climbed on the Statue of Liberty at the head of Broad Street and they proposed and conducted cheers and songs through megaphones. They had cheers for all the allies one by one, but forgot England for some time, till the Englishmen caught their eye. Then a band

came and played the 'Star-Spangled Banner' and the 'Marseillaise' and I
think it tried to play 'God Save the King' but people sang 'My Country
'Tis of Thee'. I was much squidged the crowd being packed solid, and
became more and more squidged when an Italian next to me refused to
take his hat off to the 'Star-Spangled Banner' and many men took his hat
off and stamped on it, but he retrieved it and put it on again, giving as an
excuse that the tune was 'not *officiale*'. Upon which I found myself tossed
up in a whirl of fighting and he was absolutely hurled through the crowd
by several men and shaken and his hat torn to shreds. . . . I thought
finally the yells of the crowd were rather sickening, and I longed to be
home to hear a London crowd sing, it sings much deeper than a Yankee
crowd, and much better, and probably would not sing such things as 'Over
There' all the time.

For the authentic rejoicings, which came four days later, Stella contented
herself with staying in Philadelphia, where once again her feelings were
very much frayed by what she saw as the ignorant parochialism of the
American spirit:

I did try to be charitable, but it is almost impossible to feel loving towards
a public – which has suffered and sacrificed practically nothing – [and
which chooses] to celebrate the end of a World suffering by putting on
false noses and parading the streets with banners announcing such things
as 'It took the Yanks to do it'. 'We had to show 'em the way' (!!!!!!!!).
There were no English flags to be bought anywhere, and practically none
displayed. The 'Star-Spangled Banner' was played and everybody stood
at attention, the 'Marseillaise' was played and everybody walked away,
interrupting it with 'Over There' sung with loud squealings. I shall never
forget it, and never will I regain my original feeling of pleasure in hearing
American spoken. Here is a people which is vulgar and vigorous enough
to inherit the earth, of course they will do it, they took care to keep
themselves unhurt in a world disaster, until it became obvious that
everybody was exhausted enough to make intervention pretty safe – No I
know that isn't fair. As you were. What is wrong with them is a complete
lack of courtesy, and chivalry, and idealistic international spirit. They are
a nation full of vanity and commercialism, and therefore, as I say, they
will inherit an earth which is getting farther and farther from the
remembrance of things unseen. . . . I got much worked up on these
matters, and anyway peace after four years is too much for anyone's
nerves. I just feel numb in the head.

On 18 November, with 'a slight, stunned feeling of adventure' inside her,
Stella set off west, detraining at Chicago, where she had an invitation to

meet Harriet Monroe at the downtown offices of *Poetry*, the monthly magazine of verse of which she was editor. Launched in 1912 in the improbable surroundings of a frontier town better known for industry and meat-packing operations than for culture, under her wise direction *Poetry* had gone from strength to strength, promoting such important talents as T. S. Eliot, Carl Sandberg, Edgar Lee Masters, Vachel Lindsay, Wallace Stevens. To Stella's surprise, Miss Monroe (herself a poet) turned out to be 'a very cultured, terse, unpoetic lady, like a prosperous governess' – to judge from photographs, an apt description. However, at lunch was Vachel Lindsay, and he was everything and more that a vagabond poet should be who 'tramps America with no money in his pocket, paying for food and lodging by singing his own songs, a career that would need practically no gift but cheek and unselfconsciousness, and these he has. He danced like a goat in the street on the way out to lunch, and sang "Oh the war is over, the flu is over. Oh I am so happy!"' Stella was much taken with this shambling, beetle-browed phenomenon: 'There was something very sweet and clean about him, in spite of his vulgarity and egoism. When we got back to the office he chanted some of his poems, or songs. He intones them on two notes, his head rolls, only the whites of his eyes show and the noise is deafening, especially as he forces his audience to chant crooning refrains.'

Whether or not the ebullient bard was responsible, a violent, throbbing headache that had been lurking in the back of Stella's head all day suddenly pounced, and she became 'almost collapsible'. Helen Hoyt, co-editor of the magazine and herself a poet, took her back to her 'little grimy flat – you wouldn't expect poetry of her, but you would expect great unselfishness and goodness and that you get' – showed her a bed and let her sleep for three hours. In her autobiography, Harriet Monroe gives a small sidelight on Stella's visit. She figures as a 'pale little English girl . . . charmingly keen and clever in talk . . . weary and half-starved', who was succoured by the staff of *Poetry*, and who then pushed on west 'in spite of our fervent protests'. Stella's diary overlooks the fervent protests, but records her gratitude for being driven to the station.

Two more uncomfortable nights in the train, with in between a day of midwestern corn, and then, 'I got up early and met the prairie for the first time, with a sunrise east of it and the Rocky Mountains like a dream, very far away to the west.' There, waiting to greet her on the platform at Denver, were the Goulds, she a retired cook of family friends, he a former chauffeur. With them was Mrs Gould's brother, a fellow rancher and a spare-time Salvationist, known always as 'the Brigadier'. Over the high tableland in the Brigadier's small Ford they plunged, 'a hilarious and embarrassed party', and fetched up at the homestead – two three-roomed houses, one for each married pair, with a 'sleeping porch' for Stella at the Goulds'. She was to stay a full month, and towards the end write 'I am glad I came. I have enjoyed myself. But I am not myself at all. . . . I have come to feel in the wrong almost, and always a little strained about the manners.'

At the outset she had wondered if she would be able to endure her hostess for long, 'she is such an earnest Christian. She asked me about once an hour to open my heart and take in the Lord Jesus, especially when she saw me smoking.' However, Mrs Gould was tolerant according to her lights, and said that she would not judge Stella, 'which means that I may go out and smoke in the snow'. For heavy snow and intense cold had greeted Stella's arrival. Outdoors she took to wearing sweater and breeches (her old agricultural Mesopotamians), indoors 'we sit about the stove in our shirt-sleeves'. With the drop in temperature came her first sick spell on that side of the Atlantic, and wrapped in Mrs Gould's fur coat, gazing across blinding whiteness at the Rockies, she sat in bed on her 'snowy little porch' for two days, getting on with *Living Alone*.

In nearby Golden she saw what people went west to see, 'gents cantering up and down its streets with big stiff leather trousers fastened down the outside with many buckles, and wide hats, on little horses with huge saddles'. Colorado was very much horse country still, despite motor-cars. Stella, who before had only ridden side-saddle on a leading rein, let Mr Gould put her on 'a man's saddle'. On her first ride – singing loudly – she advanced to a canter: 'It was like one of those nice dreams one has, wherein one finds that one can do easily a thing one had always looked upon as far above one's head.' All the neighbours she met had British names. An 'Americo-Cornishman' came in to kill the pig; the Golden blacksmith, who was from Sussex, drove over to get 'the last news from England' (a nice thing about him, Stella thought, was the way his eyes filled with tears when he spoke of the primroses in the hedges under the Downs).

On 19 December she was off, on a train full of soldiers on their way home from France. 'There is hope for the world when youth continues idealistic,' she comforted herself, listening to their views on the peace settlement with Germany: they were not vengeful. She herself backed President Woodrow Wilson up to the hilt, and was furious at his government's refusal to join the League of Nations.

From the observation car she watched the astonishing scenery go by, and at Pueblo a telegram neatly intercepted her: it was from Bertha (who supposedly was going to welcome her to California) announcing that she was still in the east, laid up with flu, and would not be there for Christmas; Stella would have to shift for herself.

Next morning she awoke to find herself in the Rockies, and at midday – at Oroville – the train burst out into the California of her imaginings, 'orange trees all dark, glossy green, only the most distant snows on the high peaks which receded to the west, and buildings in the cool, heavy Spanish mission style under great trees'. The train was delayed, and it was late evening when they arrived at Oakland. The station was deserted; 'I thought I should spend the rest of my life there, sitting in silence and loneliness on my typewriter'. But Laura had furnished her with a list of YWCAs, so she telephoned the local branch and was recommended to a 'respectable' hotel.

'I am so very happy to be in a big city again,' she wrote after a day's exploring, 'and especially a sea city, so that I can hear even now as I write, big voices of ships mooing in the harbour like great, bereaved cows.' She had gone to Berkeley, got the key from a neighbour, and spent hours roaming round Bertha's 'poor, lonely' house and garden: 'It was amazingly haunted, I thought. It has obviously been so much loved . . . yet on top of this background is the tragedy that I do not know, the dreadful Thing that happened to her and drove her out and away to places she hated. . . .' Romantic mystery apart, High Acres was a remarkable house, 'a darling queer crooked house, imitation Tudor with big panelled rooms and a carved staircase and big fireplaces', and it stood in 'a little young garden' with wonderful views in all directions – of the bald hills (which reminded Stella of the Sussex Downs), and of San Francisco and the Golden Gate, as yet unbridged.

Without delay, Stella took California to her heart. She liked Berkeley, 'just a great garden it is, foaming with flowers, banked round the nice, unobtrusive university building. . . . I am so happy to be here. The West is being kind to me, everyone is pleasant, and there is nothing frightening or strange as there was in the little details of New York. People here just laugh when they see you do not know the ropes.' And she was charmed by San Francisco; the ferry seemed 'enough to make a poet of every fat, vulgar businessman who uses it night and morning, seagulls cry about your head'.

On Christmas Day she was there, attending Grace Cathedral, not as a worshipper, of course, but rather because to be in church gave her a feeling of solidarity with family and friends at home. Afterwards for her Christmas dinner, she went and sat on the beach alone, reading, and nibbling apples and chocolate. In one sense she was desperately lonely; but there again she was not alone, being:

> beset to the verge of lunacy by ecstatic Secret Friends, and all to-day I hardly knew what I did until the evening when I wrote a bit and finished the book. I am a lucky woman, how do other lonely people manage who are not so befriended? . . . Both God and men may forsake me, but I – even I, only half alive, possessing only half a body and half a heart – even I am never alone.

A few days later she moved from her hotel into High Acres, 'rather happy to be here, muddling about with very rudimentary cooking in this beautiful lonely house with its incredible view. I had an evening of teeny little

adventures. All housework is that way to me.' At midnight on New Year's
Eve she was awakened by the sound of guns and hooters: it was 1919. Not a
very hopeful year, she feared: 'There seems to me no rest or peace or real
recuperation ahead. . . . As a war to end wars it is beginning to look like a
failure, although I suppose even discussion of eternal peace means the first
stirrings of an awakening.'

Chapter Eleven

On 7 January, at 1.30 a.m., Bertha Pope arrived, and promptly set about raising the emotional temperature to something approximating the level at which she herself was most comfortable. Ever since leaving High Acres, she declared, she had 'lived on dreams' of the place, and regardless of the hour began a frantic tour of inspection. Later in the day Stella was despatched to Oakland to fetch liquor (Berkeley being dry), and as news of Bertha's coming spread, the house rapidly assumed its characteristic atmosphere of high jinks and high times. The so-called Roaring Twenties had broken out prematurely in the San Francisco Bay area, at least in Bertha's set, and Stella quickly saw that she would have to lay aside her hairshirt for the duration of her stay; 'it doesn't go somehow in this nice, vague, happy California'.

Of Bertha's friends first on the scene was Peter Case, a humble adorer ten years her junior. Gentle, polite, tubercular, Peter was only too glad to devote his frenetic energies to their service; with happy heart he set to, flinging open doors before them, mending water conduits, mailboxes and stoves, 'leaving a track of improvement wherever he moved'. He was to prove invaluable in the many domestic crises that lay ahead: when the stove smoked and they woke to find the kitchen caked in soot, when the rains came and left the basement inches deep in water, the dining room a lake, and the hall 'a matter for waders or a diving bell', when someone left a bath tap running and the sitting-room ceiling turned an ominous yellow, Peter was there with shovel, bucket or mop as need demanded, gallantly playing the 'Little Mother's Help', calming Bertha's mercurial nerves, and supporting everyone with cocktails.

'Tully' Williamson looked in – improbably, a schoolmaster – 'really funny and almost too buoyant' for Stella, his *début* occasioning the consumption of 'too many cocktails and California sauternes and crème de menthes really to leave me satisfied with myself'. It was Tully who, on a trip to Napa County, pretended to the other guests at a hotel where they dined that they were a circus troupe (Stella in her breeches being 'Mesopotamian

Mildred the Contortionist'), and persuaded them all to do turns, she whistling and singing 'Little Billee'. Back from ambulance driving in Italy, medals on chest and nerves in tatters, Hugh Reid came to board. Peter moved in shortly afterwards, so 'what with our two young men and us all drinking and smoking' their maid-of-a-day mistook High Acres for an 'undesirable house' and fled, her bed unslept in (propriety was restored shortly after with the arrival of two female boarders and a whingeing thirteen-year-old boy). Then there was Austen Lewis, ex-Yorkshireman and San Francisco 'liberal' lawyer, who was intelligent company, but to Stella's distress seemed constitutionally incapable of keeping his hands off a woman, 'I really think it is a madness with him.' Accustomed as he was to 'hyper-real' women, Stella's elusive, *noli me tangere* demeanour tantalised Lewis, and as a result dining out with him was a dicey business, 'until I got on to the only tack that he and I can follow, me doing a deliberately unkissable and cynical pose just so far as to keep him amused, and him protesting humorously in different keys'. The memorable crunch came one evening when they were guests of some friends of his. Stella described what took place in a letter to Laura, adding (as she felt constrained to do in many of her bulletins from California), 'don't burble of these matters to Mother':

> It began to rain, and as I take an hour and a half to get back by car, boat, train, car, and ¾ mile walk to Berkeley, the Bs asked me to stay the night. We had all drunk some, but A was very drunk indeed, and would not go away, although the sofa he was sitting on was to have been my bed. . . . So the Bs made me up a mattress on two chairs in the dining room and I began to go to bed when A began clamouring for me on the stairs to say goodnight. (I may add that the cause of his original offence was my dislike of being touched – and more than touched – all the time by such as he. I asked him to desist.) So I went and said goodnight, rather frightened of him, but Mr B pulled him off. . . . [I then] lay awake listening to A trying the door at intervals and poor B arguing with him.[1]

'I am all unnatural in this *galère*, I respect its gaiety and spontaneity, but I can't seem to share them.' 'I don't know what I am doing with these people. I am terrified of them, and they think I am either overcultured or overprim because I speak but little. God knows I do not feel superior, in most ways. . . . I can't hear them well, I can't understand them. . . . I have lived alone too much for my own health, and can never get back to this sort of being happy.' Moments of near panic assailed her during her first few weeks, before she made her partial adjustment to 'San Francisco bohemian-ism'; Bertha, whose boasted motto was 'everything in excess', was an alarming companion even for brief periods – sharing a house with her was 'like living on a volcano'.

There was a welcome respite in early February when a kind, cultured, well-to-do couple, the Goodriches, took her to see the Monterey peninsula, but later in the month she was suffering severe headaches, the worst 'brain lapses' since before the war, and was *'accablée'* with depression. She even thought of moving on – and then remembered that she had lent all her money to Bertha. Austen Lewis, who doubled the role of lover of ladies with that of 'magnetic father confessor', took her out one evening and drew her troubles from her: 'We went to a movie, and had several cocktails, and an oyster supper, and it shows how broken down I am that I let him cling to me the same as ever, and even got a grain of comfort from the kindly touch.' Lewis pointed out that, for all her attractiveness to persons of both sexes, Bertha was 'a monopoliser and a sucker', who had drained Peter dry and would do the same to Stella if she let her. 'I went home feeling much braver.'

Bertha's tempestuous personality was a popular subject for analysis in her circle, on the fashionable Freudian lines. Stella saw the key as 'great sensuality – she is so mad with that sort of hunger that I think sometimes she is not herself. She only really lights up when she is talking of something bodily'; and she added, as if she had caught Bertha reading a dirty book, 'she sits and reads Donne's poems to herself'. The mystery surrounding Bertha had been revealed: it was simply and prosaically that she was a wronged wife. Her husband – of all things a professor of ethics, and 'a deliberate poser as one who loathed sex matters' – after twelve years of marriage had been detected in an affair with one of his students, with whom he was now living. Divorce was in the air, although he was still sending Bertha money and signing his letters 'ever-devoted'. He was hinting too that he 'knew things' about Bertha that might jeopardise her case. Stella opined that were Bertha to remarry she would 'recover from her inordinate selfishness and moodiness, and all the traits that make her difficult to live with'. In general, Stella was the last person to attribute to the sex urge the universal significance with which many at that time credited it, but clearly Bertha Pope was a special case.

Early in March she went so far as to enquire at Thomas Cook's about ways and means of getting back to England. But at present she would have to embark at New York – 'a thing I had vowed not to do as the trains are so beastly,' she told Laura.[2] The alternative was to find a job; she was placing occasional articles, and her investment income was being remitted from home, but if she was to stay abroad for an indefinite period and extend her travels, she would have to set about earning some money. Having replied to an advertisement for a domestic help (and taken an instant dislike to the voice that answered the phone), and applied (unsuccessfully) for a post as governess, she was delighted when her employment agency, with 'mysterious nods, becks, and wreathed smiles, and advice to ask as much money as I liked', despatched her to one of San Francisco's swankiest hotels with a sealed note for the headwaiter. The job turned out (she told Laura) to be that of 'companion' to an Italian woman, a Contessa Mirafiori, so-called, 'the most improper looking lady you ever saw', who interviewed her in her bedroom while getting dressed 'with several gents around, one Englishman whom she introduced as her husband'.[3] She was in fact a stage singer, and wanted Stella to come every night to dress her for performances, support her to the theatre, carry her flowers and wraps, look pleasant, dress modestly, and put her to bed, 'thus missing the last boat home, as far as I could judge – she said I would be free by 1.0 a.m.' Without uttering a word, Stella found herself engaged, and was told to ring in half an hour and name her price: 'I nipped away, wildly excited, falling off a tram in sheer absence of mind, and plucked Peter from his office and lunched with him in order to consult same. He was extremely doubtful about the whole thing . . .'; however, seeing that her mind was made up, he advised her to ask fifteen dollars a day. But when Stella telephoned, the lady had changed her mind: after all, Stella was not 'quite the companion she had in mind, which I could have told her from the first'. On the rebound, so to speak, Stella went immediately to the downtown office of the *San Francisco Chronicle* and accepted a job as bill collector in their advertising department. She was to start in two days' time.

Accordingly on 13 March she awoke early, feeling 'rather strange':

as did Peter also, (who – as ever the Little Sister of the Poor – made me some hot coffee before we started). We thought to get breakfast on the boat, but there was a queue waiting with the same intention, and no chance. I started on my job, the Chronicle office people gave me a big business building, the Phelan Building, as my district. . . . Mine was not bad work, the advertisers were all either lawyers or doctors, etc., willing to pay, some of them kind and amusing, some dreadful, facetious or ill-tempered bounders. The obviously unrespectable offices were rather a surprise to me, some of the lawyers were very dissipated looking and their stenographers unmistakably 'that sort of girl', gross and painted and insolent. I thought of poor Mrs Lawyer at home, probably well aware of what was happening. . . . Presently I began to feel very ill and faint and feverish, and unaccountably giddy, so that I began to count the doors to the doctor clients, so that if I had to faint it might be in accustomed and professional arms, so to speak. But I did not have to . . .

After handing in a hundred dollars, at considerable physical cost, and getting two dollars in return, Stella decided to resign. 'I could hardly stand up, I was so giddy and sick, and my head felt wandering.' On the way home she felt so unwell that she had to ask the attendant in the ferry building to let her lie down; a kind, motherly soul, the woman took one look at her, drew a rapid conclusion and said 'she knew I had been sick because I had had my hair cut off, but "never mind it will grow again"'.

She earned a few dollars by giving French lessons to some of Bertha's boarders, and in April secured a part-time post at the university – 'Great luck, considering I have had no education,' she told Laura.[4] She was to help students with their written English. Standards of entry to Berkeley were at that time not high. The more gently raised and academic sons and daughters of the Golden State were usually sent east to complete their education: 'This is the wild and woolly-minded west,' wrote Stella, 'and practically all these students are aiming at an out-of-door manual-labouring life.' Whereas her Chinese and Japanese students were quite easy to teach – 'their lack of grammar does not necessarily denote lack of intelligence' – her native Americans were different, 'so obstinate and established in such incredible mistakes, and they argue down to the last ditch'.

But frequently she had to cancel classes. She was not feeling well, and a consultation with California's 'best ear specialist' brought the depressing news that if she did not at once have a series of sinus operations she would soon be totally deaf, 'and probably waste away and die . . . the bad parts are infected and spreading and poisoning my lungs'. A fortnight passed, in which both health and spirits sank. On 9 April, 'I lay awake in the night and decided I would get back to my old hairshirt and Living Alone stunt, and ask for no friendship and give none, and just stand by myself until this cloud on my mind lifts.' There were the familiar symptoms of lung disease. Bertha did her best, but as Stella explained to Laura, she was 'not a specially good nurse, she is too casual, she disappears to fetch you a glass of lemonade, and when next heard of, some six hours later, has been to a matinée in San Fran.'[5] She did, however, fetch a doctor to Stella, who diagnosing bronchitis, asthma and acute pleurisy all three, sent her to hospital: 'Never tell Mother that I ever saw the inside of a California hospital,' Laura was charged.

On her first day in hospital, she would have us believe, she spent hours in a state of happy nostalgia, 'reading a bus ticket, Richmond to Charing Cross, which God by means of a miracle put upon this alien floor [it had dropped out of a pocket when she was undressing]. . . . all day I pretended to be in the bus, and remembered allsorts [sic] of little details about the places on it; Kensington Church, Sloane St., Palace Gate.' At night from the window of the ward, she looked across at San Francisco 'shining round the darkly luminous water', and wondered why she was not happier 'in this heaven'. After a week she was discharged, with a strong recommendation to come back for surgery – but 'I am a coward, I dare not think of it, with no Mother to comfort me.'

Meanwhile, social life had taken on a new and peculiar sparkle with the addition to the Pope circle of poet and playwright Witter Bynner,[6] who was putting in a brief stint at Berkeley as instructor in poetry. Handsome, witty, urbane and, though not blatantly so, homosexual, at thirty-eight Bynner – 'Hal' to his friends – was a universal charmer. Bertha was quick to succumb. On a first meeting Stella considered that her friend 'rather too obviously bowed to him, but of course that is the shortest cut to being attractive, for a woman'. He asked Stella to read and discuss her poetry with his class. Despite her 'terror' she must have done herself credit, for at the end several 'very ecstatic youths' made a pleasing fuss of her – 'it is easy to rise to the ecstasy of twenty-one' – and later, in the 'beautiful rich rooms' in a leading hotel, where the affluent Bynner was staying, a 'strange delirious lad' knelt at her feet and 'burbled rapturously about me to myself, which was interesting' (she was 'full of a frightened brilliancy', he told her).

'Nothing could be very flat with Witter Bynner present,' Stella subscribed in humble admiration after a day's outing in his company. Six of them – Witter, Hugh Reid, herself and Bertha, and a couple of visiting Bolsheviks – had piled into a rickety four-seater Chevvy, some on the floor. Unfortunately, one of the Bolsheviks – 'he was more the London type of humourless haggard earnest Socialist' – proved rather too serious for the day's festivity: 'it was interesting at first to hear about Russia, but somehow palled, as Hugh was driving at reckless speed, and the canyon was so beautiful'. They had a 'wild' lunch and all got 'a little merry. . . . Mr Bynner and Mr Tucker [one of the Bolsheviks] were both champion drink-mixers.' On the way home it rained, so they raised the hood, 'flung caution to the winds, and all clasped each other in the most loving manner . . . especially Mr Bynner, who had very comprehensive arms'.

'I seem to be a changed woman in this country,' she told Laura, 'the very air is irresponsible, and the sun undiluted makes you drunk.'[7] Stella was perceptibly uncurling her tight fronds. Simply to be mixing with people whose manners were as remote from those of South Kensington as in a civilised country they well could be was a therapy for her: 'There are no conventions here. You can walk in breeches through San Francisco without comment.' 'Rough diamondism is the western American pose. Mother and the aunts could meet easterners without surprise, but they would think the rest "not quite".' She got used to her friends' habit of frequent, casual imbibing; she joined in, and it helped her relax. Though she felt that her drinking was naughty, 'unhairshirty', it did not frighten her. She was quite sure that she would not go the way her father had gone: 'I shall never die a drunkard, because I forget between drinks how nice they are'; and, with the coming of prohibition, though she kept a hoard of alcohol in her room she never even dreamed of touching it unless she had a party.

Nevertheless, there were 'wild times', and invariably they were well moistened with liquor. For example, 3 May was 'a day of unprecedented batting', bacchic from start to finish. It began with a Martini each for herself and Bertha, for they were nervous about a luncheon party they were bidden to, in 'such a beautiful house above the bay, with a garden like an English cottage in the sun':

We started with Mexican cocktails and had an exceedingly songful lunch, Witter Bynner always leads in song . . . and I sang Londony songs, all this between mouthfuls. . . . Towards 4.30, we were all so soaked in cocktails and music that everyone's appointments began to dissolve like *les neiges d'antan*, so we caught Witter Bynner on the rebound from a duty undone and telephoned Peter to come and fetch us in a taxi, which he did. So Bertha, Witter, Peter and I taxied very brightly out to Cliff House Beach, where we found a little deserted dancing hall and we had one or two further 'old-fashioned cocktails', and turned the pianola on and danced.

I telephoned to the Pearces, at whose house I was due to arrive at 6, and told them I wouldn't come till 9, and Mrs Pearce was a little cold, and when she heard I was at Cliff House (which has a rapid reputation) advised me to 'give it up and come home at once'. However we went for a walk along the beach burbling and pleased and spent a long time looking through hireling telescopes at the interesting and romantic behaviour of the sea-lions on the rocks. Then we got on a street car and where we went I don't know, but Witter read us his poems all the way. . . . we then adjourned to a dance hall and danced much between further drinks. . . . we then most uproariously walked, arm in arm, to the ferry, singing beautifully in parts, and dancing a little, and every time we came to a high thing that could be stood upon, they stood me on it, fire-alarms and ash-cans and mail boxes, and finally we managed to stand, five of us, on two ash-cans. When we got to the ferry I was much damped by finding it was past 12. . . .

Her hostess was a kind woman. Though austere in manner as, dressing-gown-clad, she received a tipsy house guest at her front entrance at one o'clock in the morning, at breakfast she had the grace to pretend that she had found the episode fun, and to be arch about it. The culprit, for her part, was shocked – not so much by the evening's disgraceful events, as by the fact that she felt so little ashamed of them: 'It is very funny and dangerous how little a sordid bat like last night's appears when one does it with funny good friends. I know we sang in tune and danced well. I cannot imagine that we looked beastly, even standing on ash-cans.'

Up until now, no one at High Acres had owned a car. Then Hugh Reid acquired a Dodge, and Stella, who had been thinking of moving on, decided to stay: 'I can't bear to leave the family in its hour of increased prosperity.' There was no doubt about it, 'Barbara' brought new excitements. On their first trip in her they landed in trouble with the police; touching fifty-seven miles an hour, Hugh was stopped for speeding, but let off with a fatherly rebuke on revealing that he was a hero returned from the war. They were a mixed four; as evening came on and the quality of the road deteriorated – they were in Napa County – 'lightly intertwined to protect each other', Hugh and Stella settled down to sleep in the back seat. They spent the night on a sleeping bag under rugs, all four of them 'squeezed into the same bed'; it was as casual and sexless as contact between persons of different genders can possibly be, but for Stella an experience of daring liberation: 'I didn't sleep much, but enjoyed it awfully, just looking up at the night sky.'

A day or two later they were off again, this time a more flammable group. With refreshment stops at every village saloon, and a bottle of heavy port – donated by Bynner – circulating from mouth to mouth as they drove, it was only a matter of time before hidden passions came to the surface. Peter turned from being 'extremely clinging' to Stella in the front seat (she was surprised to find that she 'rather liked' being 'hugged in cars') to see Hal kissing Bertha in the back; he made an 'astonishing' dive through the air with the idea of strangling Bynner, but the poet was the stronger of the two and managed to unclasp Peter's hands. It was, however, a silent, chastened car-load that finished the journey home; 'even Hugh, who though actually well drunk did not show it much except in the beautiful speed of his driving', became 'a little bitter'.

Throughout the spring of 1919 Stella remained enchanted with bohemia. Quiet evenings at home could resolve themselves into 'steady drunks', male guests staying the night, 'sleeping around on sofas and porches.' Then she and Bertha decided to throw a properly prearranged party. They hired a drummer–cymbalist, and Stella was taught how to shimmy. 'I danced with terrible violence with everyone,' she confessed. While one young man's dances were 'orgies of touching affection', the same might be said of sitting out with another. In the arms of Tully Williamson she circled the floor four times to other people's once; someone told her she had 'oddness and fantastic charm'; she played on a borrowed guitar; she whistled and sang Hoxton songs: 'Nobody would believe what pleasure I have from little feverish happinesses. . . . I have never had my share and now I dwell on it all childishly.'

Guests who lingered late were fed cocktails, and listened to Hal singing 'extraordinarily low songs. . . . we went into the garden to hear the coyotes yelping and wheezing hoarsely quite near, such a wild, moonlight sound'. At 4 a.m. the night was yet young. After 'whiskey toddies' all round, someone proposed a car drive, and eight of them squeezed into Hugh's four-seater, five in the back, three in the front, and they drove under a luminous sky to watch the dawn from the foot of Mount Diablo.

*

On 3 June Stella was back in hospital, having her sinuses drained. It was Lausanne all over again, though on a minor scale: 'I did not cry or squeal . . . but when he used the hammer and chisel I flinched, and he was very rough and angry to me, and said he was within a third of an inch of my brain.' No sooner was she back in bed than a clergyman appeared at her side – asked on arrival what her religion was, she had replied none, and had been registered protestant. Anxious to offer comfort, 'he patted me on a little oasis where no gore was and asked if I was in pain and I said Yerce more or less, and he said "Have you said a little prayer" and I said "No", but seeing he was grieved I added "But I will if you like" so he patted me and told me to turn over right now and say it. Rather a discouraging job, I should think.' Next day her tonsils were cut out.

Possibly it was this brief removal from the High Acres scene that made her view it in a different light; certainly from now on her diary sounds a new note of weariness, even of disgust: 'I am worn out by these people, who only use these skies and this golden and intoxicating country as an excuse for hugging each other. . . . I am coming to the end of my curious delusion.' On 12 June a group of them – Stella, Bertha, Hal, Hugh and a fresh admirer of Bertha's, one Haskell – set off on a five-day camping expedition to Yosemite National Park, pitching tent in a different place each night. There was schism from the start. At Glacier Rock Bertha and Haskell elected to 'make love', while Hal, who had a bad head for heights, sat miserably pressed against the edge of the rock. Stella, 'though almost sobbing with horror', forced herself to climb to the end of the long, narrow rock and look over at the plummeting view: 'I looked over two thousand feet and nearly fainted, and the rock seemed to tip downwards suddenly to throw me off, like walking on a plank, but I'm glad I did it.'

'I have never been so dirty before or eaten off such smeary plates,' she was writing next day, 'but it is rather an adventure in a smeary way.' However, before long Bertha was showing clear signs of having a 'down' on her. She was talking about her 'detached English manners', and grumbling at her for lagging behind on hills – hardly fair, since she perfectly well knew that she had 'only one lung'. It did not help matters that Bertha and Haskell kept 'slinking off', he to propose, she to refuse. But what really upset Stella was Bertha's telling her that Hugh, whom she had believed to be her friend, had said that he did not want her (Stella) on any more of their excursions, because he wanted Bertha 'all to himself'.

On 21 June came the 'great Rift', a no-holds-barred row which took place behind the scenes of a party at which, again, Stella and Bertha were joint hostesses. Breaking out in the corridor outside Bertha's bedroom – 'as I passed Bertha's door she asked me suddenly in a voice of repressed hatred what I meant always to insult her guests by showing my damned superior English manners' – it climaxed in the kitchen in a confusion of vituperation.

Stella left the house next morning at 6.30, badly shaken. She fled to Chauncey and Henriette Goodrich, requesting solitude. They put her in their garden, in a little transparent room made of mosquito netting, with hot and cold water running into it, electric light, a soft bed, a store of cigarettes and all the latest magazines: 'I fell asleep very happily indeed in my little starlit house, and wondered why I had been so much worried, when I had the whole world still round me, and probably not so awfully much time to enjoy it.' Echoes of the row reverberated round the Pope circle for weeks, unhappily prolonged by Stella's urge to get to the root of the matter. She discussed it with Hal, he repeated what she said, and by a circuitous route it all got back to Bertha, who promptly accused Stella of blackening her name on both sides of the continent. Yet in the heat of the turmoil she could phone, and 'in a cooing voice' beg Stella to come back, saying she was 'without female society and intensely lonely' – and Stella, loving her, could almost relent.

A second operation was due, on 5 July. The moment she was discharged (the operation, on the ethnoid bone, had produced severe head pain, and for two days she had been 'all doped and packed in ice'), the Goodriches whisked her away to a sanatorium at Los Gatos, with the kind intention of footing the bill, though at Stella's urgent insistence eventually they allowed her to pay a quarter of it. She did not like her physician there, a fat, vulgar man called Boonshaft, 'a ridiculous Teutonic name'. In the presence of the Goodriches he had burst out with 'the most revolting details' about her health, 'so unnecessary and raw and dirty', and later seized upon a copy of *This is the End* that she happened to have by her, and read out page one 'like a pig'. When he had finished his reading, he said 'You have inspired me to write a book.' 'What about?' she asked. 'Tuberculosis,' came the daunting reply.

For Boonshaft was almost positive that she was now consumptive, and strongly urged her to devote a year or two to a cure. The result was the inevitable one. After a couple of slightly chastened days, during which she decided that 'TB couldn't incapacitate me much more than I have been incapacitated all my life. Indeed it only makes it a little more likely that I shan't live long, which is all to the good,' she 'lay awake at night making plans about getting some money to go to India with after Christmas'. She reckoned that by renting a very cheap room, eating at cafeterias and, in addition to her university teaching, finding a 'humble' job for the evenings, she could expect to save enough: 'I am always so lucky about money.' As if to prove that it was so, next day came a letter enquiring whether she was qualified to act as reader for the university press at Berkeley; the remuneration would be at least a hundred dollars monthly.

In mid-August she secured the job, and found her cheap room, 'a mousetraplike flat (one room and a kitchenette) measuring approximately ten feet by six', in a block overlooking the campus. The material that she had to edit was for the most part highly specialised; not much of it interested her – and she was grateful to the author of a treatise on the boring isopod for his kindly notice in advance: 'this isopod can even bore rock'. Soon she discovered a knack of focusing only half her brain on the texts, leaving the rest free for blissful intercourse with Secret Friends. Her work must have satisfied her employers, for she was offered 'a raise' in September if she would stay permanently: 'But . . . I have a sort of horror of getting tied to one stodgy respectable job, when there is all the world to see and to write about,' she told her mother.[8]

In the late autumn the first reviews of *Living Alone* arrived from England; 'I am never a quarter as clever as my reviewers are, or as they think I am,' quipped Stella. Katherine Mansfield, in the *Athenaeum*, was one of the critics to be charmed by the book, with reservations:

> We hardly dare to use the thumb-marked phrase 'a born writer'; but if it means anything Miss Stella Benson is one. She seems to write without ease, without effort; she is like a child gathering flowers. And like a child, there are moments when she picks the flowers that are at hand just because they are so easy to gather, but which are not real flowers at all, and forgets to throw them away. This is a little pity, but exuberant fancy is rare, love of life is rare, and a writer who is not ashamed of happiness rarer than both.[9]

What Stella had written was a fairy tale of wartime London. Years later, she was to dismiss the state of mind in which she walked the world when her first three novels were written as 'defensive illusionment', but at the time she felt that she had the key to a marvellous, if dangerously seductive, theatre of fantasy available only to the privileged few. Now in a foreword to *Living Alone* she warned: 'This is not a real book. It does not deal with real people, nor should it be read by real people. But there are in the world so many real books already written for the benefit of real people . . . that I cannot believe that a little alien book such as this, written for the magically-inclined minority, can be considered too assertive a trespasser.'

Very surprising things start to happen when a witch's magic comes to play upon the staid members of a War Savings committee (witches are 'people born into the world for the first time'; witches do not judge, 'they just look, and are very much surprised and interested'). A witch is questioned by a committee member as to her trade; 'I'll show you,' she replies, unbuttoning the flap of her pocket:

> She wrote a word upon the air with her finger, and made a flourish under the word. So flowery was the flourish that it span her round, right round

upon her toes, and she faced her watchers again. The committee jumped, for the blind ran up, and outside the window, at the end of a strange perspective of street, the trees of some far square were as soft as thistledown against a lemon-coloured sky. A sound came up the street. . . .

The forgotten April and the voices of lambs pealed like bells into the room. . . .

The scene shifts to the mid-Thames island of Mitten, where the witch is manageress of a curious general-shop-cum-convent-cum-hostel called 'the House of Living Alone'; we are shown a faery farm where the fieldhands are fairies, and the foreman a gentle dragon; there is an air raid in which the sheeted dead rise from their graves and mingle with people sheltering in a church crypt, while up above, on a disintegrating cloud, a German and British witch debate the rights and wrongs of war. Now and then, accurate pot shots are taken at contemporary targets, such as the English class system and the COS. The story (by courtesy so called) ends with the main non-faery character, an invalidish young woman charity worker named Sarah Brown (whose initials should be noted) sailing to the United States, 'the greater House of Living Alone', where, we can be quite sure, a great many more lonely, unexpected adventures will befall her.

Appropriately, in October Stella found herself elected chairman of a literary club. It met weekly in a small French restaurant in San Francisco for the purpose of reading and discussing verse of the members' own composition. Offerings were handed in anonymously, velvet-voiced Bertha (with whom Stella was once again on good terms) reading them out, and at the end a vote was taken on which was the best; more often than not, the choice fell on Stella's. Clearly it was an arrangement affording loopholes for comedy, and perhaps the funniest moment was when one young woman gave in by mistake a personal letter, which without hesitation Bertha delivered as free verse. At a time when almost any sequence of words could pass as poetry it was a perfectly natural mistake and, as Stella pointed out, the way the letter began with 'Hell!' gave it 'the genuine Carl Sandberg ring'.

There was a new friendship, with a handsome, intense young woman of Spanish–Irish descent called Mariquita de Laguna. 'I have been fallen in love with (if you follow me),' Stella told Laura. 'Mariquita . . . writes me letters like a lover, and leaves dark red roses leaning against my door.'[10] Together they camped out on the hills and on the beach, talking into the small hours; but as in any relationship approaching intimacy with another woman, Stella felt as though she were, in some way, deceiving her and the entire female sex, 'by pretending to be one of them'. 'I told Mariquita that I was posing when I seemed to talk yearnestly and girlishly about myself,' she wrote in her diary. 'It seems to me that I am posing when I pretend to be a real person anyway.'

If she had a doubt about Mariquita's sexual orientation, she had none about her own. Having reached twenty-seven with nothing more in her sexual biography, so to speak, than a number of male advances evaded and a bloodless infatuation for an older man, it would not be surprising if she had begun to ask herself certain agonising questions; but a year later, discussing her (as she thought) greater attractiveness to women than to men, she was serenely confident that she herself was not in the least 'sexually inverted . . . though I know I take great pleasure in the beauty of women, and am an easy spiritual victim of a woman like Bertha Pope, there is no feeling of sex in me towards women at all'.

She left America earlier than she had planned, on 16 December. To some extent it was a flight: 'It is the vulgarity that I sicken at, almost every phase of life here is tainted with it, and I resent most violently the gross, expectorating, sentimental, cheap man and woman in the street'; on the other hand, 'I have met with much kindness in America that perhaps as an alien I should not have met with in England.'

She had in fact chosen the worst possible moment to be in America, a moment when restrictions deeply disquieting to the foreign visitor were being imposed on the citizens of the land of the free. The year 1919 saw the rapid spread of a 'Red Scare' similar in many ways to that fomented by Senator Joseph McCarthy of ill fame after the Second World War. With communist revolution triumphant in Russia, it was frighteningly easy to convince a large number of Americans that international Red conspiracy was at the back of post-war industrial unrest, and to have them looking around among their friends and neighbours for its likely agents. People whose views were not 'one hundred per cent American' were finding it safer to keep their mouths shut. California had criminal syndicalist, sedition and 'Red flag' laws under which some five hundred people were arrested during the years 1919–20, and Stella had their reality brought home to her when friends took her to visit some of the political prisoners in Alcatraz jail.

All Stella's Californian friends were liberally inclined. Well before the scare was at its height she was marvelling at the temerity of a member of a left-wing group in talking in a clear voice in a fashionable restaurant about 'the fiendishness of secret government agents. . . . Russia has apparently got nothing on America for government conspiracy and brutality against progressive people. All these people in this set know that their letters are steamed open and their telephones tapped.' She admired Mr Tucker the Bolshevik for his plan to tour America to bring the Russian message to his own land, but 'he will end in prison, of course. This is a land of liberty, it does not like to hear about liberty in other lands.' Fully expecting (and probably hoping for) police intervention, Stella sat through meetings on such topics as 'The Truth about Russia', lending a fairly open ear to propaganda about the shining virtues of the new regime and the harm that Western intervention there was wreaking. Soon she was going the whole way and calling herself a Bolshevik.

Then again July 1919 saw the imposition – and very general disregard – of nationwide anti-alcohol laws.[11] To Stella the legislation seemed a grievous trespass on individual freedom, and a few days before it came into force she sat in a state of incredulous pity outside a wineshop, watching 'dumb and tragic Italians and Portuguese with their heartrendingly tiny stores hugged to their breasts, to last to doomsday, they who loved their "Dago red" so innocently and happily'. She and her friends laid up stores for home consumption, and found in most restaurants and bars that a nod was as good as a wink, and both productive of alcohol. At the restaurant where the poetry club met one simply had to ask, 'with a speaking look', for lemonades, to be promptly served with 'pisco punches', and in country parts it was perfectly possible to have alcohol offered without even having to wink.

A number of interesting experiences awaited Stella during her last few weeks in America: she went up in an aeroplane for the first time (having whispered in the pilot's ear that she was a journalist, who would appreciate 'a few thrills' to write up, she was treated to a deliciously horrifying 'wing-over', and a nose dive on Alcatraz); she saw President Wilson (who turned out to be 'a pink and middle-aged man with a too broad smile and a look of great but rather avuncular kindness'); she had her portrait painted. 'I am sure the most salient thing about me is the blurred and shut effect of my eyes, they being heavy lidded and set far back in my skull,' she wrote, feeling that the artist had missed this feature. In his studio she picked up that uniquely awesome object, a human skull, and examined it. For the 'me' who had once possessed it, this 'ivory shell' had contained – everything:

> Outside of that there was nothing. And yet inside of that what was there? Little canyons in the ivory for veins, little sockets delicately carved, a little soft quivering stuff – all substances I could have touched with my finger. These dreams, these ecstasies, these great skycrowding revolutions – nothing there that I couldn't have touched with my finger. Of course, Hamlet thought it all. . . .

California gave her a generous farewell. Ill in early December – 'such a cough and a pleurisy like an artichoke sitting on three of my most sensitive ribs' – she had, once again, been cared for with devotion and tact by the Goodriches: 'by Jove, they have been good to me'. People were predicting disaster for her in Hong Kong, from shortage of money. 'That is not worrying, but whetting,' she said, yet all the same accepted from the

Goodriches a loan of five hundred dollars; an anonymous well-wisher gave her another fifty, and – unusually for her – some of it went on 'a good velvet dress and silk stockings'.

As the time of departure drew near, as always her spirits fell. On 15 December she packed 'with the utmost hopelessness, feeling very mewish and clinging', and arrived at her farewell dinner in a weak, trembling state, rendering her more than usually susceptible to the effect of strong drink. A blend of 'rum and various wines' left her 'over-revived', 'moved', 'confused', 'watery-eyed', and she could only acknowledge with smiles 'and very nearly tears' all the kind speeches about her that her friends made: 'It is just California,' she thought bemusedly, 'a very beautiful Californian trait, to think so generously of strangers and be able to say so.' Some Chinese beads were passed around the table, and as each guest strung a bead, he or she stood up and wished on it for Stella. Wished too that some day she would return.

Chapter Twelve

On 21 December 1919 a Japanese steamship bore Stella and Mariquita – for her friend was to try her fortune in the orient too – out of San Francisco harbour into exceptionally heavy seas. 'Yesterday I saw a fried egg jump over two stewards and land on the next table,'[1] Stella reported brightly to Doris Estcourt, a friend of Hindhead schooldays, remet in San Francisco. Unlike Mariquita and most of the other passengers, who were laid low, Stella was up and about, and present at meals. On Christmas Day she joined in such festivities as were organised, trying hard to be merry: at dinner she offered to pull a cracker with her neighbour at table, an uninspiring American businessman, 'but with a reproachful look he pulled it with himself'.

The ship, the *Persia Maru*, was a floating fragment of Japan. The crew staged a fight with bamboos, dressed in quilted armour and emitting strange roars and guttural cries. A Japanese in the steerage died, and his committal was an amalgam of magic, mystery and moonlight very much to Stella's taste:

> beside him was a little meal in the light of the sunset, oranges and silver rice . . . the moonlight besides making a white road about the whole sea. . . . we thought these were the souls of dead drowned men gathering to show this newcomer the way, and indeed as he fell, with a silver noise and a silver disturbance of the water, all the souls gathered round the spot.

That disembodied, faery note sounded again, a touch defiantly, after a discussion about sex with two male fellow passengers: 'I suppose my own life and my own enthusiasms are very tenuous and decadent. Nobody ever believes that such things of foam and moonlight could ever make life worth living. Yet I know they can.'

She and Mariquita rapidly acquired attendant swains. Stella's was an

Englishman, a Mr Welch, 'a thorough gent of the greatest orthodoxy', who followed her about pitching and tossing decks, protesting nervously when she climbed up on things, 'Well relly is this quite wise?' One day, in going to the assistance of another passenger, who had been hurled against a table and hurt, she fell, was knocked unconscious, and came round – as she put it – soaked in brandy and with an arm that hurt like fire; she had torn the ligaments in a shoulder. From that day on Welch was in his element, fetching and carrying in the most chivalrous way, and indeed getting alarmingly romantic, 'so in view of the fact that he has a wife and three children in London, I get very hard and prosaic and literal'.

However, as time passed, the magic of being at sea and the flattery of Welch's doglike devotion began to take effect (Stella generally found herself more relaxed and amenable aboard ship – one of the reasons she liked them so much). Welch was an unselfconfident man, and his refined approaches made her feel more like a 'real girl' than usual: 'I came as near to being physically attracted to A.J.W. as I ever came to any man,' she wrote. 'I very rarely like to be touched, but he is so gentle and so loving and so sensitive' (in contrast to another passenger who got his face smacked when he came into her cabin and tried to kiss her). For his part, poor Welch fancied himself seriously in love, and gave her a gold lacquer cigarette case to remember him by before, hopelessly weeping, he tore himself away to Shanghai. It was a beautiful case, 'really too exquisite for an old brown-lived person like me', thought Stella. 'It ought to belong to a real lady with beautiful details to her.' The parting had upset her far more than she had expected: 'Nobody will ever feel for me again the way he did. . . . I cannot bear not seeing him again. I just feel dead and lost for ever.'

And so to Japan. She saw it through a cloud of pain and distress. Her shoulder hurt, and when it came to handling luggage Mariquita's rather casual help was no substitute for Welch's assiduity. In Yokohama 'Spanish *grippe*' caught up with her, and she learned that, for a woman travelling alone – by this time Mariquita had found a job in Kobe – a Japanese hotel was no place to be ill in. Had it not been for the ministrations of a kind young Irishman – 'I don't know why he likes me, after his full and furious life. He says it is because I am very strange and remote. I seem to have heard that before, and, anyway, I don't like it particularly' – she would have been in serious difficulty. But fortunately (as she put it to Laura) the east seemed to 'simmer in sentiment like a hot cake in maple syrup. Twinklebuds are absolutely thick on the ground . . . there must be a lack of women.'[2] Clearly the sight of so obviously frail a creature 'racketing about the world alone', as Welch had put it, made a strong appeal to the male protective instinct. And maybe California had put her in bloom.

Helped aboard ship by her affectionate Irishman, she promptly collapsed, to the alarm of the Japanese ship's doctor, who wanted to put her off again at

Kobe – he thought it more than likely that she would die as a result of the extremes of temperature encountered on the voyage. 'I don't think so,' she managed to say, clinging to the bed-rail, while inwardly reflecting, 'I would kill myself if I touched that cursed Japan again.' Probably calling to mind that discretion is the better part of valour (or whatever is the Japanese equivalent), the doctor let her stay on board. He might not have done so had he realised that she was coughing up blood, but that awkward fact she managed to conceal.

At Nagasaki she was too ill to go ashore. At Manila she was fit enough to take a quick look at American colonialism in action: '50 percent liberty,' it seemed to her to be, '49 percent equality and 1 percent fraternity. Politically a great deal is said about brotherhood – personally, almost nothing.' She had arrived during a carnival: 'Groups of virtuous businessmen and their overstitched wives stood watching through shocked pincenez a handful of young new Sammies who were making so bold as to dance with some pretty Filipino girls. The girls wore their national dress – wired gauze at the shoulders, high Elizabethan ruff behind the head, looped complicated skirt. The Americans wore their national dress. . . .'

'England at last!' exclaims to himself Edward, hero of *The Poor Man*, Stella's next novel, finding himself in Hong Kong; he follows a couple of pink, small-headed subalterns into a hotel, he hears one say 'By Jove' in a throaty English voice, he looks at cool faces in the hotel lobby: 'the faces were English and not complacent. Or even if they were a little complacent – why not? – they were English.'

Edward was doomed to a worm's-eye view of Hong Kong. Stella, on the contrary, entered British colonial society at top level. Some years earlier she had tossed her head in scorn at the 'stereotyped superior time' enjoyed by her Aunt V on a Victorian tour of India: 'Item, one tiger hunt, item, one visit to a Maharajah, etc., etc. The sort of time one would have had if one had influence enough to climb high into India, but not enough to burrow very deep. One catches an impression of a good time, from what she says, not an impression of India.' Stella intended in her travels to go one better than Aunt V, yet was not unappreciative of being met on the quay by the wife of the officer commanding the Wiltshires, and being taken to stay at her house on the Peak. There was amusement to be had in going 'in our best hats, so to speak, to the place where the Wiltshire Regiment lives to look at other people's best hats, and the regimental silver and porcelain looted from Peking, and drink cocktails and listen to the band'; some satisfaction to be found in taking one's place, with perfect assurance as far as the outward formalities were concerned, at dinner at Government House, or at the races, or at a regimental dance. No one was likely to guess that the incontrovert-ibly ladylike figure in the 'darling' little black and white dress so cleverly run up for her by her hostess felt 'almost in the running with other women but not, of course, quite'.

There seems an element of wilfulness in Stella's refusal, in face of accumulating evidence to the contrary, to accept that in ways that they found refreshingly unusual she was more than averagely appealing to a wide variety of men. She was far more likely to be mortified because her dance card was not instantly filled up than complacent because 'must the most attractive man here' chose to sit out with her. Rumour floated lightly by of several young men much offended that she had cut their dances at the Peak Club, and of a captain being in trouble with his wife for dancing with her too many times. The word flirtation had dropped from her vocabulary since Swiss days, when for a time the practice of it had been a kind of hobby, but clearly she liked men as much as ever and adored it when they liked her.

It was in Hong Kong that she discovered how much she liked sailors, both in general – 'I haven't seen such happy, simple people for years, I think. They had none of the touch of hysteria that was in Californian happiness' – and in particular: there was an uncomplicated, keen, clean young fellow, first lieutenant of a Royal Navy flagship, in whose cabin she sat on an 'unusually unchaperoned' afternoon looking at his drawings, returning home 'much smugger than I have felt for a long time'. In a safe, 'unsentimental' way he enjoyed her company as much as she did his, and together they explored Hong Kong, poking inquisitive noses into every corner of Chinese life open to them – from the wondrous, incomprehensible theatre to the 'Chinese otherwise-ladies' quarter at West Point.

Meanwhile she had descended from the glories of the Peak to live in a humble hostel for European and Eurasian women, the Helena May Institute, none too pleased to find herself sharing a table with three missionaries, 'overpoweringly chaste' ladies, one with a squint, two with spectacles, and all dressed in flannel in unnecessarily high-necked style; they had 'Christian joyous smiles, not real smiles at all', she wrote in her diary. 'What goads me is making such a virtue of being ugly. All the same, I suppose it must be wonderful, if nobody loves you, to imagine that God does – most gloriously comforting.' Stella was to meet a large number of missionaries over the years, and never to budge from her attitude of anger and contempt for them as a group. Rightly or wrongly, they represented to her too many of the things she hated: self-satisfaction, philistinism, incuriosity, the fixed mind. It was partly a question of class, for the majority of missionaries, the protestants in particular, belonged to the lower middle class, a section of society whose manners, accent and values set her teeth on edge – an effect which they had, and have, on many of her upper-class kind.

It was on the question of how far the sceptic was justified in trespassing on 'the joyous society' of missionaries in foreign lands that the conversation paused, when – minor literary lioness to visiting lion – Stella was introduced

to Somerset Maugham (she rather liked him: he seemed 'kindly and amused
. . . not supercilious as he has the reputation here of being'). Maugham
thought that the sceptic was perfectly justified in so doing, as 'writing people
were really everywhere under false pretences, pretending to be one of every
group for the purpose of getting material, and the end justifies the means'.

To pay for her passage to Calcutta, her next scheduled stop, Stella would
have to earn some money, and she found a teaching job with no trouble at
all. It has been the luck of a good many writers at some crisis of needy youth
to find themselves standing before a class of schoolchildren, posing as
teachers and feeling more like a glove that has been pulled wrong way out.
The dreadful experience befell Stella at the Anglican Diocesan Boys' School
in Victoria, Hong Kong, and her hilarious, lightly fictionalised account is
one of the high spots of *The Poor Man*. On the day she was appointed she
wrote in her diary, 'I always live so much in the moment and "right here", I
cannot remember any day but to-day, not as a real fact – to-morrow not at
all, yesterday as a dream that has ceased to amuse.' For someone with a
month to wait before tackling the largest and reputedly most 'difficult' class
in an unknown school it was surely blessed to be so blinkered.

Some fifty boys of Chinese and mixed race were to be enlightened in all
subjects from the life of Christ to elementary chemistry, mathematics
excluded. As in all schools, it was the head who set the tone, and the
temporary director of the Diocesan Boys', though 'a distinctly human
parson, with the bloom of Oxford still on him' (actually he was from
Cambridge), was hopelessly shy, ineffectual and slack. Stella spotted at once
that the teachers, past and present, had been allowed to get away with very
lax standards of tuition, though, if *The Poor Man* is to be believed, they had
precious little learning to impart in any case:

> There was one professional teacher in the school – a woman. The other
> teachers' desks were occupied by one or two unemployed merchant
> seamen, some bright young women stenographers, a stray woman
> journalist teaching 'as a stunt' [this must be Stella herself], and two or
> three sullen Chinese whose classes were always in an uproar.

While she was there one of the masters was dismissed – as was poor Edward
– for giving out a blasphemous grace when drunk.

'My work is just bearable,' she informed Doris Estcourt after a week or so,
'but my class gets larger and larger, and the more unmanageable the more it
gets used to me. I am permanently hoarse through bellowing to the
uttermost ends of the large hall where I teach, I haven't caned a boy yet, the
other teachers do, but my pupils are as tall as myself if not taller, and I would
feel silly if I tried.'[3]

'Oh, silence . . . oh, silence . . . oh, silence . . . I can't stand this,' cries the wretched Edward, until the one good little boy in the class comes to his rescue with 'last Monday we have finish Matthew-holy-gospel-according-to twenty-four chapter'. But there are pitfalls for the unwary even there:

'Excuse me, sah, what does it mean *virgin?*'
Edward's skull was sweating. 'A virgin –' he began.
'Eh -tya -tya. . . .'
'Surely the whole class has sense enough not to ask silly questions.'
'Please, sah, you shall tell him ask Ng Sik Wong. He married man.'
'Please, sah, tell him ask Ng Sik Wong wife – she shall know what is virgin – I wonder. . . .'
'A virgin is a young unmarried woman,' said Edward, petulantly damning all virgins.
'But, please, sah –'

Stella survived a term, and the secret of her survival was that she liked the boys and managed to make them like her. Nothing could stop their outrageous noise, their lying and cheating, 'but they laugh and are very genial and spontaneous and very brotherly in their kindnesses to me';[4] their feeling for her was 'a sort of mixture of the paternal with the cynical', she decided. They brought her flowers, and when she announced her imminent departure, were 'most kindly reproachful'. On the day she left Hong Kong, forty-nine of them came and swarmed all over her ship, and when she sailed followed her out of the harbour in motor boats.

She was not bound for Calcutta after all. Through a personal contact, an offer had come, impossible to resist, of three months' work in an American medical institute in Peking, and she was booked sole passenger on a cargo boat taking a load of indigo through pirate-infested waters to Tientsin.
She was not sorry to be leaving Hong Kong. 'I love the Chinese very much,' she told Doris. 'I have never felt so much drawn to a race or been so very rarely disappointed in the details of human intercourse with a people.'[5] But all the same Hong Kong was the wrong place for her, in several ways, 'partly climate, and partly because I got a bit smug, I think, owing to getting very dependent on sailors, who are a very amiable race, and bad for a severely detached suffragette'.[6] And, as she wrote in her diary, she felt a certain 'bitterness' about British Hong Kong: 'something about S B stays awkwardly outside, and does not want to edge in, and that is exactly what is wrong'.
All aboard the good ship *Chip Shing* were Chinese, apart from the skipper and first mate, who were Scots, and with them she took her meals. She discussed with them the future of Johnnie Granville, now a somewhat undersized and backward fifteen-year-old – 'I wonder what schooling he had

at Cookham' – sounding them out about careers in the merchant navy; as a result, urgent letters went to kind Laura in London asking her to look into the question of mercantile apprenticeships.

For Stella it was well-nigh impossible to be miserable in the company of sailors – but she was distressed by what was to upset her throughout her time in the east, the heartless way in which the local inhabitants treated animals. Birds clung to the rigging, getting a free ride: 'some of them had blue wings and gold breasts, and would not eat bun, and there were yellow – old gold – with red breasts, and there was one blunt-faced sparrowhawk sitting among the rest like the lion lying down with the lamb'. The coolies caught them and tied them with strings to the rigging, 'which I could hardly bear, because whenever a poor bird tried to fly away, it was hung by the leg in mid air until it recovered itself'.

At Chefu, the skipper – 'suddenly arrayed in land-lubbing clothes and looking not half so attractive' – invited her to explore:

> the town was full of gaunt, growling, ravenous looking chows, ragged with mange and obviously unfed. The puppies, little wizened insects, all head with just a wisp of ribs and mange for body, wrung my heart. The little horses, beaten and overburdened, hurt too. Some horrid little naked boys were beating to death a beautiful flame coloured lizard.

China was to cram her eyes with an infinity of sights, many of extraordinary beauty and fascination, but too many like these, paining her almost unbearably with their cruelty and horror.

In Peking the Rockefeller Foundation maintained a fine up-to-date hospital and medical research institute; Stella was secretary to the Roentgenray department, on generous pay, and lived in an old Chinese house made over to the female staff. The work was not difficult, and her colleagues were kind, but the atmosphere of cheerful American efficiency grated on her nerves: at the hostel she mourned, 'I feel left out because they are all more alive than I, at least alive to life, human life.' She found her friends in the British community, a surprising and flattering proportion of whom had read her books, or at least heard of them.

For the foreign resident or visitor, between-the-wars Peking was (in contrast with Hong Kong) a beguilingly easy, relaxed place to live. Stella loved it:

> Peking must be the most wonderful city in the world [she told Aunt Florie] and nothing will make me sorry I came. Nobody works awfully hard, it is too hot, and you have a good deal of time to let the wonder of everything sink in. I have made an investment I am glad of in the shape of a halfshare of a horse, and every other day he takes me out, either into the

little noisy gaudy crowded streets of the city, or along the cool paved walks that go around the Forbidden City – which is all tiled with gold-coloured porcelain and bristling with yellow dragons and strange curling-upwards roofs, reflected in the moat among the waterlilies.

Or else we ride out of one gate after another – against the stream of camels coming in from Mongolia – and into the shady park of the Temple of Heaven which has soft rides to gallop along, and there we ride races when it is cool – my horse Woodrow can beat nearly all the other horses he knows in a short spurt – and sometimes we come back and have supper on the outermost city wall while the moon rises.[7]

'White people', as she went on to explain, had a delightful practice of renting temples in the Western Hills: 'they are such lovely restful places to live and the Buddhist priests carry on and do not mind you at all, they like you to attend services and be interested. You live in stone-paved rooms that open out into a common courtyard which generally has a tree in it and is beautifully cool and quiet except for the soft gongs and chantings in the temple.'[8]

The climate of Peking, she assured her aunt, was ideally suited to her chest, 'almost extravagantly dry'; she played down a spell in hospital – 'almost nobody escapes a touch of dysentery, and I am lucky not to have typhoid or anything like that' (in fact she had been quite seriously sick). Aunt Florie had written offering her money, and not only money – she had offered the distilled wisdom of her Christian experience, and it was because of the love that she knew underlay both offers, that Stella ended her letter on a deeper note:

some day when I am very strong and stout and need do no other work but writing, I am coming back to China to live for ever in a little temple in the Western Hills outside Peking, with ten servants at about twopence each a day, and two horses, and then I shall get to know Chinese mountain people as I really want to. But even then I shall never know anything about peace; peace I know is too far from me, I don't know why. You can almost compensate yourself for the lack of it, I think – sometimes I believe you can quite.

But whatever happens being alive has been worth while, and though I can believe you that I have lacked the best thing of all, I just know that I have been extraordinarily fortunate and that all I have not only enjoyed but also had to bear in my life has been worth enjoying and worth bearing. Many things I have done I wish I had not done, but there is nothing that has happened to me that I wish hadn't happened. Goodbye, kind one.[9]

In July 1920 the idyll was menaced by rumours of war. In the years immediately following the collapse in 1911 of the Manchu dynasty, Yuan Shih-kai, a general of the old guard, had imposed some semblance of order on China; with his death the country fell to the mercy of rival warlords, whose armies of ruffians, when not actually engaged in fighting each other, terrorised the provinces and paralysed the central administration. The particular warlord engagement about to take place near Peking was between Tuan Chi-jui and Wu Pei-fu. Tuan's army was backed to lose, upon which it was expected to fall back on the capital and loot it. Among the populace panic spread, the richer elements making for the railway stations, the poorer placing such valuables as they possessed in the foreign compounds for safety; foreigners, in the event of violence, planned to run to their various legations, where they would be protected by their own troops. On the crucial weekend Stella and her friends scuttled ignominiously back to Peking from their temple on the rumour of attack, but in fact the city was not sacked. Instead Stella found herself sitting taking notes while doctors examined the injuries of some of the sad remnants of Tuan's army trickling into the capital – only their mysterious passivity under suffering enabling her to bear the sight of their wounds.

Then her health broke. She had a severe attack of pleurisy, and was strongly advised to go home, and at once. She gave her classic reply – 'I had always found that I had a happier and more interesting life when I went my own way. I should still be in a sanatorium ripening into an endless and hypochondriac old age if I had listened to doctors' – and spent the rest of the day 'brooding' against the medical profession.

A while later there was a recurrence of disease, she went back to hospital, and the diary contains no entry for four days. A week after that she was viewing the sunrise from the Great Wall, and camping at the Ming Tombs. Then she was off on the Yangtze River trip by way of the famous gorges, with two wives from the British community. One of them had a friend in Chungking, an Irishman in the Chinese Customs Service.

For the first three days the river moved spreadingly – dully – through flat country, but on the fifth day Stella awoke to see 'mountains steep and scarred, and with flushes of the most brilliant red'. It was 'such a lovely morning to wake up in, I was terribly happy'. At Ichang – a town said by the British Consul to be virtually in the hands of soldiery who, not being paid, were living by brigandage with the tacit consent of the Peking government – they changed boats for the transit of the gorges. There was a bewildering succession of whirlpools and fierce rapids; at one point they saw soldiers robbing a junk, but prudently passed by on the other side. After a day spent threading Wu-shan Gorge, with its incredibly precipitous cliffs, its temples perched on impossible heights, Stella was almost lightheaded with gazing:

Oh dear [she wrote once they had tied up for the night], there is a star now above the horns of the highest temple, the junks with their exquisite aspiring masts and rigging are clustered round us, and the water for the first time to-day has lost its gold, and its rose, and lies very smooth and pale-sky-colour. I think I shall never be so happy again.

By midday of the seventh day, 27 September, they were at Chungking, having a rather confused meeting with a young man eighteen months Stella's junior, 'who at first sight almost decided me to go'. Precisely why James ('Shaemas') Carew O'Gorman Anderson, a virile, moustached and monocled figure with manners strenuously polite, should have struck her with such foreboding is not at all clear; she thought it was because he looked 'so preternaturally grave and so lost in his own thoughts'. But the feeling was mutual – a few days later, when his fright had subsided, Anderson told her how one look at her had had him practically leaping off the boat: 'I was the most alarming person he ever saw!'

But of course there was no escape. Anderson on his pony, the ladies in chairs, each borne at shoulder height by four fierce-looking men, turned their backs on the river and moved inexorably away. Up flight after flight of steps they climbed (for Chungking seemed to have no streets), and, once out of the city, up higher and higher into the hills, until to Stella, gazing down, the flooded paddy-fields looked like silver eels. They travelled for an hour and a half, and came to a halt before Anderson's tumbledown bungalow. Below, enormously far, glided the Yangtze.

Before the day was out, Stella had developed a watchful interest in her host. He was plainly an intelligent man, out of the common run of officials on overseas postings. For one thing, he made no patronising concessions to the female intellect – on the contrary, 'I have to think hard what I am saying, because he is apt to say just "why" or "what do you mean by that"'; and when next day she read aloud from *This is the End* she was again struck by his knack of eager, detached interest, commenting amusedly, 'he sucked it in with such an intense face'. He did not say much, but obviously his thoughts would be worth expressing. The fact that, like her father, he wore an 'untethered eyeglass' intrigued her, as did his shy manner and his 'little, little voice':

He is shy [she confided to her diary] and yet somehow not frightened, he says little and looks pink yet what he says is quite brave, not panicstruck. That is rather like my shyness now. Sometimes the words of shy people are bolder than the words of non-shy people, because they matter more – the words I mean – so you take more trouble to free them of all trace of panic. Afterwards what you have said disconcerts you, if you are shy, but not all the time. At the same time you plume yourself rather on having said something audible and assured.

There was to be a dinner party in their honour. She watched him fussing agitatedly over the table arrangements until she and the other women came to his aid, when suddenly and unexpectedly he recovered his equilibrium and burst into loud and vulgar song 'in rather a nice voice'. In what ways he endeared himself to her during the course of the dinner is not revealed, but we do have her thoughts afterwards: 'I am getting to feel quite romantic about Shaemas O'Gorman. My heart is beginning to puff up a little, like a souflé [sic], when I see him or think of him. I don't know whether he feels romantic about me at all, or whether all these intense looks are just intellectual. I expect so, though I try to keep any blue out of my stockings. . . . I couldn't sleep when I came to bed, I was trying to make out what I really think of S. O'G.' For Stella these were unprecedented comments; and indeed she admitted that Shaemas 'intrigued' her more than any man she had ever met.

When it rained, which it did a good deal, they kept indoors, and in the close atmosphere emotions throve like exotic greenhouse plants – and were difficult to hide. There were intimate foursomes, when Stella tried to set up total 'honesty' as the goal of conversation. 'I talked too much,' she moaned after one such session, fearing lest she had exposed too much of herself, made herself ridiculous – 'deaf and emotionally deficient old woman' as she was.

But more upsetting, as the days passed it became clear that Shaemas and another of his guests, Florence Harding, were involved in some kind of passionate entanglement that predated the visit. Though Stella was convinced that on first acquaintance Shaemas had been much 'intrigued' by herself, Florence's attraction was obviously far more potent.

Yet, out walking in the hills with her, Shaemas seemed eager to know her better, probing her mind as to 'the great advantage of being thoroughly alive', for instance, and about love, 'me being darned wise and general about it, and Shaemas full of pathetic enquiry'. He talked freely about himself, sounding 'so desolate and forlorn'. It was a gloom-laden story, but Stella's thirsty ear drank it up like champagne. He had always felt unloved. His mother had ignored him, fixing her hopes on his brilliant, attractive elder brother, who had died in the war (his own loss, Stella divined, would have been trifling in comparison). Few men, he went on, warming to his theme, had been fond of him, no women. He had always been the odd man out. Now, to set the seal on his miseries, he was trapped in what was probably a hopeless passion for a married woman.

Longing to comfort him, and perhaps with some obscure idea of staking a claim in his heart, Stella summoned up her courage, 'took a deep breath, and told him that up to three days ago I was in love with him myself'. It was a charmingly girlish avowal, quite unpremeditated, and she had only a moment in which to guess at the likely response. If she feared his scorn, or

hoped that he would take her in his arms, either way she was proved wrong:
all he said was 'I don't believe you', and quickly changed the subject.

The organisation which employed Shaemas Anderson – the Imperial
Chinese Maritime Customs Service, to give it its full name (it was 'maritime' in the sense that in China most ports of entry for foreign goods were
sea ports) – was remarkable in several ways, not least in that it was a
department of Chinese government staffed, at all the more senior levels, by
foreigners. It came into being in the mid-nineteenth century, at a time when
civil disturbance, the Tai P'ing Rebellion, made it expedient for foreign
officials in Shanghai to take over the collection of customs duties. The
advantages to all parties concerned being apparent, the system continued,
and in due course was institutionalised under the highly efficient management of the first Inspector-General, the Ulsterman Robert Hart.

Initially the service concerned itself only with excise affairs, but over the
years its scope widened to include such things as harbour maintenance and
management, river conservancy, publication of maps – and even for a time
the running of the Chinese post office. In all these areas of responsibility
Frenchmen, Swedes, Americans, Britons, Australians, Japanese, Germans,
Russians, Greeks and half a dozen more nationalities worked side by side in
reasonable harmony, at the same time establishing an enviable reputation
for honesty, incorruptibility and efficiency. Though now largely forgotten,
the Chinese Customs Service was in its day widely regarded as 'one of the
administrative wonders of the world'.[10]

To the young man interested in a career overseas, a job in the Customs
was a plum. It meant responsible, interesting, generally not over-arduous
work, good pay and prospects, generous leave – twelve months' home leave,
inclusive of travel, every five years – and the sense of belonging to a
respected corps. However, when in 1913 Shaemas Anderson joined, it had
not been in the best of circumstances. He had gone up to Pembroke College,
Cambridge, from his public school, Cheltenham, with the idea of reading
classics; he had shone in the subject at school, and there was no reason to
think he would not do well at the university. But whatever the cause –
perhaps he was too independent-minded to submit to the academic strait-
jacket – during his first year up he resolutely studied not what he was
expected by the dons to study (texts that he had already done at school), but
what interested him, with the result that he pipped his exams. He was not
sent down. He could come back, provided he went over the first-year course
again. If his father would finance him, this he was perfectly prepared to do.
But, emphatically and irascibly, his father General Anderson informed him
that he would not.

So some time in the summer of 1913, Shaemas left the family home in
County Waterford *en route* to London, in the mood to move with the first

wind that blew. On the train from Fishguard he got into conversation with a man in the Customs, lending a convincible ear to his tale of the many advantages that the service offered to just such young fellows as he; he made a note of the address of the London office, paid it a visit, and in due course was enrolled. The expense to his father was a deposit to the Chinese government of one hundred pounds.

Then he went to China. In those days recruits of the service underwent for two years a kind of baptism of isolation and cold in Manchuria, while learning their job and, hopefully, mastering Chinese. Great importance was attached to knowledge of the language, and a high degree of proficiency demanded for top jobs. Shaemas had no great difficulty in satisfying his examiners in that respect. Then he was given his first post. When the European war broke out he applied for his release in order to enlist, but the Chinese asked for two hundred pounds in compensation, and this the General refused to pay. So Shaemas spent his war in China and, when Stella and he met, had not seen home for seven years.

In the tiny scattered community of Europeans of which Shaemas formed a part, it was a matter of duty as well as of curiosity to offer visitors hospitality – though it is doubtful whether a dull dinner party was worth the trouble of a chair ride in sheets of rain through mud the consistency of butter, along tightrope-like paths, and up mountain tracks at whose hairpin bends the captive passenger leaned out dizzily over space. There were daytime engagements too. At one luncheon Stella staged a display of spirit that must have been the talk of white society for days. She was piqued by what she took to be a slightly malicious challenge on the part of her hostess – and if for the sake of ingratiating herself with Shaemas she was prepared to suppress the bluestocking, she had no intention of sitting on the tomboy:

> In the middle of lunch, being at a loss for something to say . . . I said 'Do your visitors ever insist on climbing up the flagstaff between courses?' – for it was just outside with a little tantalising wire-rope ladder. Mrs Toller said, 'Yes, do please, our tiffin parties are always quite informal.' I was cold all over at this calling of my bluff, so I toiled up in the rain. It is a very high flagstaff, and the ladder is as limp in the air as a rag. I hadn't got more than twenty rungs up, before I knew that my arms were not really strong enough for such a stunt. However, Shaemas shouted up to me to come down at once, so of course I went on up, feeling very sick, and certain that my head would burst like an egg when it hit that massive stone base of the mast.
>
> My hands got too tired to hold the rope, so I hugged it to my front, so to speak, and locked my arms. The rungs in the rain were slippery, and when I got to the top it was horrible, but not so horrible as I expected, because

after all the ladder was attached there, not swinging and jerking and twisting around so that the river, and the city, and the hills were all confused in my eyes – half way down was the worst where the ladder was loosest. I thought I couldn't come down, I thought of just letting go from the top. It would have been simple, and a happy day to end on, but I was watching, without at first realising it, a tethered goat on the lawn biting at a mocking white butterfly in the air, and before I knew, I was on my way down. I was surprised when after several years I touched earth, my arms would hardly straighten out, but then I swanked, though really it was a rather senseless thing to do. It is most exciting to be senseless perhaps, and anyway for that while I was vividly alive, and the echo of the thrill went on to the end of the day.

Possibly, before she began her climb, the thought had flashed upon her that she had more to gain than to lose with Shaemas by provocative behaviour. If so, she misjudged her man; weeks later he was still bringing it up as a regrettable escapade. On the way home that afternoon, did he drop a hint of how he felt? If he did, she omitted to record it in her diary; nor did the affair stop her misbehaving – this time verbally – when a short while later he and she were guests together again:

At dinner were Captain Hall's wife and sister-in-law, such fools that they amused me rather. Mrs Hall asked me in such an exasperating voice whether I didn't think people wasted their time reading novels when this wonderful scenery was around. I said no, I always read the most outrageous novels I could find when beautiful scenery was around, she said did I never read Really Great Literature, I said I didn't know what it was. I went on grieving her to the bitter end.

Her sister was sillier still and kept on changing the subject whenever she didn't quite understand what I was driving at, but she always changed to the same 'Ah yes . . . and how have you liked Chungking?' Every time she said that I gave her a different opinion, always as if it were my first pronouncement on the subject. Shaemas got quite pink and giddy on these conversations.

At the state of affairs on the other two sides of the love triangle Stella could only make agonised guesses, and towards the end of the three-week visit was writing such painful tortuosities as: 'I am sure that to-day Shaemas really hoped for the first time that he would get Florence, as for Florence herself to-day I thought that she was discussing the matter with herself.' She was suffering acute stress, which yielded its predictable harvest of 'brain lapses' and fits of direst gloom. As the date of departure drew near, she could even be glad that she was going: 'It seems to me that China has stretched my nerves to very thin hairs. Yet there is a wonderful world here. . . .'

Needless to say, the wonderful world to which she referred was not that of the Europeans with their tiffin party small-talk, but the panorama, as she had glimpsed it, of Chinese life and landscape, which had included a good deal of horror:

> Shaemas and I had rather a beautiful ride this morning, very tiring to me but beautiful because the weather was so fair, great clouds of mist bowling along the tops of the hills and sunshine dazzling on the ricefields in the valley and on the little cottages through whose thatched roofs the smoke oozes very blue. . . . On our way home we passed crowds of soldiers, most of them engaged in making the poor peasants work for them, mostly at the point of the bayonet. The behaviour of the soldiers was sickening. I saw a poor coolie boy who had sunk down under his load, exhausted, the soldier was hitting him with the carrying pole on the head. Another was sticking his sword into the leg of an old man. . . . The soldiers themselves looked as if all humanity had been beaten out of them, quite empty faces, they stared at us with wild red-rimmed eyes. [The soldiers were the scattered remnants of a defeated Yunnanese warlord army on their way out of Szechwan.]

One day when Stella wanted to use his office typewriter, Shaemas took her into Chungking and they went for a boat ride, passing the street of the prostitutes, 'the lowest prostitutes of all, whose price is forty cash (about two coppers). I could see some of those women in their doorways . . . they had obviously hard faces, and stonelike eyes.' Further on, in a spot where all the dirt and rubbish of the city seemed to be accumulated, half-naked women and children were plunging their hands into the welter, searching for stray bits and pieces to sell for a copper. One boy, who had stolen some treasure that another boy had found, was being held down by half a dozen of the pack, while his kneecap was repeatedly hit with a stone: 'I was nearly sick with his screams' – the fine edge of the horror being her inability to do anything about it.

When animals were the victims, sometimes she could help:

> I saw a bat brought down by a Chinaman with a long bamboo, poor little thing, just mixing harmlessly with the stars and the sunset and then so outraged, I ran after the man and held out my hand for it, it was not hurt but could not fly from his hand – no bat can fly unless it has a take-off. He would not give it to me at first, but on my asking him again he most courteously did, so I carried it – it gnawing my finger nervously the while – till we got to a tree and there I left it letting the blood run to its head so as to revive itself.

*

On the day of departure, their ship being delayed, 'Shaemas and I crossed the river to Chungking to see what we could see. All down the river the poor dead soldiers were floating face down in procession.' They found the city in turmoil, with the Szechwanese army at one set of gates, and the Yunnanese 'with curious, choked, insane expressions on their faces', rushing to the opposite ones in the hope of making their escape across river. Stella found herself unceremoniously pushed behind a shop counter by Shaemas. When eventually they reached the riverside, firing could be heard from both ends of the city and bullets were splashing into the nearby water, which was full of drowned men. It was only thanks to a European motor boat that they got away.

In moments of danger, Stella behaved with exemplary calm. It was only afterwards that sometimes she collapsed, as she did that evening – in the most 'disgraceful' way – at a farewell party, fainting and fainting again in her hostess's bedroom, having fled there in the nick of time. Many a woman would have stayed there until the party was over; not so Stella. 'I made the greatest effort I ever did against my health to come in to the sittingroom to the others. I managed to dance with Shaemas . . . and then to sing my songs on an even sillier bleat than usual. . . . By God, I did feel beyond the end.' To cap the drama, they heard next day that one of the men who was dancing that night had been shot dead on his way home.

That same day, they got off in earnest, a party of three: Shaemas, his term of duty at Chungking being at an end, Stella and Florence. The third woman, Gladys, had already continued upriver. The evening of the first day brought its drama, when it was discovered that under cover of the previous day's commotion a large quantity of opium had been smuggled aboard. The British captain confiscated it, and no sooner had he done so than the ship was invaded by soldiers demanding it for their officers, and on the alarm's being sounded to summon a gunboat, one of them pulled out his knife and plunged it into the chief engineer 'almost to the heart'. By now the soldiers had retreated to their boat, but were still hanging on to the ship's side. 'In our superior British way,' Stella told Laura, 'we all stood looking at them and . . . they suddenly whipped out their revolvers and covered us':

You have no idea how our superior British manners collapsed. Shaemas tried to trip up and knock down me and Florence on the deck, I jumped with ease and grace about twenty feet and got behind the saloon door and looked from behind it at stately Shanghai businessmen entwined with stewards and Chinese sailors flattening themselves on their tummies behind the deckchairs.

The soldiers began to row round the ship and my saloon door began to seem inadequate as cover, but the Captain turned the searchlight on them and the gunboat crew was heard puffing towards us so the boatful of soldiers whisked off downstream without actually firing. I must say the time has seemed pretty tame since we left Wahusien.[11]

With the ship once more under way, Cupid began to have fun. Shaemas and Florence retreated into quiet corners of the deck to gaze into each other's eyes and 'coo', while Stella – her attractions perhaps enhanced by the passions surging within her – inadvertently made a conquest of the ship's captain. In off-duty moments he sat holding her hand and whispering sweet nothings in her ear, and before the trip was over had actually proposed, and been rejected.

At Wuhu Florence disembarked to rejoin her husband, and Stella had the pain of seeing Shaemas rush in despair to his cabin and fling himself face downward on his bed: 'I could see him through his half-open door, and his legs so limp. . . . It is no good, I am sick with wanting him.' When they reached Shanghai, 'a shade pink and blinking beneath his eye-glass', he vanished into the roaring city in search of somewhere to live. Watery-eyed, Stella went off to stay with her old flame A. J. Welch, who greatly to her relief seemed to have outlived the *tendresse* and tears of *Persia Maru* days; between themselves the episode was by tacit agreement buried – and of course was not to be revived in the presence of his charming wife Rosalind, who had come from England to join him, and to whom Stella took an immediate liking.

In any case, Shaemas Anderson was soon on the scene. The 'devastating discussions' about his hopeless romance began all over again, and he told her, though not in so many words, that he had in fact slept with Florence. For an intelligent man, Shaemas seems to have been extraordinarily obtuse as far as the state of Stella's emotions was concerned:

Shaemas said I seemed incredibly sympathetic, he didn't know that friends could feel each other's troubles so acutely, I admitted it did seem a little incredible and suddenly began to be squeaky and hysterical again, but I swallowed it and pretended it was a choking fit. Shaemas, looking at me with a startled eye-glass, suggested we should go home and talk there, so we did, and there he said, very kindly, that it had occurred to him that I had some secret sorrow and could he help me at all? He said it was his turn to help, and by God it certainly is somebody else's turn now.

I said that I had a secret sorrow sure enough, but that I would not burden him with it, except so far as to say that anybody in the world except himself would guess what it was. He looked puzzled and said it was either my health or money affairs, probably. He was offended, a little, that I would not confide in him, so I told him to imagine that we had all been acting out parts in a play – what would my part be, I asked him, just the part of an Ear? He thought it would be the part of an extraordinarily sympathetic yet detached friend. So I said he might go home now and try a little guessing.

His last words were that he was a timid guesser, so I told him he was a fool if he didn't know what I was driving at, and a brute if he did. He went away looking kind and perplexed.

Two days more of this frustration and the strain began to tell. On 30 October she wrote:

When I woke up this morning a thing happened, while I was thinking and wanting, that you would hardly believe – my head broke. I felt something quite definitely happen inside my head – and after that I was not acutely worried any more, but the most curious feeling was not being able to imagine anything or think ahead, or know anything except what I could see. I could not conceive the wish to write, the scattered lines of a poem I have thought of seemed to mean literally nothing. . . . Now looking back I think something like this may happen in a breakdown.

At their next meeting Shaemas was as much wrapped up in his own misery as ever, as clueless as ever as to the nature of hers. Stella tried a different tack: 'I made so bold as to say that when he lost hope of Florence in about five years' time he was not to marry some County Waterford young lady until he had come and consulted me, and I would show him another kind of girl, so he promised, although he said that all intelligent girls except me made him look and feel a fool.'

Next day she went down with pleurisy. She stayed in bed, and the letter that arrived from Shaemas, though it showed quite plainly that her broadest hints had failed of the mark, nevertheless had a note of tenderness, of amorousness even, that must have sent her temperature shooting up; it read as follows:

My dear little Stella,

(You will probably resent the implication of 'darned womanliness' in the word 'little'.) I am awfully sorry to hear that you are in bed to-day. Yesterday I wanted so much to brush back your charming boy–girl hair from your forehead and kiss you, but if I had you would have accused me of being kind.

I don't want to be kind and anyway kindness from me would be a presumption, but I would like to be a little tender and affectionate with you. It would be such a pleasure to me to caress anyone I am as fond of as I am of you. I suspect you are bored. I wish I could think of something that would have on you the effect of a really good non-soapy cocktail. But I can't. [12]

Stella wrote in her diary:

> When I look at this letter I think one of two things has happened. Either
> he knows what I feel like and is trying to comfort me, or else I have
> managed this thing damned badly, and if I had known the things that
> other women know I could have made him love me. I think we have been
> two shy people longing to comfort each other, and I ought to have known
> that, and been the first to kick my inhibitions away. I say that now, but
> when he is there I am afraid of being trodden on and repulsed. I am full of
> fear, even of his eye-glass, even when I would give anything if he might
> be a little thing so that I could hold him tight and comfort him.

On 3 November, she was up, but feeling 'a maniac and fierce tiredness
. . . a sort of active fever of panic that paralyses my mind and my feet'.
Shaemas took her to dine with friends, and in saying good night 'suddenly
kissed me in a most fatherly way, and I could hardly bear to let him go, and
he said I was like a nice sad child'. Two days later he took her out for a day's
boating. They had made a pact to try and enjoy themselves, and 'not to be
unhappy or talk of unhappy things'. Stopping to explore an attractive grove
of pine trees, they found that it concealed a graveyard; and it was here, in
this suitably melancholy setting, that Stella and Shaemas had their first
physical contact of any length:

> Shaemas and I sat down against a grave and held and comforted each other
> a lot. . . . I do not know whether Shaemas hurts me more than comforts
> me by holding me and kissing me, and doing my hair different ways. I
> know that I pretend terribly then, and afterwards it is worse, but Shaemas
> himself, I think, is a little comforted by letting me hold him tight when he
> cries. . . .

In any case, the relationship, with all its torturing irony, was pathetically
near its end, for in two days' time Stella was due to sail for Hong Kong. The
eve of departure, 6 November, inevitably was 'a wretched day', and in the
evening Shaemas gave her a farewell dinner at the Carlton Hotel:

> It seemed too noble a dinner just for me. We had very luscious cocktails,
> and champagne – the latter I didn't seem to want much of, being too dry at
> heart even to want to be happier, so Shaemas drank most of it, and for the
> first time in my knowledge got rather maudlin. We tried to dance . . . so
> we came home, and by Shaemas's orders I changed into my Chinese suit
> [a tunic and trousers of blue brocade]. I look as nice as I can look in that.
> But it was a very dreadful last evening; Shaemas stayed till half past
> two, and I think at any rate at first he didn't know altogether what he was

saying. He said that to him it was virginity that was a contemptible thing in a woman. He said that if I had submitted to a real sex experience I should never feel aloof or lost any more. He said that he couldn't love me that way now, because he could think of nothing but Florence, but he said in three months he would be wanting to make love to a Chinese woman, or me, or anyone handy. He didn't really put it so brutally as that – even half-drunk he was interesting and logical – and I think that there is more than a little truth in that point of view. It is true that the experience seems to have more part in making men and women complete than any other factor in life.

I also know well that were he sober, and if he wanted me he could have me now or at any time, whether he cared for me or not. I know that I, who thought myself so aloof and so boylike, am a woman as much as any other woman. Almost as much, but not quite perhaps, for I can get more emotion out of bodiless things than most women, or almost any man. But yet a great hardness and redness in Shaemas almost swept my mind clear of words, especially when he spoke of virginity in a woman being almost an insuperable barrier (quite insuperable, he said) to an imaginative man.

That rawly sexual image, inescapably a phallus urgently demanding virgin tribute, was thrown up from a level of Stella's subconsciousness hitherto untapped; alone, it shows how cataclysmic was the experience that had overtaken her.

All these things [she went on] I was unable to answer at all beyond admitting anything I felt instinctively was true, I was not shocked or anything like that but I couldn't say anything. I could have borne it better if he would have left me alone. I do not know why if he feels as he says he should want to hold me and kiss me. I asked him that, I asked him if he felt he had behaved quite fairly to me all this time in Shanghai, or whether he need have hurt me quite so much, he said he could not see what else he could have done, since we both get pleasure from kissing each other we might as well do it which is in a way true. . . .

The wild sea of Stella's passion had only a few moments left in which to dash itself hopelessly against the breakwater of Shaemas's matter-of-factness; next day, 7 November, they parted. It stood out in Stella's mind as 'the most appalling day I have ever spent':

I came on board the 'Porthos' for Hong Kong, and Shaemas came to see me off. He gave me things too womanly for me – long string of carved ivory beads. We sat in a little eddy place in the saloon, and Shaemas cried, and said he thought he had been a cad after all, and he would not allow himself to say anything, because he said he had said so much, too much, already. I felt sick. I only cried a little until he had to go away. I wanted him to go away while I looked out of the window, but I looked round and he came back, and then he went away. I cried then. And after a bit I thought I had missed a chance of seeing him as he crossed the wharf, and me never to see him again, so I ran to the deck but he was gone, and the ship moved away, and I swear with my real eyes I saw him again coming on the lower deck, and I ran down but he was not there. I am haunted. My brain is falling down.

Letters from Shaemas met her at each port of call, and at her final destination, Calcutta. He was starting for England in a few months' time on long leave, and over and over again he urged her to join his ship at Bombay so that they could travel the rest of the way together; but, shattered and humiliated as she was by their terrible eve-of-departure conversation – 'some of the things he said seemed for some reason to penetrate into the region of festering complexes' – she did not find it in her to reply. His scathing remarks about virginity had made her feel contemptuous of herself; she could hardly bear to look at women on the ship who seemed full-blooded, sexually ripe.

For his almost lover-like attentiveness in Shanghai she could find only one explanation: while he loved Florence with his body, he loved *her* with his mind: 'If I were an optimist I would say that it is possible he might some day wake up and realise not only that he had a love that is not body-love, but that I – even I – am not bodiless . . . but being me, I think he is a very full-blooded and sexually passionate creature who may always find the best of life in bodies.'

At the best of times, letter-writing did not come easily to Shaemas (no more did speech), but when his subject was delicately emotional, when states of mind and heart required definition, he was stretched to the limit. However, his effortful phrases – he never resorted to cliché – and pinched, rather childlike hand had a moving eloquence all their own.

Doggedly, humbly, he strove after honesty of word; even on the subject of his present misery over Florence he must surely have touched a chord of pity in Stella with his 'I doubt if I feel as much as you do, I haven't enough imagination. But all the same I am wretched enough in my own way.'[13] On the subject of herself he was just as true: 'I don't meet people like you once in twenty years. Do you think I can't recognise superiority when I see it? . . . Look here, I wish I could talk to you because I can express myself with a pen about as well as I can with a piano. But then I can't talk much either.'[14]

He was reading *Living Alone*: 'I'll write again and talk about it, and that will give you a chance to despise me. . . . Stella you know you are charming, I expect it's an unusual faery charm, silken hair, beautiful fay eyes (the latter I expect cultivated by your Nana), feverishly thin wrists and general air of I-ought-to-be-looked-after-but-I'm-damned-if-I-want-to-be. . . . I like and admire you enormously.'[15] On his hopes for happiness: 'I've a big capacity for resignation, I don't really expect anything, this is what some people call being a worm.'[16]

His fifth letter, which met her in Calcutta, listed the ways in which he thought they were alike: scepticism – 'we don't believe in anybody or anything, least of all ourselves'; unshockability (how wrong in a sense he was) – 'you don't judge people by actions or rules, only by your feelings'; self-pity – 'both damned sorry for ourselves, though in quite different ways'.[17] What marred this letter for Stella and provoked a crushing reply (though perhaps even that was welcome after her long silence) was his assurance – too baldly, too unimaginatively expressed – that when he had got over Florence (they had had a decisive meeting and she had rejected him), he would seek her out in England: 'I'll try and find you, and see if I can't be some use to you. I'll ask you to marry me.' Passionately involved as she still most certainly was, Stella had no desire to catch him on the rebound, to be a mere second-best.

Chapter Thirteen

Ahead lay India. Stella was conscious of arriving in the colony at an acutely sensitive time; indeed, in the light of recent happenings there some of her American friends had been predicting, not without a certain perceptible satisfaction, a speedy end to the British Raj.

In 1919 a new constitution had been proclaimed, which offered Indians a larger say in their own affairs than they had yet enjoyed under British rule. It had been well received. However, some incidents of unrest following shortly after had led to the swift passage of bills restricting civil liberty. These had been strongly resented. The new spirit of indignation had found a new leader in Mohandas Karamchand Gandhi, already proclaimed Mahatma, Great Soul. He had proposed a *hartal* (a traditional method of protest by cessation of all activity for a day), and it had led to riots. Amritsar proved the flashpoint. In April 1919 a prohibited meeting was dispersed by gunfire with large loss of life. The man who gave the order to shoot, General Dyer, was censured and retired, but India was shocked when the House of Lords voted in his favour, and a generous fund was raised in appreciation of his services. 'Cooperation in any shape or form with this satanic government is sinful,' declared Gandhi in quick response, launching a movement for non-cooperation which included resignation of government office, withdrawal from government schools and colleges, and the boycott of the forthcoming elections. Wherever she went in India, Stella was to hear the state of the nation warmly debated, the consensus seeming to be 'that the British era is coming to a close'.

Meanwhile, waiting on the dock at Calcutta to welcome her, a bright dot of orange, copper and scarlet, stood Miss Cornelia Sorabji, a friend of her mother's who had stayed with them in Norfolk Square days, a civil servant, a devout Anglican, a fervent champion of British rule. To Stella she was to prove most Christianly kind, though her domestic difficulties – she had not the knack of managing male servants – were to make staying with her a rather nervously exhausting experience.

At her flat above the Army and Navy Stores in Chowringhee, Stella opened her mail and found to her relief that it contained a largish sum of money; she would not have to draw on Aunt Florie's munificence after all. But she had to admit that she was not feeling well, and quickly found herself in hospital under the usual suspicion of being tubercular. As always, it was merely a question of lying still and trying to be patient until such time as the doctor told her what she knew very well already, that she was suffering another visitation from her old friends Julia the pleurisy and Bill the bronchitis. She was in hospital for a week, and it was probably while she was there that she started work on *The Poor Man*, the novel in which she was to draw on her American and Chinese experiences.

Cornelia's friends proved interesting, a satisfying blend of brown and white. There was a little rani in purdah aged twenty-one, who arrived in a sealed car, getting out of it into 'a sort of bathing machine of canvas without a floor, so that Chowringhee could see nothing but her modest brown bare feet. The stairs were cleared and our menservants warned, so all went well.' Married at twelve to a lunatic raja who died a year later, she might never see another man, never have any amusement more hectic than coming out to tea. There was an old Prince of Oudh, who called with his son, 'but the latter being a good Mahommedan son (though apparently about thirty years old), made no sound throughout except heavy sniffles – he had a cold'. Staunch British loyalist, the Prince hated Gandhi – 'catch him – hang him – hang all seditious leaders', he said – and predicted the massacre of four million Britons if the transfer of power was carried any further; the new Indian councils he thought useless: instead of putting in positions of power low-caste and out-of-caste scoundrels, the British should have invited princes and rajas to step forward (i.e. people like himself). There was a venerable swami of ninety with a face radiating perfect happiness and a shrewd notion of how to please Stella: 'The *sahib-log* become insincere through being in India, nobody could tell why,' he said, 'but she was fresh, and so sincere that he had not words in his tongue to say how sincere.'

Mindful of her duty to the London evening paper, the *Star*, to which she was supplying a series of articles on her travels, Stella persuaded Cornelia to take her to hear Gandhi address an open-air meeting of non-cooperating students. Expecting hostility – after all, Cornelia was a civil servant, and Stella British – they were charmed to find themselves courteously beckoned into a raised pavilion by some of the students, but above the noise of the thick-wedged, violently excited crowd, they nonetheless could hear nothing of what Gandhi said. Stella was determined to take a closer look at the great man. She applied in writing for an interview, saying that she was a journalist, and in reply Gandhi's secretary left a telephone message granting 'Mr Benson' an appointment that very day at the house of C. R. Das, a prominent member of the Congress Party. Arriving before time, she had leisure to note handweaving looms being carried about, and a library filled with English books, before she was ushered – a series of written questions gripped nervously in her hand – into the presence of 'a bent, rather pathetic looking man, apparently about sixty [he was fifty-two] with hollow cheeks and grey cropped hair and very bright smiling eyes'.

Donning benevolent horn-rimmed spectacles, Gandhi studied Stella's questions and answered them in extremely accurate but careful English. (Naturally he assumed that she wrote shorthand, equally naturally she was indisposed to admit that she did not; 'perspiringly' she took his words down in a make-shift shorthand of her own, and was hours deciphering it.) His answers conveyed radical hostility to the existing regime and the material-istic philosophy that underpinned it; on Amritsar, he quietly said that there was only one opinion conceivable.

The interview over, getting to her waiting taxi presented a problem: there was a garden to cross, and it was occupied by a large crowd calling for the Mahatmaji. In a moment he appeared, 'smiling such a broad smile at the people that it was very nearly a gently mocking smile', and immediately saw her predicament. He gestured to Das, who 'in a voice of thunder' issued a command, 'and the kind crowd in silence made a broad road for me to the door of my taxi'. Stella felt that she had been more courteously treated than she would have been as a hostile journalist in either England or the United States. She felt too that she had won an inner victory: 'I came home rather triumphant, for I had been so much frightened and yet so loth to funk the experience, and now my hunger for non-funking was satisfactorily appeased.'

The therapeutic effect of travel on an aching or a broken heart has long been understood, and at first it worked a half-cure on Stella – 'Only in the night I think and think of Shaemas,' she was writing early on – but after a month or so there was a total relapse and she admitted, 'I have Shaemas in my thoughts sleeping and waking.'

Of course there were plenty of distractions. A Lady Sanderson appeared, claiming cousinship – 'certainly our family seems to collect grotesque relations' – and invited her to stay. Fresh as she was to India, Stella knew not how honoured she was by Lady Sanderson's attention, until considerately informed by the lady herself. As consort of the Chief Justice of the High Court of Calcutta ('the fourth man in India' as was repeatedly pointed out), Lady Sanderson could make or mar a social reputation with a flick of her pen. Stella was quick to spot the devious self-flattery in her complaint of how very snobbish the ladies of Calcutta were: 'often they would not know people until she (Lady Sanderson) had set the seal of her approval on them by asking them to dinner'.

To Stella, Lady Sanderson was merely another in a string of ludicrous, self-important women whom fate had elected to throw in her path, and whose patronage irritated; persistently she refused to be impressed. As it happened, a surprise lay in store for both of them at the races. Having trailed humbly through the crowd in 'the foaming wake' of her hostess and arrived in 'a noble No I box', Stella was brought up against no less a personage than the Governor of Bengal, a brisk-looking, youngish man with crisp golden moustaches:

> at first Lady Sanderson left me out very much, and did not take the risk of introducing me to anyone, but – this is a dramatic and Cinderella-like story – after a bit the Governor, Lord Ronaldshay, caused me to be introduced to him, having heard of me I don't know how, and said be seated. So I sat on his right hand feeling exactly like Cinderella, I almost stuck my foot out for the glass slipper. . . .
>
> Forgetting that I had just been reading his speech on non-cooperation, I burbled about my anxiety to get to the bottom of Mr Gandhi's views, and said I was anxious to write him up from a rather sympathetic point of view for my newspaper – the Governor said 'Oh please, not too sympathetic.'

Titillated rather than shocked, it would seem, by such temerity, Lord Ronaldshay graciously invited Stella to come and talk to him again when she should have returned from Christmas camp. It was at a Government House dinner early in January that, confident for once that she was looking 'rather nice like a real girl in my new gold frock, my first shoulder-showing frock, oddly enough', she caught the seigneurial eye and was 'sent for': 'I sat augustly on the sofa like a real Calcuttarian, and he asked me how my revolutionary activities were getting on, and I burbled rather cheekily – somehow he instils cheekiness in me, I think it is his sparkling pincenez. . . . He said Gandhi was a very honest man.' Whether the Governor's condescension reflected greater glory on hostess or on guest is not easy now to judge, but Lady Sanderson could have had no further doubt about the presentability of her eccentric little cousin.

Christmas had been passed in the company of Cornelia, her brother and a large party at Bharatpur, as guests of the Maharaja. The Maharaja himself, 'a most beautiful, fawn-coloured young man', had met them at the station, and driven them to the camp with startling speed in his Rolls-Royce; he was a Maharaja with a particular interest in motors.

A huge marquee, hung with starred fabric, soft-carpeted and with windows of glass, real doors and a vast, castellated fireplace, had been erected to receive them. The private tents, laid out in 'long, echoing streets', were complete with verandah, electric light, small bathroom, writing table, notepaper and gold-printed programme of events. Soon guests were fraternising; Stella chatted with a good, submissive daughter of the Raj, 'of the kind that would conceal her wits and her more interesting interests with British bashfulness, pretending that she preferred tennis to reading, whether she did or not'. On Christmas Day there was church and Stella, who had not attended service for two years, took communion for fear of offending Cornelia. Afterwards she watched polo, and helped decorate a guava tree (apparently the nearest thing to a fir that Bharatpur could produce), from which later she was to receive a gift of a pearl brooch.

The Maharaja was anxious to indulge his guests in all their traditional customs, and at Christmas dinner there was a flaming plum pudding and plenty of champagne. At the appropriate moment he arrived in person, exquisite in a silver robe, 'a diamond tassel in his turban swinging over one ear, and all his breast tinkling with diamonds. Polite speech followed polite speech until we were soaked in port wine and politeness.' Stella had drunk more than enough to dispel her inhibitions, and without a qualm took a leading role in charades, which demanded that she jump on to the table and sing 'Heaven will protect the working girl'. She also rendered a 'rather shocking' song about Mr Noah that was one of her favourite setpieces. Retribution followed, and she felt 'rotten' all next day.

A note of lavish, and to European eyes slightly zany, extravagance characterised all the Maharaja's proceedings. There was a torchlight tattoo. The Maharaja had had each of his glittering Rajput warriors electrically wired up the back and along one arm; 'looking a little bashful at being thus turned into chandeliers', they executed lance exercises while the Maharaja at a central battery worked all the torches, of various and changing colours, that they held in their hands. There was a new extension to the palace, run up in a fearful hurry only a month earlier, when it was rumoured that the Prince of Wales was coming to Bharatpur – 'it was quite hideous', thought Stella. There was the ceremonial opening of the Maharaja's new motor transport works, when (her small son having blessed the silver key) the Maharani arrived in a purdah car to unlock the doors, and commemorative gold chains were distributed among the onlookers, while the Maharaja in a Ford did 'stunts' on a very sharp ramp. There was the day's hunting, with hawks and a caged lynx, which turned out to be 'a large fuss about nothing', for there were no kills. Intrepidly, Stella chose to sit not in 'a sort of motor car body on a high elephant as the olders and wisers did, I bestrode a saddle on a little elephant, and a mahout with a sort of pricker sat on its head'. If the hunt provided nothing else, it provided a picture: returning, 'we filed through Bharatpur city amid the cries of Salaam from the citizens under their torches in their booths, and outside a temple there were fierce, clashing yet sweet, bells ringing, which we heard as a background to everything else, until we went under the great pointed gate (like an ace of spades) into the moated fortress'.

Stella 'got up' a collection of limericks to present to their host in appreciation of his spectacular generosity, and (though he did not seem to understand quite what limericks were all about) he gave instructions for them to be printed in gold by his state printer.

Stella went on to Delhi, to Agra, to Allahabad, staying with British acquaintances. They showed her the sights, took her to the Club to dance and play bridge; it seemed to her that India was 'a country run entirely on gossip'. Into her flatteringly interested – and flattered – ear large numbers of Empire-builders, most of them 'morning posters', conventional people, anxious to conform, poured their life histories, the more willingly perhaps in that she was a rather unusual passing outsider; one man told her that she amazed him – 'so like a child, murmuring sweet nothings to a buffalo at one minute, and breaking out into remarks about God the next'. At Benares, 'globe-trotting with a cold eye', she stayed on her own at the Hôtel de Paris, but even then she was everywhere escorted by kind Britons: 'One of the reasons why I should like to be very strong and brave is to go by myself to Tibet. I will do it some day, if I live.'

At the end of January she was back in Calcutta, seated beneath an awning among other 'perspiring patriots', watching the arrival of the Duke of Connaught, an elderly son of Queen Victoria, who had come to India to open the new Bengal parliament. (Despite Mr Gandhi's best efforts 'quite a crowd' of Indians were present, she observed.) The opening ceremony made her cross, for women spectators had been given seats out of the chamber and out of hearing: 'We were allowed to see the pretty uniforms and curtsey to the Duke.' And she had a radical criticism to make of the ceremony itself, which might have pleased Gandhi, but if confided to Lord Ronaldshay would certainly have caused him to flash his pince-nez in her direction: 'I thought how dramatic it would have been if the new democratic Indian council had been opened by a man in the street, a little sweeper, dust-coloured and one of the millions, instead of by a pink royal duke, representative only of the paperweight era of the nineteenth century.' A few days later, representing the press, she managed to gain entry to the first session of parliament – whose members struck her as self-conscious and ill at ease, as well they might be on such an occasion.

At Cornelia's flat tension was building up about – of all things – mice. Implacably Cornelia was laying down traps, while the *khitmagar* was protesting that by so doing she was violating the laws of hospitality, 'since the mice are the miss-sahib's friends, and she talks to them all day'. Stella thought that anyway the mice were probably non-cooperators, who would retaliate by lying down all round the traps so that no one could get at them. For the sake of almost any animal Stella was perfectly prepared to look ridiculous, as she proved when in the full glare of Chowringhee she rushed to the rescue of a dried-out buffalo with buckets borrowed from the Army and Navy Stores: 'A buffalo always wrings my heart, it is so unlovable. Nobody ever thinks it is beautiful or pathetic, its figure is so ungainly and unsuitable for hot weather, its eyes are always crying, and everything it does is wrong.'

Before she left India, the loan of a book on psychoanalysis set her probing for the root of this chronic tenderness of heart, the acute sympathetic pain that she felt in the presence of any distress, human or animal, and she thought that she had found it in the stark contrast, in this respect, between her sleeping and waking selves:

> all my mind in sleep, and in the Secret Friend-making side is, unless I make an effort, full of thought of – and even joy in – pain, physical and mental. To my Secret Friend I am worse than God was to Job. This is how I know that Secret Friends are bad for me, and I think my conscious mind, conscious and ashamed of this subconscious and demonian dwelling on pain, and inducing a sort of rapturous cult of pain, rushes to the other extreme when it – the conscious mind – is in power. I carry my waking tenderness to the point of imbecility, I . . . actually feel the pain – physically feel it – that I see inflicted. . . .

The next step was to ask why it was so, and she found an answer in what Shaemas had said of her:

> I am thwarted in my sexual side – thwarted by my own intellectual inhibitions – I suppose Freud would discover what it was in my childhood that made me so walled away, so unable to be a real woman and express womanliness and receive manliness. I think the sleep-cruelty therefore is a form of subconscious revenge on the world because myself has walled me in, the tenderheartedness is a reaction against the vengeance.

Probably the experience that excited her most during her time in India was when she slipped her rein at the end of a boat trip with friends through the Sundarbans, the mangrove swamps south of Calcutta. Alone but for her manservant, she cadged a lift on a broken-dynamoed boat being cautiously returned to Calcutta by a morose Glaswegian engineer. It had no passengers other than she, no beds, no lights, and over their dinner together in the dark the Glaswegian told her many thrilling things: how a cholera case had been aboard the previous night, had been removed to hospital and had since died; how the ship's papers said she would capsize in any but calm waters – 'high waves were rushing in from the sea'; and how there were quicksands about, which, should they run into them, would suck them down. In conclusion he confided that he didn't think the engines would hold out, and he shouldn't have asked her, 'but he wanted company'.

Essex Benson, Stella's mother, at about the time of her marriage.

Ralph Beaumont Benson, Stella's father.

Stella, aged about nine.

Stella at about twenty-one, posing as a 'real girl'.

Laura Hutton in 1916, aged twenty-seven.

Witter Bynner, Bertha Pope and friend, California, 1919.

Stella with some of her pupils, Hong Kong, 1920.

Wedding day, 1921. Stella and Shaemas leaving St Mary Abbot's church, Kensington.

Stella at about thirty-nine.

Stella Benson. *Oil painting by Cuthbert Orde, 1929.*

Above: *Count de Toulouse Lautrec de Savine, KM, ex-Tsar of Bulgaria.*

Above right: *George Benson, Stella's elder brother, in his early forties.*

Below right: *'I saw a photograph in the* Tatler *or something of you and Cuffbut looking noble almost to excess...'. Cuthbert and Lady Eileen Orde, 1930.*

'In China ... where I shall probably spend the rest of my life, more or less, I hope to acquire that serenity of poise which only the Orient can give.'

Stella Benson. *Drawing by Wyndham Lewis, 1932.*

Stella with Penko on the verandah at Pakhoi, 1933, shortly before her death.

He gave her food for thought on another subject too, when he threw his knife and spoon across the cabin because his servant had not washed them properly: 'what an incredible fierce mysterious thing a sahib must be to that little boy [she reflected], full of ominous starings and swearings and menacing silences and strange quick angry actions. . . . we don't behave uncontrollably to each other, why should we to Indians, why not say in simple, and if necessary strong, words what we want . . . ?'

More offensive was an incident at Calcutta station involving Cornelia Sorabji. Stella was about to depart for Bombay, and Cornelia had come to see her off. She entered the carriage to help arrange her things – and 'a fat Irishwoman was rude to her, and said she wouldn't have natives interfering'.

Chapter Fourteen

On 10 April 1921, Stella left India 'without tears'; after nearly three years away she was anxious to be home. Having abandoned her Cunarder at Marseilles (for she wanted to 'buy a couple of hats' in Paris), she landed at Dover on 26 April.

England as viewed from the train was 'unexpectedly exciting. I saw real little lambs, and primroses in some cut down woods, and bluebells . . . everything was extraordinarily green and wet looking. . . . I thought the Thames had shrunk very badly – these Yangtses and what not have thrown my eye out.' There was a miners' strike in progress, and at her mother's new flat (she was now in Kensington Court, close to the Gardens) there was very little coal and no baths: 'Bloodless revolutions and what not are all very fine,' reflected Stella, 'but it is certainly trying to be a bourgeoise in these days.' She found the Gardens shut and, peering through railings, saw soldiers encamped, and horses picketed along the avenues leading to Kensington Palace.

Her mother – like the Thames – seemed to have shrunk. Stephen, reading for the Bar now, still lived at home; handsome, charming, 'clever in a smart way', he struck his sister as objectionably snobbish and shallow – saying, for instance, that if Cornelia came to London he would not receive her, as she was Indian. Laura, studying medicine at London University and undergoing psychoanalysis, introduced her to her college, Westfield – 'Oh such innocent jokes and bridling, virtuous ladies', Stella scoffed, disliking the place. In Hoxton Mrs Oneleg (who was now married to an octogenarian coster-monger) treated her to one of her tragedienne's welcomes: 'She was standing in her doorway and saw me coming, and then she looked hard the other way, and when I came up she shrugged her shoulders and shrugged her mouth, so to speak, and fell on me.' She went down to Hampshire to see Johnnie, who was enrolled in the *Mercury* naval training vessel at Hamble: 'I have little impulse of emotion towards Johnnie,' she confessed. 'I am a little afraid of him.' In Shropshire she found George struggling to keep alive a small engineering business that he had set up, which employed machinery of his own invention, and which he had been convinced would make money. Olive was expecting their second child. Lutwyche Hall was let and being beautifully maintained by, ironically enough, a *nouveau riche* family from Liverpool.

Nervously she went to Cookham Dean to see David. After so long an absence, would he remember her? She need not have worried:

When I whistled in my old way, he was struck to stone with his head on one side: 'Where have I heard that sound before and why does it thrill me?' Then he came, doubtfully and trembling, and when he saw it was me he jumped at me once or twice, and then he hid his face in my skirt and stood quite a long time rubbing his head a little in [it]. . . . He made me feel more as if I had come home than anyone or anything has since I came back.

As for Shaemas O'Gorman Anderson, he was a thing of the past: 'I want more than anything to be free of the thought of that unhappiness, and of anything connected with Shaemas,' she wrote, 'especially as it is now unlikely that I shall ever hear of him, much less see him, again.' There was no pressing reason for lingering in England, and six weeks after arriving she booked her passage to New York on an October sailing. America had no associations with Shaemas – and, besides, she had been promising herself a return trip to California: she wanted to camp out on the high sierra.

But it transpired that fate had something else in mind. On 25 June, returning to Kensington Court to change for an evening out in the West End with friends, Stella discovered on the hall table an envelope in a 'dear little schoolgirlish writing' that took her breath away. The letter within, inscribed on the stationery of a London hotel of no great note, suggested in tentative terms that she might care to contact the writer, might care to meet. 'I found this letter at home,' wrote Stella, carefully placing the treasure between the relevant pages of her diary, 'and was instantly nearly sick.' How many minutes passed before she was in a fit state to pick up the telephone cannot be known; but she spoke to him, and they arranged to meet that evening at ten o'clock in Regent Street, outside the Café Royal.

'The time went somehow,' and at the appropriate moment she parted from her friends in the cellar restaurant beneath Piccadilly Circus, and made her way to him. 'I was very polite and frosty and jovial in spasms. He said would the politeness wear off, and I said never again. . . . I am not even sure I care a damn now, I could have been sick at any moment, I am not sure of anything except that I was so excited all the time my heart was roaring like a wind in my ears.' The tone of their courtship duet was set: she the nervous, volatile soprano, with 'I want him to want me as much as I want him' as her tortured refrain, he the steadfast bass.

To Shaemas's first proposal of marriage, which thrust itself somehow into the middle of a stormy telephone conversation, 'I said no of course, and we went and fortified ourselves with cocktails at the Royal Palace' (a Kensington hotel to which he had moved). The idea of 'setting up together' for a trial period, mooted by modern-minded Peggy Boulenger, seemed rather a good one – before Stella reflected on how deeply it would hurt her mother.

In mid-July Shaemas went to Ireland to see his family. Frequent letters crossed the sea in both directions. At first he was very circumspect in tone, as if anxious that she should not form a false estimate of his feeling for her: 'I am thinking of you a good deal with pleasure and affection' were hardly the words of an ardent lover. Indeed, Shaemas himself seems to have realised that they would strike a chill, for next day he was writing again, this time weighing up their prospects of happiness together. Here again, no one could accuse him of being over-sanguine:

> It's incredible that your feeling for me should be at all a lasting one because I don't stimulate anything in you except perhaps the yearning to be loved. Am I at all your sort of person? I should say it's very doubtful. But let's try it, there's always divorce if we make a fearful mess of things. And after all fundamentally I'm decent enough, or I think I am, and I don't expect too much, and I shouldn't want to claw at your independence; and I shouldn't be jealous of your success. I could be very fond of you, Stella dear, but I'm suspicious of you, it seems to me I'm only a sort of disease for you.[1]

Alas, Stella saw in this honest and conscientious epistle chiefly 'semi-contemptuous pity' for herself, and pity still acted upon her psychological wounds like acid. Even so, she went to Dr Monckton to ask if marriage for her would be medically wise. He told her that it would involve a risk to herself, but that there was no reason why any children she had should not be healthy.

Within his matter-of-fact limits, Shaemas had begun to wax tender: 'I can't visualise your nose,' he confessed on 22 July, his twenty-eighth birthday, 'but I have your obstinate, almost ferocious little mouth, and the characteristic lines of your jaw and the jolly tilt of your chin. And the delightfully schoolgirlish effect of your slim little body.'[2] Next, he was wondering 'which of sixteen Stellas holds me most. There's the absurdly and charmingly soft-hearted child, the fierce, bridge-playing Stella, the mischievous, knee-crossed, chin-tilted, gay Stella, the sad Stella, the light-hearted Stella who shakes her goldy hair from side to side, the boy Stella in trews. . . .'[3] 'I love him more and more,' a bemused Stella confided to her diary, 'but I can't think what I shall say to him for the rest of my life.'

Evidence of his affection was accumulating certainly, but she wanted more, she wanted evidence of 'love'. It was beyond her to bear, she cried out confusedly in a letter that was never posted, that he might come to tolerate her (physically, she meant) only by pretending desperately to himself that she was Florence: 'You see, I am very much me, you couldn't have selected any "woman of the street" – any comforter – more furiously herself, more furiously unwilling to be anonymous.' But the best that Shaemas could do in that direction was to move cautiously from 'I don't love you',[4] on 9 August, to 'I'm half way to being in love with you',[5] two weeks later, making it sound uphill work.

Frighteningly rather than reassuringly, he added, 'I'm hungry for you physically.' 'I wish I knew more about bodies,' Stella put uneasily in her diary, 'but even if I did I suspect I should never be so conscious of my body as Shaemas is.' Unable to bear the suspense – she was not sleeping – peremptorily she summoned him to Cornwall by express letter, to Tintagel where she had come on holiday with her mother, Stephen and Evelyn Bengough; they had been joined there by her transatlantic friend of 1917, Brooks Henderson.

Over the years she and Brooks had kept in touch. His letters, warmly affectionate, rather fey, literary as befitted a college instructor in English (he had a way of commencing 'Bright Star' or 'Star of Stars') had pleased and flattered her; but she saw Brooks as something of a lightweight, an endearing eccentric, someone not to be taken quite seriously. Now – suddenly – 'little Brooks' was talking of love. 'Who is Brooks?' Shaemas had enquired more than once from across the Irish Sea – for somehow Brooks's name had slipped into one of her letters, and somehow – subtle is the game of love – when she had replied she had omitted to explain.

To complicate matters, another voice joined in, to make a quartet of it. A rhapsodic tenor, it wafted over the ocean waves from the eastern seaboard of the United States, from New Hampshire, and belonged to one Swinburne Hale. This curious character, radical lawyer by profession, romantic loner by pose, had first written to Stella when she was in China, extolling her work in high-flown, gushing style, and had kept up the correspondence, and the style, ever since. Stella was his little secret pen friend, with whom he enjoyed a bogus, make-believe intimacy that appealed to the Peter Pan in both of them. He had sent her his photograph. Uncannily what one would expect, it is the portrait of a not-so-young romantic actor – lean, finely chiselled features, burning eyes – and the odd thing about it is the way it has at some time or other been torn across the middle by a deliberate hand.

Up to this time Swinburne had told Stella little of his circumstances – writing to her was essentially a means of escape – but now, sensing from her letters that she was on the eve of committing herself to some other man, he was in a hurry to disclose his present dilemma. It was strikingly similar to that of the unfortunate husband of Lady Chatterley. His wife, a poetess obscurely unsatisfied by all he had to give, had absconded with a lover – 'a Russian Jew boy', 'mystical', 'unkempt' – who had been employed in his vegetable garden, 'just such a Russian as I have met a hundred times in deportation proceedings'. Nobly he voiced the hope that the gardener's 'great and silent love' would help his wife 'find herself'. Then he went on, 'I beg you, Stella, Stella, make no disposition of your life till we have at least met and touched hand. . . . If I cannot come to you, come to me. Beloved, I beg you.'

Stella was by no means the first woman to discover that when eventually lovers come, they come not single spies but in battalions; the irony, of course, was that the one she wanted seemed to be the least impassioned.

In response to her express, on 19 August Shaemas, looking white and strained, duly arrived in Tintagel. On being introduced to her mother and Stephen, he trembled visibly, but Stella did not mind: 'He looks very glassy but to me adorable when he is shy.' He had good reason to be strained, for he had come to England resolved to clinch matters with Stella, knowing that the only way to do it was somehow to convince her that he wanted her as much as she wanted him, if not with the same passionate intensity at least powerfully and sincerely. It was not a task he felt cut out for.

In fact he managed it rather well. He found words to soothe away her doubts, and a style of lovemaking that put her on easier terms with her own physicality and his. Though he may not have realised it, he had helpers in the sea, the skies, the rocky coves of north Cornwall. Historians may well be correct in insisting that the stone pile that rises above Tintagel has no right to its name, nevertheless King Arthur's Castle did very well as a setting for romance: 'after dinner he and I bullied the old castle keeper into letting us go on to the castle by moonlight. It was a bright crimson moon. We just loved each other – indeed Shaemas claims to – and seems to – love me now.'

On 24 August he took her to County Waterford, where at Ballydavid, a long, 'kindlooking' white house overlooking the Doone estuary, his mother and aunt were living out a typically Anglo-Irish rural existence: 'I think we do the poor but respectable business better in Ireland than they do in England,' Shaemas had said. Lady Anderson (General Anderson had been awarded a knighthood in 1919, a year before his death) was much as Stella expected – 'still and shocked' at the death of her favourite son, full of grievance against life, giving the impression to the people around her 'that it is tiresome of us to be alive when he is dead'.

As it happened, she was a woman who set great store by looks, and

Stella, neither conventionally pretty nor well dressed, will not have given satisfaction in that regard. To judge from snapshots, at around this date she favoured the earthy, 'peasant' look – homespuns, gathered skirts, folk embroidery. (At the first excuse, of course, she would be into her Mesopotamians, though doubtless they did not accompany her to Ballydavid.) Well as the style suited her, it was not elegant.

As to her coiffure, 'short hair' had scarcely reached rural Ireland, and the country people, seeing her cropped locks, thought she had been caught 'walking out' with an English soldier or policeman – in County Waterford such heads were found only on girls who had been summarily cropped by Sinn Fein.

Shaemas's sister and her husband were there, and quantities of friends and relations lived round about; but Stella was not amused at meeting so many 'toothy-smiled subalterns and screaming girls in chintz dresses. . . . I must say I felt cross, and crosser still when I thought of living in this appalling, uneducated, shrieking and slanderous society. . . . I think I was never in a circle I wish to see less of.' (Shaemas would come into Ballydavid on his mother's death, and there was talk of his taking up residence there.)

All in all it was not a merry visit; Stella was frisky even with Shaemas, giving him back his ring – a temporary one of jade, 'the same colour as a big wave as it curls over to break' – when he showed her the letter of renunciation that he had written to Florence. The letter had to be stiffened considerably before she would take the ring back. On 6 September they left Ballydavid and travelled back to England together. There they chose a proper engagement ring, a black opal set in diamonds, and a wedding ring. Then she took him to Shropshire to meet George.

In one sense the visit was a torment, for it showed Shaemas in a very poor light. 'It is almost impossible for a person with my weakness of character', Stella confessed in shame and exasperation, 'not to begin to wonder whether Shaemas is really as stupid as he seems here. . . . My God, shall I die of boredom married to a man who not only can't answer me back in a worthwhile way, but also might – as we loved each other less feverishly – damp down all my rather precarious little shoots of flame?' It was George's fault. With his engineering project on the verge of collapse, and a new mouth to feed (Olive had just had a daughter to whom Stella stood godmother), perhaps he was not in the most charitable of tempers. Whatever the reason, according to his sister he had no compunction in running conversational rings round Shaemas, and no scruple in showing his contempt. George was a 'brilliant' talker, Shaemas 'a very poor one'. He groped for words, and stuck doggedly to his line of thought against the current of the talk. Appalled at her disloyalty, Stella decided that he had 'very little sense of humour indeed'. If they had not been able from time to time to steal away to secluded spots and be happy 'loving each other', who knows how the visit might have ended.

The fact was that Shaemas's nervousness with George tended to dry up his words at the source. With Stella he had uncovered a thin spring of purest eloquence, on paper at least. When they were briefly separated he was writing: 'It will be so wonderful to love this fierce and beautiful Stella, and to live in a world refreshed by Stella's wand, never a tedious world, but a world softened and yet quickened and alive,' and – sloughing off the burden of his years of disgruntlement, confirmed pessimist transformed by Stella's wand into astonished optimist – he wrote movingly, 'To-morrow isn't the to-morrow of all the world except me. It's mine too.'[6]

When it came to arranging the wedding, Shaemas, who had no time for religion, wished for a registry office ceremony. In all probability Stella felt the same, but they yielded to family pressure: a church wedding it would have to be – but not an elaborate one, Shaemas insisted. 'An ordinary suit of clothes with a soft tie' was what he proposed to be married in, and positively there was to be no 'throwing of rice, old shoes, or such imbecilities. And I will make no speech.'

Only relations and close friends were present at the ceremony, which took place at St Mary Abbot's Church in Kensington High Street on 27 September 1921. Though no reference is made in Stella's diary, it is hard to believe that bride and groom were unaware of the significance of the date: it was a year to the day from their first meeting on the banks of the Yangtze, when they had recoiled at the sight of each other in such an inexplicable way.

Now in Stella's eyes, Shaemas, in a dark-grey suit, looked 'beautiful and calm but pale'; and she:

> felt truly well dressed for the first time in my life, in a sort of Beggar's Opera highwayman style, cut away velveteen coat with frilled front and cuffs, etc. It all seemed to happen rather from behind a veil from my own consciousness. It was like coming to from an operation – something very important seemed to be happening to Stella Benson but Stella Benson wasn't me. . . . I felt very giddy and dazzled all the time and at the altar nearly fell down a step but Shaemas neatly caught me.

As they came down the aisle Mrs Oneleg, in a new white hat, stumped out on her crutches and thrust three white roses into Stella's hand.

> We came down to Cookham Dean in the afternoon. I am perfectly happy, Cookham Dean was in a sort of serene mist of October sunshine, and we saw the sun sink through the beechwoods over Marlow.

For a week the diary entries cease.

There is ecstasy for me in the thought of giving you a happiness in your body [Shaemas had told her]. I will make you love your own body as I do. My starry friend, there can be such happiness of the body if it is a real love. At least for me physical love means so much, it means tenderness and courage and unselfishness.[7]

But on the honeymoon Shaemas may not have had much chance of making his promise good. On the day after the wedding, Stella went down with food poisoning ('ptomaine poisoning' in the medical language of the day), was 'terrifyingly ill for some hours, fainting and fainting again . . . and for the rest of the week was most depressingly exhausted and upset'. Her sickness apart, it was, Stella reiterated, 'a perfectly happy time'. The only inharmonious note was struck by David, who recognised in Shaemas a serious rival for Stella's affection, and did not scruple to let him know it.

Back in London, Stella was writing with a yearning compassion of this new husband and his struggles with life. Compassion is a fine thing, but it can easily turn to belittlement; it would be reassuring to hear from time to time of some of the things that Stella found in Shaemas to admire:

Often it touches me in some very tender and inarticulate place to think of the 'me's' of all creatures. Of everyone trying his best to be inoffensive and even pleasing, of everyone puzzled to think – how can they hurt me so – this me which is my only me, the only aspect I have to present to the world, my only asset. . . .

When Shaemas talks about his me, it makes me want to cry, there is something so childlike and groping about the core of everyone's personality, once you begin imagining it – Shaemas behind his darling little anxious eyeglass trying to be a normal and valuable member of the community is so adorably pathetic, somehow.

Part V

Writer and Wife

Chapter Fifteen

On 28 October, after a fortnight at Ballydavid, Stella and Shaemas set off for New York, their intention being to spend part of the winter of 1921–2 driving across the United States by the southern route, the only route practicable at that time of year.

At that date it was rather a daring plan. Nowadays someone wanting to drive from New York to California by way of the Deep South has only to point his car south-west on US State Highway 95, head to Philadelphia and continue on roads of similar status as far as New Orleans, where he turns west on US 10 and carries on to Los Angeles with little, as far as road surface is concerned, to worry about. In 1921 things were very different, for although, with almost nine and a half million motor vehicles raring to go, Americans were well aware of the need for new and better roads, and plans for federal highways and integrated state road systems were under urgent discussion, not a great deal had actually been done. The Lincoln Highway, envisaged as a hard-surface road running from coast to coast, existed only in fragments and (as Shaemas and Stella learned from two girls who had braved its perils) petered out altogether as one went west and became 'only a blazed trail'. The journey that *they* had in mind, in the eyes of most of the Americans they met, was adventurous, hazardous and tough.

Their first necessity was of course a car, and in New York they picked up a Model-T Ford, a 'Tin Lizzie', the unadorned, functional little four-seater that had made its appearance in 1908, and since then done more than any other single car to put America behind the steering wheel. A humble black box fitted high on narrow wheels, it was designed for reliable performance on the nation's farms and in small towns in an age of impassable roads, isolated farmsteads and garageless villages. It was simple to drive – with its three pedals for forward, reverse and stop, its throttle mounted on the steering column – and indeed the Andersons were told that it was 'fool-proof'. The obvious choice for them was the touring car with its fully collapsible roof; they called their particular model 'Stephanie'.

With very little experience of driving between them, and no knowledge whatever of motor mechanics, they drove Stephanie round and about New York for a few days by way of practice (no doubt taking for granted the noisiness of the engine and the comparative bumpiness of the ride), and then hired a chauffeur to drive them on the first lap of their journey (as far as Philadelphia, where they were to stay with Miss Mott) and explain the car's mechanical mysteries on the way. Expert instructor no doubt Al was, and should not be blamed for the panic that overcame Stella (as she told her *Star* readers in an article reprinted in her first volume of travel sketches, *The Little World*) when he abandoned them in a wet Philadelphia. At that date, a windscreen wiper was an optional extra on a Ford, and the Andersons had not had one fitted:

all the outside world was a-dazzle and a-squirm through the glass. But still we moved successfully.

Something was wrong. I had committed a crime. Two policemen were running towards us gesturing insanely, each shouting something different out of the corner of his mouth. Stephanie suddenly fainted, and, as she did so, the position became dreadfully clear . . . Stephanie had fainted on a tram-line. . . .

'Well say, what's eating you? Step on her can't you?'

'What do I step on for God's sake?'

I stepped on everything, I tore everything from its socket, except the hand-brake, which I left gripping Stephanie's vitals. Yet Stephanie woke to the fact that she was foolproof. She moved in a series of appalling spasms with a loud grinding noise. We were safe in a side street before she fainted again.[1]

On 21 November they were off in earnest. As far as Richmond, Virginia, Stella reported 'good' or 'fairly good' roads – though taking a wrong turning out of Annapolis they landed up 'axle deep in red mud'. All through the South, mud ('gumbo' to the natives) was to be the chief hazard – some places were 'absolutely bog . . . two very deep ruts filled with rushing water', and if a couple of cars met head on there was nothing for it but to dismount and hoist one of them out of the way. In Texas, Arizona and New Mexico, sand and the 'living rock' took over.

Frequent punctures were normal, expected mishaps. Normal too was difficulty in starting, for which the Model-T was notorious. 'Something in Stephanie's front' snapping, and brake failure were more noteworthy, as was the occasion when Stella miscalculated in trying to overtake, jumped a ditch and ran 'violently' into some woods, smashing Stephanie's windshield and lights. Fortunately for them a nationwide network of Ford repair agents existed, with a fixed scale of charges for dealing with every emergency.

It was in a dried-up, bouldery river-bed in Arizona that late one evening Stephanie stuck, the petrol in her tank too low to allow her to take the steep ascent out. It was unwise to camp, for a sudden rainfall in the hills could make a river-bed a deathtrap. What were they to do? Suddenly Stella had an idea: if they half-filled the tank with water from a nearby pool, perhaps Stephanie might reach the top of the bank. She did, and there she 'died'. They slept amid the cactus, and in the morning Shaemas struck out across the desert to the nearest town, eventually reappearing in a car, in company with some travellers from Montana:

'Why, look who's here!' said the chief gentleman from Montana, speaking out of Stephanie's digestive organs. 'You got water in your tank.'

We said no word. 'It's these garages – they're all as slick'n crooked as they can be these days. If a guy looks kinda green these garages'll hold him up for his bottom cent. . . .'

We said no word. The kind man from Montana let the water out of Stephanie's tank and gave us enough gasolene to take us to the next town. He left us still green but grateful. Even more green and more grateful than we gave him to suppose.[2]

It was at Montgomery, Alabama, that Stella first fell ill, vomiting repeatedly: 'I hope I am not going to have a baby, but I don't think I could be so violently ill if I were' (she very much wanted a child, but not just yet, and not despite precautions). And it was at New Iberia, Louisiana, that she went down in a more serious way, with bronchitis. They were trapped in New Iberia for seven days, and Shaemas got desperately bored (though he was 'so darling and kind and careful'). Lying in bed, Stella had leisure to ponder their relationship, to wonder if in fact they were 'the right people for each other, whether perhaps I sometimes worry him, and he sometimes damps me. However, he is very good to me, and though he is slow and often overpoweringly immovable and silent, he is never silly and never hysterical or unreasonable or childish as I am.'

It was in Texas that they had their first row, a dispute about driving, Shaemas complaining that Stella was giving him an 'inferiority complex' by insisting on taking over whenever they came to 'difficult bits'; he had no confidence in himself, he said, unless other people had confidence in him. Stella countered that his extreme shortness of sight worried her. But it was too late for reasonableness; they 'hurt each other very much, nearly decided to sell the car and part, and were extremely miserable'. However, they were pals again for Christmas dinner, taken in the desert among cactus and prickly pear – 'an immense store of Xmassy foods', topped up by bacon and potato chips, fried on an open fire.

When not camping, they sampled a variety of overnight accommodation, from the very occasional sophisticated hotel to the humblest shack offering beds. They met much kindness and some quirkiness too. There was the gentleman at the Dixie Hotel, Andalusia, Alabama, who upped and asked, 'How much more do you like this country than your own?', to which Stella replied: 'No better, of course. England is my country and I like it best, just as if you went to England you would naturally like America best.' Metaphorically speaking, he spat, and came back – 'Yes, I reckon I shouldn't think much of England!' Rashly, Stella made a remark to the effect that some Americans seemed hardly to have noticed the war, to which – to her extreme indignation – the patriot replied: 'Not notice it! I should say we did notice it. We won it.'

By 10 January they were in California, and by 12 January it was recognisably the California that Stella loved. She was 'bursting with happiness to be back'. Driving was easy now, and on 14 January they scored their record run for the trip – Santa Barbara to King City, two hundred and fifty miles. At Saratoga were the kind Goodriches, and 'for the first time for months we were really easy and comfortable and under no strain. A perfect bedroom too, even cigarettes supplied.' They had covered four thousand miles, and with pauses it had taken them fifty-five days.

After a week they moved to a 'funny little flat' in Berkeley. San Francisco was 'enchanting and exciting', and most of Stella's former cronies were around (fortunately for their married harmony, Shaemas was not much taken with Bertha Pope), so that for the whole of their three months' stay they never lacked company. The poetry club resumed sessions, there were excursions to the mountains, and a great many parties.

Stella tried and failed to secure a job for Shaemas at the university as instructor in Chinese; his 'inferiority complex', she complained, made him 'a deplorably abashed and ineffectual candidate'. She settled down to work on *The Poor Man*, fed and refreshed by her surroundings. For in one sense *The Poor Man* is a love song for San Francisco and the Bay area, their visual splendours contrasting with the pettinesses and squalidities of the human actors. In this connection one is reminded of her outburst of disillusionment two years before: 'I am worn out by these people, who only use these skies and this golden and intoxicating country as an excuse for hugging each other.'

The story is set in the spring of 1919, the time of Stella's first visit to California. It opens on a party in a studio high up one of San Francisco's hills:

It was night-time and the great California stars hung out of a thick dark sky. Perhaps the stars gave the waters of the bay and of the Golden Gate their luminous look, as if there were lights set in the floor of the world, a great light overlaid by fathoms of dark vivid water. Lights were spread like a veil over the hills on the near side of the bay and, on the far side, the mountains stood ankle deep in stars.

Inside the flat a group of bohemian third-rates are busily downing cocktails and asserting their egos ('what interesting people they were trying to be', as Stella remarked in a different context). One is Rhoda Romero, a socialist artist, 'insolent, handsome and contented' (except that she was rich), who shares the flat with a Russian Jew: 'They had married in a moment of inconsistency but had since divorced each other in order to live together with a quiet conscience'; another is Mrs Melsie Stone Ponting, a divorcée who lives mainly to be kissed.

Seated on his own, a despised 'poor thing', is a youthful Englishman, Edward Williams, the spectacularly unheroic central character. He is deaf (and we learn what it is to be deaf at a party – one overhears a perfectly prosaic and ordinary person say, 'That was the song of the twelve eagles after the emeralds of the South Sea lost their fragrance,' and another add, 'They were crushed the day the love-tinker died on a hill of violets in Vienna'), he is spotty of face, he has a despicable inferiority complex and a weakness for cocktails. Later, we have him pledging a borrowed bicycle and sponging off the husband of a friend. Yet with all this he manages to be not unsympathetic, and one critic, the novelist Forrest Reid, put his finger on why: 'We all carry Edward within us . . . the potentiality to become Edward, and gradually while we read we begin to feel that perhaps, even now, we are a good deal more like Edward than we know.'

Into the room walks Emily, the beautiful English girl with 'fierce, almost agonised eyes', for whom Edward will soon be prepared to chase half over the Far East. Instantly he thinks 'What a miracle', and chokes on a gin-old-fashioned. When she leaves, he follows:

Before Edward R. Williams had time to think another thought, there he was looking down a precipice of street at a deliciously small Emily a hundred feet below. San Francisco streets often nose-dive like this. The grass grows between their cobble-stones because nobody dares to use them except pulley cars and persons with very strong ankles. Emily was walking gingerly down. Beside her, plucking protectively but ineffectually at her sleeve, was Banner Hope. . . . Edward followed. . . . when he reached Emily she was alone.

'Wez Bope gone?' asked Edward.

'His tram came first,' replied Emily. 'I'm waiting for a Ferry tram.'

'Tram . . .' triumphed Edward, who had long been exiled among mere street-cars. 'That's the stuff to give 'em. . . . Tram . . . Do 'em good, by Gosh. . . .'

There was no Ferry car in sight.

'Would-nibby fun,' remarked Edward, 'if we had supper at Jove Pinelli's? Night yet young. . . .'

Emily paused a minute. 'Yes, would-nib,' she agreed.

Emily, though born in Kensington, had no ladylike instincts.

The Poor Man captures memorably what it is to be young, alone and pretty much at sea in very foreign surroundings. When, later, Edward escorts Emily home to Berkeley on the ferry, we are back with the love song for San Francisco:

The air was full of lights and stars, but the water remained sombre except for a white strip spun across the bay by the moon. The noise of the water growling at the bows of the Ferry so slightly occupied the silence that the screams of the trains on the Oakland side were clear to the ear. Clear to the sight were the trains themselves, little swift snakes of light pursuing one another about the bay's edge and out on to the distant piers.

On the human scene, Stella is at pains to let us know just what it is in American culture that she detests. The satire is corrosive. Edward gets a job as door-to-door salesman, touting *Milton for Our Boys*: 'It was not, of course, "in poetry". Poetry is unhealthy for children, unmanly for Our Boys.' He is taken up by 'a typical young woman of the Wild West', a Jewish girl called Mame, who boasts all the time of her 'beaux'; she introduces him to her Pop, a retail merchant who picks his teeth a great deal and spits, and calls his house not a house but a 'home': 'We who can live in houses and can see the word Mother in print with dry eyes or hear the glugging of someone else's baby over its food in a cafeteria without vicarious domestic ecstasy, must seem very coarse to Americans. However, the missionary movies are with us now. We shall all no doubt eventually suffer a change of heart.'

The Poor Man has no coherent plot. All one can say is that Edward's will-o'-the-wisp, hard-shelled, suffering little Emily disappears China-wards, hopelessly in love with another man, and that Edward follows and (after threading various oriental scenes and adventures) eventually catches up with her, broken-hearted in a dingy hotel in Shanghai. He offers her his love, but he would not be the hapless 'poor man' of the title were it not furiously, cruelly rejected.

Shaemas and Stella left San Francisco on 22 April 1922, paused in Philadelphia and New York to see friends, and took ship for Ireland on

5 May. On the voyage Stella completed *The Poor Man*, and did the final retyping while staying at Ballydavid. For both of them it was a duty visit, holding out no hope of pleasure; this time they found Lady Anderson engrossed in trying to make contact with her son's spirit with the aid of a Ouija board. Stella left Shaemas there and went on to London on her own, delivering her typescript to Spenser Curtis Brown with 'a few deprecatory remarks'; they were probably about its causticity – for in her diary she had put, 'I think parts of it are very good, though I am in some ways sorry that it has to be occasionally spiteful.' Without examining the book, Curtis Brown took her at her word, shook his head regretfully and said, 'loveable books are so much more saleable'. But when he came to read it he was delighted, called it 'amazing', and thought 'it ought to make them sit up'.

From Dr Monckton Stella came away 'feeling complacent, he thinks I am such a plucky sort of bean'. In Hoxton Mrs Oneleg, bosom prominently adorned with a locket showing Stella 'with a very shiny nose', gave her a warm cockney welcome, and together they sold fruit off her stall in Pitfield Street, and drank cups of thick, sugary tea with 'false milk' in it at a coster dive afterwards. Her mother was anxious to be kind and helpful, but there was a hiatus of communication between them (which amused Stella) on the question of marital sleeping arrangements; at her flat Mrs Benson had only a *double* spare bed, and this, she strongly felt, would hardly suffice when Shaemas arrived. She wondered whether Shaemas would very much mind putting up at a hotel – after all he and Stella would be able to meet every day. 'What is this older generation made of?' Stella asked herself. 'Do the women even forbid themselves to think of wives "behaving married" with their husbands?' When Shaemas finally appeared, she moved with him into a hotel.

Alas, in London he was proving less than satisfactory as a husband, and in new ways – though among complaints Stella has the grace to interject 'I hope he is more or less satisfied with me, I shouldn't be.' But Shaemas had no 'foreseeing imagination', no 'London instinct' (an Irishman long exiled abroad, why, one asks oneself, should he?), and very little energy. She was even having to help him buy collars, and put him on buses. Moreover she was suffering complicated agonies at seeing him out of his depth with her 'gay, clever friends' – people like the Boulengers:

It hurts me dreadfully to see Shaemas not understanding them – them incredulous of his seriousness and despising his heaviness, their trying to persuade themselves that his is perhaps a subtler playing the fool, trying to adjust themselves to his lack of response. When at times he understands that people are not serious in something that has been said – when he even perhaps responds, I feel as proud and surprised as though he were a baby saying first words. But it isn't often.

And there was another worry: Florence Harding was in London. From Ireland Shaemas had written, very matter-of-factly and no doubt thinking that he was being splendidly honest and straightforward, to say that when he got to London he meant to look her up. Perhaps understandably, Stella had been very much upset:

> She has been his mistress and I am convinced wants to be again. . . . I wish terribly now that the adventure of marrying Shaemas could be over. . . . any love he has for me – and I really know he loves me now – doesn't seem to make him at all imaginative about what loves owes or love expects. . . . it isn't his seeing Florence I mind, it is his wanting to see her.

Such woman's subtleties bored and depressed Shaemas. Convinced that no harm could come of it, he was determined to see Florence. In bed at their hotel, Stella brooded into the small hours, and then bethought her of the hurt wife's classic recourse, 'so that at last I dressed and went away meaning to go back to Mother, but when I got to the hotel door I remembered I could not get into Mother's mansions much less the flat, as I had no key and it was 3 o'clock'. Though Stella felt it to be 'outrageous', Shaemas met Florence and went on meeting her.

Then, on the last day of June, the painful business of Florence was swept aside by a much greater trouble. Later Stella ran a line of loops through a few consecutive lines of diary here, though she allowed passages to remain that clearly indicate what the new trouble was. Shaemas had reason to suspect the recurrence of syphilis, contracted during his early years in China; he feared it would put an end to their marriage, by making her refuse to live with him, 'but of course it does not'. She did not blame him, either for the original slip or for not telling her what its consequence had been. Instead she blamed his mother, '*she* with her idiot adoration for uncontrolled "manliness", for Byron – Don Juan – brought him up really to bring sorrow of this kind upon himself – a child of twenty-one, untrained in self-control – in a lonely port in China'.

But she was overwhelmed with grievous emotion and, very much upset and coughing up blood, on the day after receiving the news was removed to her mother's where she stayed in bed for three days in a state of acute depression; when Shaemas came to see her, she was not always 'kind'.

But when once he was safely cured – 'which they say he can be' – she would have a child, she decided. A day spent in the company of George's children had made her see that 'heartless' as she might be towards adults, she was not, 'somehow, heartless about babies or little children'. The risk to herself of bearing a child she was prepared to face, 'as long as it wasn't born slack or half-alive mentally – or very moody, like me'.

There was another attractive encounter with a slightly older child, when she went to Sussex to visit the Welches, who were on leave from Shanghai. Denton,[3] the youngest of their three sons, she recalled, 'was always my friend'. He was seven now. 'A flea would despise the amount of lemonade I've got, Mother,' he quaintly remarked, 'in a slow, earnest, thoughtful voice . . . which is most charming'. Stella was to meet Denton Welch again in 1925, and pronounce him 'the nicest little boy I have ever met . . . he always wants to understand everything to the last degree. "How did they know, Stella, at the beginning, that a terrier's tail would look nicer cut short? Did one have its tail cut off *by mistake*? Or did they take two dogs and cut off the tail of one and put them *side by side*?" All very determined and emphatic.'

Her own adopted Johnnie Granville seemed to be shaping well too: 'Johnnie', she decided, 'is the most hopeful of my hobbies.'

The blow that Shaemas and Stella had suffered jointly had not, unhappily, drawn them closer together. Her feeling of shocked dismay, his feelings of shame and hurt pride came between them in a way that would have seemed inconceivable eleven months before, when they were preparing for their wedding. There were 'devastating' scenes, and when on 1 September they boarded the *Dongola* at Tilbury for the voyage to Hong Kong, Shaemas's leave being nearly over, for her part Stella was profoundly depressed, deeply pessimistic about what lay ahead:

> I get no pleasure at all out of going to China with such a glum grievance-monger as Shaemas repeatedly shows himself to be. It seems to me that by some horrible accident – the fault of which rests on me, for it was I who loved him – I have given up everything – my friends, my health, my amusement, my adventuring and the pleasures attendant on my writing – for nothing – to spend the rest of my life in a filthy climate with an unimaginative gloomy fussy and absolutely unsympathetic companion, only quick to speak when he has a grievance. I was mad last year.

When the Andersons reached Hong Kong they learned that Shaemas was appointed Assistant Commissioner at Mengtsz (pronounced 'Meung-tse'), a small town in Yunnan, the most southerly province of China, bordering on French Indo-China. It was the station that he had applied for on account of Stella's health, and 'the only really healthy station in the Customs'.

One would give a good deal to know what Shaemas was feeling – about his marriage, about Stella, about their prospects of happiness together in China. In tracing the emotional chart of their marriage, one has only Stella's reports to go on; and – perhaps on the principle that good news is not news at all – she has more to say about Shaemas's shortcomings than about his strengths, dwells more on the times when things are going badly between them than on the commonplace times when they are going rather well. But when she does find occasion to praise him it is for warmth of heart, honesty, kindness, courage, readiness to forgive, all of which would surely come high on anyone's list of qualities to be desired in a companion of lonely exile.

Chapter Sixteen

It was not at all unusual for a Customs man to return to China from home leave with a bride in tow, and a question in his heart as to how she would settle down.

Mr and Mrs Anderson left Hong Kong on 17 October 1922 with a fairly lengthy journey before them. To get to Yunnan Province in those days meant a two-day voyage to Haiphong in Tonkin, French Indo-China, followed by a long rail-trip north. Alas, the journey did not augur well. On the boat Stella went down with bronchitis and high fever and had to be painfully cupped by the ship's doctor; at Haiphong Shaemas and a steward between them assisted her down the gangplank into a ricksha, which whisked her off to hospital, where the *médecin supérieur*, who plainly thought she was consumptive (she was coughing up blood) detained her overnight. (In the ricksha she had been sufficiently *compos mentis* to note that Haiphong was 'a rather pretty, clean looking city', and to make detailed observations of Tonkinese dress.) The outlook was further dimmed when Shaemas heard that Eddie Pritchard, whom he was to replace at Mengtsz, had no orders to leave, and presumed that the Andersons were posted to an outlying bungalow.

When, two days later, they set off along the Red River valley on a 'primitive' train with 'grotesque' food, Stella was still by no means well. By the time they reached the 'very dirty' Tonkinese inn where they were to spend the night she was exhausted; Shaemas too was fretted beyond endurance, and kicked a tiresome waiter out of the room: 'the first time I have seen this done, and I hope the last', acidly commented his wife. Next day she was still very poorly, but at least had the consolation of a puppy on her lap to fondle as, dizzily and spectacularly, they climbed into the Himalayan foothills, penetrating tunnels and skipping gorges in a triumph of French engineering. At 4500 feet, they had their first sight of the place where they were destined to spend the next two and a half years:

our train seemed to have reached the sky, and ran mildly and austerely over sort of downs of grass and flowers, perforated with great gashes of bloodred earth, and suddenly we were looking from very high up over an enormous plain set in a ring of mountains like long red receding waves on a beach; in the middle of the plain, among crops and beside an indeterminate lake, was Mengtsz, a round town set in trees.

Yunnan Province is blessed with moderate temperatures, clear skies, and rich, covetable mineral deposits. It was with the exploitation of the latter in mind that the French, at the turn of the century, had pushed through the railway. But the region had to wait until the establishment of the People's Republic to be systematically developed. In the 1920s it was still an industrial backwater, its hinterland home to tribes of shy semi-nomads, and infested with gangs of bandits who periodically issued forth to plunder the villages and waylay, and sometimes capture and hold to ransom, the unwary foreigner. Mengtsz, some fifty miles up the line from the frontier, served as a border post of the Customs; it was manned by five Europeans and a handful of subordinate Chinese.

Stella's first impression of the staff compound (where at Shaemas's positive insistence they were after all to be temporarily housed, in three rooms in the house of a French bachelor colleague, Monsieur Dunod) was rather encouraging:

a fine well-treed compound full of birds and shade and the sweeping lines of eucalyptus trees and big rose trees, and rather dull flowers in pots. The birds are magpies and egrets and hoopoes and there are unseen birds singing constantly. The three houses . . . are built Chinese style with upturned wavy-tiled roofs and whitewashed walls and rough wooden pillars with a little blue and green painting beneath the eaves.

But she was deeply depressed about her health, and on the third evening 'rather collapsed nervously': 'I cannot breathe without so much wearisome effort, and cannot feel anything but sick and weak and deaf and done, and seem to get no better. Shaemas was very good to me. But it seems to me I have outlived myself. I am only a quarter alive now. . . .'

Her heart had sunk on meeting the two English couples who, she presumed, were to form the staple of their social life in Mengtsz. Commissioner and Mrs Bethell were a kindly, shy, middle-aged couple, who struck her as quite commonplace. Eddie and Betty Pritchard belonged to precisely the section of society she most disliked, the class she designated 'Lower Tooting', and saw as philistine, overmindful of its Ps and Qs, unbearably self-satisfied and complacent:

Mr Pritchard looks exactly like a seaside young man and has that accent and brisk cocksure manner, you can see his unformed insignificant face on any promenade or in the expensive seats of any Pierrot show on the coast of Britain, and he wears the orthodox tweed coat and grey flannel trousers. Mrs Pritchard has a pretty but mean face and is quite illiterate. They both – though in some ways kind – took great trouble to discourage us about everything at Mengtsz, there was not a single domestic or intellectual or social essential for our future about which they would allow us to harbour hope – again the lower middle class love of imparting bad news.

Pritchard improved on acquaintance, but Stella never liked his wife; a few weeks later she was to note with annoyance how 'Mrs Pritchard is really proud of her shortcomings, though she always introduces them with an "I'm afraid": "I'm afraid I like things new and spruce, I don't like all these antiques. I'm afraid I'm always busy with the children and housekeeping, I don't have time for art or any fal-lals."' The proud summit of the Pritchards' literary taste, she was to discover, was the popular light fiction of Hall Caine, Jeffrey Farnol and Ian Hay.

Their first week at Mengtsz saw them provided with cook, coolie and boy. Stella seeming stronger – though in a few days she was to go down with pleurisy – they exchanged courtesies with the small French community, the consul, doctor, railway manager, schoolmaster, bank manager and their respective wives. It was a period of intense strain for both of them, and culminated in an eruption of matrimonial bad feeling, their most serious to date, Stella descending to saying that she hated Shaemas, and he, alternately angry and tearful, telling her that she humiliated him, that she did not know what tenderness was, and that they had better part. The 'horrible fight' and the heart-searchings it provoked in Stella are the best clue we have to the state of their relationship after just over a year of marriage. It suggests that Stella had arrived at the stage of disenchantment that awaits many of those who marry when they are 'in love'; and that Shaemas was finding marriage to a temperamental woman in perilous health a more difficult proposition than he had bargained for. At Haiphong he had been shocked at how ill she was, and hardly thought she would recover. There is no knowing how much or little she had told him about her state of health before they were married. It was a subject about which she was defensive, and she may even have thought that she would lose him if the whole truth were known. And the question of her health apart, he must have realised by now that he was not going to find in her the enthusiastic sexual partner he was hoping for.

Next day, the waters of reconciliation closed over the quarrel. They took a ride together on their new ponies into the mountain-enclosed countryside, making their way along roughly paved roads towards rice-fields where buffalo wallowed, coming back on a tiny path running along a dike between waving tobacco plants.

Almost at once they started on the treadmill of the tiny European colony's formal social life. It was the function of the wives, English and French, to provide an endless round of At Homes, teas and dinners – not so pointless an occupation as might appear, because it was a means of preserving sanity in a situation where, apart from directing their servants, they had virtually nothing to do. For some it provided a chance to dress up – one of the Frenchwomen had her dresses direct from Paris, no woman thought of going out to tea without putting on gloves and wearing her best hat. If the Andersons' inaugural lunch party on 10 December is anything to go by, the alcohol flowed freely: they felt obliged to offer cocktails, champagne, two kinds of still wine, as well as whiskies and sodas and 'gins and bitters'. One never hears of anyone getting drunk, though at one dinner party all the men 'got a shade binjed', and some of them (not Shaemas) 'rivalled each other with stories and allusions of a shadiness that was even apparent to Mrs Pritchard and me, though we couldn't keep up with the French'. At most social gatherings some game was played – tennis, which at least had the virtue of providing exercise, or chess, poker, bridge: 'I never play cards when I'm happy,' Stella moaned, not quite truthfully, to Laura.[1] Cards were played for money, a regular source of friction and resentment, particularly among the French. Though Stella was unaware of it, the low calibre of petty overseas officials was a standing joke in France; however, she soon had them placed: 'I don't know if you have ever met French colonials,' she wrote to Sydney Schiff (the novelist Stephen Hudson, who began a correspondence with her in 1924), 'one never seems to in France. It is not really an exaggeration to say that any one of our half dozen neighbours would conspire with his familiars for hours to avoid paying a debt of forty cents, and would slander his wife for the gain of a dollar.'[2]

Stella's Mengtsz experience left her in fact with an anti-French prejudice that lasted all her life. Only a month before she died she was expatiating to Essex Cholmondeley:

I think living with French people would harden the most tender heart. It seems unlikely somehow that nationality should be so very far-reaching and important, but French people really are national to the point of mania, it seems to me, or at any rate French colonial people are.

There is only one thing that we have learned to depend on from our neighbours here – and that is that they will always, always, take the narrowest, most ungenerous, most exploiting dullest stand, on any subject. Offer a Frenchman your last penny and he will *always* take it. But quite apart from the weariness of being always exploited, one finds oneself soured by the simple dullness of such *extreme* materialism. I am no mystic myself by any means, but I continually want to think about, and talk about *things I am not sure of*, things I wonder about, things that have no definite answer – above all, *self-made* ideas. If you confine yourself – as all these gross French people do – to things that can be known only – not *thought* – you have to be resigned to dealing with food and money and copulation *exclusively*, as they do. Really nothing else can be known for *certain*.[3]

In Mengtsz the French kept up a strict outward *politesse* that made the British feel uncomfortable – they had to be 'so damn careful' of their manners. Gallic formality of dress was maintained, though according to Stella only at the expense of hygiene – 'no baths, women in slovenly kimono all day, except when they expect company, in which case they appear in exquisite but unwashable satins and silks in sweltering heat – men playing tennis in coloured shirts, braces and stuff trousers (non-washing) with glimpses of sky-blue underwear at the ankles'. There was also a language difficulty. The Consul at Mengtsz was, admittedly, *vif* and *charmant*, the sort of person to make a party go with a swing, but with the best will in the world it was not easy for the British to be suitably 'lightsome' and responsive in their 'careful' French.

Not that conversation among themselves was in the least sparkling. It ran on 'safe though suburban lines', dwelling much on the possible choices of bride for the Prince of Wales, now twenty-eight years of age and still apparently heartwhole; or sank even lower in the retailing of imperfectly remembered jokes from dead *Punches* and *Tatlers*. 'It is over two years', Stella was to complain to Schiff in 1925, 'since I've been able to say anything or answer anything that seemed to me worth saying or answering. I've never been a stranger in the world before.'[4] It is an interesting reflection on the period that at the height of the jollifications the Mengtsz crowd does not seem to have been on Christian-name terms.

In spite of her sense of alienation, Stella contributed more than her share to the social merry-go-round. She gave her dinner parties like everyone else, and her monthly At Homes, but she also jollied the Customs staff, on her first January, into putting on a matinée performance for the French – some comic sketches and dramatised nursery rhymes – that went down quite well. She gave a party at New Year for which the Anderson drawing room was wittily transformed into a smugglers' cave, and the Customs personnel came disguised as lawbreakers. For a fancy-dress party she even persuaded Shaemas, whose style of looks was nothing if not maturely masculine, to dress up as Cupid – 'very sweet, slightly swathed in spotted muslin, with a great deal of meat showing . . . gray wings in feathers, and a little bow and arrow.'

There were enjoyable moments, and minor triumphs to relish, but from most social events Stella came home unrefreshed, and wounded in her self-esteem. She candidly admitted that, mixing as she was only with people who despised or thought irrelevant the things she valued, she was not getting the reassurance that she needed if she was to be moderately content: 'Everyone', she wrote piteously in her diary, 'except Shaemas would rather I were a different kind of person.' She was probably right.

Apart from him no one cared about the new books that arrived in regular parcels from friends in England and America – her Christmas present to him, *Ulysses*, 'the suppressed book by James Joyce, now printed in Paris. . . . it makes you notice the dirtiest in everything and everyone, and hear a filthy entendre in your most faery thought. Still it was worth doing – it may encourage someone to analyse a less salacious mind'; Sinclair Lewis's *Babbit*, 'almost too prying for non-Americans to read it'; the *Last Poems* of A. E. Housman, 'so exquisite I can hardly bear to read them'. Apart from Shaemas no one cared when Katherine Mansfield died, 'the cleverest woman in England. Would her enchantment have grown if she had lived? Or is it young in essence?'

Apart from him no one knew about the reviews of *The Poor Man*, some of them highly flattering, that arrived in the early months of 1923 and interfered with the writing of a new novel – 'if the review is favourable I try to hit the same appreciated note again, or if it is bad I feel too much flattened to hit any note at all'. In the *Nation and Athenaeum* (which had incorporated the Athenaeum in 1921) novelist Forrest Reid placed it 'among the very finest of modern novels', and opined, absurdly, that 'probably no character in fiction has been more completely realised, more faithfully presented than the "poor man"'. The *Spectator* focused on Edward too, and thought that his history challenged comparison with the theme of Dostoevsky's *The Idiot*: 'Miss Benson has written the novel no one could have anticipated, much less hoped for, even with her former admirable work in mind.'

The response of her California friends was naturally rather different. Stella was more shocked than reasonably she should have been by the degree of their hurt, for while she could be honest and say that there were no 'offensive portraits' in it, she ought to have realised that parts of it read like an *exposé* of manners and morals in the Bertha Pope set. Moreover, her scathing attack on American popular culture, however clever and apt it might have seemed had it come from a native American, had a very ungracious air coming from a foreign visitor.

It is easy to see how betrayed her friends felt: had the fey little English girl who had joined so gaily in their binges, had played the guitar so charmingly and sang, had seemed so willing a convert to their radical ideas – had she in her heart been mocking them, judging them, all the time? That she had come back and actually finished the book in California was a particularly sore point.

Piteously, Bertha wrote in September to say that when she had been in England in the summer she had not cared to take up the introductions that Stella had given her: 'I thought that we must look vulgar and ridiculous to all English people, who do not like us and couldn't be expected to, and even while they were pretending to like us were making notes for ridiculing us in the future.'[5] Even Witter Bynner, from whom Stella had hoped for more constructive criticism, wrote her a letter of stiff disapproval seasoned with complaints that her Americanisms were not correct.

Stella wrote Bertha a very lengthy apologia for what she had done. 'I see now that I must not come back to California,' she said. 'I realize well that I have lost many friends there and I admit that this is hardly surprising'; but she did not retract one word:

> It seems to me that nothing is too strong to be spoken against the spreading of cheap art, cheap semi-education and cheap morals. . . . Of course it is true that anywhere in the United States . . . one may meet groups of Americans of refinement, education, subtlety, and that subsoil of fantasy in which real art grows – *but this is not the American spirit that is spreading over the poor world.* . . . The American culture *that reaches us in Europe and in Asia* consists partly of short cuts to bad art – of which the movie, the gramophone, the radio, the lusciously illustrated Home Magazine are superficial manifestations. . . . Chief and – to us non-Americans – the most ominous of all, is the spirit of cheap intolerant uplift and the democratic upholding of mediocrity and material prosperity and advertisement. . . . I can only say that the spreading spirit of which I speak is the thing that makes me thank God I shall not be alive in fifty years' time.[6]

That the European nations had their 'middle class', regretfully she had to admit, but there it was under some control, whereas 'your middle class is so enormous that it has burst the bounds of America and is peopling the world'. When seriously challenged, Ellis Roberts assures us, Stella would agree that she cherished indefensible prejudices, but he adds that the admission did not produce any permanent change of heart. When it came to American vulgarity, French sex-absorption and the behaviour of the middle class everywhere, clearly she loved to hate.

Meanwhile the British in Mengtsz steered clear of the writing side of her life, and the French (naturally) were worse, 'definitely repelled by any hint of intelligence in a woman, unless it goes with sex-lusciousness. They are kind to me considering, but make it very clear that I ought to have either babies *or* a great variety of good clothes.'[7]

For month after month passed, and Mrs Anderson failed to become *enceinte*. Her disappointment must have been compounded by the knowledge that whatever the gossips might be saying it was not by her own choice. Her diary entry for 31 January 1923 begins: 'We had a great blow to-day'; four determinedly blacked-out lines follow, and then 'I must forget about a baby.' Evidently Shaemas had a recurrence of syphilis. Stella does not comment in her diary on the danger to his health or hers: her emotion centres on the fear that it may never be wise for them to have children. She cannot hide her deep disappointment, though she puts a consoling gloss on the news:

> I can't say it is so sad to me as it would be to many women who are stronger and more full of life. I feel very strongly that having a baby might have gone hard with me, and perhaps my life is saved by this obstacle. It is like the War with Shaemas; he tried to be in it, but his failure probably saved his life – but like that again, I shall always feel that I have missed a privilege and a great and fine ordeal, just as he feels about the War.
>
> I would like at least to have *tried* to prove myself a woman, I would have liked to have assured myself that even my kind of rather moonlight life can be handed on – but I shall never know now whether I would have been worthy of that. This way at least I am more free. Perhaps it is deliberate on the part of Fate, this insisting on keeping me footloose and soul-loose and in and out of everything.

Shaemas, no doubt profoundly troubled, sought advice and treatment from the French doctor at Mengtsz.

If 'Fate' meant to deny Stella babies, as compensation of a sort there were always puppies. Almost as soon as she got to Mengtsz she acquired two, Cowslip and Josephine. The latter – 'daughter of a French pointer who made a *mésalliance* with a Chinese wonk' – after maturing, was ever in litter. With a facetiousness ever-more-strained, Stella called the puppies after popes or well-known makes of cars: Rolls-Royce, Buick, Dodge and Ford followed Innocent, Clement, Boniface and Pius in swift succession, and then came a brood named after characters in *Pride and Prejudice* – Darcy, Bingley and Collins. When the offspring of two pointers grew up mysteriously into a setter, she wished she had known earlier, and christened him 'Poinsettia'.

'I love all puppies with great facility, but delicate or very loving puppies seem to break through the bounds of ordinary canine charm and become like babies in my heart.' At a low ebb herself, she was to sit up with Bingley night after night in a hysterical, vain attempt to keep him alive. To Laura she confessed that puppies to her were 'a kind of ghost of real babies', adding pathetically, 'that's quite a big thing – to be a ghost'.[8]

The reason for what she termed her 'obsession' with older dogs was rather different, she felt: 'I think it is a kind of inferiority – I can't feel so lovingly about people in general as I do about dogs in general. Perhaps it is only because I so much want to be loved and admired – dogs always do – and people seldom.' Yet she suspected that deep down there was more to it than vanity or frustrated mother instinct, 'something apart from that, something that is to me exquisite in dogs'; it escaped final analysis, like most of our deepest preferences.

She found in Mengtsz another use for her practical tenderness. The *New Atlas and Commercial Gazetteer of China*, a weighty volume issued in 1920 to apprise British businessmen of the rich possibilities of trade that awaited them among the teeming yellow millions, gives a list of the staple exports of Yunnan (the trade in opium – Shaemas's chief headache – though flourishing, was illegal and could not be included). Along with hides, horns, tobacco, maize and tea, feathers are mentioned. Stella was horrified by the nasty facts of the feather trade: in the nesting season, when the plumage was at its best, female egrets were captured and robbed of their single fine feather, then broken and cast aside for dead; the nestlings starved. Stella collected destitute nestlings, founded an 'orphanage', fed them forcibly on raw fish and brandy, and (as with the puppies) loaded them with 'amusing' incongruous names: Osbert, Sacheverell and Edith recovered under treatment; Egberd, Egbreda and Egintruda sadly perished.

In April the Pritchards left and the Andersons moved into their house – another Chinese-style house in the Customs compound – and for a few days Stella busied herself in making it look 'more human, less suburban'; she enjoyed herself machining curtains, 'the thing completely filled my mind all day'. There were other occupations to part-fill her mind – she gardened, she taught drawing to the children of an American missionary, and English to a French child, she took lessons in Chinese from one of the Customs clerks – but in all of it she had plenty of leisure to scrutinise her marriage, to wonder what held her to Shaemas now that she was 'no longer in the slightest degree in love with him'. Simply her compassionate understanding, she decided. She knew him so well in all his sensitive places, all his reticences, that to see him hurt would be like being hurt herself. That did not mean that she was always gentle with him; on the contrary, 'I am tenderhearted in a shallow way to everything and everyone always, but to Shaemas only sometimes, because he can make me hate myself, and that hurts me so that I hurt back.' When quarrels flared Shaemas showed himself the finer character: 'I never humble myself to Shaemas, Shaemas is much more generous in admitting he is wrong.' One of the most painful facts about marriage, she was learning, was that it 'shows one up not only to the person one loved [*sic*], but also to oneself'.

The only use that Stella would have for her Chinese would be in dealing with her servants and with shopkeepers. The Andersons had no contact except of the most formal and official kind with the citizens of Mengtsz, and Stella had no occasion to go into the little town (threading the dark gate in the thick wall) unless it was to inspect the market with Shaemas, or stroll about the streets with him sightseeing.

In the evenings along quiet back streets they would watch grand ladies on modestly bound feet taking their rare walks 'under great petticoated apple-green and crimson umbrellas, the frills of which hang all round and hide their faces and shoulders from the public'. 'Half-witted looking' soldiery hung about, dressed in uniforms several sizes too big for them; they were mustering for an attack, which never came, from a Szechwanese warlord. Sights of horror were ubiquitous: chickens, alive, hanging upside down; carp gasping in packed masses on stalls; ponies and donkeys bleeding under enormous burdens; an aged beggar carrying on his back his skeletal mother; another, blind, crashing his bleeding head on the cobblestones, shrieking for alms.

Throughout their time in China articles on local life and customs, and on their personal adventures flowed from her pen to end up in the pages of the *Star*, the *Nation and Athenaeum*, the New York *Bookman*, the *South China Morning Post*, and other periodicals. Some of them, with her own pen-drawings by way of illustration (her talent was strictly limited but – just – adequate) were reprinted in volume form in *The Little World* in 1926, and *Worlds Within Worlds* in 1928. Stella pooh-poohed her journalistic articles, on the grounds that they were written strictly for money and with great ease. She was 'genuinely sorry' when flattering reviews of the two books appeared in respected journals; why, she wanted to know, could not reviewers, even the best of them, discriminate between 'newspaper stuff' and her novels, which at least attempted to express 'something permanent and true'? She thought her travel articles 'desperately sprightly', and indeed there is a straining after amusingness in some of them (especially the ones tailored for the popular press) that is not attractive. The charm of the diary narratives, the sharp immediacy, the casual felicities of phrase and rhythm, get lost in the process of transformation into printable copy, and given the choice one would keep the diary versions, discard the articles.

One significant thread running through the diaries is not made much use of in the articles, and that is the record that she kept of sights that had delighted her eye, precise notes of scenery, light, weather, particularly in terms of colour. 'I think the only excuse for my being alive', she had written, 'is that I do so terribly enjoy seeing things, seeing the brushing of waters by the wind, and the brushing of the sky by the clouds. . . . People are a temptation and a torture to me, and I don't know why I find so much pain in them.'

Several times a week – usually with Shaemas, never alone – she rode out through the flat rice-fields towards the hills. There were longer excursions too, involving a night at a native inn, like their visit to the tin-mining town of Ko-chui, twenty-three miles distant on a road notorious for brigands, when they had to hire an escort of four armed Chinese soldiers to protect them. Early one morning, as they came home after a night away:

the sun found itself as a vague indefined bright region in the mist, and all the cobwebs and gossamers – perfect cartwheel webs everywhere from flower to flower – were of polished silver, and like little white flames were the heads of the pale grasses up towards the sun. Finally in a breath – without apparent movement – the mist was gone, and the mountains, clothed in pale grass, were sheeny yellow, and grey rocks like seated elephants were about the slopes, and the shadows, in the grooves and streams and little canyons in the bodies of the hills sprawled like spiders. There was a caravan of ponies and men aslant up the tree-crested mountainside.

One evening as they were riding home:

the sky became a deep subtle brown–purple towards the fringes which met the mountains, and the sun set leaving two burnished sparks of cloud-dust between the peaks. A crane, wailing its creaking cry, navigated round a star, and on one hillside they were burning grass, and making a great arch of fire glitter against the dark. The black silhouette of all the world was blind, except for the occasional glint of a star in water – and dumb, except for the mysterious hidden talk of unseen passersby.

If one compares these loving descriptions, the product of a painter's eye and a lyricist's pen, with the language dipped in vitriol that Stella was using in her diary for some of the human beings she was thrown with at this time, one cannot help feeling that without the solace of the pony rides she would have collapsed; emphatically, it was a case of (in the words of her ancestor Bishop Heber's hymn) every prospect pleasing and only man being vile. Take for example her almost phobic reaction to some of the protestant missionaries she met. Not only did they speak with 'Tooting' accents and demonstrate 'Tooting' manners, they wore in their eyes the 'very irritating Christian loving beam, which produces a mote in mine at once'. She pilloried some hapless female missionaries met at a tea party in an article for the *Nation and Athenaeum*, remembering too late that the piece was likely to be reprinted in a China newspaper. Did she care? Not very much, she confessed, for 'side by side with a feeling that it is cruel to hurt and despise them, I feel such an overwhelming repulsion from their ugliness, complacency, and manner of unjustified authoritativeness that I do not mind' – and the fact that she let the article go unamended into *The Little World* shows how little contrite she was.

By August 1923, when a hiccup occurred in her supply of books, Stella was chasing her tail in an agony of self-deprecation:

> It is the first time in my life I have ever been thrown on my own inward resources with nothing to read and no one to talk to – Shaemas being at the office all day and no one else in the place being able to conceive of any conversation more subtle than a discussion on the cost of living or the meretriciousness of servants. . . . The effect of this isolation is to make me ponder a great deal on myself in an entirely unproductive way – and to make me hate myself most bitterly. I see how much I have depended on outside approval and flattery all my life and how nothing I am without it. And it is dreadful to come to the time of life when one realises suddenly that one can't change oneself. It would be no good to put on a hairshirt after one had realised that a hairshirt might be rather becoming, and might – failing more concrete benefits – earn one a pat on the back from God.

She was expecting visitors – a Colonel Nicholson, who had been flatteringly kind and attentive when, heartsore, she had stopped off briefly in Hong Kong on her way from Shanghai to Calcutta in the autumn of 1920, and Doris Estcourt.

> I am looking forward to my visitors coming – and then spoil my looking forward by realising that I am practising my songs and my guitar to make them think how versatile I am, and inventing things I might say to them when I first see them, and generally prinking again. I should think no one had a more humiliating self than I have, and when I am shut up with it I can't get away from it. I am writing a bit but even that is prinking in a way – I say to myself 'people will think that clever', therefore I also think it clever – what I see Katherine Mansfield says in her diary is the fatal sin in writing.

The advent of Nicholson at the end of August, soldierlike, reserved, 'very polite with an extravagantly Piccadilly voice', was enormously welcome. Shaemas suggested – hoping perhaps that forewarned is forearmed – that he could be looking for a love affair, and that Stella herself might be ready to fall in love. But she knew it was impossible: she could not love so confident and successful a man, drawn as she was by her 'need to dominate' to 'failures and sorry people'.

For a month Stella basked in the Colonel's attentions, a welcome change from Shaemas's recent worse than casual manners; according to her, he was getting more and more glum and slack, dropping off to sleep in spare moments, failing to offer guests drinks, even deliberately dropping things for her to pick up. (It was part of Shaemas's 'feminism' not to dance attendance on women as if they were incapable of doing things for themselves.) Then Nicholson proved the ideal sightseer, ever brisk and keen. Shaemas, disquietingly flaccid, was quite likely to keep his eyes fixed on his newspaper in new and interesting surroundings.

But Nicholson's visit was not all tranquillity. He and Stella had an argument in public about 'friendship'; it was fierce, perhaps unnaturally so, and it shook her so much that after he had retired to bed she felt impelled to go and knock on his door and sue for peace: 'After a bit he came, poor little darling, in his shirtsleeves all rumpled, looking as if he had been crying.' She apologised for her rudeness, he for his. Conscience still unsatisfied, she wrote him a letter to be taken in with his early-morning tea.

To Shaemas, intently watching the charade unfold, it seemed as if they might be falling in love. But he was mistaken: it looks more as though, naughtily, Stella was using her undoubted emotional hold over Nicholson to torment him and to break down his gentlemanly reserve. For the eve of his departure she arranged a charming surprise: a sumptuous champagne dinner, set out of doors and lit by lanterns strung between 'faery' eucalyptus trees. All the diners wore mandarin coats, and in a pool of moonlight Stella sang to her guitar. A typically Stellarian game was played (it may have been of her invention), people challenging each other to be 'honest' about themselves. Nicholson scarcely uttered; instead, he gazed fixedly at Stella from under his hand. It was the state to which, years before, she had reduced Nigel Bengough. Nicholson must have been uncomfortably aware, during the visit, that she was probing him, for his bread-and-butter letter includes an apology for being so 'hidden'.

After his departure Stella wept (Shaemas caught her at it and was hurt), but hers was a light, post-flirtation sorrow, not real grief. While the thought of taking a lover did not 'outrage' her, she simply did not want one: 'from some radical and unhealthy defect in my nature physical things that ought to be essential are not essential. I believe I could be content if I never had those physical experiences again'; Freud had by this time turned topsy-turvy the nice woman's ideas on sex: far from shutting her eyes and concentrating on England during intercourse, she now felt she should be revelling in it, and feared that there was something seriously wrong with her if she did not.

When after a month she read in the paper the announcement of

Nicholson's engagement to a Miss Phyllis Biggs of Hong Kong there is no sign in the diary of pique.

At the end of October Doris Estcourt arrived – self-assured, kind, irritatingly fussy, but by and large an agreeable companion; this was important, as they intended to take her with them on a tour of French Indo-China. Alas, for three weeks of her stay Doris had to amuse herself, for her hostess was in bed with congestion of the lungs, the culmination of an autumn of sickliness. She was up for Christmas, however, and at New Year enjoyed juvenile romps, and another truth-telling game which involved each player's declaring what he thought to be his three main virtues and defects: Shaemas put intelligence, kindliness, quietness as his virtues; intolerance, laziness and temper as his defects; Stella 'keenness', courage and sense of humour alongside egoism, ungenerousness and intolerance. As a measure of their self-knowledge, all four lists were correctly guessed.

In January 1924 Stella on her own took Doris to Hong Kong. No sooner had they paid a few Peak calls in the 'heartless' Hong Kong way – 'dropping cards into boxes marked "Out"' – than they were caught up in the social swing. Colonel Nicholson was gratifyingly friendly – at least at first – introducing them to his Phyllis, a radiant and charming girl with 'very brilliant pink and white complexion and brilliant golden hair', quite unlike Stella. Thereafter, his manner altered. He became distinctly cool, and one can only suppose that Phyllis scented a rival. Stella sent him a letter saying how snubbed she felt, and the Colonel was no doubt relieved when the Haiphong steamer bore her and Doris away.

Hanoi when they arrived (Stella reported in an article for the *Star*)[9] lay limp under *le crachin*, its periodic malaise, a drizzly, overhanging cloud. They were joined there by Shaemas, and a little later by Charles Davy, a young man met in Hong Kong who was to travel with them. On 5 February they travelled by train to Vinh in Annam, where they put up at a Chinese hotel with the ominous name of the Inn of Harmonious Repose, tossing and turning on jointed wooden mattresses to the tune of wailing mosquitoes.

Next morning 'a little goblin of an Annamite chauffeur' with a native mechanic at his side drove them along a brand new road to the Laotian border: Stella and Doris were to be the first white women to explore this, the least-known province of French Indo-China. The natives, small, brown, handsome, with big sentimental eyes, were dressed in brilliant sarongs and lived in palm-leaf huts on stilts: 'everyone looked shocked to see us and – with the universal human instinct of preoccupation with the shocking – settled down on haunches to take a good look'.

The French officials they met gave a pleasing impression of efficiency and dedication. The *chef de poste* at a jungle prison station mustered some of his chained and manacled convicts to prepare beds for them; he was a kind man, with a great affection for his people and a high regard for native justice. He cited an example: if a man touched a woman's breast he got ten years in prison, if he raped her, only five. *'Car, en effet – n'est-ce pas, mesdames? – en ce cas-là il y a toujours un peu de bonne volunté. La dame se donne un peu a ça. . . .'* M. *le résident* at a village on the Upper Mekong River had married a *laotienne*, had not seen France for years and showed no inclination ever to do so again: he was obsessed with love of Laos. Turning back towards Annam on an ancient jungle track about which no one knew or would promise anything except that it was interrupted by swing bridges that might not support a car, they lurched and heaved their way to a remote outpost where the *délégué* cycled forward to meet them. He was 'a big, beaming buck nigger', perhaps from Martinique, and his face 'shone with the happiness of achieved mastership'. In buoyant, emphatic French he told them about his work, and the story of his life. Intelligence, he said, was not a matter of race, but of contact with civilisation. Looking out of the window at the Laotian villagers, 'gracious, sleepy, lovely as bright lizards in the sun', and looking again at the *délégué*, 'black, thick, energetic, and completely prosaic in buttony khaki', Stella pondered his words, and experienced a bewildering 'mental squint'.

Hué, the Annamite capital, was hot. Round and round the bandstand strolled the representatives of France and their well-corseted wives, round and round in an outer circle went Annamites in orange, green and purple robes. The British party visited the palace of the Emperor, who was out of sight, nursing bronchitis. His throne seemed sadly symbolic of his status – 'gaudy and solitary and a little rickety about the legs', its gorgeous brocade cushion 'only slightly dinted by the ghost of empire'. Saigon, the capital of Co-Chin China, was hot, ugly, disappointing; the city of which French colonials spoke 'with pride', and French novelists wrote 'with succulence and daring', was full of degenerate types – 'hardly proper ladies and luscious men' – and there were 'a great many obvious Britishers about . . . all of the most depressingly angular, spectacled, gawky English type'. She was seeing them with the awakened eyes that one brings back to England from trips abroad, when one marvels how a race of such anti-aphrodisiac appearance has managed to perpetuate itself down the ages.

Next day, the *bureau de poste* at Phnom Penh, the Cambodian capital, yielded a telegram recalling Shaemas to Yunnan to sit an examination in Chinese. What ought they to do? The trip would have cost them two hundred and fifty pounds, and Angkor was to be its high spot. Stella proposed they make a dash for it, even if it meant a couple of sleepless nights. A new motor road was supposed to exist, though the *chef de police* had never heard of it: 'One goes by *boat* to Angkor. *Messieurs, mesdames* deceive themselves, by automobile nothing marches.'

But the road did exist, after a fashion and – 'rolling and roaring and bucking through the dry bridgeless stream-beds in the streaked light of the tepid Cambodian moon' for twelve hours non-stop – they were to be the first tourists in the world's history to use it. By moonlight they explored the ruins of Angkor Wat, feeling like shadows, and then snatched a few hours' sleep. Day came up dull, hot, banishing mystery, encouraging hasty photography with the 'rude eye' of a Number One Brownie; but Stella thought that it would take more than a camera's winking to desecrate this 'quite young wonder of the world'.

Back to Phnom Penh, only to discover that their ship left Saigon, some hundred and thirty miles away, in eleven hours' time. They found another car, this time with driver, and dozed uneasily through another Cambodian night, their one thought to arrive at the boat in time: 'It is nothing to us that the *Bureau de Tourisme* is in ecstasies over the pioneering feat we have performed in the car it hired to us. We droop over passport formalities, we pillow our foreheads on our omelette at breakfast in the hotel. . . . having at last boarded the dirty little ship, we sleep and sleep and sleep.'

Home again to a rapturous welcome from the dogs, and, for Stella, a fresh look at a manuscript that she had completed before they set out. Having discarded the one that occupied her in the spring of 1923, she had written another in the autumn, in only three months, after Nicholson's departure and during Doris's stay – 'very quick for me',[10] she told Aunt Florie. Every morning Doris had found her hostess sitting on the edge of an arm-chair – one of her dogs occupying the greater part of it – writing rapidly in an exercise book, and seeming to reconcentrate instantly after any interruption.[11] 'I think it is not very good,' she went on to her aunt, 'unfortunately neither good nor likely to be popular, so I fall between two stools.' The book already had a name, *Pipers and a Dancer*.

Alive with wit, filled with lucent and lovely verbal watercolours of the Chinese scene, *Pipers and a Dancer* is a brilliant, flawed, disturbing little novel. In its sour way it is a comic book, and the comedy arises from the mispairing of fiancés. Ipsie, the female of the pair, is a creature so taken up with dancing a different dance to every piper she meets that she is scarcely a person at all, least of all to herself: 'Where am I all this time? Who is this person in my skin?' These are the questions with which she torments herself. In the very first sentence she is catching herself out posing:

Ipsie suddenly stopped speaking and heard with horror the echo of her own voice saying, 'You see, I lost my three brothers in the War.' 'How damn pathetic,' she thought, and she reminded herself for the thousandth time that she had determined to be reserved.

She is an artist, we learn, and lives most vividly in her eyes and her imagination – 'sometimes she thought that she could hardly consider herself virgin, she lived so intensely in Conrad' (Conrad being her elder brother, killed in the war).

Ipsie has come to China to marry Jacob Heming, a fat, middle-aged electrical engineer, with whom she is not in love. (Asked how this could be, Stella replied, 'Ipsie got engaged to Jacob because she was never real or grown-up enough to be alone – or to realise that she could never be turned into a real grown-up person even by a real grown-up husband. I do not believe this to be far-fetched or impossible.')[12] Heming is, in fact, her opposite in every way – philistine, blind to his beautiful Yunnanese surroundings, with no trace of self-criticism or humour or imagination in his large head. He honestly cannot understand why people do not like him:

> His mind was an incessant tangle of 'He ought to have known. . . . What did she take me for. . . . 'Tisn't as if I. . . . A man of my standing. . . . Speaking as if I was his servant. . . .' All the world, it seemed to Heming, spoke to him and had spoken to him always in an insulting voice . . . through the thunders of these changing remembered voices he could always hear his own voice replying reasonably, gently, never insisting on any thing but bare rights. . . . He seemed to himself to be an excellent fellow, only too ready to take his part in any clean fun, a ladies' man, no vices.

As for Ipsie, she 'haunted him more kindly than did most of the other ghosts', and for that reason he very rarely thought of her. She was a good homely little body, and he had no doubt that she would, when properly trained, make a good little wife. If he had any misgivings at all about her, it was simply on the score that in the early days of their engagement she seemed to be asking too much of him:

> 'We ought to know each other . . . we ought to know each other better. . . .' He could hear in his head now the voices of those letters, demanding, demanding. . . . 'Such nonsense,' he thought. 'I simply don't know what girls are coming to nowadays. Hysterical I call it. Why, we might be the first couple that ever thought of getting married.'

'I am a little more of an Ipsie than my husband is a Jacob,' Stella told Sydney Schiff, 'but that is saying nothing as anyone could tell you who knew him.'[13] Of course Jacob is not Shaemas in any crude sense, yet Shaemas provided the germ of the character and living with him enabled her for the first time to create a convincing male portrait. Jacob is extremely well done, and his elaborate preparations for a farewell party to which in the end, because everyone dislikes him so, no one turns up, is a gem of comic pathos.

As it happened, Ipsie does not see Jacob alive in China, for first he is captured by brigands, and afterwards dies of dysentery. No sooner does Ipsie know that he is safely dead than she enthrones him alongside her brother in her inner heaven of abstract, disembodied lovers – 'How far', she reflects, 'were these lovers from a mystery in a double bed.' She is faced now with a choice: either to marry a pleasant, conventional young American called Rodd, or to retreat into the suffocating embrace of Jacob's large, dreadful and (query) lesbian sister Pauline. She chooses the latter, and as she does so something in her face shows Rodd the truth: 'Why, she's not alive. There was nothing to hold on to. . . . Reality's the only thing she can't imagine. She's a fairy. She's a fairy. Nobody can hold a fairy.'

'I may have been more or less an Ipsie seven years ago,' Stella conceded, 'though I think I was braver than she was.'[14] Brave enough, certainly, to face the mystery in a double bed.

The Andersons were to wait almost a year for news of their next posting. For both of them it was a dreary time. There were changes in the Customs staff, but essentially life dragged on the same. For Shaemas, with his job to occupy him, things were never too bad, but Stella sank very low indeed; from May to September 1924 her diary ceases altogether, ever a bad sign. When it resumes she is 'ill and very much depressed . . . very much underweight, and often full of pain and weariness' – her physical condition plainly a mirror of mental distress.

Needless to say, she had not been in bed all summer. There had been a Frenchwoman, abandoned by her husband in a ramshackle hut and half crazy with loneliness, to whom she was kind; and a colleague of Shaemas's had involved both of them, drainingly, as confidants in his excruciatingly long-drawn-out relationship with the wife of a French official – until Stella upped and said that she was no longer willing to be 'a receptacle for amorous yap', and he fell silent. *Pipers and a Dancer* had gone to Curtis Brown (it was published by Macmillan in September 1924), and early in 1925 she signed the contract for *The Little World*. Meanwhile she had written the greater part of another novel, which had to wait its turn behind the travel book, and so did not appear until October 1926. It was called *Goodbye, Stranger* and, like *Pipers*, was set in China.

To read *Goodbye, Stranger* in conjunction with the contemporaneous diary is to find it almost indecently self-revealing. 'The book is acid,' writes Ellis Roberts, 'it leaves on the palate that odd, wrinkled sensation that the persimmon leaves in the mouth. . . . It is a story of exile and frustration, an angry story in which the satirist and the victim are one.'

Into it Stella has tipped ingredients noxious to her – missionaries, the values of the American middle class – and out of her desperation added, nostalgically as it were, the element of faery that was missing from her two previous novels; but she has thrown in too her self-disgust and her deep doubts about herself as woman.

Her chief male character, Clifford Cotton (one-time missionary but now odd-job man about a mission station) is a 'changeling': for seven years past a fairy has inhabited his healthy virile body, making him an uneasy stranger in the world. During this time his marriage has survived, but purely on the level of affection and physical desire: for his sweet, pretty, shallow, all-female, all-American wife Daley, with her Victrola (a mechanical piano) and her glossy illustrated magazines, asks no more of marriage.

But when one day a tatty troupe of travelling entertainers arrives on the scene, Clifford (yearning for the 'wisdom' that a fairy invariably lacks) falls for the miserable little pianist of the group, Lena, an English girl, a haggard, dry, tart little creature with a frail body (soon she is tucked up in bed in Clifford's house, with pleurisy), and a 'strong mind'. Compared to Daley, a 'real' woman if ever there was one, Lena is doubtfully sexed. She has, indeed, once managed an affair with a 'thin Fulham poet', yet her reaction when introduced to Daley is unusual for a woman: 'I wish I needn't be hiding my life from her,' she thinks. 'I wish I were eighteen and a virgin. . . .' And Daley, noticing Lena smile at her 'with a boy's smile', thinks 'I wouldn't like to undress in front of her, somehow.' However, despite her sexual ambiguity Clifford becomes, briefly, her second lover. (Sex is always coyly handled in Stella's novels, but when Clifford is discovered late at night stealing from Lena's bedroom we are to understand that they have been making love.)

The discovery precipitates a crisis on the morrow, and Clifford, the changeling, is sent away by Lena. Neighbours find his clothing abandoned in a bamboo grove. He has been seen running naked in the woods. What actually has happened is that, having discarded his clothes, the changeling has been reclaimed by his fairy people. The person who finally comes back to Daley is her seven-years-absent husband, the 'so manly – so practical – so good-hearted . . . fool' that he was before, in the words of his cronelike old mother:

'Perhaps,' said Lena, slowly lifting a distraught face, 'perhaps the world's a little better for the loss of a stony-hearted fairy. . . .'

'Perhaps it is a little better,' said old Mrs Cotton. 'A little ki-hinder. A little more American. But oh,' she cried, raising her knotted hands before her face, 'but oh – there are so many men, and so – few – fairies. . . .' Her voice died away on a low murmur, 'No more . . . no more fairies. . . .'

It is a tragic ending, and disillusioned. But there was no alternative right ending for a novel that was an accurate print-off of the writer's state of soul.

In the Chinese-style house with the curved roofs, matrimonial squabbles flickered and died. One row began with a complaint by Shaemas that he had never once enjoyed his breakfast while in Mengtsz because of a certain checked tablecloth they used; it ended in an ice-cold discussion of divorce. Plainly it was high time they left. 'I am looking forward so violently to getting away,' Stella wrote, 'that I am sure God will do all he can to stop it.'[15]

The news that Shaemas had passed his Chinese language exam with the highest possible honours had been very encouraging: 'He is much the most junior man in the service who has succeeded in doing this,' Stella had told Aunt Florie with wifely pride, 'and it will probably mean a good job – it must mean Peking for us sooner or later.'[16] But not yet, it seemed. Great was their disappointment when in March 1925 a telegram came ordering them for six months to – of all places – Shanghai. International, commercial, meretricious, the Paris and Chicago of the orient, Shanghai was a city they both detested.

When on 4 April the moment of leaving came, the sadness was in parting with the dogs and ponies, especially the dogs: 'I can hardly bear to think of them, going through their lives looking in vain for all the love and notice and talk that I have given them – and all the joy, the bouncing and whinnying, that is lavished on us whenever we come in must be bottled up for ever now. The little funny special voice that belonged to each dog will never be heard again.'

There was the now familiar journey to be traced again: Hanoi, Haiphong, Hong Kong – then on to Shanghai. There they parted on 14 May. For Stella was going home, and Shaemas was to have six months there on his own. 'I feel now as if there was no excuse for me to leave him,' she wrote. But with her ship under way it was too late to change her mind; all she could do was rest in the consoling thought that 'loss is so much more healthy than staleness'.

Chapter Seventeen

On the voyage Stella had deep talks with a Viennese psychiatrist, Willi Gutmann, a colleague of Freud's, who, while finding her 'a profoundly interesting subject', warned that if she were to undertake analysis she would 'certainly lose her husband, probably her art, and perhaps her life'. As the ship drew near the States, passengers were faced with the problem of what to do with their precious liquor, either drinking it themselves, pressing it upon the empty-handed, or – last resort – throwing it overboard (though many kept it with intent to smuggle); Stella traipsed all over the ship led by mysterious signs 'getting drinks just to save them from the sea'. Drawing in to port she was appalled to find that her last visit, with Shaemas, had 'spoilt her memories': 'he loves facts and actualities so much, and I can always find foothold on a pretence and in foolishness. I won't look at the real world, I'd rather pretend desperately to be a fairy, and Shaemas won't let me.' However, the sight of a deputation of friends come to meet her (Bertha Pope prominently armed with 'red roses and great lovingness') uplifted her spirits; generously, California had decided to forgive her for *The Poor Man*, if not quite to forget.

She stayed a fortnight with the Goodriches, and then set off for Miami, *en route* for the Bahamas, where, on the island of Eleuthera, George, with Olive and the two youngest of their children (they now had four), was pursuing a new money-making scheme with, as Stella feared, his customary 'undue hope'. It had no connection with the supply of liquor to thirsty Americans, an activity that was bringing prosperity to a good many Bahamians at that time. He had invented a machine for cutting smooth, prepared blocks of building stone out of the ground, which he reckoned he could sell at about a seventh of the going rate; on Eleuthera grew 'the world's best tomatoes', the only obstacle to a flourishing trade being the want of a harbour. If he could construct one with his 'Rocplow' (which he saw a way of doing) then, in one imaginative gesture, sell off the resultant stone and open the harbour, and afterwards apply himself to harbour management and tomato growing, he was positive he could make a fortune. Stella was affectionately sceptical, having noticed that George's circumstances tended 'never to have a Now, always a Very Soon'. In the Bensons' 'nice very tumbledown white house' on the edge of the sea, she idled a week away, swimming, exploring, toasting sausages in the open with the Governor, Sir Harry Cordeaux, who seemed 'an extremely easygoing creature for a Governor'. On 1 July she left for Miami, New York and home, finishing *Goodbye, Stranger* on the way – and meeting on the Atlantic crossing some dozen of her readers, not to mention 'thirty or forty persons who fell on their knees automatically to anyone whose name has been in print'.

Stella reached London on 21 July 1925. Aunt Mary had died the previous week, and her mother was looking 'rather sad and worn out'. Stephen, however, was in fine form, 'more and more sure that he is the best person to be'. Hoxton seemed over-full of half-forgotten old ladies, 'mostly in half-expressed need of money'; Mrs Oneleg's aged husband had died, and she was 'on the parish – this family that I have bolstered up with so much care for so many years'. On the spot she decided that Mrs Oneleg was not going into the workhouse, and set about getting her a pension. Johnnie, still at Cookham, seemed 'very good, I think, and "grateful", but not an interesting boy at all – not grown up enough to take a lonely place in a lonely world' (she and Shaemas had been wondering whether a job on the engineering side of the Customs 'outdoor' staff – the NCOs of the service – would suit him). Her goddaughter and niece Georgina, a babe-in-arms when last seen, was grown into an enchantingly self-sufficient four-year-old: 'the little air in which she moves contains all the jokes and sorrows and thoughts she needs. She can be heard all by herself in a distant corner of the garden pealing with laughter at – perhaps – the expression of a cabbage.'

Dutifully she reported to Dr Monckton for a check-up. He thought that she had lost a lot of ground, 'and obviously doesn't think I shall live long – but he says I made my choice long ago between prolonging life and living it. . . . China is as good as any other bad place, he says.' However, the particulars of Shaemas's new posting – to rugged Manchuria, with a climate similar to that of northern Canada – so alarmed the ear specialist to whom he sent her that Monckton was prepared to join with him in cabling the opinion that it would be death for Stella to live there. Her reaction was the predictable one: she 'refused their kind offers. . . . I insist on ignoring the whole condition. Since I can't cure it, I won't be patched up. If I must die, I'll die as alive as I can.' There was no necessity to mention the other arguments for going: 'I need him to sustain in me the delusion that I am a real woman just like the others,' and 'he couldn't live for a minute on dreams – if I were away another month he says himself he'd have Chinese women in the house'.

It was on this trip that Stella began to meet writers. Two days after her arrival she took tea with the Woolfs in Tavistock Square, the invitation the result of Leonard's acceptance for the *Nation and Athenaeum* (of which he was literary editor) of some articles of hers. Conscious of her lack of formal education, doubtful if she could hold her own in argument and discussion with a trained mind, Stella was ever nervous of what she termed 'highbrows', yet glad of the chance to meet these well-known twin pillars of Bloomsbury. Virginia – inwardly aglow with the recent success of *Mrs Dalloway* and *The Common Reader* – was leading a busy social life that July, at the same time energetically writing articles and labouring for the Hogarth Press, housed in the basement; but, as she later observed, she was 'riding a flat tyre', and next month was to go to the country and collapse, with a solicitous husband to monitor her progress to recovery.

Stella watched the couple with an attentive eye, especially Virginia, ten years her senior, in whom she saw physical frailty comparable to her own, but not the same headlong defiance:

They seem a rather tremulous but extraordinarily intelligent pair. Both are a little *maladifs*, somehow. He had some kind of a jerking illness [he suffered from a lifelong tremor of the hands] and she looks terribly strained. She, in a day of mannish short clothes and clipped hair, wears untidy trailings and a large heap of faded hair behind. But she has a curious serenity behind her anxiousness, somehow – the serenity of great understanding – in spite of her rather distracted look I don't believe the world is so difficult for her as it is for me, because she is bigger and never unnerved by little things like the tea being beastly and what not.

Of course she leads a physically easy life more than I do – she is more nervously fragile – she doesn't challenge physical difficulties as something drives me on to challenge them. It must be a great ease to leave go and suddenly think – well, I'm not strong enough to do that – I can't go down to Hoxton, I'm too tired – I can't go back to Shaemas in China, I'm too ill.

Leonard Woolf looked very sad and physically so disabled that you feel you ought to be very gentle, until he speaks and then you feel that you needn't be too darn gentle. He is a very gentle person himself and not weakly, doesn't need any cottonwool buffers.

She went to Chesham in Buckinghamshire to meet Sydney Schiff. They had been corresponding for about a year, ever since he wrote to congratulate her on *The Poor Man*. He had said he would like to meet her, but 'If I do come home next year,' she had warned, 'I shall not dare to meet you. Your letters give me the impression that you think I am the kind of person you would like to know, but your books give me the impression that you wouldn't like at all the kind of person I really am. You are much more alive than I am. Words and eyes and imagination are very much alive in me but nothing much else and that isn't enough to make friends with.'[1] She liked this urbane, elderly semite with the soldierly look. They continued to correspond – but she doubted if he was 'a very real artist – if he is, he is in some way antipathetic to me'. And her verdict on him had a little kick in the tail (different from a sting, and often a feature of her summings-up of people briefly met): 'charming manner – sober and understanding sympathy, which is very delightful and soothing, and really means something – though not as much as it seems to mean'.

Naomi Mitchison, ten years her junior but already the author of a novel, had sent her a letter of appreciation, irresistibly naive, on *Pipers and a Dancer*:

> I don't think anyone has ever quite caught that terrible showman before and you've done it perfectly; it is so infinitely more intelligent than the James Joyce method [Stella had given the name 'the Showman' to that part of Ipsie which made her dance to every piper]. But of course – as far as I am concerned at least – you have done it in every book: just got hold of something unsaid about life and crystallised it. . . .
>
> I love all your Chinese descriptions, the people passing, the clothes, the weather; I don't know if you want people to like your descriptions as much as that – I don't think it interferes with one's acute pleasure in the story.[2]

Graciously, Stella had replied:

> It was an enormous pleasure to me to feel that my books are liked by the kind of person I imagine you to be. I *do* like people to enjoy the descriptions of the things I see. I should not mind if the descriptions drowned the story since to me my own eyes seem often to drown my own life. That is the only reason why I write; sight is the only magic thing I have.[3]

She added, since Naomi spoke tentatively of their meeting some day, that she hoped they would, perhaps under the auspices of mutual friends, the Spring Rices,[4] 'only I imagine I am rather a disappointing person to meet'.

Now she joined the Mitchisons and Spring Rices on holiday with their children at Varengeville on the Normandy coast. Naomi Mitchison remembers Stella as pale, rather thin, a little ill-looking; yet she would join with enthusiasm in parties and 'silly games' – though she did not like games that had a sexual content. She never spoke of her husband, giving the impression of being a single person. To Naomi she showed reserve, but that, Naomi now freely admits, was probably because she alarmed Stella by her puppyish enthusiasm; Stella, after all, was one of the first writers she had met and she had ardently loved her work ever since she was sixteen:

> For seven years,
> Oh, seven years, princess!
> I have thought about you – pictured you.
> And now you are here:
> Green cloak and silver flowers.
> Oh you pale fairy,
> Have I no power to bind you to me now?[5]

Stella liked and was interested in Naomi: 'very shy and full of quirks, but has a witty mind . . . she blurts penetrating remarks. She was very much afraid of me because she feels rather emotionally about my books.' Stella herself was moved to compose a poem, or set of verses rather, while at Varengeville, but not in compliment to her hostess or any of the company. The subject was an inflatable rubber horse, Épinard by name, which she had fun with, romping in the sea:

> When I once more to China's shore
> With great reluctance must return
> You'll keep, of course, your rubber horse
> And I will buy a rubber mare.
> A rubber mare that lives on air
> Will come with me (by C.P.R.)
> And every day, upon the way,
> I'll talk to her of Épinard.
> When she would sup, I'll blow her up
> With hot romance that burns within her;
> With every puff I'll sing of love
> And breathe her Swinburne for her dinner.
> So she will swim to seek her him
> After her last inspiring meal,
> And I, astride my rubber bride,
> Shall see again Varengeville.[6]

It was here that Naomi's brother Jack Haldane sat down beside Stella on the beach and suggested Cambridge as a suitable depository for her diaries.
Back in London, a meeting awaited Stella with another writer who loved

her books. Winifred Holtby, six years her junior, a rising journalist, a speaker on feminist and League of Nations topics, and herself the author of two novels, had been sending her 'excellent letters' for months: 'she has an extravagant feeling for my work'.

'I want to know her,' Winifred told a correspondent. 'The thing that I cannot understand is that she seems to want to know me. I never sought her acquaintance – only wrote once and told her not to answer. Her letters are unexpected – gentle and less uncompromising than her books – more ordinary, lacking that fierce sweetness but gaining in humanity and approachableness. I think that she is good as well as brilliant. . . .'[7] After their meeting, Winifred reported: 'she is nicer even than her books, kinder, less ruthless, extraordinarily personal and real somehow. But she looks horribly ill. . . .'[8]

Stella, for her part, had liked Winifred; 'rather charming', she had found her, 'very intense and very much withheld'. Winifred's friend Vera Brittain, shortly to depart for the United States with her new husband, she liked less. Because all three were scribblers, we have a triple view of that droplet of time, that meeting over tea in the mansion flat in Maida Vale on the afternoon of 31 August 1925. Vera Brittain describes the occasion in *Testament of Friendship*, her biography of Winifred Holtby. Stella had arrived so quietly, she recalled, ushered in by their housekeeper, that both she and Winifred had sprung to their feet in speechless embarrassment. The visitor was well dressed, in 'a charming, expensive wool suit', but as the afternoon progressed Vera was to detect an incongruity in her having chosen it: the suit 'belonged entirely to the gay world of extravagant reality, but she herself did not "belong", though it was a world that she loved. Delicate, witchlike, remote, with her penetrating blue eyes and the chill whisper of a voice that her deafness gave her, she seemed a spirit from some distant planet temporarily inhabiting a crude, material universe.'[9] 'Witchlike' seems a little hard, and it may be that Vera Brittain took to Stella no more than Stella took to her.

On 8 September, the day before she sailed, she called at the British Museum to see Arthur Waley, the eminent translator from the Chinese and Japanese, who was employed in the Department of Prints and Drawings. There was no doubting Shaemas's scholarly and linguistic ability, and Stella liked to think that his knowledge of things Chinese and excellent command of the language would one day gain him an academic or museum post – 'I hope to God Shaemas will in the end chuck all these fat Customs prospects, and find a job in which he can keep his soul alive,' Stella had cried out to her mother in a desperate moment a year earlier, at the same time fearing that his was 'too worrying a mind to allow him to start again at the bottom lightheartedly'.[10] The hope now was that Waley would point the way. But there was nothing at the Museum, he told her. Why not try Cambridge, where Professor Giles,[11] at eighty, was due to retire? The position was a sinecure, it seemed: Giles had 'never had a pupil during a score of years, only potters about among Chinese books. . . . It sounds an ideal job for Shaemas.'

As she boarded the *Empress of Scotland* at Tilbury, a photographer from the *Sunday Pictorial* stepped out and snapped her: she was a minor celebrity! 'Noted Authoress to Travel Again' was how she envisaged the caption, if in fact they were to use the picture. In its journalistic way the phrase neatly sums up her life, past, present and to come, though the implied suggestion that she was footloose and fancy-free and travelling purely for amusement no longer met the reality of the case. As she was quick to point out when congratulated on having married a man who could show her exotic quarters of the globe, being tied to one place was not travel. There was another word for it, with a less attractive flavour, and she used it in her diary now: 'I do so much hate going back to China this time, Mengtsz has shown me too much about exile.'

The journey from London to Seoul, where Shaemas was to meet her, took four weeks. Viewed from the railway, Canada flamed with autumn colour. The Pacific was rough, and she was penned in her cabin with pleurisy. At Yokohama there were press reporters to deal with; at Kobe she entrained for a wonderful ride alongside the Inland Sea, with 'smoke-blue mountains and white scrawled seas and birdlike flocks of fishing boats' passing her carriage windows. At Seoul it was 'very comforting' to be with Shaemas again, 'even though everything seems to have conspired to prevent him from being any more a wonderful creature to me'. It was 'very good' to have someone near at hand who thought well of her, 'very cruel' too, in that 'it shewed my heartlessness anew to me, and my lack of emotional vitality'. They lingered in the city a day or two, seeing the sights and hiring a Korean cook to take back with them to Manchuria, one Yi Meung-sik, who, anxious to do the right thing, on entering their service, to his mistress's grief discarded his 'nice ridiculous Korean black top hat', and appeared in a dark-blue 'livery' much too big for him, brass buttons and a jaunty tweed headpiece. On 21 October they set off by train northeastwards for Gensan, where they took a night sailing and woke to see 'real snow mountains towering above the far cliffs at Seishin, a new little pioneering town'. In a rackety train they rattled towards the border, stopping at a Japanese inn, where the lavatory was so placed as to be in full public view from three directions. Stella drew a neat little diagram to illustrate their dilemma, but how (or indeed whether) they resolved it is not revealed. Next day saw them travelling in a cold little train along the bank of the River Tumen dividing Korea from Manchuria, crossing it on foot, and taking a yet smaller, yet colder train north to the town of Lung Ching Tsun, where they pulled in at 4 p.m.

The final lap of the journey was unexpectedly bleak, for while the Korean side of the river was well wooded, the Manchurian mountains were stripped of timber. Just as on arrival at Mengtsz three years before, Stella's heart sank, and she 'got dreadfully depressed at the prospect of living in such a colourless, endless, shaven country'. But however verdant the mountain-sides she would have felt much the same: it was exile and loneliness that she feared. Yi the cook, quietly weeping in his corner of the carriage, miserably echoed her feelings: 'This place bad place. . . . Very much bad place. Missy more better go back Seoul.'[12]

On the platform, waiting in a queue to greet their acting Commissioner's lady – for Shaemas was top man in Lung Ching Tsun – were two European 'outdoor men' Love and Dulham, and two 'assistants' (juniors on the 'indoor' side), Li and Yamaguchi, a Chinese and a Japanese, with their respective wives. The town, a burgeoning new settlement, at first glance looked highly unpromising. There were no trees at all, except for 'a few skeleton poplars', and the place:

> all seemed to be in process of building, scaffolding and half-baked Japanese imitations of ambitious foreign houses were everywhere. . . . We live at the top of a bald hill, just behind a hideous mission school which blocks out our view. Outside our gates are four little mission houses built to match the school. Our house is a four-square villa with four rooms and an attic, the garden is quite bare and untended. . . . good heating system, nice fireplaces, plain comfortable furniture.

On Stella's pronouncing the place 'horrible' Shaemas, who had gone to some trouble to make the initial impact as painless as possible, 'rather naturally lost his temper and we had a miserable evening and I gave myself a great headache by crying a good deal, and Shaemas was very much disappointed and annoyed, poor thing. But really the place seems to me unbearable. Even four dogs do almost nothing to console me, they are inhuman outdoor dogs.'

Their missionary neighbours – apart from the outdoor men the only native English speakers in the place – were a group of presbyterians from Canada, four families in homes 'stuffy with bright goodness and comic cushions', and four 'virgin lady workers' in a house to themselves; at a discreet distance from the protestants was a small community of German Benedictine fathers.

When Shaemas's assistants came to pay their formal calls, Stella found Yamaguchi a pushy young man, with 'the superficially bright manner of all the sillier kinds of Asiatics, very anxious to impart information which he had only partially mastered'. Li was intelligent, but 'looks cynical and talks with a shade of insolence, dislikes the English and belongs to various Young

China movements towards independence' (to rid China of foreign interference was the aim of all forward-looking Chinese). Neither of the wives
knew any English, and it seemed to be part of their code of manners to admit
no interest in anything: 'If I handed them a picture or an ornament or an
illustration to look at they handed it back instantly without glancing at it,
but bowing politely. They also put down all food and drink untouched.'

The obscure part of the world in which the Andersons found themselves,
known to the Japanese as 'Kanto', was in the extreme south east of Chinese
Manchuria. The only viable link with the outside world as far as Europeans
were concerned was the railway, but at best its service was irregular, and
could be interrupted for weeks on end when the winter snows came. Internal
communications were primitive, the roads mere wagon tracks, whose
rugged realities Stella was to experience at first hand when she accompanied
her husband on some of his inspectorial missions.

The society of Kanto must have been one of the most oddly constituted in
the world. In descending order of numbers, it comprised Koreans, most of
them farmers; Chinese, mostly officials or vendors of one sort and another;
and Japanese, who were there because their country had imperialistic
designs on the area – and was to invade and take over in 1931. The Japanese
ran consulates, hospitals and schools for the benefit of their own nationals,
operated railway and mining concessions, and even ran the police. Japanese
currency circulated equally with Chinese. Finally, there was a sprinkling of
Russians, all of them stateless and there on sufferance only. Some had been
in Manchuria before the revolution and had opted to stay put. Some were
White Russians who had slipped over the border from Siberia in the nick of
time. Some had come as fugitives, the remnants of a defeated army that
poured into Manchuria after the collapse of the short-lived Far Eastern
White Republic of Siberia. Trying to look on the bright side of her coming
exile, Stella had told her mother: 'anyway, we shall have more money and a
furnished house, and maybe we shall have Russian neighbours'.[13]

Stella was to experience glooms while at Lung Ching Tsun, but never to
reach the depths of depression that she knew at Mengtsz. For one thing the
life was not so laboriously social – though she had been there only a week
when she and Shaemas, along with nearly two hundred Chinese and
Japanese guests, attended a grand celebration banquet – with geishas – laid
on to mark the birthday of the imbecile Emperor Yoshihito (he would die in
a year, to be succeeded by his son Hirohito).

Next morning she was off with Shaemas to inspect a Customs barrier
some four hours' ride away. She was driven by their *mafu* in a trap, while
Shaemas rode; the weather sparkled, and as she jolted along a road that 'in
any other part of the world' would have been called a donkey track, she sang
to her ukelele. A rapt audience followed on behind – 'a Korean in his white

baggy clothes and inevitable top hat . . . mounted on a donkey which slobbered on my shoulder blades'. Having slept at the barrier, 'a little blowaway looking new house in a compound with high round mountains shrugging their shoulders before and behind it', they were home again in time to welcome a visitor.

Maria Aristidovna Nadarov was a Russian of good family, but not of much culture, who had worked in London as a governess and was strongly anglophile. An ugly, weatherbeaten woman in her late forties, she was full of good sense, and took an endless interest in the Andersons' affairs. With an elderly, sick husband she had been living since the revolution in a nearby town on the charity of the *tao yin* (the local magistrate) and on what she could make by the sale of her eggs, butter and vegetables. Maria Aristidovna was by no means the ideal companion for Stella – but in her situation she could not afford to be fussy.

The next Russians to appear were the Polykovs, mother and son; she came to sew curtains, he to interpret. In Russia the Polykovs had belonged to the prosperous merchant class, now they lived in a two-room Korean hut. 'She looks as though she would be satisfied with only animal necessities,' Stella wrote, 'and she hardly has those.' There was mutual embarrassment when they all sat down to eat, the Polykovs trying hard to show restraint and indifference in face of the food set before them, Stella pretending not to notice their 'ravenous' feeding. It took her a while to adjust to the humble status of the Russians generally: to find Shaemas's Chinese assistant employing a Russian girl as maid seemed topsy-turvy after what in Hong Kong and Peking she had come to accept as normal in race relations.

By mid-November winter was well advanced in southern Manchuria. One wonders how powerful a plea Shaemas made to his wife not to accompany him on a tour of inspection, necessarily prolonged, of a series of Customs barriers to the east of Lung Ching Tsun. Perhaps it was beyond him to dissuade her, for certainly she went.

On the first night they put up at Hunchun, some fifty miles distant, at the house of a French colleague, Lancournet, and two mornings later, under his escort, they set off on their tour, Stella in a cart that was 'springless and uncompromising', but bearable with cushions and rugs. Ahead lay the mountains of Siberia; behind, the mountains of Korea; all around, the South Manchurian range. Next day, with Manchurian suddenness, the weather worsened. Out of deep-frozen Siberia blew a wind that Stella described eloquently as 'indescribable', bringing 'horizontal sparse snow'. 'I got very cold, I felt pretty bad,' she wrote; and, as though suddenly reminded, bethought her of the fact that 'great cold was always to me the kind of hardship too unbearable to be adventurous'. However, there was nothing for it but to press on in face of 'a screaming wind that went through

my layers – silk – wool – leather – corduroy – wool – fur – as though they
were muslin'.

Rivers were freezing overnight now, from three to six inches deep, but
not yet freezing solid: they were full of small drifting icebergs. In some
places, however, it was not considered lunacy to attempt a crossing by boat,
and this they did the next day, only to find themselves wedged in 'great
grinding sheets and blocks and rosettes of ice with no water in between'.
They were rescued by a man with a rope who hauled them to an island, but
they were not safe yet. The only way to reach the far bank was by crawling
on all fours across an iced-over bridge, one plank wide and several planks
long, 'and the water here was so swift and deep that it had not frozen at the
edges. It was a nightmare crossing.' (In fact it was a horribly exaggerated
version of the ordeal to which her father had put her as a small girl, and
which remained a bad memory.) The next river – the area was abundantly
supplied with watercourses – was too full of ice to permit an attempt by boat.
It was just possible to cross on foot, 'as long as one was quick to move at the
sound of a crack', and in the middle it was 'all smashed and one had to jump
across a hole on to a round ice-covered log which was frozen in'. (Even in
these circumstances Stella found a moment to observe with delight that 'the
edge of that river was all steepled with little reeds and weeds which had
become coated with ice and stood up gleaming slenderly, glazed with
pinnacles of ice'.) Next day wisely she stayed indoors at their Chinese inn,
'lying on the big *kang* oven, and eating two most noble Chinese meals'.

Barring accidents, the worst was over. Lancournet's comfortable house
beckoned, and then home. As he strode on ahead with Lancournet – Stella
following in her cart – Shaemas was no doubt congratulating himself on
having steered a gallant if headstrong wife through a series of entirely
unnecessary adventures; he was unaware that the cart had slipped off the
road, overturned, and snapped its axle. Stella was in fact not greatly
troubled. Her men, though beyond hailing distance, were still in sight, and
she decided to continue on foot and signal as soon as one or the other of
them turned round. Neither did. She traced their footsteps for *three hours*
until, worn out and furiously upset, she resigned herself – somewhat melo-
dramatically perhaps – to 'a night on the cold ground. I had no food, however I had my fur coat. However when I had lain down for half an hour, very
much depressed at the outrageous unapprehensiveness of Shaemas and
Lancournet, I got very cold, and began a most piercing pain in my side.'
It was at this juncture that her driver, with the same horses harnessed to a
different cart, luckily caught her up.

What passed when eventually she overtook the men can confidently be
left to the reader's imagination. No doubt Stella made her opinion of their
dereliction abundantly clear, no doubt they put up some sort of abject, male
defence. What the men said to each other later on, with Stella safely tucked

up in Lancournet's spare bed (where she was to remain for three days), is not difficult to imagine either. No doubt it turned on the expediency or otherwise of husbands allowing wives to join them on winter expeditions over rough country.

On 7 November she felt capable of moving on. Again a frozen river had to be crossed, the only safe way being to rise at 5.0 a.m. and walk over before the sun was up. It took them half an hour, over 'cracking, twanging, creaking, patchy ice. . . . one had to run quickly yet smoothly so as not to break through'. Once over they sat down to rest, watching 'a beautiful dawn and a fiery sunrise, but it was pretty cold'.

For six days after their return the diary is silent. When it resumes Stella is 'feeling pretty ill still with the pain in my side and full of a depression most difficult to cope with. I feel dreadfully humiliated that I cannot face life here better.' It seems to have escaped her memory that according to medical opinion in London she should have perished ere this.

By now the snow was three feet deep round their house, and looked as if it had come to stay. Christmas was on the way, prompting Stella to bring up with Shaemas the subject of childhood memories – unwisely as it turned out, for what ensued was by no means a happy, heart-to-heart exchange:

> [Shaemas] says he has never felt glorious at all – he has no glamorous remembrance at all – nothing corresponding to my sort of secret glamour about Christmas days in anticipation when I was a child . . . or Bible stories very intensely imagined – or first bodiless romantic love. He says he remembers nothing glorious in his childhood except the day he won his football colours at school.

And Shaemas's want of imagination extended into more delicate areas. Just before Christmas they went to stay with the Nadarovs in their 'rambling spidery casual house' where everything went on in a 'huge confused but clean hot room, at one end of which an immense Russian brick stove breathes heat'. It was an agreeable visit, but the day they came home ended miserably, 'Shaemas seeming to me very unkind because I was feeling too tired and poor to – do as I ought, as it were, at bedtime. He is so very unimaginative, but it is true that I am often weakly and should never have married. We both decided that it would be better for us to part and let him have a docile Chinese wife. I was very unhappy.' Next day was better: 'Shaemas makes up very generously . . . he is more warmhearted than I am – anyone is that.'

On Christmas Eve they gave a party for the Canadian missionaries which went off fairly well, though 'the division between Christian tee-totallers and heathen bingers was very strong from the first'. Rather to her surprise, the missionaries produced perfectly acceptable Christmas presents. It always surprised Stella when missionaries behaved in a way that seemed at all 'human'; for example, when a 'Pan Presbyterian Conference' assembled in Lung Ching Tsun she was quite taken aback to come across a member with a genuine interest in China 'regardless of the heathen question'.

Won over by their consistent kindness, she did in fact come almost to respect her missionary neighbours here, though not their brand of Christianity, which struck her as being 'like children playing at church. There is no notion of the difficulty and ecstasy of religion, or any attempt to understand mysteries.' Like many professors of no religion, she had a clear image of what religion should be – unlike her husband who, she said, 'simply could not conceive a hunger for religion or any interest whatever being taken in religion by an honest or intelligent person'. Another black mark for Shaemas.

For the Christian Orthodox, religion and good cheer went hand in hand. Days after their Christmas was past the Russians were still celebrating, keeping open house as best they could in rooms that measured eight feet by ten:

It was so cold outside and so hot within [Stella explained, in an article]. The candles of the Christmas tree, the candles round the ikon which enshrined a portrait of the Tsar, seemed to burn our eyes as we came in out of the snow into the brilliant little oven of a room. . . .

'Ver' sorry – ver' sorry,' said our host, 'ver' small house.' But obviously he was not at all sorry. Obviously the party had all the glory of those long-ago parties one used to give in the nursery to groups of guests – real or imaginary – squeezed cosily into a house made with three chairs and a table-cloth. . . .

'Of all things there is not enough,' said the host, looking down with an excited look on the groaning board. There were enough sausages and cakes of curd, enough songs, enough bottles of vodka and sweet port wine – but what he meant was that there were not enough eating utensils. The tops of cigarette tins make quite grown-up looking plates, however, and you can pretend they are priceless family plate. Our host ate curds and nuts out of the lid of a saucepan and drank his vodka out of a jampot, but he didn't eat or drink very much because he was singing and playing the guitar at the same time.

'Spasibo, spasibo – horosho, horosho,' we murmured – thus rashly squandering half our Russian vocabulary in a breath. . . .[14]

In Lung Ching Tsun there was friendly contact if not intimacy across the language barriers. It added enormously to the interest of life. 'I believe that an analyst would find much more unconscious hostility between men and women in Japan than in any other race. In public at least they never consult their wives or allow them to express an opinion. I am sure that the women have something to say – though never in history have they said it.' Formal occasions could yield scenes of pure comedy, as when at dinner two Chinese ladies were observed in a brisk skirmish about their respective underwear:

> Conscious of her own splendour below, Mrs Kao said (evidently) 'My dear, you haven't half enough on,' and lifting up the flap over Mrs Chia's tight satin ham disclosed red satin embroidered underclothes – and, the red satin flap being lifted, a layer of black satin. Mrs Chia was very proud to be thus examined but her face fell when Mrs Kao lifted up her flap and showed *white fur* underclothes. Neither were anything that would wash.

And the heartbroken grief of the Japanese barber's wife on the death of a puppy swept aside the obstacles of national formality and their mutual pidgin Russian, to bring Stella to the astonishing discovery: 'Why – but this is another me!' They were both of them childless, and that was the point. However, decorum soon reasserted itself:

> gradually her face set again into its discreet Japanese mould. . . . I ran after her with a handful of sweet peas – the only comment I could think of – and she bowed again, and I bowed again. It was as though a ghost of lovely and sorry unreason had shimmered itself into two, and the two halves walked away from each other in the form of an English female novelist and a respectable Japanese tradesman's wife.[15]

By midwinter getting about became easier, as people took to the ice-bound rivers. In January Stella was off on another inspectorial mission – 'I had not meant to go with Shaemas . . . however the weather was so beautiful that I went' – driving in the car along the middle of the river on a smooth black passage with an inches-thick cover of snow that prevented too much skidding, Koreans whizzing by on rudimentary wooden skates.

By early March there was a transformation in the weather. It was much warmer and they began to garden. By summer Stella was to report to her Aunt Florie, herself a keen gardener:

> we grow all our own potatoes, tomatoes, cabbages, beans, peas, marrows, pumpkins, cucumbers, lettuces, radishes, carrots, corn. . . . we have also had much more than we could eat of plums, apricots and loganberries, and the cook and I made 27 pots of jam, bottled dozens of bottles of apricots and plums, dried several pounds of fruit in the sun for the winter and

made a lot of candied plums from a Russian recipe. I feel quite a Haus-frau![16]

She was growing stocks, and snapdragons, and verbena and lupins, 'also my sweet peas have been very lovely and are still giving me several vases a day'.[17] Kanto was marvellous for wild flowers too – for azaleas, iris, wild roses, tiger lilies, wild lupins, and her own favourite, a flower with only two petals, 'like a butterfly exactly, with deep rather greeney-blue wings and a white furry body. . . . I never saw so many flowers – even in springtime Switzerland.'[18]

Apart from gardening, Stella was taking lessons in Russian, she had four dogs and consequent puppies to concern her, she was dabbling in photography and developing her own prints; and in September she and Shaemas took Mary Nadarov on a trip to the Kongo-San, the Diamond Mountains of Korea.

A month later she was packing her bags again. She had survived one Manchurian winter, but she was not going to tempt providence by risking a second, and besides she was ripe for a change. Shaemas would not be left on his own. An English customs man, Landon, who was undergoing treatment from the mission doctor, would be staying for some of the time, and out of the kindness of her heart Stella had invited her Russian teacher for the whole of the winter. An ex-cavalry officer, he was a dismally pathetic figure, 'a drooping young bulrush of a man, longnosed, over-polite' and consumptive, who lived alone in a Korean hut, earning just enough to keep body and soul together by teaching Russian, mainly to Japanese policemen – and he overwhelmed Stella with tears and handkisses when she invited him.

All the same, she felt that it was only right to tell him what he was letting himself in for: 'I told him that Shaemas was very absent-minded and unsociable, but had a good heart, and Vorotnikov said that many Russians were like that and he was used to it – but I doubt if he is prepared for Shaemas' unusually bad manners and inadaptability.' (From Vorotnikov's comments to Stella when his stay was over – that he had had a 'humiliating' time, and that 'if this had happened to him when he was seventeen it might have made him a much wiser person' – it is plain that temperaments clashed: '[Vorotnikov] says he sees now that Russians are essentially silly people, and that all their opinions are emotional'.)

The Russian community in exile arranged a farewell party for Stella, but as it turned out were not present in full strength, because one of its internecine feuds was in full swing. However, a spokesman for those who did attend made 'a very sentimental and exaggerated speech, with tears running down his face and billowy tremors in his voice', about the extraordinary virtues of her mind and heart – but inevitably designed to let the assembled company know ('as usual') that he was holding himself in readiness to lay down his life for his Tsar, and so might never see her again. Day by day Stella was learning more about the Russian character, but feeling as affectionately indulgent towards it as ever.

Chapter Eighteen

Stella was in San Francisco in late November 1926, soon to be settled, sharing with another woman, in 'a steep cottage on a ladderlike stair on Russian Hill'. Early on, she looked up some of her former left-wing friends – only to realise how much her political colour had changed: 'I am no longer an instinctive radical,' she decided, 'I have come to think that the mass cannot think things out for itself or look after itself.' During an evening spent with 'a proletarian circle' who sang the Third International while eating their dinner, she caught herself thinking it 'an unusually uncatchy and prosaic tune – only communists would think it worth singing, our old imperialistic and capitalistic songs are far finer' – sentiments that would have been heresy in times gone by. Nor was she impressed when all the working men present, who had come in their own automobiles, stood up 'and hissed through clenched teeth that in no country in the world is the workman so much of a s-s-s-slave as in this so-called democracy, etc., etc.'

She made a new friend in a lively young American girl, Marie Welch, a writer of poetry, a practising Catholic, a multi-millionaire's daughter, who, when she went off to Paris, allowed her the use of her fascinating, high-powered automobile, 'Innocent' by name; this was an enormous treat, as Stella loved cars.

There were interesting encounters with two visiting Englishmen. She had a rendezvous with the young Cambridge don I. A. Richards, 'who wrote me that he lectured on modern literature (including me) and had written a book called *The Meaning of Meaning*' (semantics, the 'science of meaning', was to be one of his specialities in the years ahead). When she first caught sight of him, in a San Francisco store, he was caught up in an ambiguity of an embarrassingly practical kind, for house detectives were accusing him of stealing a book from the counter. But when once he had the situation clarified, by sending the book round for identification to the shop where he had bought it, they plunged into a stimulating conversation ('he has read everything and is never at a loss to understand anything, however vaguely expressed', wrote Stella) on the abuse of language in American advertising, and other matters of current intellectual concern.

Surprisingly to her, Richards maintained that the phase of 'bogus personalness and explosive emptiness' through which America was going was something necessary, and should be hurried along, not stopped. Europe had been through it, he said, 'but the Americans, having arrived late, are crushing into scores of years developments that with the rest of us were spread over thousands', an argument that smacks of the facile perhaps, but certainly impressed Stella: 'I have rarely met such an obviously brilliant person,' she enthused respectfully, 'so alive mentally'.

Hugh Walpole's books she did not care for – 'except perhaps *Mr Perrin and Mr Traill*, and I was a little excited over *The Old Ladies*' – but person to person at a literary party they got on rather well. 'A shy, honest, funny little thing', he called her in his diary on this first meeting, 'the image of Jane Eyre'; a lifelong bachelor who was rarely at ease with women, probably Walpole found her air of asexuality reassuring. For her part, she was surprised at how well he knew her books, and how much he liked them. And she discovered that this 'complacent looking . . . bluff large smiling creature' was not in the least conceited about his own work: 'He says he is only a story-maker and his novel writing is only a continuation of a childhood trick of inventing stories – not *imagining* them or really *being* them – just stringing them together deliberately.'

Stella greeted her birthday with buoyancy – 'I am thirty-five and I don't mind. A day's march nearer home' – but next day her cheerfulness was dashed to pieces by a letter from Shaemas, 'a very hysterical letter', she called it, though it is certainly not that. In urgent, but affectionate and reasonable terms it discusses their sexual difficulties and his present celibate predicament – and raises the question of his taking a temporary mistress:

My dearest Stella,
    . . . You know that continence is a sore to me at any time. And for 6 months at a stretch in this place, where one sits all day indoors in stuffy rooms, listening to the wind blowing outside, it really is awful. . . . But if my having a woman means putting the lid on to the extent of killing a hope which I cling to, that you will in time find it natural and pleasurable to be loved, I must do without or tell a lie about it, which I have not done yet.
    I love you very much, more than I am ever allowed to show, but in my own way. Not a romantic, but a tender and of course sensual way, which I think a pretty good way of loving. Listen, Stella, you must let me love you my way. Such love as we have had so far has too often been shamefaced or perfunctory or frustrated. Unless you can feel pleasure in my loving, I

shall never be more than half happy. You must let me see and touch and kiss your body, and you must be happy in letting me. And why not? It ought to be easy for you to be proud of and happy in your darling little body. . . . (You won't let me kiss your mouth even, which is the prelude to lovemaking all the world over!)[1]

Distracted with worry about what was the proper response, she broached the subject with Henriette Goodrich: 'This is the first time I ever dared to talk frankly to anyone about being married – Mother would never let me – and it was very relieving.'

Henriette thought it 'very honest and just' of Shaemas to have discussed his dilemma with Stella, and not simply gone ahead and found himself a woman, in the hope that she would never find out. She did not think it 'specially dangerous to consent to Shaemas having "a safety valve" in the form of a Chinese extra wife: she thinks it hopeless for a rather underbodied fragile person like me to expect to satisfy Shaemas – even if I were to exhaust myself trying to live up to him'. But was Henrietta's the right advice? Stella was not so sure: 'It still seems to me dangerous, because Shaemas has so often insisted that the physical side is the only gateway to all his emotions – that it is the temple which sanctifies all intellectual and social intercourse – just as imagination is my temple. In this case if the gateway – to put it crudely – led to someone else, would he cease to need me?'

Having thought about it for another two days, she sent a 'guarded, disguised' telegram, giving Shaemas permission to take 'a proxy wife'. Then she took out and read his earlier letters to her in San Francisco, only to be appalled by what she saw as:

his obsession with the physical side of our meeting in March. . . . I cannot bear to face that horrible train journey again and meet him – as he hopes bright and unfatigued – at Seoul after forty-eight hours on a Japanese train. To be desired *only* for the purpose of getting into bed is horrifying to me – I can understand it as a point of view, that it is his only form of love and a form to which I have never given adequate satisfaction – but it is horrifying – perhaps only humiliating – because this is the side on which I am weakest.

Having brought herself to speak about marital sex with Henriette, it was comparatively easy to open the subject with Bertha. Surprisingly, considering her reputation as an amorist, Bertha thought that '*every* woman is cold compared to every husband'; the two 'most physically luscious' brides that she had known had confessed that they were bored by 'that side' of marriage, especially when, as was Stella's case, 'it didn't result in babies . . . they had to pretend always'. 'The worst of it is,' Stella cried out in passionate despair in her diary, 'I can't pretend – not often – and oh for God's sake not forever.'

Early in March she sailed, and on 31 March was reunited with Shaemas at Seishin. He looked 'very large and kind and excited . . . and I was quite thrilled to see him again'. When, next day, he revealed that he had been making love, 'physically only', to a Russian woman during the winter, and before he got her letter telling him to 'comfort himself if necessary' with another woman (he never got her cable), at first she thought she didn't mind:

> but somehow the more Shaemas said I had no right to mind, the more I did really mind. But the minding cannot be very fundamental or relevant, since it is very obvious that he has no love for anyone but me – I couldn't be deceived in that. . . . I suppose my minding is just vanity – yet even vanity has no right to protest, logically – since he feeds my vanity with so much love, and gets so little demonstrative love in return.

With logic and with self-analysis she tried to dull the pain, but she did not succeed; at some deep level beyond the reach of reason she felt betrayed.

When they reached home the dogs took her reappearance for granted, and did not seem to recognise the glory of the occasion; Communitska, her horse, had a boil on her chest; and the garden was entirely frozen and bladeless. Li the cook – astonishingly – had been sober ever since she went away, and the woman who had been Shaemas's mistress was still coming in to do the ironing.

Almost at once Stella fell ill and spent several days in bed. Shaemas was 'sweet' to her in her illness: 'I am very fortunate, seeing what an incomplete person I am – in having a husband still in love with me after five and a half years.' But sadly the harmony was not to last. Shaemas in turn got ill, and lay in bed reading an American sex manual from which, in what she thought a 'bitter' way, he selected passages to quote at his wife, 'notably the contention that men and women have equal sexual appetites and that to be sometimes reluctant – as I am – is a deliberate affectation or some remnant of a tradition of coyness that can easily be overcome'.

Shaemas's mistake was to probe into areas which even Stella, with her passion for 'honesty' in relationships, preferred to keep inviolate:

> When, trying to be honest, I say that I do not always get much delight out of our relations, though in many cases I do – and when I also say – being pressed by him to tell the truth – that when I am away from him it is not in bed that I most often miss him – he says that this admission spoils the whole of our marriage for him and accuses me of never really enjoying what we should share of joy. An argument like this simply sullies the whole thing for me – makes it all too conscious and Marie Stopesey.

Though sexual intercourse was to remain for Stella more a burden than a solace, more a duty than a pleasure, the Andersons were not to settle for separate bedrooms and a *mariage blanc*, with Shaemas seeking comfort outside. Apart from her fear that in that way she risked losing Shaemas's love, there was the Cholmondeley voice within her, bidding her persevere. And she may well have felt that to renege in this matter of sex would be to classify herself once and for all, and in the most basic sense, as 'not a real woman'. In a paradoxical way, to do so would be to concede her body the victory – and that was what she never would allow.

However, there was more to life than bed. There were dogs and puppies to tend, parcels of books to open with delight, the proofs of *Goodbye, Stranger* to correct. There were articles and short stories to keep her pencil occupied, and the germ of a new novel working in her mind – for she had taken up a Bible, read over the story of Tobit in the Apocrypha, and been seized with an idea: 'I should like to crib the plot – and if one did, one needn't add anything essential for the purpose of modernising – the whole thing is here.' In October their long home leave would start – and always there was the comforting thought that in Manchuria they were out of the way of the civil war that was tearing apart much of China south of the Yangtze.

In fact, Lung Ching Tsun had a commotion of its own in July, though a minor one. It heaped first honour and then ignominy upon the head of the acting Commissioner of Customs, the glory of the decoration conferred on him by the Chinese – for courage and devotion to duty – being more than cancelled out by the very nasty rocket that the Inspector-General sent his way to mark his strong disapproval of his wife.

The local *tao yin* had imposed a surtax on goods entering his domain, a modest, perfectly legal tax, but one deeply resented by the Japanese business community. As Stella nicely put it, 'if you have been accustomed to treating your neighbour's property as your own, his action in plucking a daisy on his own lawn will seem to you as presumptuous as though he had blown up his own house over your head'. The new tax was no concern of Shaemas's, but that did not prevent an angry mob of Japanese shopkeepers breaking open the Customs godown and removing their cargo, thus avoiding both customs duty and surtax.

The senior Japanese official in the town, the Consul-General, took the shopkeepers' part – 'the Japanese, a race of bureaucrats and team-thinkers, cannot even lose their heads without losing them officially and all together', bristled Stella – and from within his fortified, bastioned new consulate – 'built, so the Japanese say', she went on, 'as a symbol of friendship between two great nations' – he discreetly fanned the flames of unrighteous indignation, and blew them in the direction of Shaemas. In the consulate-controlled local newspaper, Shaemas was represented as a 'viper' and a 'bourgeois' (the ultimate insult, Stella gathered), and in cold print his very life was threatened. Moreover, messages from the consulate-general kept arriving at his office to the effect that a dangerous mob was roaming the streets, thirsty for his blood. In a final throw, a warning was delivered one evening to his home that the mob, armed with bombs, was on its way to blow him and his wife up.

The Andersons received the news with scepticism, but took sensible precautions just the same:

> we sent the dogs and horses away to a place of safety, committed my jade beads, synthetic pearls, and priceless Stella Benson manuscripts to the missionaries' care, hid the safe in a thicket in the compound, decided on the point at which we could most easily climb over the compound wall should the Mob come in at the gate, dressed ourselves in dark clothes (and any woman will realise how difficult it was for me to find a pair of low visibility stockings in these days of insolent champagne-colour) and sat down to wait, reading *Northanger Abbey* with ears pricked.[2]

From the first Shaemas had suspected that the scare was engineered by the Consul-General, so as to frighten him into persuading the *tao yin* to withdraw the tax, and the non-events of the night tended to prove him right. Next day, the affair came to a peaceful conclusion, with the despatch by the Chinese Chamber of Commerce of a large number of telegrams reporting the hostile Japanese attitude; fearing a widespread boycott of their goods, the Japanese capitulated and accepted the tax.

It made a good story. Now, though Customs employees gave an undertaking not to publish matter relating to their work, or with political implications, no such undertaking was made by their wives. With untroubled heart, therefore, Stella set to and wrote up her account of the imbroglio, posting it to the *Nation and Athenaeum*, who printed it in their issue of 27 August under the light-hearted heading 'Storm in a Manchurian Teacup'. From the extracts given above, it will be seen that she took a by no means flattering view of the role played by the Japanese in the affair. This, alas, did not escape the Japanese ambassador to the Court of St James when he came to read it, and he issued a formal complaint to the Inspector-General, with the result that a positive thunderbolt of a letter met the acting Commissioner's return to England: if the acting Commissioner's wife were ever again to publish such an article, the acting Commissioner would be sacked, and in any case her crime would prevent his being appointed on his return to China, 'to such posts as his abilities would otherwise qualify him to fill'.

Stella gives no account of the tortured matrimonial discussion that must have followed receipt of this letter, but since the article had been despatched with Shaemas's knowledge and consent, the *mea culpas* ought not all to have been on her side. (To anticipate, the Andersons were on visiting terms with the previous Inspector-General, but if they were looking for sympathy when they visited him in the New Year they were disappointed; retirement to peaceful Wimbledon had not softened him, and he enthusiastically supported his successor's line, his only criticism being that it was not tough enough: he himself would have given Shaemas an even fiercer rebuke – why, hadn't he once sacked an Assistant Commissioner for having a wife who opened a hat-shop!)

'Goodbye, Manchuria':

> When I arrived in Manchuria two years ago, it was like straying into a nightmare. No train, it seemed to me, had ever inflicted upon its passengers so many frozen draughts, so many unwashed fellow-travellers, such uncomfortable and verminous seats or such a treeless, bladeless, khaki horizon. . . .
>
> But two years have passed since then, and across our khaki Manchuria flowers have come and gone as sunsets came and went, the rough cheerless trails lead my memory now to charming destinations. Even the train, on the day of our departure, had a noble, sophisticated look to me, coming, as I did, from constant painful journeys in springless Manchurian carriages-and-five or broken-down droshkies.
>
> Once more Yi the cook was with us – dismissed two days before for dancing in among our guests with the words, 'Missy, I am plenty drunk, dinner no can do.'[3]

Goodbye, Manchuria.

Chapter Nineteen

It was late autumn, 26 November 1927, when the Andersons moved into Stella's cousin Hugh Cholmondeley's empty bachelor flat in Cornwall Gardens, South Kensington, and Stella, with the enthusiasm of the returned exile, threw herself into the pleasures of 'roaring, confused, but enchanting' London.

There was her first-ever ball, the Liberal Ball at Claridge's, to which she went feeling like 'a débutante of sweet thirty-six'; her first-ever lunch at the Savoy, with well-heeled Marie Welch; a mannequin parade; Edith Evans, 'enchanting' as Millamant in Congreve's *Way of the World*; Ruth Draper in her celebrated one-woman show. She dined at Laura's 'Bolshevik' 1917 Club, 'a dirty little place, pimpled with dusty-haired earnest or olympically sneering young men and women', Laura 'a sharp little white skeleton' herself. She heard Ramsay MacDonald debate socialism with Winston Churchill at the Inns of Court; Churchill, 'being unprincipled, unkind and a gentleman', made mincemeat of the Labour ex-Prime Minister, at the same time uplifting his audience with 'some fine English self-congratulation about our England – we are nationally cynical now about our own glory'.

Down in socialist Hoxton, Mrs Oneleg (though a-brim still with 'goodness and essential humorous gentleness') was proud to relate how she had thrown her crutch at various inquisitive 'charity gents and guardian fellers'. She was partially paralysed now and blind in one eye, and Stella waited for an entire morning with her outside a Blind Pension committee room, watching the other 'old wreckes of humanity', hardly bearing to imagine the details of their lives. Up west, she chose her Christmas present from Shaemas, a modern silver tea-set in a Queen Anne design; 'but', she reflected guiltily, 'I haven't really any right to presents from Shaemas, since I am not going back to China with him'.

They had arranged an early appointment with Dr Monckton to discuss the question of their having a child, and Stella's comments suggest that he was encouraging. He examined them both. There was nothing apparently wrong with Stella 'from the baby-bearing point of view'. Nothing wrong with Shaemas either: 'I saw the source of life on Monckton's microscope, after a test of Shaemas, and it was alive – all the potential life that might have been immortality for us – and can't somehow reach life.' The only reason, it seemed, why they could not have a child was that they had not had one.

Stella was living at a fast pace, and already by mid-December she was feeling jaded. 'I get tired of looking in at other people's shop-windows – especially as what I see is always mostly window-dressing. . . . I want somebody both honest and wise to tell me how to catch hold of life again – but that's the same as wanting God – there isn't any answer when you cry for God, or for honesty and wisdom – the wise people are never quite honest – that's part of their wisdom, just as honesty is my main folly.'

Her next day's engagement (she was to be guest of honour at a tea party given by Curtis Brown) was hardly likely to offer what she craved. Inevitably it was a very 'shop-window' affair:

> I was planted on the sofa and highbrows loomed up one by one to bow over me. May Sinclair was the most disconcerting – she has the psychoanalyst's unblinking manner – volunteering no remarks, only Yes? to whatever you say, like a fledgling bird always gaping for another worm. . . . William Gerhardi,[1] a bulbous-browed delicate looking young man, pink-eyed, looking about nineteen, was led up and I began to tell him how much I liked his *Futility* and *Polyglots* and how I came from a near-Russian country – when he suddenly walked away. Feeling that my shortage of sex appeal was being almost indecently emphasised by this, I struggled on. . . .

She talked for a while to Rose Macaulay,[2] whom she thought had 'a governessy manner', and then:

> I was clapped round the shoulders with some violence and there was Gerhardi again crying 'I didn't know you were You, Stella Benson, I want to talk to you' . . . and he was very friendly and wilfully naive which was rather a nice experience.

Stella's *Goodbye, Stranger*, Virginia Woolf's *To the Lighthouse* and Storm Jameson's[3] latest offering, *The Long Ship*, had been shortlisted for the *Fémina–Vie Heureuse* prize. (From 1925, two Parisian reviews collaborated in making this annual award of £40 for the best work of imagination by a younger British author or a British author who was considered not to have received adequate recognition, regardless of sex. An English committee submitted three works to a French committee for final judging, and the

winners up to now had been E. M. Forster with *A Passage to India*, Mary
Webb with *Precious Bane* and Radclyffe Hall with *Adam's Breed*.) During
the course of the afternoon, Storm Jameson, with what she no doubt saw as
exemplary tact, confided to Stella that if *she* didn't get it she hoped Stella
would; 'very smartly' Stella replied that they neither of them had the
slightest right to it 'since we could neither of us unlatch the shoe of Virginia
Woolf – the cleverest person alive to-day, I believe'. One almost hears
Storm Jameson's shop-window glass cracking. (In fact, *To the Lighthouse*
would be the winner.) It is salutary to note that of the novelists whom Stella
met that afternoon, she, the guest of honour, is the one whose name has
been buried in deepest oblivion – and the only one not accorded a niche in the
1985 edition, compiled by Margaret Drabble, of the *Oxford Companion to
English Literature*. Not much enlivened by the festivity, she went straight
back to her 'dreary home – there is a sort of temporary quarrel going on
between Shaemas and me just now, and I feel sour with the business of being
married'.

Dutifully, Shaemas went to Ballydavid for Christmas, and Stella to the
Cholmondeleys' new house in Dorset, where she had a time after her own
heart. It snowed heavily and they were incarcerated, most of the cousins
were there, and all of them in the mood for nostalgia. Details of childhood
games came tumbling out of the recesses of memory, they turned the
drawing room into a nursery, got out chessmen and spent hours re-enacting
an elaborate medieval adventure game with donjons, keeps and oubliettes
laid out all over the furniture and carpet; while it lasted it was total, blissful
escape. Reality was quite another thing. When she got back to lonely
Cornwall Gardens, disconcertingly no letter from Shaemas awaited her.

Early in 1928 the Boulengers took the Andersons to the Gargoyle Club, the
restaurant-cum-nightclub (then three years old) at 69 Dean Street, Soho,
already an established haunt of writers, artists and intellectuals. By means
of a small and temperamental lift, members and their guests rose to the top
of the building where, by daylight, a choice of views lay before them: the
chimney-pots of Soho, or a Mauresque interior designed by Matisse, walls
of mirror mosaic reflecting in fragments the dance floor and surrounding
tables. It was a club of two distinct moods: at lunchtime it was quiet,
decorous; politicians and civil servants came with their wives. At night it
was a melting pot, where interesting encounters of all sorts were possible.

Shaemas and Stella liked the place – they enjoyed dancing 'to a whispering band which left most of the beats to the imagination' and – boggling
rather at the height of the membership fee, seven pounds – decided to
join for the year. Presumably they passed muster with proprietor David
Tennant: he did not admit everyone.

They were seeing a good deal of Stella's friends Dominick and Margery Spring Rice, whose marriage was under acute strain from Dominick's drinking, and they struck up a new friendship (boon companionship may be the apter term, since the relationship throve on a shared enjoyment of cocktails and poker), with friends of George's, Cuthbert and Lady Eileen Orde. The Ordes were artists and lived in Chelsea; they were sometimes mentioned in the society gossip columns and their photographs occasionally decorated the *Tatler*. Cuthbert was a portrait painter,[4] Lady Eileen was less interesting to the press as an artist than as the daughter of the fourth Duke of Wellington. Handsome rather than pretty (she had her grandfather the Iron Duke's nose), witty, amusing, mondaine, in the eyes of some her attractions were rendered more interesting by virtue of her physical handicap: she was a victim of multiple sclerosis, and her recent paintings had been done by mouth. Undoubtedly she had courage. Stella admired her pluck and pitied her at the same time – to her an irresistible combination – as she watched her weaving her way through the tables at the Gargoyle, quivering and shaking on her escort's arm. Eileen had a make-no-bones-about-it outspokenness that Stella particularly enjoyed: 'She almost cultivates the special frankness of those near death,' she wrote, awed, on a first meeting. 'Both Ordes terrify and interest me.'

In spite of the fact that he was 'too good-looking to be human', Cuthbert did not terrify for long. Soon she was to find out two reassuring things about him: first, he was scarcely conscious of his good looks; second, he was not very bright. In fact she was to go so far as to call him 'chicken-brained'. However, he was wonderfully convivial and debonair, and after the chaste society of missionaries even his risqué-est stories came like a breath of fresh air. Nor did one have to be long in company with Lady Eileen to realise that she too had a lively taste for sexual and lavatorial innuendo.

This bright and brittle modernity was not, one would have said, quite Stella and Shaemas's scene, and the fascination that the Ordes exercised over them was perhaps to some extent an effect of exile; rumour had reached them, even in Manchuria, of a new, anything-goes style of London social life, and the Ordes seemed to typify it.

One day in February, when Stella's back was turned, Cuthbert switched on his wireless, 'and someone suddenly began telling us the price of broccoli sprouts'. Stella had happened to mention that on the very next day she was to make a broadcast, by invitation of the infant broadcasting corporation, and that – believe it or not – she had never heard a radio.

Her audition at Savoy Hill some time earlier had nettled her, for instead of allowing her to follow her natural bent, 'emphasis by understatement, in voice, in wit, in manner, in soul, in everything', her producer Lance

Sieveking[5] had asked her to read in a 'chatty, overemphasised, sprightly way'.

On the day of the actual broadcast she retired with her announcer and a 'kind' young Mr Hibberd[6] to an inner room with a gaudy red electric light bulb over the door, and soon her voice floated out over the ether on the subject of, of all things, rugby football: 'deliberately ignorant observations about that game I saw between England and the Waratahs' (she had watched this New South Wales team play at Twickenham). Listeners may have remarked some variation of tempo in Stella's reading, for from time to time the announcer had waved a yellow paper at her, saying '"Slower, please", on which I hiccoughed, faltered and slowed up, only to get faster and faster until the yellow paper waved again'.

An SOS from Johnnie Granville had Stella rushing down to Maidenhead, taking with her Shaemas for moral support, and Stephen in his capacity as lawyer. Twenty-two now, Johnnie had got a girl 'into trouble' and – though he now said he no longer liked her – reluctantly he had promised to marry her the very next day; the girl and her parents were on picket duty outside the garage where he worked so as to keep him up to scratch. Johnnie had been terrified that he would be sacked if the garage proprietor got wind of what was up, but in fact – while deploring such goings-on – his employer took his part, and was prepared to send for the police should the family trespass on his property. Meanwhile he was allowing his foreman to drive Johnnie home for fear of assault.

Obviously Johnnie hoped that Stella would act like a fairy godmother – wave her magic wand and somehow rescue him – but this was not what she had in mind: she and the two men made a compact between them to present 'three blank stern faces' to Johnnie when they arrived, and leave him with the 'dreadful necessity of having to make his own decision'. However, Stella sought out in Maidenhead a 'rather facetious' young lawyer (who evidently enjoyed the comic aspect of this bucolic tragedy), commissioning him to protect the lad's interests should the girl sue him for breach of promise or – as she did – in a bastardy suit.

Nigel Bengough put in an appearance, 'very middle-aged and a bit bald' – and married; Stella had not set eyes on him since 1918. There was no need, she felt, for his wife to be – as she was – 'not very pleasant' to herself: 'I am a very safe past for him to have.'

Possibly the meeting had the effect of ruffling her own spouse's feelings, for it was on the same day[6] that he broke out in complaint at the way Stella was 'thrusting her friends on him' so that he could not 'be himself'. It was a serious enough upset to have her running back to her mother (now in a flat in Drayton Court, Drayton Gardens, South Kensington): 'I can't live with someone so steeped in prosaic gloom and grievance. . . . What he so resents is the fact that I don't depend at all on him, and he does on me. We being what we are, it can't be helped. We oughtn't to have married.' Mrs Benson was 'very kind' but 'a little confused' by her daughter's sudden descent; Stephen, at thirty-two still living at home, was very kind too, 'but did not stop playing the ukelele'.

In Mrs Benson's view a permanent separation was the answer, but Stella was not so sure: 'there are really a lot of things I value in Shaemas – chiefly his honesty. If his honesty only led him to like or enjoy things and people sometimes, instead of always frankly detesting, life would be bearable. . . . Shaemas feels that the fact that he is very fond of me ought to compensate for his lack of imagination, joy or enthusiasm.' After a week she relented, and went back to a chastened Shaemas, suitably contrite and anxious to amend his ways: 'He says he can't do without me, and in a way I need him. He can't grow humour or imagination of course, but he knows and thinks interesting things, and I can't think it is anything but slackness and mental indolency that makes him such a sullen and dull companion. He has promised to try to open his mind more.' Shaemas had a good deal to put up with in his marriage to Stella, and it is well from time to time to remind ourselves that in the nature of things the evidence is all one-sided.

Halfway through February, Dr Monckton sent for Stella. He told her that in his opinion, what with parties and late nights, she was 'running herself to death'. It was a shrewd prognosis, for only a few days later she took to her bed with pleurisy, was ill on and off for nearly two weeks, and then went back to her mother to be 'fattened up'.

It was a week or so after leaving her mother's care that her heart began to trouble her, not the physical organ but the metaphoric one. The occasion was an antarctic explorer, 'Bill' Bickerton,[7] whom she met through the Ordes. (As Leonard Antequil, sardonic observer of the goings-on of an immoral, self-indulgent Edwardian upper class, he makes an appearance in Vita Sackville-West's *The Edwardians*, a book, incidentally, that Stella thought 'very cheap and dishonest'.) Darkly handsome, romantically scarred, with a look of Ernest Hemingway (Stella cut out and kept a magazine photograph of the author which reminded her of him), he was – or seemed to be – the complete 'he-man'. Othello-like, he recounted his experiences at the extremes of human endurance; Desdemona-like, she listened enthralled. He had spent the best part of two years in Antarctica, one year simply killing time (he had been a member of the ill-fated Australasian Antarctic Expedition of 1911–14 under Douglas Mawson, and was among those selected to await Mawson's return to base camp, involving twelve months' unscheduled delay). He had got his scar while serving in the Royal Flying Corps during the war.

Yet he was more, Stella felt, than the plain and simple man of action: there were hidden sensitivities of mind and heart: 'He is intelligently – even subtly – interested in people. . . . besides going about hunting risks, he hunts understanding of people and new aspects of people. People, in fact, are more to him than a kind of by-product of a life of exploration and battle.' After only their sixth meeting, always in the company of others, she was writing, with a fervour distinctly girlish, 'without being really emotionally involved – he seems somehow so exactly what human intelligent *Man* was supposed to be in the beginning – a rare success, in fact, on the part of God'. What Bill felt for Stella it is impossible to know: his letters to her are lost, as hers to him. But all the signs are that it was no more than friendship.

Soon Stella was ill again, coughing up blood, confined to her bed. It meant that she was missing chances to see Bill – and this was especially galling as in a matter of days he was due to depart on a three years' expedition to Brazil. (On the day she heard the news, Stella had written: 'I had quite a sore throat about his going, all day' – one of the rare occasions when she admits the link, which is clear to the observer, between her emotional and physical distresses.) However, sickness had its compensations: Shaemas came back from playing squash with Bill to say that he had talked exclusively of her, and next morning a large bunch of her favourite (brick-red) sweet peas arrived at her bedside.

'Pooh at thirty-six' she writes in the margin of her diary that very evening. Though her wiser self whispered that it was better that 'no real feeling' should exist between 'a very real person like him and a very unreal person like me', the almost-conviction that she attracted him intoxicated her. Having risen from her sickbed to go dancing at the Gargoyle with the Ordes, Shaemas and him, she had driven home alone with him in his Bentley feeling 'like one of those hot chocolate dishes encased in ice cream'. Next day he sailed – for Newfoundland, not Rio after all. Such nonchalant changes of plan were a feature of his romantic life-style.

Bill had driven them down to Kent to see Vita Sackville-West at Long Barn, only a mile or two from her ancestral home, Knole; Stella had found Vita 'easier to be with than most highbrows since she seems better-bred and not so busy being clever at all costs'. In theory, 'highbrows' frightened her, in practice she coped with them rather well: with Arthur Waley, for instance, whom she admired enormously – 'he is a kind of Bloomsbury saint – he lives in a cloudy ecstasy of cleverness – and looks like an angel, such a perfect, longlashed, chaste face'; or Aldous Huxley, whom she was determined to hate, having recoiled in horror from the cynicism of *Those Barren Leaves*. When met at the Gargoyle, he turned out to be human after all – vulnerable, frail, nearly blind: 'I could only be very gentle, and contented myself with saying that I couldn't bear his books, and took it for granted that he couldn't bear mine'; before they parted, the Huxleys had invited the Andersons to stay with them in Italy.

She had already met and liked the doyenne of Bloomsbury, which made her invitation to dine in Tavistock Square ('without dressing') less alarming than it would otherwise have been. 'Would your husband come in afterwards?' Virginia Woolf enquired, adding – somewhat disingenuously perhaps – 'We have only a small table, so I'm afraid I can't ask him to dinner.' There seems no good reason, if she had really wanted Shaemas to dine, why she could not have asked him instead of the painter William Arnold-Forster.

Before the party was over, however, Virginia had cause to congratulate herself on her choice, for she had discovered that, as far as she was concerned, a little of Shaemas O'Gorman Anderson went a very long way. Nor had relations been entirely easy between herself and Stella; on one topic the ground had opened between them, and there had been a quite heated exchange:

> It was a dreadfully sticky party at first – all three were suffering from the kind of shyness which precludes them from looking at one when they speak to one. However wine warmed up their courage.
>
> There is something very fine and true, though perhaps a thought too rarefied, about Virginia Woolf. She doesn't look or speak as if she had any contact with any but intellectual life at all – she is very honest but she can't be human. She is a little hurt if you suggest this. She is for instance embarrassed by having won the French *Vie Heureuse* Prize – saying that to win prizes is a mark of mediocrity and almost an insult. I accused her of being inhuman in this – what does she write books for if not to be read – and to be read *not* by gods but by men and women. The English committee of the prize – and presumably the French one too – is not made up of geniuses, but it is made up of reasonably intelligent women interested in books – in fact of the public for which – lacking gods – she has to write. I should be delighted even to get a prize from a committee of costers, myself – I like being read and praised, so long as I may write in my own way in order to earn it. She admitted that her point of view was illogical.
>
> Shaemas came in later and a rather tiresome not too amiable argument sprang up – V W having parried the shy question as to whether she was writing another book [*Orlando* was published in October 1928] – (he has a great admiration for *Mrs Dalloway*) – with the accusation that *that*, she supposed, was his stock remark on meeting a female writer. Shaemas was ruffled thus to be treated as a low-brow China-hand and accused her of being a highbrow and inhuman – much as I had done but in less delicate terms.
>
> V W hotly denied inhumanity and was resentful, but every word she says shews her interested in penetrating the motives of people, and as never tired of watching the completely aimless yet hysterical activities of

women in Oxford Street who seem to be matching materials and studying clothes in the shopwindows without ceasing, yet never in themselves becoming beautifully or vividly dressed – that kind of thing is the remark of someone who is *watching*, not living. She has no sense of living with people – *life* being the exciting thing, *not* reasonableness.

A few days later Virginia wrote to her sister Vanessa:

we had a most curious wizened monkeylike woman, Stella Benson, to dine. As you are now a library subscriber, perhaps you can tell me about her books. She was second for my prize; and she took it very seriously; but I had to admit that I had never been so sneered at in my life as for getting it. Why does almost every bodies [*sic*] intelligence stop short beneath the chin? One finds somebody intelligent, amusing, educated, and then Hey Presto (as you would say) they take the *Fémina* prize for the voice of God, and become no better than a suburban lodging house keepers [*sic*] scullery maid. But she has seen rivers in Manchuria freeze from side to side in ten minutes, and is of two minds whether to leave her husband or not.[8]

Stella would have been mortified to know the impression that her looks made, furious at the tone of ivory-tower disdain, and would have hotly resented being likened to a scullery maid – but to have been deemed 'educated' by Virginia Woolf would have seemed an astonishing accolade.

H. G. Wells was a celebrity whom she rather dreaded meeting, not on account of his cleverness, but because she 'couldn't bear ladykillers'. However, when she met him – at a tea-party given for her by Ella Hepworth-Dixon, to meet 'various people whose names I did not catch, though they were all very great' – she found him:

rather easy to get on with and not the traditional ladykiller at all – rumple-haired and schoolboylike and with a high falsetto voice (which gives him a great start in comedy stuff, as it were) and a very charming eager interest in and appreciation of anything said by the person he is speaking to. He seemed to like me but I daresay this seeming is a habit with him. I dare say he wouldn't long like an unseducible woman. He asked anxiously whether there was a Mr Stella Benson always at hand.

She would have been surprised to know that, when juggling with the names of female novelists on an occasion a few years earlier, he had put Katherine Mansfield above Virginia ('a too-well-educated woman writing her best') – and then gone on to claim that her own *The Poor Man* proved her 'a more considerable person' than the author of *Jacob's Room!*[9]

Stella had written some articles while in England, she had arranged for the publication of her second volume of travel sketches, and seen to the press a short story (entitled *The Man Who Missed the Bus*, it was to appear in a choice limited edition in time to catch the Christmas market; hardly Christmassy in theme, it is a fantasy touched with nightmare, about the horror of possessing separate identity). It was not until mid-May that, ignoring the signs of the English spring outside her window in Cornwall Gardens, she made a start on a major new enterprise, her Manchurian novel; she called it provisionally *Tobit Re-Told*, and 'it was very exciting to be writing again'.

In June the Andersons took Dominick Spring Rice (still having matrimonial troubles) and Winifred Holtby ('the Perfect Fellow Traveller')[10] on a tour of Ireland in 'Arthur', their new Armstrong-Siddeley. 'Stella Benson and her husband are darling people,' Winifred wrote in a letter. 'They are so charming together. He is clever and extremely well-read and interesting to talk to; but he thinks himself a dull dog compared with her.'[11] Then Stella went on her own to Lutwyche Hall, sad to find the grounds grass-grown and deserted, and all the house's fine possessions sold to feed George's ill-fated ventures.

In mid-July she and Shaemas set off in Arthur for the Continent, and on 12 August were in the fashionable Riviera resort of Antibes. The Ordes were on holiday there – in fact they met them by chance on their way into the little town. Cuthbert quickly had them sit down to cocktails in the hotel garden, and then set about giving them the latest gossip of the place, ' "illicit couplings of old and honoured names", etc. . . . I must say I was not madly amused. I never want to be outside as a sightseer – I hate watching and whispering at anything – even lions at the zoo. . . . Eileen is a much finer person than Cuthbert – an enchanting person she is, and with ten times his brains.'

They met some of the Ordes' Riviera cronies, not much liking what they found: 'They don't seem to have the knack of picking up real people for their friends – these people were busy being lido-esque and "in with smart society".' There was a 'millionairey' dinner, at the Cap d'Antibes restaurant:

Thirty or forty people there, and not one Pure Woman. I had a great many people twined round my neck with loud refined cries – not because they liked me but because I have just reached that point in literary success that makes silly people know my name and feel they ought to pretend to know my writings. Michael Arlen I sat next to at dinner, he having made a great splash of kind words about me – in these unlikely seas – ever since he came here. He is an ugly, underbred looking little man and a great poseur – probably for my benefit only – a sort of St John the Baptist stunt – not worthy to unlatch, etc.

Humble obeisance from Michael Arlen – even if not entirely sincere –
would have been subtly pleasing to most novelists in 1928, for four
years earlier his *The Green Hat* had taken him to the dizziest heights of
fame.

If the Andersons were, and felt themselves to be, out of place at Antibes,
quite as much so, one would have thought, would have been the George
Bernard Shaws. However, apparently not so. Judging from Stella's account,
the great man, at seventy-two, was sufficiently encapsulated in egoism to be
at home anywhere, and Mrs Shaw, 'a very well-trained wife for him, calm,
smiling and selfless', would have little say in where they spent their
holidays.

Squinting from the sea, Stella saw Shaw arrive on the beach, 'looking
superb in a hooded dressing-gown – very devilish with his huge white beard
and upturned eyebrows'. With the Ordes, she went and sat down beside
him:

while he showed off – superlatively well. He talked for a long time about
music – like a brilliant baby – singing motifs – tara-ra-tum-TUM – and
stamping and declaiming – criticizing (he does that about everything)
without the slightest suggestion that he could possibly be wrong. . . .

    Of course though his hands tremble and he is not such a rock of
complacency as he pretends, he makes a great pose of infallibility. . . .
when he mentioned about nature imitating art in the matter of female
beauty which obviously changes as the fashion in painters changes –
Eileen said 'Yes, Whistler said that,' and Shaw answered quite tartly – 'if
Whistler said it, he got it from me!' He said also that wherever he went he
was haunted by a sibilant – sh – sh – sh indicating that everyone round
him is always saying – There's Shaw – That's Shaw – Look, there's
Bernard Shaw.

Once Shaw had got going on the subject of himself, there seemed to be no
stemming the flow:

He was more charming when he was imitating himself as heard on the
gramophone. He has, actually, a strong Dublin accent – but he says a
gramophone magnifies a brogue. Regulate the machine to *slow*, he said
(in a sepulchral groaning brogue) and I sound like a Killarney beggar –
turn it up a bit (accelerating his voice) and I am Dublin middle class – but if
you speed it up yet more I yap like a Belfast caddy.

When young, he said, he had been deeply affected by Gounod's *Faust*. It
had even affected his face: 'he had one profile that was definitely Judas
Iscariot – though the other profile, fortunately, was Jesus Christ. Unluckily

he never could remember on the spur of the moment which was which. Etc.,
etc., etc. We laughed obediently until our sides ached.'

Later on, Ordes and Andersons got together and composed a letter asking
Shaw and his wife to dinner, and took it round to his hotel. 'He came out and
said he would be damned if he would dine with us, since he could not get food
he could eat anywhere outside [he was, of course, a vegetarian, and
abstained from tea, coffee and spirits], but he would come round and sit with
us to-morrow night.' True to his word, he came, 'and declaimed again, about
boxing and about Ireland, etc., etc. During which I went to sleep until
Cuthbert scratched my ankle.'

It was lucky that he did, for suddenly Shaw turned to her and said, 'in a
horrifying tone of indulgent contempt, "I hear you are one of the modern
highbrow women writers, but I have never read anything of you." I thought
it showed lack of imagination not to realise that I might be affronted by this
discounting of my despicable gifts.'

Just before this remarkable encounter, Stella had had an unfortunate
accident, tripping over a tramline when rushing for an appointment at the
barber's, and skinning her knees and shins. Typically, the wounds refused to
heal. A doctor was called, who murmured the sinister word 'suppurating';
the legs were agony, the wounds showed yellow bubbles and dripped blood,
and the victim was having to be carried about by Shaemas or Cuthbert –
except when she was swimming in the sea.

It rendered the return to England trying, even though Laura, who had
also holidayed in Provence, was there to lend a professional eye. At the best
of times Shaemas found Laura difficult, and he drooped a little in company
with her and a disabled wife, seeming to 'wake up' only when the conversation happened to turn on Eileen Orde. Stella flattered herself that she
'completely understood' Shaemas's 'feeling of throat-yearning back to
yesteryear', for was she herself not feeling exactly the same about Bill
Bickerton? And wasn't 'our dear Eileen', after all, 'a truly resplendent
person'?

Two months devoted exclusively to the pursuit of pleasure is enough to
try anyone's nerves, and one senses a definite *froideur* between the married
pair. However, when they got to England and Shaemas crashed the car
through driving on the wrong side of the road – 'Shaemas wasn't hurt but
Arthur's keen, beaklike face was squashed in' – Stella was moved to relent,
momentarily at least: 'Somehow after this heroic feat I felt quite a glow
towards Shaemas again – a thing I haven't done for a long time.'

George was in England and had with him a home-made movie showing
the progress that the Hatchet Bay Company (of which he was resident
managing director) had made in developing Eleuthera: 'George talked about
it to me in the dark – as usual in a subdued white heat of confidence and

enthusiasm.' Next morning the newspapers reported that a hurricane of exceptional violence had devastated the Bahamas, presumably sweeping up George's island in the way: 'I can't describe these days,',Stella wrote in her agony. 'I simply can't bear George's despair. . . . I mind more what happens to him than to anyone else on earth. . . . he has carried the gospel (which is also mine) of taking risks always – to absurd and heroic lengths, and he has mercilessly been beaten.'

In the midst of his personal misery, George took a few moments off to talk about Bill Bickerton, whom he knew and, to Stella's consternation, considered a fraud, 'a theatrical poseur, posing as a he-man. . . . If George thinks Bill's apparent nobility assumed, this gives my little sprouting faith in human fineness quite a jar.' But really, any warning about Bill had come too late:

He has wandered in among my Secret Friends – where very few human friends have ever been – and there must he stay. Maybe that's the safest place for my noble ideal of him, and then the real Bill can be what he likes and not hurt me (by mistake) as he might otherwise have done. . . .

Curiously enough, though, I heard from him to-day, the honest-to-God he-man letter he generally writes, and that made me revert for a little while to my faith in him.

Chapter Twenty

Autumn in London. Poker sessions with the Ordes resumed. And parties. Parties where prostrate couples lay amorously entwined on divans, and Stella, bolt upright among them, endeavoured 'not to look too chaste'. A party at the artist C.R.W. Nevinsons',[1] where 'a dirty old street musician' was brought in to play the guitar, but had his efforts much hampered by 'a blotto young lady in red satin, who sat on his knee kissing his nose, and combing his dusty beard with her fingers'; it was 'not a merry binje at all', Shaemas and Stella decided, coming away sober and ruffled. Bloomsbury parties with the homosexual element much in evidence – young blond men with wavy hair and made-up faces, wearing no coats over thin silk shirts: 'on the sofa near me sat a male husband with his male wife at his feet, the husband running fond fingers through the wife's hair'. (Stella was pleased with herself for thinking up the expression 'Bloomsbury intersexuals', and then decided that probably it had already been coined by someone else.)

There were new acquaintances in Eddie Marsh, Rebecca West, Elizabeth Bowen; 'honest' Winifred Holtby remained very high in Stella's esteem, her friend Vera Brittain less so – and on a first meeting she took a positive dislike to Vera's 'dreadful young husband, George Catlin. . . . he is so excessively posed, so full of Bloomsbury affectations and Cultchah through being English on American university staffs (staves?). He annoyed me dreadfully. . . .' Ellis Roberts, her future biographer, a freelance journalist, and his American wife Harriet, were the kindest and most appreciative of new-found friends.

It was they who arranged a meeting between the Andersons and the de la Mares over lunch at the Gargoyle, guessing that Walter and Stella would like each other, knowing that she loved his verse. She found the poet, at fifty-five, 'very gentle and honest – I should say not at home in the grown-up world, but rather calm and tranquil and therefore not afraid of that world'. The conversation went deeper than at the average luncheon party: people asked not merely what each other's opinions or convictions were, but *why*, and Stella had recourse to her everlasting notion of a fundamental self-pleasing vanity:

> I think myself that all convictions arise from vanity – something about that conviction flatters some little tender area of self-doubt in us, and so we build our ecstasy and enthusiasm on that, and nag our perspiring brain with inventing logical arguments to protect our little quivering edifice. Vanity, I suppose by the way, is all the superstructure of self-doubt.

By this time Hugh Cholmondeley had returned to London and reclaimed his flat, and the Andersons had moved into a furnished house in Southwick Street, quite close to Marble Arch. It had 'good rooms enough but furnished in funereal purple – the beds disguised as purple velvet coffins in the daytime'.

Hardly, one would guess, an erotic setting – and after the second night there Stella had to confess, 'I disappointed Shaemas with my lack of love.' Next day, in a confusion of apology and self-justification, she went on, 'I'm tired to death, Shaemas treats my weariness and lack of response as a personal grievance. . . . I'm sorry I can't love – but I can't – I'm not proud of it, I feel it as a deficiency – but I have to put up with other people's deficiencies – why can't they allow me mine? If I were a male artist I should have someone who would coddle me through these darknesses – but a woman mustn't be coddled, she must live ready to coddle others.' And on 27 September she wrote sardonically in her diary: 'This is my Leaden Wedding – seven years married.'

Two weeks later, Shaemas came to her with the admirably honest though deeply disquieting announcement that, while 'remaining devoted' to herself, he had fallen in love with Eileen Orde. It was not altogether a surprise: 'Of course, I knew that he was goo-gooing at her, but I supposed, and still half suppose, that this could do no harm – one would have felt a man was fairly safe with a woman if he had even to help her blow her own nose.' But a facet of Eileen's gallantry under affliction was evidently a conviction that it did not put her out of the running as far as love affairs were concerned: when Shaemas had declared his love, she had 'challenged him to carry it through', and having gone so far (he had been permitted to kiss her), he did not see 'how he could pull up'. Stella for her part did not see, if the affair was to develop, how she would be able to bear Shaemas's 'habit of absolute candour' – a word-by-word, caress-by-caress account of his amorous progress: 'It is the first time since I grew up and dropped pretences that I have wanted not to know the truth.' She felt angry and disillusioned about Eileen; that her friend was 'sensual almost to the point of obsession' she already knew, but 'I would have expected her to play fair and realise how

unfairly easy it is to attract a man if you start on a basis of beauty so
pathetically in distress.'

On reflection, the best plan seemed to be for her to go to the Bahamas for a
while, ostensibly for the sake of her health, but really so as to leave the field
clear for Shaemas. It was a plan that seemed to her to combine the virtues of
generosity, detachment and modernity – and when Shaemas reacted to it
unfavourably she was both indignant and astonished: 'He was very much
hurt, and thought me very heartless, especially as he could not be sure that
Eileen will admit him to her full favours – and then he might be left without
a bed companion – a terrible possibility.'

It was at this point that Shaemas, who had no inclination or capacity for
intrigue, made a fatal error. Candid as ever, he told Eileen of Stella's plan,
and she – whether from a sense of shame or because she saw that the affair
was likely to take her into deeper waters than she had anticipated – dismissed
Shaemas, and said that she would never see him again. She then sent for
Stella and, over tea, 'very affectionately' volunteered her apologies and
explanations: she had not thought Stella would mind, indeed she had not
thought she would *know* – she and Cuthbert made a habit of not telling each
other of their love affairs. Surprisingly, Stella lent a calm and docile ear to
this rigmarole, merely pointing out that 'what Shaemas and I had in
common was honesty, and that it rather took the place of tenderness with us,
perhaps wrongly'.

It was a triumph of womanly sweet reasonableness. Stella devoted herself
to 'trying to be sympathetic and cheering' to Shaemas, 'and sleeping with
him twice in three days'. All the more upsetting then was his outburst when
it came. He had been brooding on her motives, and had come to the
conclusion that her threat to go away was a deliberate 'putting a pistol to his
head'. He accused her of arrogance and vindictiveness. Psychologising in
her turn, Stella decided that the reason why he had sought an affair in the
first place was in order to avenge 'the injuries marriage has inflicted on his
ego. . . . he didn't want to be in love with Eileen unless he could make me
stay here to feel humiliated by it'.

They had a wretched twenty-four hours in which they talked of separation, and then – suddenly – came reconciliation. One does not know what
deeper influences brought it about – even the actors in this melancholy little
comedy had but a limited grasp of why they performed as they did – but a
superficial motive would seem to be the 'huge' cocktail party that they were
hosting that evening. In the event it was a successful party. With the
exception of Arthur Waley and Eddie Marsh, everyone present got 'rather
tight', and the intrusion of a policeman – 'I don't know what crime we had
committed' – set the seal on its success, as in those days and those circles it
did.

Stella wore a new lace dress, designed for her by Peggy Boulenger, with 'puffed Elizabethan hips and pointed stomacher'. It made her feel 'very womanly after these striding years', and everyone liked it. The Ordes were there, and next day, very properly, Eileen sent her hostess a thank-you note, to which this was Stella's reply:

> Dearest Eileen,
>
> Your letter pleased me most awfully – and so did the presence of you and Cuffbut at our party. . . . I need hardly say it would have been very flat without you – but apart from the actual fun of having you with us, Shaemas and I are both enormously relieved that you did come, and that the unhappiness and discomfort he had feared were smoothed away by this easy and natural meeting.
>
> Maisie tells me she has collared you both for poker next Thursday. We shall look forward to that.
>
> Blessings on you.
>
> Stella.[2]

Mercifully, mercilessly, the women had swept the tiresome rubbish of Shaemas's shattered hopes under the drawing-room carpet.

Early in December 1928 the Woolfs once again asked Stella to dinner, and again without Shaemas. It was a more successful occasion than the last:

> Virginia was much more human and looked less worn and wild than usual – she hinted at – and even put into words, a few human womanly feelings and inconsistencies. I liked her very much to-night, probably only because she flattered me by liking and listening to me a little more than usual. Leonard Woolf looks decimated with melancholy and ill-health, but is always kind, and extraordinarily understanding of any half said thing.

This time the second guest was 'an ardent faunlike young man . . . full of knowledge and fancy', Lord David Cecil; many years later Cecil remembered the evening, and what happened when at about ten o'clock the husband of his fellow guest came to fetch her away – something that Stella omits from her diary:

> He was an unromantic figure, a philistine man with a toothbrush moustache and a square face. But he wanted to do his best: so he said [to Virginia Woolf], 'Are you writing anything now?' and she replied, 'I don't suppose you're very interested in writing,' with her ironical smile. He took that rather well, and about a quarter of an hour later he said, 'I

think we must go. I will have to go and wind up my car.' She said 'What kind of a car have you got?' and he said, 'I don't suppose you're very interested in cars.' I thought he won that interchange. But she took it with a smile.[3]

How to account for Shaemas's ricking his ankle in the same hole twice, so to speak? Could he have forgotten that the identical question had earned him a snub last time? Did he do it on purpose to annoy? Or was he gripped by that fatal magnetism that draws us to mouth the very words that we know at all costs must be avoided? Whichever way, it is pleasing to see a man with no pride in his way with language triumphing even momentarily over such a mistress of words as Virginia Woolf.

In fact the Andersons did not go straight home. With the Woolfs, they went on to Clive and Vanessa Bell's in Gordon Square, where Stella was at pains to look about her, noticing 'a great many very h.s. looking men and normal looking women (imported apparently from Kensington) not one of whom did I know. . . . Shaemas was so obviously miserable that I had to leave early.' Her hostess, Vanessa, had been 'shy and sharplooking – silent in gulps', her host impressed her favourably, particularly since the evening before Arthur Waley had told her '(rather cattily) that he was a buffoon, and had really got by mistake into a highbrow Bloomsbury world – he was really a "country gentleman". But no one can look at Clive Bell's face (so like an ironed out Winston Churchill) or listen to his pointed, mocking talk, and believe this.'

That was on 11 December. On 21 December Bill Bickerton was back, and Stella was saying confidently to herself, 'I can see him straight now,' and giving him a copy of *The Man Who Missed the Bus* as a Christmas present. Then Shaemas left for Ballydavid.

Stella passed Christmas Day very happily with her Aunt Phyllis, and on 28 December, since their subscription was about to expire, threw a 'goodbye binje to the Gargoyle', her guests the Ordes and Bill.

Now – though her diary was not taken into her complete confidence over this – it is perfectly clear that during the months of Bill Bickerton's absence Stella had allowed, indeed encouraged, herself to build up an elaborate fantasy about him as the ideal friend and lover, a kind of Conrad-made-flesh. The fantasy was based on very little: their pleasant acquaintanceship in the spring, the fact that he had bothered to write. But it had taken strong hold, and another couple of meetings with him made nonsense of her boast that she could 'see him straight' now. It was with palpitating heart, therefore, and a confusion of hopes and wishes that she looked forward to this evening where, Shaemas absent, she and Bill were to be thrown into the most interesting, possibly challenging, relationship.

It is possible that Bickerton read her mind, and acted deliberately to disillusion her (there were rumours that he had a new girl friend); whatever his motives, he behaved badly at the party. For a start, he had too much to drink; and then, by means of looks, gestures, nuances of phrase – who can tell? – he conveyed to her a something that produced in her an accumulation of irritation, mortification, pique. It was the last straw when he disparaged *The Man Who Missed the Bus*. Her hurt feelings broke their bounds and she lashed both him and the Ordes with what she confessed to her diary was 'unjustified' rudeness:

> I become a great ego-exhibitionist on these occasions, and especially with a little champagne taken – and no food. I felt too ill to eat – and I get an absurd craving to claim attention (intellectually speaking) and put all my naturally scratchy oddities on all my more prominent angles of personality. The result was I was horrible, and I feel sick with humiliation now. . . . About Bill . . . I see a sort of vulgarity about him now that I really secretly knew about before – and I am free of wanting him. . . . Do you know, I have to confess now that I had made a great resolution during these sleepness nights to ask Bill to be my lover – on condition that I didn't draw at his freedom at all – and give me a baby [the first of several such comments in the diary. The medical picture is obscure, but what is clear is that Stella laid the responsibility of her childlessness on Shaemas] – how ridiculous – what a mistake – how childish and uncomprehending I am about men. Who would want a scratchy, thin, poor mistress of thirty-seven?

Her letter of apology to 'Dear Eileen, Cuffbut and Bill' was designed to lay the blame for the outburst entirely on her hurt feelings as a writer (she enclosed an article of hers which had appeared in the *Nation and Athenaeum*):

> the thing is, you see, that up to now I have really been Tickled Pink (to excess, as I now see) over the man who missed the bus, and took such a dam [*sic*] lot of trouble to make it lucid that if it is not articulate – well damn [*sic*] it all, I can't talk any clearer. However, I now see that the trouble lies not with the Matisseyness of the author, or (god forbid) with the obtuseness of the reader, but with the fact that the experience suggested is not so widespread as I had supposed. To me a description of that sort of slipping of the cogs of identity is practically commonplace, but you are more securely enthroned and so the thing seems false to you. [The article] is only another way of putting the man who missed the bus. If you are sick of the subject tear it up. But don't think it's dam [*sic*] clevah because god knows I am done with being clevah, I do only want to

say the things that everybody knows, there's no point at all in writing otherwise. I mean everybody *who faces themselves knows*. To other people one might as well be damn [*sic*] clevah as not, and presumably that's what Mr Matisse feels. . . .

    Yours With Sincere Repentance (no but really sincere, wash out the capital letters)
      Stella.[4]

Soon afterwards, sitting beside her on a sofa at a party, Bill ostentatiously made love to another woman. 'My feeling now is nothing but acute humiliation for having made such an idiotic mistake,' she wrote. But erotic dreams about him troubled her nights, and early in the New Year she wrote to George in Eleuthera to say that she was coming to visit him. When in due course she gave Shaemas some of the particulars of the Bill affair, he would have been superhuman if something in him did not cry quits.

Viewed from an objective standpoint, it was possibly the best thing that could have happened: a married woman of mature years was relieved of a fantasy that was adolescent in nature and could very easily have run her into danger. From her own point of view, alas, Stella felt the rebuff as a deep insult to her feminine pride: she had offered her love and it had been rejected. The effect was to last the rest of her life, sapping her already frail confidence in her attractiveness as a woman. Ellis Roberts knew her only during those years, and he writes:

> It was as unfortunate as it was tragic that she should have decided that she was unattractive as a person; it was incredible to her best friends that she should think of herself as especially repellent to men; it was hard for them not to think that was a pose, and when that opinion was dismissed we were still left guessing why a woman with so much charm, wit, intelligence and gaiety, with no social disadvantage except her partial deafness, could think of herself as a notorious pariah.[5]

In mid-January Bill left the country. For Stella an autumn of neglected ailments – she had had bronchitis and a series of colds – culminated in a bad attack of flu, and she was in a nursing home for a week. On the day that she came out, Shaemas – with what seemed to her a cruel want of consideration – told her how badly he felt about their marriage. It was an 'unhealthy' marriage for him, he said. Her cleverness and reputation made him feel 'inferior', and he thought they should part, this being a good moment to do so, as she was about to go abroad.

Stella was in Eleuthera on 11 February. The Hatchet Bay Company had in fact suffered little as a result of the hurricane, but that she knew already. What struck her now as a greater hazard than hurricanes was the calibre of man whom George had working with him: there were far too many 'neurasthenic gents', not enough 'roughneck working men'. And in the schedule she drew up of sensible improvements to be made by George if he was to see a return on his investment, the enlistment of 'a kind of Shaemas' to handle finance had high priority.

But the sleepy spell of the place caught her, and she even toyed with the idea of settling: 'If I am to live alone – if the climate proves to suit me. I'd be out of everybody's way here.' In the balmy air she explored caves, got on with *Tobit*, swam, began to see the 'Bill-craving' in a different light – as 'baby-hope', her last chance before middle age: 'My feeling about Shaemas is largely embittered by the frustration of baby-hopes, too.' Deeply un-decided about the future, she opened the oppressive topic of marriage with her sister-in-law. But what Olive had to say gave her no comfort. 'Only if I learn to cook, and learn to pretend a rapture in bedwork will our marriage continue. This, as Olive says, *is* marriage after first love is past.'

Meanwhile, letters between her and Shaemas criss-crossed the ocean – 'reasoned, impassioned, imploring, sardonic and grateful' on her side (wrote Ellis Roberts, who, unlike her present biographer, had the benefit of reading them), affectionate, guarded, deliberately low-key – we may assume – on Shaemas's. On the ship to New York – for she had decided to go back to England, even if it was only to say a proper goodbye to him – the last of the series met her, and she gave it a characteristically biased reading: 'kind but quite obtuse', she found it; 'all that Shaemas wants is a female hole – one that he can use without losing his self-respect'. However, their reunion at Southampton on 14 March was affectionate, and when on 7 April he sailed for China, his leave being up in May – he was to travel this time by the Trans-Siberian Railway – she was 'sad to see him go. He has been very kind lately, and I dare say if we didn't talk things out so much, we should be happy together.' It was a sentiment directly contrary to their creed, but perhaps the beginning of wisdom.

On 1 May Shaemas cabled that he was appointed acting Commissioner at Nanning in Kwangsi Province, South China. It was a hopelessly hot and damp place in summer, he explained in following letters, but healthy enough in winter, and he expected to be transferred in the spring. In fact, with the sinocisation of the Customs now well under way, he had hopes of early retirement on a part pension: 'If you hear of any job *in London*, keep it open for a bit. . . . It would take £500 a year *in London*, if I could get a little scrap of pension from the Chinese. . . . Goodbye, my dear little Stella, I do want you, my dear little pretty, there is no one in the world like you.'

In other letters she is his 'little pheasant', his 'little fish'. 'Please write me often and gently,' he pleads, 'I miss you fearfully, my little wife', 'a kiss for your darling little breasts'. When a letter from him has sounded self-reproachful, depressed, she writes, '*Of course* I don't regret being married. I am dam [sic] lucky to have a husband who isn't sick of me by now. I truly am very fond of you, dear, and always shall be, in spite of quirks.'

Those last weeks in England had sealed a fresh compact between them. 'Do not come unless you are well and strong,' he tenderly urged. But her mind was made up: no mere physical considerations, no considerations of health, would prevent her from persevering with this marriage – which was now, it seemed, about to offer her 'a life between a swamp and a mudflat'.

Her remaining months in England, the months of spring and summer, she spent out of London. In May she was in Tenby, South Wales, with Marie Welch. Marie took her to stay with the Robertses at their cottage, High Croft, The Edge, in Gloucestershire, overlooking a deep green valley and the pretty steepled town of Painswick. 'Almost embarrassingly friendly', she found them, and most kind: 'one couldn't have more inspiring and hopeful friends'. In fact, the Robertses and Marie had, as Ellis puts it, laid a plot 'to protect her from her own indomitable pluck, her own insatiable inclination to waste her time and energy on people who, except as might a drink or a wild party, could give her nothing but loss of energy and waste of time.'[6] (Perhaps he had the Ordes in mind.) They prevailed on her to stay with them for the rest of June – but only on condition that they let her pay her way – and remain in the cottage when they went abroad in July. She saw it as a chance to finish *Tobit*.

There was another sad sortie to Lutwyche, 'the air in it like a ghost in itself'. Brooks Henderson came to stay, and Stella's mother, and Laura – poor Brooks crushed into the ground by the disastrous reception of an ambitious and indigestible epic poem, *The New Argonautica*, which had taken six years to write, and on which he had staked his all[7] – 'he really *knew* it was *superlatively great*, he really knew that he was a second Keats', Stella mourned. She went to see Susan McLeod, who was living out her last years in Cheltenham (she was to die in 1930); and for love of George she set to and edited a tiny pamphlet giving an account of Eleuthera, and pointing out the advantages, ripe for the picking, that it held out to settlers. *Come to Eleuthera, or New Lands for Old*, it is called, and a notable item is a 'letter to an ideal settler', plainly from the pen of George:

> There is everything here for the man who is willing to start from the foundations, and build his opportunity with his own hands. . . . Aeroplanes sound good, but a little previous perhaps. Are you a pilot? . . . Have I mentioned the possibilities of a restaurant? . . . And – Great Scott, man – don't you want to work in the sunlight for a change, and be never too hot, never too cold? And to work on something *new*, something just beginning? Hold that thought! Something beginning – in the sunlight! Yes, do come.

It was printed in an edition of one hundred by the local printer in Stroud.

In August she stood in for her mother (who was nursing a sick Aunt V), and took charge of the four eldest of George's children – he now had five – at Sutton-on-Sea, Lincolnshire, 'a most dreary place, but the kind children love, with miles of sand'. Stella had a name for being good with children, but never before had she had ultimate responsibility for any (a nanny and nurse-maid were in attendance, but she had the final authority). The result was remarkable, even a little comic. She got inordinately fussed and bothered over their misdemeanours, took them heavily to heart, and – fleeing to memories of her own Victorian upbringing – adopted a gravely moralistic stand. 'You can't get out of it,' Stella cried to Shaemas in a letter, 'that having a family, whether husbands, mothers, nephews, nieces, is for a woman artist extremely demanding – life in fact is one long fight for one's right to create.'

She had made this feminist point rather neatly in an article written in Manchuria. The time is the remote future when, as Stella supposes, gender roles will be reversed. Two women, Belle and Remi, are discovered in conversation, when there comes a knock upon the door. It is Belle's husband, and – 'not forgetting to smile sweetly in the direction of his wife's guest' – he askes her permission to use her study for his work, as the children are distracting him. 'Of course, dearest,' says Belle,

> 'Only remember not to disturb the papers, dear, won't you?' And as her husband disappeared, she called after him, 'And dearest – I have to fly over to Bombay this afternoon to see a woman on business. Like to pilot me?'
>
> 'I'd love to, Belle dear, only . . . it's this work of mine . . . I did want to finish this article. . . .'
>
> A shade of disappointment crossed Belle's face. 'Oh very well, dear . . . of course the work comes first . . . if it's so *very* important as all that. . . .'
>
> And only when she heard her husband's eager – 'Why no, darling, of course it doesn't matter. I can finish the article another day. I'd love to come' – did Belle's eyes resume their beam of tenderness.[8]

Feminists had discovered fresh areas of male dominance to be angry about, now that the electoral battle was won. Stella continued to rail at Shaemas now: 'the only thing I cling to in the last resort I *must* put my writing first. . . . I insist on being a writer first and a wife second: a man artist would insist and I insist,' and she went on insisting:

> I insist that I have a right to a married life, to be fond of you and be faithful to you, and have you fond of me and faithful (more or less) to me, as long as your feeling warrants this. . . . I wasn't *born* to be a wife to anyone,

but to be a writer – however I am your wife, and I'm very glad I am; and if only you would realize that I can only be the kind of wife I am – only secondarily domestic – it would be much better. . . . Spiritually I am not independent of you: but am much more of a Little Wifie than you allow me to be. I really am fond of you, and only wish you would clear your mind of what you think a wife *ought* to be, and just think of what I am. All husbands seem to suffer from the delusion of thinking that other men's wives are wives, while theirs is unaccountably and unwarrantably a person. All wives are persons, really. . . .[9]

The fact remains that at Sutton-on-Sea, while suffering the penalty of being an aunt four times over, she had found time to work on *Tobit* and bring it to within two chapters of completion. It is not always easy to sympathise with the complaints of the better-off among the women writers and artists of those days, who were in a position to pay other people to attend to the practicalities of life. In Nanning, Shaemas told Stella by letter, she could look forward to having no less than ten servants – an unprecedented number – to look after her house and garden.

Tobit Transplanted was the novel that established Stella's reputation. By any standards it is a formidable achievement: over twice the length of any of her previous novels, it is solid in construction, well plotted, with painstakingly delineated characters and finely evoked foreign backgrounds. Readers of her earlier work may have missed some of the old bittersweet zest and bravado, and even from time to time have yawned over a certain self-indulgent over-generosity of phrase – a convolvulus of longwindedness that wreathes it about – but they cannot have failed to be impressed.

What had struck Stella when she picked up a Bible in Manchuria and lit upon the story of Tobit was the curiously exact parallel, as she saw it, between the situation of the exiled Jews in Assyria of Tobit's day and that of the White Russians in Kanto of her own. In briefest outline, the story runs thus: old Tobit, living in exile with his wife and son Tobias, suddenly loses his sight. In nearby Media lives another unfortunate, Sara, daughter of another Jewish family in exile, who is possessed of an evil spirit: all of her bridegrooms – there have been seven – have died on the wedding night, the marriage unconsummated. Hearkening to their prayers, God sends the Angel Raphael in disguise to help them. Under his escort, young Tobias travels to Media, where he has business, and where he meets, woos, wins and – having been provided by the angel with a specific for driving out evil spirits – safely beds Sara. He takes his bride home to his old blind father and – again with the angel's aid – cures him as well.

It is easy to see the attraction of the story for Stella: in essence it was a fairy tale; transplanted in time and place, it enabled her to write about her beloved Russians; and in Sara (who becomes Tanya) it offered her ready-made one of those strangely-set-apart females with whom she so readily identified. Tender-hearted yet detached, intensely alive yet 'fanatically virgin', morbidly sensitive to pain both in herself and in others yet so preoccupied with the thought of pain that she invents stories about pain and death in the night 'to make her body thrill', in many ways Tanya is Stella herself:

> Love of her neighbour was a thing felt stilly, thinly diffused among pitied lovers – puppies – parents – flowers – insects – even things. . . . She drew no ecstasy except from her eyes. And she felt a little giddy always because she saw so many things, and had so little known self – or such a wide unknown self – to see them out of.

The good angel of Stella's story is the diverting Mr Wilfred Chew, a mission-educated Chinese of fervent Christian faith who (besides being a barrister of the Middle Temple) knows a thing or two about Chinese medicine. However, what brings it to pass that docilely and willingly Tanya marries earthy, healthy, boyish Seryozha and both survive the wedding night unharmed, is not Chew's prescription of the fumes from the burning heart and liver of a fish, but Seryozha's own bright skin and lissom body (resembling an animal's), and a something in his character that draws Tanya. She recognises in him a willingness to let other people be, to leave well alone: 'I could leave you alone,' said Seryozha. 'God knows it is a thing I ought to understand. I only want things to walk and fly about by themselves. . . . I like my dog to go on laughing at its own jokes without me.'

It is over the birth of a foal that they come together, closer even than on their wedding night; and it is at this key moment that Stella articulates ideas that were to dominate her thinking for the rest of her life – ideas about 'being' as a value in itself, a value that transcends all 'oughts':

> After a few minutes, the foal lay free. . . . with a little soft falsetto laugh, the mare began to lick it all over, snuffling with delighted tenderness into every cranny of its body. 'Oh joy – Oh joy,' whispered Tanya for her. . . . This joy was their meeting place at last; to this trysting-point the compassionate, cold, complicated heart of Tanya ran to meet the direct, greedy and simple heart of Seryozha. Living was what things *were* after all – living – and nothing else, really. . . . This *being* was the Unknown God, to whom both, obscurely, owed homage – this exquisite inhumanity – immortality – oblivion – urgency – this tremendous relevance called life. To the admission *It Is*, nothing is irrelevant except *It Ought To Be*.

But the whole novel exemplifies this idea. Seryozha owns a dog. Every now and then Stella pauses to investigate what it is to 'be' that dog, and at one point gives a riveting three-page account of its nose-led progress through the geography of an unfamiliar house in search of its master. She is good, too, on a caterpillar saved from drowning, and on how a poor bullock behaves, marooned on a river-islet; and on how a flurry of hens let loose on a road feels. In exactly the same way she strives, with humans, to present each 'me' as it is, to get behind its eyes, above all to pass no moral judgements.

One notes how triumphantly her attraction to Russians survived actually getting to know some of them in Manchuria. To judge from the book, the male half are a compound of vanity, self-pity and self-delusion – but these were props that everywhere Stella found shoring up the frail human ego. What she particularly admired in Russians, she told a 'nice Russian Customs man' met in Hong Kong later, was that they were a nation of individuals, 'they recognise *separateness* and separateness admitted seems to me the peak of civilisation'. The Customs man was politely sceptical about this, but he did concede the accuracy of her Russian portraits: it seemed to him almost incredible that a non-Russian could have depicted Russians so well – every Russian knew examples of all the types she drew, and he himself was married to a Tanya!

In *Tobit* Stella is at pains to lay an exact finger on the actuality, the thisness of things: from the domestic manners of Russians, to the way a weaning kid sucks at a milk-soaked rag, or how the flesh on a man's skull quivers as he talks; and she is memorably successful. Yet in spite of all, a spirit of ethereality pervades the book. Full as it is of creatures and things existing in close proximity, close relationship, ultimately what *Tobit* is about is their separateness – what, somewhere in the book, Stella terms 'the giddy spaces' in between.

Mrs Benson was in poor health, and Stella had already arranged for a cousin, Ivy Cayley, to go and live with her for a while. Before she sailed, she had Johnnie Granville to tea (with him he brought a new 'True Love', but Stella did not see how he could afford to marry her, when a large part of his wages went on supporting his previous true love's child). On 14 September George escorted her to her ship at Liverpool.

After four weeks afloat she was at Hong Kong, 'bitterly disappointed' that Shaemas, who was held up in Nanning by fighting, was not there to meet her – and that instead she was greeted by 'a very stupid, chalkpowdered woman called Lady Craig'. When eventually Shaemas arrived, it was 'very good' to see him: 'I felt guilty that perhaps I take too much for granted the support he gives my vanity.'

Chapter Twenty-One

Meanwhile from Nanning Shaemas had been despatching letters to Eileen Orde, warm, friendly letters designed to amuse, but strictly non-amatory in tone, letters to which no reasonable wife could take exception.

> I live in a very comfortable largish house, rather modern, with wide cool verandahs and electric light. There are three bathrooms in the house, each with near-porcelain bath, but (and I put this in in deference to your known interest in such matters) wooden commodes instead of what are sometimes called flush closets. At 9 a.m. the commodes are carried out and dropped in the river. . . .
>
> I am looking forward enormously to having Stella here. . . . The journey is marvellous and she will love it. And I really think she will rather like this place.[1]

She did. No sooner was she embarked with Shaemas on the voyage up the West River, and then overland for a hundred miles in a smart 1929 Ford than one senses a lift in her spirits. There was the scent of danger in the air, and Nanning when they arrived was 'stuffed with soldiers'.

Since Stella's first arrival nine years earlier, many shifts of power had taken place in China, much blood had been shed. In 1923 the Kuomintang or National People's Party under Sun Yat-sen had turned for an alliance with the infant Chinese Communist Party and to the Soviet Union. An expedition against the military commanders and warlords of the north was planned – but before it could move Sun Yat-sen died. The leadership passed to his military adviser, Chiang Kai-shek, who during 1926–7 marched as far as the Yangtze; China's richest city, Shanghai, fell. In Shanghai, under pressure from right-wing interests, Chiang broke with the communists and turned to massacring them. He formed a Nationalist government, went on to capture Peking, and in 1928 became President of China. Membership of the Chinese Communist Party became a crime punishable by death.

In 1929 Chiang Kai-shek was still busy exterminating communists, but they were not his only foes. There were warlords in the provinces with minds and ambitions of their own, and currently Kwangsi, of which Nanning was the capital, was in open rebellion. However, within the Nanning garrison there was division, and a few weeks after Stella's arrival a mutiny took place, the troops loyal to the Kuomintang getting out under cover of darkness and escaping in purloined river-boats. What rendered the Nanning situation even more confusing and confused was the fact that it was in conflict with Canton, some 350 miles to the east, while Canton in its turn was opposed to the Kuomintang.

The great dread of the peaceful citizenry of Nanning was that *all* the troops within its walls would depart, leaving them to the mercy of brigands, or of a communist peasant army that was on its way from the west, trailing ruin in its wake. Early in the New Year, Shaemas's opposite number in Lungchow, some eighty miles upriver, was lucky to escape with his life when communists sacked his quarters. He walked directly into the hands of brigands.

There were very few foreigners left in Nanning – a young English petrol salesman, a Swede on the Customs outdoor staff, an English missionary doctor and his wife, and a handful of American and French missionaries. Stella settled down to work on *Tobit*, and by Christmas had it finished. She acquired a dog, a pointer called Folly ('she spells it "ffolly" like the ffoliots') and a pony named Fanny Price after the heroine of *Mansfield Park* (Shaemas's mount was Edmund Bertram).

Almost every day they went for rides. There were morning rides: 'I love the early light and the cobwebs lying like lace hankies all over the grass against the light, and the young rice just showing above the water in the rice-fields, like green dust on glass.' And evening rides: 'the most beautiful cloud I ever saw, just at sunset – a huge massif of a cloud – tremendously thick – pierced by shadowed passes, crags, glaciers. . . . if it had been a mountain we should have remembered that view for ever – but since it was only a cloud, the memory is as transitory as a flower.'

After last year's crisis Stella and Shaemas were emotionally exhausted. While they recovered, it was essential that they jog along with the minimum of friction, the maximum of goodwill, and in war-torn Kwangsi this proved to be not too difficult. Certainly they must have appeared a happy couple, for at Christmas 'Nick' Humphreys, the young petrol salesman, presented them with a pair of toy birds, the Chinese symbols of Darby and Joan. A simple young man, Humphreys would have been surprised to know the effect on Mrs Anderson of his shaving his beard: it started a train of thought in her that led to the terror of ultimate aloneness, as she told Laura. A bearded Humphreys the female missionaries held in some awe. Come the day of the shave, and he was transformed in their eyes into an ordinary, approachable young man: 'It is quite horrifying', wrote Stella, 'to have it brought home to one how wholly one *creates* one's neighbours . . . how intensely and freezingly alone one really is in the world . . . one's friends being ghosts of one's self really, with or without beards.'[2]

Early in 1930 Stella had an asthma attack, and was still unwell in mid-February, when a couple of deserters from the French Foreign Legion in Tonkin appeared on their doorstep. Big, amiable boys, they hung about the house for a day or two doing odd jobs, and then Shaemas escorted them on the first lap of their long road east. In doing so, he was fired upon by soldiers of the Nanning garrison. 'Shaemas is brave,' Stella wrote admiringly, 'I am nervously reckless rather than brave – I am terrified of getting hurt, but crave hysterically to get close to being hurt.' This being so, she must have been sorry, when the Cantonese came a-bombing Nanning, that the Customs residence was at a safe distance from the town; however, the incident made a good story to tell Eileen, in the tone of desperate sprightliness that she reserved for this particular correspondent:

> We Nanningers are all of a doo-dah, having been bombed yesterday. A Cantonese aeroplane came over and laid two *very* bad eggs on us. . . . The bomber dropped beside his bombs messages to say O People of Nanning – *do* be good and loyal, and cease your rebellion . . . very poor psychology on their part because of course there's nothing we Nanningers would like better than to be good and peaceful and make money – but warlords make rebellions over our heads. A warlord called Huang Shao Hsuing [*sic*] came to our tennis tournament the other day, and I sat side by side with him, making myself a new pair of cami-knickers – *too* Mrs-Patrick-Campbellesque, don't you think?[3]

Another diversion was a plot, involving one of their house-boys, to kidnap Shaemas and hold him to ransom. It was uncovered in the nick of time, and it left Stella feeling jumpy: 'going into our bedroom to-night, I saw a cord being stealthily drawn under the bed. I thought it was a brigand preparing a noose. With a yelp of horror I threw myself upon it – it eluded me, and proved to be the tail of a large rat.' With so much going on, there was scarcely time to be depressed.

Stella wrote some short stories during this time, including her best known, 'The Desert Islander', a wry tale of an Englishman in a remote outpost, who tries to help a sick stranger and loses his own life for his pains; it was suggested by a gallant, vain attempt on the part of Shaemas to get the Swede, Einarrson, who needed treatment for syphilis, through the fighting to hospital, the Nanning doctor having already obeyed orders to quit.

For by April, with the Cantonese advancing from one direction and the communists from the other, the net was closing fast. Letters and newspapers rarely got through, food was short, alcohol had almost run dry. The only strong drink left in Nanning by the end of May, Stella told Winifred Holtby, was 'one bottle of gin, two of whisky, and one of very glutinous "Hunting Port" (but we don't hunt). . . . A loaded revolver now lives in the nose-powdering drawer of my dressing-table – a mingling of face and gun-powder which causes me often to leave my nose shiny rather than have to see the beastly thing (the revolver not the nose, silly).'[4] Shaemas, more at his ease in a tight corner of this kind than at a London literary party, was being British almost to excess in face of future possible danger, 'always very phlegmatic and unapprehensive. . . . though I believe he is very level-headed and well-informed, I think he is too unimaginative to have very good judgement about danger and when to flee from it (*never*, he thinks).' What *she* dreaded, Stella decided, was not being killed – 'if I can get *Tobit* off to England' – but 'being frightened by seeing murder in a man's eyes – to think of being run at by someone with intention to destroy me has always horrified me'.

But it was not to come to that. On 19 April a telegram transferring them to Hong Kong arrived. Stella's reaction was mixed: it would be 'refreshing' to be once again in a safe, organised society, but she felt 'very much frightened' of community life, 'especially life in a tenth rate community. . . . my indolent and afraid heart has enjoyed Nanning'. On 2 May the British Consul at Canton wirelessed an order to quit Nanning at once, as a Cantonese attack was imminent. How to get out was the problem. They were thoroughly besieged now – surrounded by fighting, all roads destroyed, the river too low to permit rescue by gunboat. The only possible escape route – though that way too there was danger from brigands and communists – was upriver to Lungchow. On 6 May Humphreys took it upon himself to 'borrow' his company's launch and he, Stella, Shaemas and Einarrson got off, escorted – in theory – by Rebel Gunboat No. 6, a slow, unwieldy craft overladen with scared peasants, which the tennis-playing General, apparently out of the kindness of his heart, had designated for their protection.

Despite the high degree of tension and discomfort, the escape was a glorious thrill to Stella, and she took the unprecedented step of making out several copies of her long and detailed diary report of it, and sending them to friends and relations at home. They were never actually fired upon, but the propinquity of brigands lent 'considerable zip' to the four-day voyage, and there were places where it was thought prudent to dawdle close to their slow escort. Once, they spotted a brigands' lair, and another time a dozen furtive heads gazed down at them from behind a barricade. The presence of Einarrson added greatly to the strain. Hysterically demanding five shots of morphia a day, he used up a fortnight's supply in three days, and thereafter was either dying or pretending to be dying, Stella could not be sure which.

He got wildly distressed, was constantly sick, and monopolised both the cabin and the washplace.

At Lungchow, blessedly, there was morphia; and they went sadly to view the remains of the Customs property – 'not one spot of anything of poor O'Kelley's possessions . . . car hacked to pieces, sitting outside in the rain'. A ramshackle motor convoy took them to the Tonkin border, and once across their first thought, after their Nanning deprivations, was of food. They 'gorged a GLORIOUS French tiffin', followed by a champagne dinner eaten to the tune of gunfire: the French were celebrating the feast of Jeanne d'Arc. Mindful of Einarrson's shattered nerves, Stella sent back a message to the inn to say that the guns were fired only in fun.

In Hanoi she bought nine Paris dresses and two hats, which cost forty pounds, a large sum: 'I felt guilty, but Nanning clothes certainly won't do in Hong Kong.' Einarrson now had his drug, but not always an *infirmier* to inject it: 'I am getting better at it, but hate doing it – his arm is nothing but bone, and so discoloured, and he cries and dithers so hysterically, reproaching you for not being quicker.' On the ship to Hong Kong (a French ship taking some 'strangely-sexed' people to Saigon) it was rough, and they were all so ill that Shaemas crawled to the bridge and asked the captain if he would give the *piqûre*; but the captain said 'not in such rough weather', so Stella had to do it. Between spasms of sickness she managed to boil the syringe and fill it: 'Then I staggered to Einarrson's cabin and plunged the stuff in, on which Einarrson succumbed into James's arms [for no explained reason, Stella had recently dropped the use of 'Shaemas'], and I into Humphreys'. . . . It sounds rather funny now, but actually it was a nightmare day and night.' In fact it was just the kind of nightmare she enjoyed.

In Hong Kong the Swede was admitted to a secular hospital, having refused a Christian one on the ground that, given the nature of his disease, he would be preached at – a plea with which Stella could sympathise. The rest of the party was taken into the hospitable embrace of the Commissioner of Customs and his lady. And then the Andersons went to view their future home, 509 The Peak, a colonial-style house with verandahs. They found it 'superficially filthy, but fundamentally pleasing'. Two days later they moved in, with Humphreys as their guest.

Stella had no illusions about what life in the colony would be like. 'I shall hate Hong Kong's rounds of calls and meannesses of indolent and unkind and overdressed women', she had told Winifred. 'Hong Kong is an island of tenth rate men, married to eleventh rate women. However,' she went on, 'I daresay there are ten just men in it and four or five just women.'[5] Thus it was in a spirit of only very moderate hopefulness that she set up the 'At Home' sign at the entrance to No. 509, and awaited her first Peak calls.

*

Hong Kong – British Hong Kong, that is – in the between-war years had many of the less attractive features of a small provincial town: the cultural deadness, the snobbery, the gossip. The officials of the colonial civil service formed the elite of society, with at the very summit the Governor and his wife, next, the Colonial Secretary and his, and so on down in a clear order of precedence. Somerset Maugham's Kitty, heroine of *The Painted Veil*, discovered this shortly after her arrival:

> Of course everyone had been very kind, and for two or three months they had gone out to parties almost every night; when they dined at Government House the Governor took her in as a bride; but she had understood quickly that as the wife of the Government bacteriologist she was of no particular consequence.[6]

Soon Kitty knew the shame of being taken in to dinner by the agent of the P & O line. (A point to remember is that the P & O agent's wife might well have two or three *amahs* for her children, and other staff in proportion, which could mightily assuage the pain of being low on the ladder of consequence.) Stella, as wife of the Number Two in the Chinese Customs – an employee of a foreign power – was not high up the ladder; but there is no sign that she cared. What did irk her was the unremittingness of the social round, the preoccupation with games, the philistinism.

It was not that the Hong Kong British did not read; they read a great deal. Homes on the Peak (indisputably the best place to live) were full of out-of-date copies of *Country Life*, the *Strand* magazine, the *Illustrated London News*, and *Blackwoods*; and the English newspapers, arriving via Siberia two or three weeks late, were eagerly scanned, first for the news, then for the advertisements, the best means of keeping abreast of the changing tastes and fashions of home; and there was a surprising number of English-language newspapers printed in China. A great many books were read too, of a 'middle-brow', mentally untaxing kind – emphatically not the sort of books that Stella was interested either in reading or in discussing. A university existed (it had been founded in 1911), but it was little more than a technical college for the local Chinese, and did not attract European scholars of the quality likely to leaven the pudding of the colony's intellectual life. When a person of intellectual or artistic distinction happened to alight in the colony – as did Maugham, and later Shaw – invariably it was as a bird of passage. As yet there was no theatre. The amateur stage flourished for social rather than artistic reasons, and on the lightest of diets. (Of one offering, a 'roguish' farce entitled *Art and Mrs Bottle*, Stella was to note that it 'upheld sanitary engineering at the expense of ART, *Art* being synonymous with velveteen coats and flowing ties and loose morals – obviously the stuff to flatter a community of business people like Hong Kong's'.)

It took ten minutes by cable railway to make the ascent of the Peak, or one could mount by car – and for the first time in his life Shaemas had a chauffeur. If one took the railway, awaiting one's choice at the terminus was a selection of sedan chairs or rickshas, their bearers eager to whisk one away to one's destination, often through mist.

The main reason why Europeans had colonised the Peak was that it was cooler up there than in the town of Victoria below; for that advantage they were willing to put up with up to eight months a year of damp obscurity, and the inflated fuel bills that went with it. For every Peak house had a 'drying room' equipped with stove or electric radiator, and fitted with numerous racks and shelves on which clothing, leather goods, books, soft furnishings, possessions of all kinds could be stowed to preserve them from a damp that could reduce a cake of soap to pap and a bag of sweets to a sticky lump, cause glue to melt and pictures to fall from their frames, and was to have a predictably deleterious effect on Stella's lungs. During her first winter on the Peak she was at times 'half suffocated by this thick, wet fog that wraps us round', 'wholly unable to breathe more than an inch deep', and she suffered frequent attacks of bronchial asthma.

On clear days the views from the Peak were ravishing. Stella marvelled that 'we English colonials should build on the Peak such hideous and *blind* houses – houses that don't *look out* at all, except, as it were, by accident'. 'From my bathroom,' Shaemas told Eileen, 'I can see the harbour with ships and ferries and junks darting about, and from the other side we look out across a fast-dye blue sea at remote, hardly inhabited islands. The harbour at night is like a Christmas tree, lights spotted about everywhere.'[7] He went on: 'The main amusement here – apart from golf, which I loathe – is launch picnics with surf-riding. Surf-riding is dam good fun, though one swallows too much water. . . . I expect Hong Kong won't seem so good after a bit, but at present I am keen on being left here. The interior of China is getting a bit too hot.'

He might have added how much they appreciated the convenience of electric light, running water, fresh milk and cream, daily ice and a telephone after seven years 'in arid outposts'. But already he had found that there was a price to pay: 'somehow one leads rather a dull life here . . . everybody seems rather careful and tidy, if yer know what I mean',[8] and he told Stella that he feared they were 'getting into the clutches of genteel people only'. True, the necessity of having her silver tea-set by her had struck Stella almost as soon as she arrived on the Peak: 'I sent a hasty S.O.S. to Mother for it,' she told Winifred, 'as soon as I realised how refined we were going to have to be.'[9] It was permissible to drive down to the beach clad only in one's bathing costume, but that seemed to be about the only casual, post-war thing one could do; in other respects Hong Kong preserved the formalities of the day before yesterday.

Other wives clearly enjoyed the life, and were only too anxious to conform. They 'adawed *bridge*', they insisted, and were 'oh-my-dear-terrified' of Chinese. Stella met them at Ladies' Day at the Hong Kong Club, an event laid on in honour of King George's birthday – 'I can't say I ever celebrated it before, or even knew it for a date at all' – and many and many a treat of lesser note. Her Paris dresses were an asset in the life she had to lead – for watching polo, tennis, racing, or for partaking in a 'ladies' tiffin (menu: lobster, teal, pancakes and mangoes). But appearances were not all. Her reputation as a 'nawthoress' had gone before her. She was felt to be 'clever', some people found her 'alarming', and a minority let her know it. 'I felt dreadfully cut off among these selfsatisfied provincials,' she wrote miserably in her diary, after hearing that a man to whom she had an introduction did not want to meet her, because he disliked 'clever' women. 'Only the ones who are too stupid to know that I am intelligent will know me.' Almost as trying were those – like a certain otherwise pleasant colonel – who, knowing that she was clever, talked to her with 'a careful intelligence – a lamentable form of indirect flattery to which all writers, I suppose, are subject' (though even he was to be preferred to another well-meaning military man who asked her if she were currently writing any more 'pretty tales').

Certainly it did not pay to seem in the least profound. Most Hong Kong people, she told Winifred, were content to answer the first word only of any remark: 'Just a few of our intelligentsia wait for the second word before saying – oh *don't* – that's too *deep* for me. What do you take me for? A *highbrow*?' When recklessly she quoted a line of Housman to some women, she met the response, 'Oh, my dear – *poetry*? I should have to read it again and again for days before I knew a *scrap* of what it was about.'[10] In vain she insisted that the particular quotation was about what it seemed to be about – bones, simply bones; they would not have it.

As it happened, there *was* another woman writer in the colony, Bella Southorn, a sister of Leonard Woolf, but as the wife of the Colonial Secretary she was to an extent above criticism, and, besides, her volumes of essays – *Chips of China* and *Under the Bamboo Curtain* – were so nicely poised to flatter both herself and her readers, tinkled so charmingly with superior British amusement at the quaintnesses of the Chinese, that she was felt, though undeniably 'clever', to be scarcely alarming at all – or, at least, not on that score.

At thirty-eight, Stella was looking more than her age. Illness and hard climates between them had given her a dry, bleached look, and during that first Hong Kong autumn she lost weight. When, later, Shaemas insisted on taking a photograph of her nude, on a secluded beach – 'nothing could be less characteristic of inhibited me' – she was shocked to see that she had lost the pretty body she once had: 'It has a haggard look, like my face. I didn't value it enough when I was young. I have so few beauties, I should have valued it more.'

There was certainly an element of regret for lost youth in the feeling that rose up in her for young Nick Humphreys, one night when Shaemas was away, and this perfect physical specimen and nice boy – with his 'thick black hair and proper robust fittings' – seemed suddenly accessible, only yards away along the verandah. But even as she desired him she was analysing her feeling, and seeing that it had a bifurcated root: 'a little of my Bill-sickness seems to have got involved with Humphreys, and O, I would have liked a strong little blackhaired baby before it is too late'. Nothing happened, of course, and so slight was her confidence in her power to attract or even interest him, that she was astonished when next day he asked her out for tiffin and a drive. They sat and looked at the sea at Repulse Bay, and it was all very strained. Shaemas came home at tea-time, and that was that.

During that discontented autumn her thoughts took on a parched look, like her face. Again and again she came back to the idea of 'bones':

Love and the flesh don't matter – nothing matters except bones – multiplying bones on the earth, and presently under the earth – that is the only indisputable purpose of life – that's all this ferment inside the strong young hairy body of Humphreys will lead to – the multiplying of moving bones about the earth. I am a ghost by the way – an irrelevant ghost not even haunting the high road – a ghost seen faintly in the fields from that high road which is paved with the stedfast [*sic*] and enduring bone and only marched upon by what is left when all the skins have gone.

Unable to sleep one night, she came downstairs and took from the shelf Housman's *A Shropshire Lad*. There was a poem, the one which she had quoted from with such notable unsuccess, that she wanted to look at. It was called 'The Immortal Part', and its central image, bone, though it underwent a sea-change in the depths of her mind, was to preoccupy her to the end of her days.

Housman imagines his 'immortal part', his 'stedfast and enduring bone', his skeleton – conscious that with it is the ultimate victory – as every day of his life asking the same complaining question, urging the same terrible advice:

> 'When shall this slough of sense be cast,
> This dust of thoughts be laid at last,
> The man of flesh and soul be slain
> And the man of bone remain?

'Lie down in the bed of dust;
Bear the fruit that bear you must;
Bring the eternal seed to light,
And morn is all the same as night.

'Empty vessel, garment cast,
We that wore you long shall last.
– Another night, another day.'
So my bones within me say.[11]

The burden of that macabre poem, a hymn to all-conquering nothingness, is not Stella's; at her lowest she was not as negative as that. The bright certainty of an afterlife that once was hers had faded with her youth, but she still passionately affirmed the reality and value of life on earth. One sees it in her response to the news of her Aunt V's death earlier this year:

this life is only a flash of something between *nothing* and *nothing*. It only remains for us to value enough this only flash . . . to recognise it as the *one treasure*, wherever it gleams . . . in a cloud – in a dog's panting – in a leaf's growing – in our own quick moments. There is no other treasure – only ashes will fall blindly over flowers in the end [her aunt had asked that her ashes be scattered in the countryside] . . . we waste so much time letting the precious fact of *being* slip by us.

As Stella used it, 'bone' could be a positive, even a seductive thing – the sweet essence of personality that remains after all pretence is stripped away, the pitiable 'me' residing, hidden, in the core of all sentient creatures.

In the spring of 1932 she sent to the *New Statesman and Nation* (which since 1931 incorporated the *Nation and Athenaeum*, and of which Ellis Roberts was now literary editor) a remarkable piece about bones, which arose from the experience of seeing her body duplicated over and over again in a room lined with glass. If she lifted her right hand, a massed rank of Stellas lifted a hundred right hands; and yet, she thought, as they all lowered their arms and pinched their elbows until they – or, as she hoped, hers alone – tingled, with *her* was the leadership, with *her* the bone:

Certainly these glassy thin women lied if they claimed the bone. . . . Show their teeth as they may they lie in their teeth; their teeth, claiming to be bone – lie. Teeth, I sometimes think, are like those small trivial atolls of islands that show above the surface of oceans – islands that, we are told, are but the topmost crags of immense submarine mountain ranges, whispered clues to the secret substance of the world; all that the simple sun can understand of the dark, fearful solidity of earth. And so, I think, teeth prick prettily through the flesh as mere hints of the submerged, barbarous bones of man. Only when the world is dead and the veins and arteries of the world's waters dry away, will the drowned mountains confess themselves to the stars; only when death calls the bluff of the skin and flesh and bone and brain, when the dry skeleton snarls between naked teeth, will man's single truth be finally declared.[12]

For a moment or two she triumphed over these false, boneless, substitute selves in the mirror, making faces at them and seeing them obsequiously copy what she did. And then suddenly it struck her that even bone was not the ultimate reality, it too was a mere substitute, there was a something beyond:

as chairs are substitutes for thrones, and thrones for godship; feet, bony feet, are substitutes for wheels, wheels for wings, and wings for omni-presence; dolls are substitutes for live pets, pets for babies, babies for immortality . . . bones then are substitutes for souls. . . . My scaffold-ing of bones crumbled within me; what proof had I now of my own lonely solidity in a world of mirrored myselves?

This is not the place for a study in depth of Stella's ways with this many-sided symbol; yet one idea that again and again occurs in relation to it, we should notice: her conviction that in a universe of 'bones', moral imperatives and moral judgements are totally irrelevant. Early in 1932, for example, she writes:

No, I have suddenly thought how to express it better. It is the bone that is the axis of the world of each thing and each creature. In each of those billion worlds – yours – mine – the dog's – the hawk's – the sonata's – the engine's – everything must be allowed to move in a way *consistent to itself and none other* – in a vacuum of licence, as it were. We may be glass to one another – we may see one another's systems and be astonished, but we mustn't get in – the glass must be unbreakable and *ought proof*. Our *oughts* shatter one another's glass integrity – our bullets shatter the exquisite privacy of animals – *but this is the sin.*

In the gentle, humanistic creed that Stella was evolving, original sin had no place. Man was not fatally flawed, a battleground of good and evil. The damage that he inflicted on his neighbour was not malicious: rather it was the consequence of self-absorption, of failure of imagination.

Meanwhile everyday life went on, and everyday relationships, imperfect and ought-ridden as they were, were to be pursued. Now that she had decided that life for the foreseeable future was to be lived at Shaemas's side, she had become less critical of him, more accepting. When she complained to her diary that there was no human being in Hong Kong whose company she preferred to her own, she was forgetting that often she preferred his (in another bad hour she wrote despairingly, 'How could every minute not inevitably be a minute of loneliness for James and me – him so full of reading, and me so full of thinking?').

For their companionship was real. After he got back from work they went swimming together, or for walks on the rural Peak with their bulldog bitch Tulip Camilla, named after a character in a David Garnett novel. (She was to produce for them two litters. One was named after former governors of the colony – 'To me there is no greater pleasure in Hong Kong', Stella assured Eileen, 'than going to watch the six tails of Robinson, Kennedy, Stubbs, Nathan, Lugard and Clementi, all pulsing in the same rhythm as they lie in a neat squashed row all binjing the maternal binje'[13] – the other after typewriters – 'they all have Universal Keyboard, and Remington especially has peculiarly easy action'.)[14]

There were inspection-jaunts together to lonely little anti-smuggling posts on 'darling' silent green islands with monkeys in their trees and big, shiny cowries – dappled like deer – on their beaches. There were cosy evenings 'playing (and singing) on the guitar, playing chess, and talking'. And Shaemas was her sympathetic ally in their constant socialising. A considerable part of every week, and most of every weekend, was given over to this, and a Sunday consisting of cocktails in one house, lunch in another, tea and tennis in a third and dinner in a fourth was not so remarkable as to be considered worthy of an exclamation mark. Even though Stella was bleakly conscious that 'the aspect of people that faces oneself is a wholly illusory aspect . . . *nothing* in anyone faces a neighbour – any more than anything in the moon has any facet directly turned upon one', she had to admit that 'from the point of view of a watcher and imaginer of the hearts of aliens, I rather enjoy meeting people'.

'I don't know why I feel so tender to party-givers,' she was writing in July 1931, after a year or so in the colony, 'they seem to me such a poignantly vulnerable class – all the little evidence of their putting their best foot foremost wring my heart – even to the best toilet paper in the bathroom, and the servants' lips moving as they try to remember all the last frenzied instructions.' They mixed a good deal with service people, in preference, one suspects, to what one colonel's wife dismissed scathingly as 'the serviette civilisation of Hong Kong'. But it was becoming a matter of indifference to Stella whether people were genteel and serviette-ish in the Lower Tooting sense, well bred in her mother's, or wild in her own (by which she meant outside the fence of convention), 'if only you meet them and watch them – they can't be so genteel that they have no bones, however hard they try. Of course, if you are going to get to *know* them, it is different – but people capable of the mutual genius of knowing and being known are too rare to be reckoned on.'

Halfway through January 1931 Shaemas's chief was transferred, and until such time as a new Commissioner arrived, he would be 'queen bee'. His normal work kept him very busy; now he would be under extreme pressure – 'my job is to control some 20 odd stations, some on land and some on sea,' he told Eileen, when once his Commissioner had left. 'I have a fleet of 5 miniature gun boats, armed with 3 pdrs, machine guns, etc. and manned by Europeans, whose job it is to patrol and fight pirates and smugglers. We operate the movements of these gun boats by wireless, and the whole thing is rather amusing. . . .'[15] With a very good grace Stella postponed a trip home – she had meant to look for a house, see about a school for her niece Georgina, the expense of whose education she had undertaken on George's having finally severed his connection with the Hatchet Bay Company – 'but James dreads too much being left alone in this difficult place, and I cannot do otherwise than sympathise with this fear – there is nothing more lonely than much talk and nothing said'.

One of the rewards of Shaemas's temporary apotheosis was an entertainment allowance – 'but there is no one whom it would be fun to entertain' his wife remarked – another, the retention for his personal use of the Customs launch, 'the prettiest and best launch in Hong Kong', he boasted to Eileen, 'a superb thing in white and gold, with shining brass everywhere, and a beautiful Chinese crew, all in white with crimson tummy bands'.[16] Surfing parties and picnics achieved in such style could hardly fail to be delightful, even if the company was not quite what one would have chosen.

And by the time the new Commissioner arrived to snatch the bauble from them, the Andersons had found a different way of passing their leisure hours. Near Stanley Village they had come upon a tiny stone temple perched on a cliff-side, with rought steps leading down directly into deep water. In the curious Chinese way it was available for hire as a bathing-cum-picnic place; the priest–custodian did not in the least mind if Stella and her female guests undressed before his altar, or hung their petticoats on the horns of it – in fact, as Stella noted in an article, he generally saw fit to perform his religious duties just when they were getting dressed from their swim. After a bathe, the terrace was a 'magic' setting for drinks or supper in the light of the setting sun. The fishing boats in the bay lit lamps 'with which they lure the silly fish out of the sea, and the whole mountain behind our temple shimmers with lights lit to lure the silly breadwinners and guests home from club and bar and the seashore'. Once, a boat lay fishing almost directly beneath them, its bright acetylene lamp shining on the water, 'no glimmer of light looking upwards towards us at all – the light seemed to permeate the water and disperse its substance, so that the boat, with its spidery, lazily moving rower, seemed to be flying lightly on a cloud of pale green air, spangled with fish'.

In August 1930 the proofs of the American edition of *Tobit Transplanted* arrived for correction; as might be expected, Stella disapproved of every alteration made by the Americans, from the title *The Far-Away Bride* to the fact that the text had been 'interfered with' and her introductory note on the situation in Manchuria (carefully composed with Shaemas's help) relegated to the back. In September came the proofs from Macmillan. Then in December Shaemas announced to Eileen in none-too-respectful terms an unlooked-for success for the book. It was to be chosen by the English Book Society, 'an institution you have probably never heard of, which forces masterpieces down the throats of anxious-to-read-the-right-thing sub-scribers. It should therefore bring in more money than previous books have . . . should make a difference of £500. . . . I say, how mercenary we are becoming.'[17]

Stella had done some writing in Hong Kong – some articles, a short story, 'Tchotl', a satirical fantasy about half-baked uplift and bogus idealism (American-style, naturally) – and had made a start (in June 1930) on a larger venture, a novel called *The Bones*. It came to nothing at the time, but the idea continued to work in her mind, and on 7 May 1931 we find her writing to Laura for particulars of 'stunted bone disease'. Achondroplasia was the disease she meant, Laura told her in reply: it went with sexual precocity and great virility, as well as the characteristic 'pugnose' face; it was not associated with mental deficiency, though mental development might be 'quaint'. Primed with these facts (though ignoring the sexual implications), on 31 May Stella started work in earnest on a novel which was to have as its central character an achondroplasiac dwarf. She called the book $\nabla\triangle$.

Glancing along the spines of Stella's novels, one notices that she lacked the happy instinct for hitting upon attractive titles, and it may be that this tells us something significant about Stella vis-à-vis the world. From *I Pose* to *Tobit Transplanted* her titles read like an obstacle course designed to puzzle or irritate the book buyer, and send him along the shelves in search of some more accessible-seeming author; but even Stella knew that $\nabla\triangle$ was going too far, and she joked to Eileen, 'I don't know how one will ask for it in libraries – just draw the mystic double triangle in the air, I suppose.'[18] What does the hieroglyph mean? Nowhere does she tell us, so we cannot be sure, but a not unlikely guess would seem to be that it represents a pair of bones seen endwise, and perhaps in cross-section, their separation symbolising the doomed loneliness of creatures, their pairing, the spiritual need that draws them together, always in vain.

Stella was deeply committed to writing this novel, which as well as incorporating her intuition about 'bones' was to embody her notions on the

needlessness of 'oughts' – and yet, very early on, she allowed herself to be
diverted from it to a literary adventure of a quite different kind. 'I was
nagged to do it,' she explained in a letter to Vita Sackville-West, 'and it
seemed one way of saving myself from being worried to hurry with my *real*
book – as one throws (I am told) one baby to a pursuing pack of wolves, to
pacify and delay the animals.'[19]

What caused the diversion was a visit that she paid in April to an old man
lying in a free bed in hospital, said to be the author of some 'very shocking'
stories. Not that there was – or was ever to be – any authentic contact
between them:

> I was a ghost to him from the first. 'I have ever been a great admirer of
> ladies,' he said, looking through me at be-bustled, be-fanned, be-
> diamonded frou-frou memories, as I arrived in a damp mackintosh and
> muddy shoes at his bedside. With his white beard he tickled the pages of an
> album. . . . With his white beard he tickled the pages of an album. . . .
> 'This is a portrait of the Princesse de —, lady of royal blood, who was
> crasy of me in Vienna,' he said, indicating a photograph – clipped from a
> newspaper – of a female face with an oblong dimness over the mouth,
> entitled *Get rid of that film, You can see the difference in three days.'* . . .
> 'This is my dear, lovely Marie – the *prima ballerina'*; he had scratched out
> the printed name and written: 'Marie my dear tru sweatheart – O
> Womens, the perl of the Nature'. . . .
> 'Two million roubles,' he said, 'have I spent on ladies in my life.'[20]
> 'The food is not fit for gentlemen stomach here, madame. Only fit for
> common loo class men stomach.' There was a stirring among the loo class
> men in all the beds within earshot. Oh, how tired his fellow-paupers were
> of the sound of that bold old voice! 'Lend me some money, madame,
> please, to buy some fruit for my sick stomach. I have not a cent . . .' He
> turned the pocket of the tartan infirmary dressing-gown inside out to
> show that he had not a cent – and from it two dollars fifty fell loudly to the
> floor. 'Not a cent,' repeated the Count, firmly, replacing it in his pocket.[21]

Stella could forgive the Count his lies, for her 'heart was wrung' by the
old man. He seemed to her a free spirit broken by adversity, a brave
adventurer cruelly trapped, in his piteous old age, in a sick body, and when
she left his bedside she carried away a pile of his manuscripts with some
vague idea that it might be possible to convert them into cash.

The idea of selling his stories was not new to the Count – indeed, Stella
discovered that they were his currency, and that he would say 'I give you
here a story, you can please give me ten dollars,' as another man might say
'Can you change this ten-dollar note?' She herself was convinced that some
of his stories would turn out to be good ones the moment he told her that he

arrived in Venice, a penniless fugitive from Russian justice and, on being advised by a friend to go on to Bulgaria, asked 'Why Bulgaria? Is the thron vacant there?' (It was, and he sat on it for a few days.) However, it was some time before Macmillan issued her edited version of the memoirs of Count Nicolas de Toulouse Lautrec de Savine, KM, Knight of St Vladimir Cross, St Anna, etc., etc., 'for long yahrs martyr of the Tsar's tyrany, exiled three times to Siberia . . . twice escapet from Siberia and trampet the world over'.

An early problem was how to head him in the direction of his exploits as a 'millitairey men' in the Russian–Turkish and Spanish–American wars, and as a nihilist revolutionary under the Tsar, and away from 'loving storys'. For it was as 'the Don Juan of Our Days' that the Count liked best to remember himself: 'All my adventures are loving adventures, madame,' he firmly maintained, 'there is planty lovings in all of them.' Indeed there was. He had been 'intusiast of womens' ever since his green, cadet days in the 1870s, when no single set of 'blu eyes', 'gold hairs' or 'smole fiets' had power to attach him: 'The most ones of our officers had sweathearts, but I was to yang and to inconstant to bound me with a gerl; prefair to flay from one to another, as a butterflay who flay from one flower to another,' he candidly confessed in the sentence that Stella cherished above any other in his works.

She quickly realised that the only way to serve him up to the public of the 1930s was as a grotesque, a figure of fun, an exotic treat. There was no question of correcting his broken, headlong English, his fanciful spelling; both were essential to 'the raciness and rapture' of his style. But he needed editing, and eventually she hit upon a way: she would present the Count's tales in all their original glory, but embedded in a commentary by herself. The outcome was a very odd book indeed, with a very odd title, of whose derivation Stella had only the vaguest idea, but *Pull Devil–Pull Baker* does very well as a name for a book that is in effect a literary tug-of-war. For Stella's interpolations are never respectful, never po-faced; in alternate paragraphs and chapters she plays merry hell – as, being a devil, she is entitled to do – with the preposterous old Count's gimcrack Ruritanian world of venal sex, vicious anti-semitism, pasteboard militarism – his 'gay gerls', 'crooky jews', 'hyg fecheneble regiments'. For example, his story of heartless good-time-girl 'Lili, a Noty Gerl' she 'outshoots' with a monstrous fantasy about a man who falls in love with a charmer equally ruthless and commercial – Co-Co, the Co-operative Stores.

In mocking him thus, did Stella in fact reduce herself to the level of the 'crooky womens' who all his life exploited and deceived the trustful Count? Before passing judgement, one must remind oneself, first, that had she been scrupulously faithful, he would never have got into print at all; then, that unlike the majority of his 'sweathearts', she left him very much richer than she found him. She kept to the letter her agreement to pay him a third of any profit accruing from their collaboration which, as things turned out, was a tidy sum (Stella was always honourable and punctilious to a degree over matters of money). Moreover, she was as indulgent to the old rogue as a devil well could be. She did not pass judgement on him; the harsh epithets that crowd the mind of the candid reader of his unedifying reminiscences do not soil her pen. In a word, she tried not to injure his old bones.

By the end of June the Count had sheered off to Macao, from where he was sending her daily, twice-daily even, begging letters. Already she had advanced him fifty pounds and could offer no more until a batch of his stories – 'very mockingly edited by me' – had been accepted for publication in England (in fact they were not placed until 1932, when the *English Review* carried them).

Then suddenly he was on her doorstep, and her heart was 'wrung' all over again, because he looked 'so old, and so ill and so expectant'. She gave him a dollar and sent him away, only to have her heart 'smite' her that 'lack of money, and dirt, and smell, should prevent me from asking an exhausted, very old, hungry and courteous old man to dinner. . . . I felt raw and sore with self-reproach.' She invited him to lunch on another day, but the comments that she made on him afterwards ('so self-assured and bird-witted', 'dated (1876) silliness', 'the perfect cadger') suggest that the meeting was no great success – at least, not for the hostess.

She had taken the opportunity of his visit to examine the sheaf of papers that he carried around with him in a greasy satchel – the Benevolent Society that was currently struggling to unravel his affairs having asked her to do so, in the hope that he could be shipped off to France. But none of them seemed valid or interesting, and none proved the American citizenship that he claimed. However, splendidly impervious to discouragement, the Count continued to offer papers:

> 'I have here too a letter of recommendation from a famous American bishop.' He showed it. It said: 'Dear Sir, I must ask you to cease importuning me for money, otherwise I shall be compelled to take steps to protect myself from this nuisance. I have given you a ticket to the – Institute and done all I can for you'. . . . 'Here is a letter from a famous editor of newspaper' ('Your manuscript is illegible and quite useless to us – like others you have sent us') 'and a card of recommendation from an American millionaire,' added the prince, producing the muddy card of Howard B. Katsheimer – evidently picked up from a trampled wet wharf – '*Bon voyage*, Madge dear – a few flowers with my love.'[22]

Stella was to tire herself out doing the rounds of consulates, trying to get his Russian passport visa-ed. Finally the German consul consented to give him a visa, but would not assist with his passage. It could well be that the Count viewed these bourgeois efforts on his behalf with some contempt. He was quite used to moving from country to country without either documentation or money, by means of a simple 'triky'. Having squeezed sufficient cash out of some charitable individual or institution to buy himself the cheapest available ticket, he would commence a sea-voyage. Where the ship was headed was no great matter, for once at sea his genuine disabilities – old age, bronchitis, worn-out digestive system – would suddenly take alarming hold, and at the next port he would be placed on shore in a free hospital by a harassed ship's doctor. It was by means of this or some similar 'triky' that he had come to Hong Kong in the first place.

Chapter Twenty-Two

The woman who could persuade a British army colonel to put his yacht about in Hong Kong harbour so that she might go to the rescue of a beetle marooned on a derelict hamper – 'the chances were about a billion to one, I suppose, against anyone seeing its antennae, SOSing from the wreck, but I did' – would seem ideally fitted to serve on the committee of the RSPCA, and this is where Stella found herself within weeks of arriving in the colony. Soon she was putting her pen to their use, in an appeal (typically Stellarian) to readers of the *South China Morning Post* to support the coming financial drive: 'There are few situations more enjoyable than finding oneself in a position to play a god's part, and to animals we necessarily appear as either gods or devils. . . . the difference between heaven and hell lies in our hands, and this week our hands have nothing more difficult to do than to dip into our pockets. . . .'

She was also on the library committee of the Helena May Institute, where one of her duties was to help choose new books – not always a straightforward task, since the library had been founded in the first instance for the religious and moral improvement of young girls. Early on, Stella felt in conscience bound, 'if innocence *must* be considered', to veto Colette's *Chéri*, though later, when the committee threatened to return to its origins, she decided that she would have to resign (in fact they voted against reform, and she stayed on).

She also helped out as library assistant, which proved to be an eye-opener. The first time a coolie came to her with a chit which read 'Please give bearer two books', she turned it over looking for further clues: 'Two books! What two books?' 'Missee wantchee two piece book,' the coolie confirmed. She had had half a mind to hand him two volumes of a children's annual – they were certainly books, and probably the trustful subscriber had not already read them – but after a while she realised that this method of random selection ('trial by coolie', she called it) was Hong Kong's most usual way of choosing its reading matter.

Even subscribers who did take the trouble to turn up in person – 'the busy, confident matrons of Hong Kong, hurrying to the library with a bunch of chrysanthemums dangling from one finger, a rattan basket containing a change of shoes and stockings under one arm, and a library book that they haven't enjoyed clasped to their bosoms' – even these had no more idea of what they wanted. Most stood twenty minutes looking along the shelves at the titles (one woman took out *This is the End*, leafed through it, muttered 'Oh, no,' and thrust it back), and finally, as they left, pounced on a book that was handy on the library table because someone had just brought it in.

Most of the above strictures occur in an article that Stella wrote for the Anglican Cathedral magazine. On reading it over she asked herself whether its tone might not seem unpleasantly 'superior', but since it was at bottom a feeling plea to subscribers to choose books on more rational principles (which she proceeded to indicate) she believed that she was justified in letting it go. But it was hardly likely to endear her to those same matrons, some of whom may not have been quite so self-confident and hard-shelled as she took them to be.

In December 1931 she was fetched into murky waters: 'I found myself upon a committee for enquiring into the International Traffic in Women, by order of the League of Nations.' It was a committee in a hurry, for its brief was to prepare a report to present to a travelling commission of the League, due in Hong Kong later the same month. At the first meeting Stella was 'outraged' by what she heard – 'things that made my blood boil'. It was not prostitution as such that angered her – she claimed to have no moral objection to that – but the circumstances in which girls were drawn into the prostitute's life, and held there virtually as slaves: 'the coercion of a living creature to unnatural courses. . . . I just want everyone to have his own self-respect.'

There was very little 'international' traffic, properly so called, in Hong Kong. Most of the prostitutes were Chinese girls from other parts of the country, who had been sold to procuresses by poor parents, often in infancy, trained to prostitution in China, and brought into the colony when ripe for the work. The colonial government was prepared to license them, after a rather perfunctory ascertaining that they were over twenty-one years of age, had already practised prostitution, were continuing in it of their own free will, and owed no one a proportion of their earnings. A judicious bribe to the Chinese, Indian or British clerk of the Secretariat for Chinese Affairs conducting the interview ensured that, however improbable a girl's answers might be, she got her licence. On average, six young girls a day were registered, and later Stella was to see a copy of the questions and answers that 'the poor little slave candidates' were made to commit to memory.

Once licensed, a girl was sold to a brothel-keeper, herself the proud owner of a government licence, who took anything from seventy-five to a hundred per cent of her earnings and split it with the procuress, or *amah*. The girls believed that repayment in full of the sums that had been laid out on them was their only means of escape, but since the tide of their debts was constantly rising – they had to pay out of their own pockets for such essential items of their stock-in-trade as clothes and singing lessons – release in that way was virtually impossible.

The full facts of the grubby trade were gathered by Stella and a comrade in arms only after the committee had concluded its rather shallow investigation and, thankfully, disbanded itself. Truth to tell, the committee, several of whose members were wives of men in government employ, were not anxious to probe too deeply. The Governor, Sir William Peel, had made it quite clear that he regarded the League's enquiry into 'tolerated brothels' as an unwarrantable interference in the internal affairs of the colony – and already in his brief time in office he had sent home men whose wives had shown lack of 'tact'. But Stella and a certain Mrs Gladys Forster were not under the same constraint, since Shaemas's masters were in Peking, and Professor Forster was an employee of the university. If the Governor wanted to discharge his spleen on them, he would have to go about it by rather devious means.

It was at Stella's suggestion that she and Gladys took the enquiry a stage further. Gladys, fat, perspiring, 'manly', powerful in debate and transparently sincere, was the ideal ally in a skirmish of this kind. The fact that as a Christian she had a horror of unchastity worthy, according to Stella, of 'a burning fanatic' was no great obstacle: Stella and she respected each other, and were content to pursue the same objective for different reasons, 'so I don't intend to drop my enquiries after all'.

Their first step was to approach the head of the SCA (the Secretariat for Chinese Affairs), whom they knew socially. But they found him entirely unhelpful: he would not even divulge the age at which girls were eligible for licence. (Stella was later to refer to this honoured official as 'Number One Brothel Master'.) Next they did what few women in the colony, white or yellow, would have been prepared to do, or perhaps thought worth doing: they went to the 'red light' district at West Point to see for themselves. Armed with the facts, they thought, Gladys as a good churchwoman could communicate them to the Bishop, who might be prepared to pass them on to the Governor over dinner at Government House, 'between the soup and the fish, as it were'.

They called on a school run by a Chinese Christian woman for the benefit of prostitutes, which opened at midday to allow the pupils to make up for lost sleep. It was plainly a worthy venture, but on the afternoon they were there only nine, out of a population of some 2600 licensed girls, were in attendance. Next they were conducted by two of the pupils to some brothels, where they were given a warm reception, sweets, tea and cigarettes being thrust on them by the bored inmates, who were obliged to hang about the places all day in case an inspector called. If he found a brothel empty he could put in an order for its closure on the grounds of lack of use.

In cool, objective terms Stella recorded all she saw. The cubicles, cleaned daily by the *amahs* (who slept in the corridors outside), were neat and tidy. They contained bed, dressing table, two huge spittoons, a small wash basin and 'a perfect incrustation of gaudy pictures'. The nightly role of these girls was to sing and chat with Chinese guests at nearby hotels and restaurants, and almost invariably to bring a guest home. In the eyes of the girls themselves, to be under age was so usual as to be scarcely worthy of remark. Medical inspection was very occasional, and then not compulsory: thus, as Stella triumphantly noted, 'tolerated' brothels were no more hygienic than unregulated ones, although health was a main plank in the government's case for licensing.

Even so, these girls considered themselves vastly superior to the 'Big Number' girls, who catered for non-Chinese clients, and to visit whom Stella and Gladys now bent their steps to Nathan Road. Except that the girls seemed just as pleased to see them, things there were completely different. These girls were painted, dirty, brazen, and – though it was by now late afternoon – their cubicles were dirty and tumbled, the sheets drab with dirt, pillowcases stained, spittoons not emptied. And these, wrote Stella indignantly, were the houses 'to which the soldiers and sailors are recommended as being "safe"'.

Before they left Nathan Road an incident occurred that typifies Stella's and Gladys's differing attitudes to the whole business of prostitution. They were sitting in the entrance room of one of the brothels when an English sailor in uniform passed. One of the girls ran to the door screaming stridently at him ('none of your seductive whisperings') but he turned in at a door further on. Minutes later they passed the house, and glanced in. There was the sailor, seated on a bed between two *amahs*, watching the antics of two drunken prostitutes: 'I was embarrassed at catching his eye and passed on; but Mrs Forster insisted on going back and catching his eye again, so as to make him feel uncomfortable. She brings *morals* more into this than I do.'

As a mere woman Stella had not presumed, even in the privacy of her thoughts, to question the underlying need for prostitutes. 'I have been so well brought up by James to understand that chastity was impossible to the normal healthy young man – and that when attempted it led to morbid repressions, etc. – and that it was unnecessary to be attempted as repression robbed a man's life of much spiritual joy,' that to hear the opposite proclaimed one evening over dinner ('that nature of the kind that could not be controlled was an exception in a man' – and this not from a man of 'the missionary type', but from Major Harris, 'a military doctor, a normal looking healthy athletic young man') was almost past belief, 'it seemed like a dream'. How Shaemas bore the overturning of his teaching is not revealed, but a short while later it was his turn to disconcert Major Harris with a modest proposal of his own for making prostitutes redundant: 'James's point of view of course is that . . . if respectable girls were less chaste, no harm would be done and much suffering eliminated – now that birth control is within the power of all and also now that early marriage was economically impossible. Major Harris was very much shocked at this idea. He thinks that every bride – at any rate every *gentleman's* bride – must be virgin.'

Further visits to West Point did little to modify the impression gained on that first visit. What did outrage and horrify Stella almost unbearably, and confirm her in her campaigning, was seeing and talking to some of the little 'brothel slaves' in hospital. One in particular grieved her, a girl of sixteen who had been worked as a prostitute since childhood, for years beaten into submission if she refused a man whom she knew to be diseased, and who now – unsurprisingly – was suffering from almost every known form of venereal disease; her eyes and nose were 'almost eaten away' with syphilis. Stella undertook to pay for her treatment, but she had arrived on the scene far too late – after six months the girl was totally blind, and would spend the rest of her life in hospital.

No doubt her story figures in the report with which Stella busied herself in May, and which was read out in June before the committee of the Hong Kong branch of the League of Nations Society, who welcomed it, and voted to send it after revision and verification to the Hong Kong government. If they got no satisfaction there, it would go straight to Westminster. In due course, in shortened and somewhat emasculated form, it went to the Hong Kong government. (A copy lies in the League of Nations Archive in Geneva, and will be open to inspection in 1995.)

Already Stella and Gladys had reason to congratulate themselves, but they had no intention of stopping there. With the Governor publicly referring to their campaign as 'an outcry of hysterical women' (and looking 'icily' through Stella at a fencing display at the Yacht Club), and the Colonial Secretary writing to say that 'nothing would be done before the League's commission of enquiry reported in two years' time', it was clear that the central bastion had yet to be undermined. On 27 June, Stella was writing to Winifred Holtby:

If the Government here buries its head in sand still, after being appealed to, we personally are going to send our report on the subject home to as many people as we can think of – the Anti-Slavery people – Lady Simon – Lady Astor – Lady Rhondda – Dame R. Crowdy – etc., and then I will send you one to see if you can get publicity for it (but anonymously as far as I am concerned, or I shall get James sacked – at any rate anonymously until we get transferred from Hong Kong). I'd love to send you the report now – but we feel it must wait till the League of Nations Society has done its damndest.[1]

In October a powerful reinforcement came in. Hot from an inspection of Singapore, where licensed brothels had recently been abolished, the chief of the Social Questions and Opium Traffic Section of the League of Nations, the only woman head of section at the League, was due in Hong Kong. Dame Rachel Crowdy (several times mentioned in despatches) had headed the Voluntary Aid Detachment nurses on the continent during the war. She was a past mistress in the art of circumventing male officials, and no doubt the Governor and the head of the SCA were wishing her anywhere but in Hong Kong.

As far as Stella and Gladys were concerned, it was of paramount importance that Dame Rachel heard their side of the case before she heard the government's, and on the day she was due to arrive Stella prepared a summary of it, and determined to put it into her hands the moment the ship docked. Already she had written urgently to Dame Rachel at Singapore and wirelessed to her at sea; now she planted her wilting body on a sweltering dockside in order to intercept the distinguished visitor before the Governor's aide-de-camp could nobble her.

In a final bid for attention, she sent on board a note signed 'Stella Benson', hoping that the name would act like an open sesame. It did. Pushing on board second of anyone (and outmanoeuvring the ADC), she found Dame Rachel, pressed the report upon her, and had a triumphant twenty minutes' conversation with her before anyone came up: 'It was like a good dream, the way she welcomed me, said she liked my books, especially *Pipers and a Dancer*, and announced at once that she intended to come and lunch with me that minute, saying "she could lunch with the Governor any day, but might never get a chance to lunch with S. Benson".'

Collecting Gladys, they repaired to the Hong Kong Club, where over the lunch table Dame Rachel came out strongly on their side. There could be no two opinions, she said, about state regulation, and delay in reform could only be accounted for by commercial expediency – that is, the profit accruing to landlords, and hotel and restaurant proprietors. Stella was completely carried away: 'To hear sense and imagination and good information coming from the lips of a woman – not to have to make allowances, or to be patient and tolerant – seemed so wonderful.'

It was three o'clock in the afternoon when eventually they drove Dame Rachel to Government House. And it was only then, seeing on the august steps a usually-so-beaming ADC with 'a wholly frosty face', that Stella realised the enormity of what she had done: entertained a Governor's guest before the Governor had had a chance even to offer her a biscuit! 'I became sick with horror for fear lest I had injured James's career just at the moment when he is left in charge here, and hopes to make a little splash [he was to stand in again briefly as senior man]. . . . I wept a few tears secretly.'

Once at home, she hastened to compose a letter to Lady Peel, expressing humble apology, and at the same time giving her a dignified let-out if she felt like being merciful: Dame Rachel when she disembarked had thought that, as her ship had been late docking, it was already past lunch time at Government House, and that her taking a 'snatched' lunch with Stella Benson would incommode her hostess less than a dinner taken with her on some other day, etc., etc. But alas, Lady Peel was not to be mollified. The acknowledgement that she returned was quite disagreeable, so that when next the Andersons were invited to dine at Government House, on 13 October, Stella asked the ADC in confidence whether it would be diplomatic for her to have an influenza attack. Evidently he said no, for she went, only to have her 'heart wrung' by the sight of Shaemas, 'in spite of his being about to be Acting Commissioner here . . . seated so far down the table as to be to all intents and purposes under it – he wasn't given a female to take in, poor lammo, and it seems very odd that pork-butchers, men who mend the electric light, insurance touts, etc., should all be placed above the representative here of the Chinese Government'.

If, as seems likely, Shaemas had been the recipient of a deliberate snub, it was ominous for the prostitutes' cause. However, behind the scenes the influence of Dame Rachel and the League, backed by the threat of Westminster, would seem to have been at work. A month to the day from the snubbing dinner, Gladys flew joyfully to Stella with the news that the Governor, with Lady Peel and an entourage, had actually paid a visit to the prostitutes' school. 'He really seemed *shocked* to see how young and naive they were,' said Gladys, '. . . candidly admitted that he was much impressed . . . most fatherly.' Some of the girls had ventured to ask him to pose with them for a group photograph, and after some hesitation he had agreed; then unfortunately the camera had been found to be out of order.

But it really did not matter. Nor did it matter that the head of the SCA had looked 'hostile' throughout the visit and would not address Gladys, or that Lady Peel looked 'indifferent'. The fact of the visit was the thing. It could only signify that official opposition to their cause was lessening.

A few days later, the Governor made a point of being 'kind' to Stella at the races. Emboldened, she and Gladys drafted him a letter seeking an interview so that they could put their case personally. But an interview proved not to be necessary. On 1 December, at a dinner at Government House, Sir William found an opportunity to talk to Stella alone; in the course of the next few days, he told her, an announcement was to be made of the abolition in stages of both classes of tolerated brothels: the 'Big Number' houses were to close in six months from 1 January 1932, the Chinese probably not for three years, but meanwhile no new girls were to be registered. He felt bound to say, however, that he was pessimistic about the likely result: as things stood, at least if a girl made a complaint her owner could be brought to book. Stella considered this to be nonsense, since no girl ever dared complain – but she did not say as much: 'being not at all a lucid talker, I was rather overpowered by the Governor's serene, austere and authoritative monologue'.

Nothing had happened to change Sir William Peel since the moment Stella first set eyes on him. He was still the same 'handsome stolid old man, almost exactly like any other amiable orthodox old man controlling any tassel of the fringe of Empire'. But tonight he shone in the bright glow of her approval. From what he had been saying, it seemed that the victory was theirs, and she could afford to be generous: 'He is an honest and truly just man, I think – and we have worried him perhaps beyond what he has a right to expect. . . . I rather liked the Governor to-night.' This was magnanimous of her, particularly as he had been at pains to point out that the reform had been in his mind for six months – in other words, well before her and Gladys's campaign had begun to bite.

At Christmas Gladys gave a party, in her own home, for some of the little prostitutes of her acquaintance. To friends who marvelled that she let her young daughters meet them, she explained that they took them for ordinary Chinese girls, and indeed in the school uniforms that they had asked for – neat grey blouses and black skirts – they looked so clean, young and shy that it was difficult, even for those in the know, to bear in mind their 'sophisticated and tawdry' nights.

At the party they made a great noise of enjoyment, played games, got presents off a Christmas tree, and ate a huge tea, just like Stella's East End girls. Later, it was hard to know how to react to the news that every one of them had purchased a baby girl for a few dollars, and was having it brought up for sale to a brothel, as an insurance against old age. Or to Gladys's revelation that her wedding ring had disappeared at the party – and she knew how: she had taken it off for a game of 'ring on a string', and when the lights went out for a film show, one of the girls had burned it off with a cigarette. The only just and reasonable response must be a mild one: 'Of course, what could be expected? Such girls have been so much exploited, they must feel that everyone owes them something.'

Stella had some remarkable dreams that autumn, about bodies, about 'bones', about death. One seemed to be telling her that a person like herself, with 'no body' but 'a strong brain', ought to kill herself; from another she awoke with her ideas about 'bone understanding' beautifully clear: she had had a vision of 'sending the skeleton out of doors':

Imagine a body in a room – seeing through eyes hearing with ears – feeling with sex organs – thinking with brain – and then suddenly seeing the easy and absolute air through the doorway, and going towards freedom – *undressing as it goes.* This is not a mystic thought – not one of those turgid mysticisms about the Otherness of the Uttermost, etc. – it seems to me a practical possibility and an idea *necessary to me* – it really must be done, if not by me then by some other set of bones – some day, in a true civilisation, all skeletons will stand out of doors – naked of senses – their senses left like clothes in the dark house – bone receiving news about bones with nothing between them but air. It isn't clear now – but something that I swear was true, shewed me those free bones in this morning's darkness.

In mid-January she embarked on the voyage home by way of the United States, on the long Pacific crossing writing some articles and reading and re-reading Virginia Woolf's latest novel, *The Waves.* She lingered a month in California, seeing old friends: 'It was great fun,' she told Shaemas, 'having Californian ramshackleness again after Hong Kong refinement and tea-napkins.'[2] (Bertha Pope was there, having just completed a drive across the States on the Andersons' old route, the Santa Fé trail, now paved all the way. It had taken her just nine days.) She enjoyed excursioning to the country areas she loved, and she felt better physically – though the pace of Californian life proved too rapid for her forty-year-old nerves: 'I am having a pleasant but rather confusing time, everybody talks too much and also there is really too much binje, and always at such unsuitable times of day it seems to me.'[3] It was while she was there that she heard that the Royal Society of Literature had awarded her the A. C. Benson silver medal, and, after conflicting stories from different correspondents, knew that the French committee had unanimously voted her the *Fémina–Vie Heureuse* prize for *Tobit.*

With her she took the manuscript of $\nabla\triangle$, her last, never-to-be-completed novel, and now as she travels by stages home (she stopped again in New York), working on it on the way, may well be the moment to consider it. As she moves into her middle age, Stella writes a sad, wise, compassionate, sardonically funny book, redeemed from harsh satire and free of 'faery'. She writes of life on a crowded, lonely planet, where the sentient creature is in constant threat not from the malevolence but from the terrible separate egoism of its neighbour:

A million separate men are a million separate vanities, and a million separate vanities are really a million separate gods; each of these gods creates a separate world and peoples it with humble lovers, defeated enemies, listeners and other unsubstantial supers. And all the time, the million separate men remain, solid, inconvenient and terrible to another, crashing in and out of one another's thin glass worlds.

At one point in the novel a small black beetle, which has been clinging to the leg of a man's trousers, unnoticed by the wearer, who is striding about a room talking vociferously, falls off and lands with an unexpectedly clear little tap upon the floor. Forlorn and upside down, it lies in the path of the talker's return:

'The end, the end,' thought Francis, as George's heedless foot descended. One Absolute Importance – One Number Oneship – had gone from the company. Curious how steely tough these absolute importances seem – and how brittle they really are. Curious what a very discreet pop a *me* makes, when it bursts.

Mundos is 'a tragi-comedy of separateness', as Hugh I'Anson Fausset was to write in a review of the novel.[4] The locus of the story is a small island somewhere in the tropical Atlantic, and in calling this speck of land Mundos (which seems to conflate the name of the largest of the Bahamian islands, Andros, with the Latin *mundus*, a world) Stella was no doubt making a quiet point. A British Crown Colony, Mundos has for Governor Sir Victor Cole, 'in whom', says Fausset, 'the industriously well-meaning but totally unimaginative administrator is brilliantly caricatured'. As the book opens, trouble is brewing on Sir Victor's usually peaceful island, on to which, thinking that they will be of benefit to the natives, he has recently introduced buses. In fact they provoke a good-tempered riot in which all the motor vehicles on the island are destroyed.

If Sir Victor is serenely ignorant of the wishes and motives of the coloured folk he rules, he is equally unaware of those of his wife Phoebe, who arrives in Mundos to join him on the day of the riot, and whose gawky English womanhood Stella explores with wry understanding. It is not surprising that on the voyage (at the age of forty-seven) she has reached out for involvement with another man. However, she has not chosen well. Sam Wylie, an ineffectual Bloomsburyite spongey with noble ideals and sentimental illusions, has no need of women, and is drawn to Phoebe because he fancies that she is a woman who knows how to leave a man 'free'. Sam is a man who refuses to put all his eggs in one basket, 'and if a man (or a cuckoo) is in habit of not putting all his eggs in one basket, it may, I think, be taken for granted that none of the eggs is called Love'. His emotions are invested in his childlike, half-educated island university students, who painfully let him down.

The shipboard intimacy between Sam and Phoebe has been a mere fiction:

'They were sustaining between them an ideal air-born couple of ghosts. They were not aware of each other's bones.'

'Which brings us to the most interesting character in the book,' writes Fausset, 'and the only one who does achieve a vital contact out of the very extremity of his separateness.' Francis Cole, the Governor's son, is a dwarf with a grotesque body and little flapping arms. All his life he has had to make elaborate plans to avoid being hurt by people's reactions to his appearance. For example, he means to greet his mother's arrival not on the public quay but in the drive of Government House. At a carefully selected spot, invisible to the sentry and the servants standing at the front door, he will park his specially adapted Austin Seven car, and when his mother, rounding the bend, sees him and causes the Daimler to stop, he will leap on to its running-board: then Lady Cole, craning lovingly from the low seat of her car, and her son, towering above her window – his ridiculous stature forgotten – will meet on equal terms.

His eyes, at a level of some three feet from the ground, have tended to be more acutely focused on bodies than on faces. Quite early in the story, when a native half-caste rioter, Jim Fanna, is approaching him threateningly, suddenly he experiences a sort of extension of vision, the consequence of this abnormal point of view:

> Francis saw now that the man was wearing one sock inside out, and as though in an X-ray beam, under that inside-out sock, the bone of a hostile body; he saw the other side of this barrier that divided life into *this* side and *that* side. For there in that foot was something never seen before – the motive power of *that* side – the uncompromising bone moving in a leg that had brought a man running to attack *this* side.

The revelation of the secret bones of people opens a new world to Francis, a world in which bone looks at bone, without judging: 'The look of seeing eyes [says Francis] is the rarest look in the world – the look of one seeing from a point outside his own vanity, registering everything, accepting everything, from a cockroach to the face of another man's God.'

Ironically, it is Francis who, in seeking to protect Jim Fanna from the consequences of his actions during the riot, brings about his murder. And from this point the plot resolves itself into a wild-goose chase in the course of which Francis ends up shipwrecked in a distant part of the island. Now it is his turn to be sought. When the story breaks off Sir Victor is searching Sam's flat for his wife, she is being led on a fool's errand by one of Sam's students, and the boy who carries Francis's letter describing his own whereabouts is asleep under the pier.

Meanwhile – remote, inexorable – the natural life of Mundos pursues its separate existence: in their tens of thousands crabs migrate, ants march, frogs decamp, parakeets fly from one feeding ground to another, and remorselessly the harsh, irritating wind blows.

'[Stella Benson's] talent never found more brilliant expression than in the haunting, disturbing cadences of her swan song,' wrote L. P. Hartley in reviewing the book. It is an opinion that the present writer would endorse. Even if Francis's – and Stella's – wonderful new vision of 'time in the bone, light in the bone' eludes our intellectual grasp (as it did that of Sam Wylie who, like most of the rest of us, suffered from having been fed on books and so did not know how to 'think wild'), we can yet be strangely moved, feel ourselves mysteriously enriched, by *Mundos*, the title under which the novel was published in 1935.

It brought the almost certain promise of better, more assured things to come, had Stella lived. 'I feel I have got my tools now,' she said to fellow novelist Phyllis Bottome later in that summer of 1932, 'but I'm only just beginning to know how to handle them.'[5]

Chapter Twenty-Three

Stella was in London on 22 March, staying at Drayton Court with a mother who had aged a great deal in the last two and a half years (she was seventy-one now), seemed more mentally confused and not very happy. The only way to comfort her, her daughter decided, was with lies: 'Of course, I pick and choose among the lies, and lay awake to-night trying to think of ways of making Mother feel like a working cog, a valuable piece of machinery still, but she is very astute.' Only love, convincing love, would reassure her, 'and I haven't the words of love – perhaps I haven't the fact of love either – I have only a painfully tender impersonal heart.'

George's news was very bad – 'all Benson news is necessarily bad news' – he was having to sell off part of the Lutwyche estate, and he and Olive were camped out in a difficult, damp, cold, tumbledown wing of the house. And she was extremely cross with Stephen, who she thought was exploiting his mother; at thirty-six he was still living at home and spending the major part of his income on bachelor pleasures. Stella had abundance of 'oughts' for him, strongly recommending that he set up on his own, without, it seems, reflecting how finally useless this would leave their mother.

Laura was emerging from a liaison with a man, entered upon at past forty 'for the sake of experience'. Unsatisfactory as the affair had been – not what Stella would have wished for Laura – she could not but be glad that it had happened: 'I myself probably place sexual life too low in the scale of necessities now – but I should certainly have placed it too high if I had remained a reluctant virgin.' Mrs Oneleg and Rosie seemed fairly prosperous and comfortable down in Hoxton. On her second day back she went to see the Ordes, and it seemed 'pleasant and natural being with free-spoken people again'. Cuthbert had things to report of Bill Bickerton that further defaced her image of him; he was 'insanely conceited', formerly a homosexual and 'a virgin until he was forty'. For him (as opposed to Stephen) her mercy flowed easily: 'it is his *bone* that is a cad's bone – no *ought* applies to him – as a bone-cad he is doing his best'.

On the same day a cable from Shaemas announced that he was promoted Deputy Commissioner, and posted to Hoi-how on Hainan, a big coastal island between Hong Kong and Haiphong, 'a lonely place', said Stella, 'but I feel I wouldn't mind loneliness for a bit, now'.

Shaemas wrote to Eileen:

I live in a rather ramshackle but airy house with a wide jaloused verandah looking out to sea over low flats and creeks. Hoi-how itself is rather a poor place, as it consists of salt-pans. . . . But there is a biggish town with one sky-scraper, at least six petrol pumps, eight sing-song girls (the politer kind of harlot, and the measuring rod of the degree of civilisation of a town to many Chinese), two Cantonese restaurants, a public snooker room, any number of wizened motor cars, and so on. You would love this kind of place – for about five minutes.[1]

Then came a letter to Stella saying how lonely he was: 'But I have learnt more about this *soulmate* stuff now,' she commented ungratefully, 'and know that between James and me there is really nothing but candour and tenderheartedness on my side, and bedhankering and tenderness on his.' Finally came news that her dog Remington had died, and this produced a great keening lament.

What dawned on Stella only rather slowly was the fact of her literary celebrity in London that summer. She found herself a kind of Queen of the May of the book world.[2] It first struck her at a dinner of the PEN Club,[3] where, 'overwhelmed but pleased', she was shown a place among the 'friends go up highers', on the right hand of the president, John Galsworthy (his references to her work in his shy speech were, she felt, all the more of a compliment since the dinner was in honour of Goethe not Stella Benson!).

That day, 5 April, was a thriving day for vanity altogether, for in the morning she treated herself to a session with 'the grandest, most expensive hairdresser in London', blueing £1 8s 6d on learning how to treat and arrange her hair from a kind old Frenchman; and her new part-time secretary Joy Scovell arrived, a friend of Ellis Roberts' just down from Oxford, who was to assist with a massive fanmail – so many envelopes were arriving every day that she had time to open only the ones in handwriting she recognised.

On 4 May there was a price to pay for success: 'I worked hard all the morning trying to keep calm before my terrifying ordeal.' It was *Fémina– Vie Heureuse* prize-giving day at the Lycée Français in South Kensington. For the occasion, she had chosen a dress at Jay's in Oxford Circus, soft blue, with a crossover bodice that had silver buttons cutting diagonally, and with it she was to wear a small hat rakishly tilted over her nose (and if the press photograph is reliable it was not becoming).

The dress did not arrive from the shop until half an hour after she had meant to start dressing. And then the lunch was not easy. Present were Jean Schlumberger, who was to receive the Northcliffe Prize, a British award offered on similar terms to a French author (he won it with *Saint-Saturnin*), Harold Nicolson, who was to hand out the prizes, Rebecca West, G. B. Stern,[4] and Amabel Williams-Ellis;[5] they chatted away in a language that was somehow not quite hers: 'I thought they were all too civilised for me. I don't seem to be civilised at all, perhaps it is only not being educated. . . . I didn't know the names of modern people they all mentioned – but as it was simply gossip they discussed – in Harold Nicolson's case always gossip to his own credit or advantage – I didn't feel much hankering to know.' It seemed to her that Nicolson and West dominated the table with 'trying-to-be-clever kind of talk': 'Rebecca West did it by mistake, because she is really so humble and shy and doesn't know how to be calm, and Harold Nicolson did it on purpose, because he has a very glittering picture of himself as a very cultured cosmopolitan, and so he can't be calm.'

Among the audience to hear Nicolson praise her writing skill 'in terms that I would hardly have thought credible had a prophet foreshadowed them ten years ago', were her mother, a couple of aunts, Laura, Olive, the Ordes, the Ellis Robertses and Spenser Curtis Brown. Her own speech (Nicolson noted in his diary that she was very nervous and read from a trembling paper) began with an apology for her deficiency in voice, and went on at once into a feeling exposition of her present passionately held belief that everything under the sun, from warthogs to primroses, drainpipes to sunsets, had the right to be, and would one day be, written about 'really and truly without prejudice':

> Someone will be born who is really unable to conceive of these irrelevancies we call *better* or *worse* – *the thing I like* – *the thing you like* – someone who genuinely sees only a difference in shape between a living cockroach and a living rose. That person will be the first absolute writing *creator*; that person will not write *about* things, but will write *things-in-themselves*. And if things-in-themselves could really be put direct into our minds, without the intervention of eyes and ears and prejudices – I suppose we should never again need to be taught lessons, or to draw morals, or ever to hear the grisly word ought again. That would be the new Genesis.

How Mr E. M. Forster, a 'very crooked, gentle-looking man' to whom Stella was afterwards introduced, and the rest of her listeners received this proposition is not revealed; but it disconcerted Stella when, in rising to thank her, the chairwoman, Mrs Williams-Ellis, took occasion to demur at it. (Her 'coronation' at the Royal Society of Literature three weeks later was painless in comparison – she had only to ascend a platform and receive graciously a medal 'like a large silver saucer', and afterwards sit through a lecture on an obscure seventeenth-century poet.)

On 13 May, in her second-hand Morris Cowley two-seater 'Pimples' (purchased for £20), Stella drove herself down to Parham in Sussex to stay with friends, the Pearsons, 'eating a pork pie very happily in a bluebell wood on the way.' It was peaceful at Parham – so 'excessively peaceful', in fact, that she found herself wondering 'what is the point of peace from my point of view. . . . Somehow to live I must be conscious of mortality – there is a sort of ceaseless sub-risk the taking of which in itself constitutes the feeling of living for me.' On 17 May she drove over from Parham to Sissinghurst to lunch with the Nicolsons. On previous occasions she had thought Vita 'intelligent, solitary and sombre . . . not out-looking in any direction', but now she was 'very friendly and *me-looking* (i.e. adjusted to promoting interest in me, for the duration of the meeting)' – another consequence of sweet success, perhaps. Harold, on the other hand, seemed as before, 'rather heartwringing . . . like many showers-off on touchingly flimsy grounds':

> he would like to show off . . . and none of it really *quite* gets across; his failure makes him seem abashed like a thwarted child. He can be very amusing, but only if a successful *me* comes into his stories naturally – if his *me* has to be dragged in irrelevantly (and by hook or by crook his *me* has to be there), the story hangs fire, and disappointment clouds his pink face.

'Certainly my stock is oddly up at this moment,' she remarked in her diary on 7 July, 'it is not every woman of forty-one (rising) who gets so much flattery, and whom people really seem to wish to see, quite often'. Invitations to literary parties kept arriving. She met David Garnett, 'whom I have long wanted to meet – but one doesn't meet him much even when one does – he is armoured in a stout, slow, grave shyness, like a bear'; and Ralph Hodgson, reputedly 'one of the most irresistibly charming' men in London, Kingsley Martin, Charles Morgan, Phyllis Bottome, Helen Waddell, Sylvia Lynd, Lord Dunsany, Forrest Reid. On what was their second meeting, Lord David Cecil liked her enough to invite her to lunch *à deux* at his house in Edwardes Square; both he and she could 'imagine being each other', she thought.

On 7 June she was at a cocktail party given by Nina Hamnett, a celebrity of bohemia, then aged forty-two: 'Nina Hamnett has the reputation of being either drunk or stripped (usually both) at all parties,' Stella noted, 'she herself fosters the reputation.' Outside the house an unknown woman approached Stella and asked if she would deliver a message to Nina, for her ear alone; 'oh no, she wouldn't want to see *me*', the woman said. Stella entered and introduced herself, at the same time saying '*I have a message for your ear alone.*' She was taken behind a bar, where Nina poured out two sherries to fortify them for the crisis, but on hearing the message, she said 'Oh God, is *that* all', walked out from behind the bar and never spoke to Stella again. The room was full of writers she knew and artists she did not; Augustus John appeared, 'very selfconsciously the great man' and looking 'like the Leaning Tower of Pisa'. 'Loudly' he wrote his name in the visitors' book and then walked out.

It was not long before literary parties came to seem a mere 'passing of literary people before one another's eyes', not parties of potential friends. And she soon found that the constant flattery about *Tobit* that came her way (at literary parties and elsewhere in that 'summer of flattery') was having a strange effect on her 'vanity': it was developing a callous spot, so that she could feel detached from the pleasure of being flattered, and see its effect on her. She did not like what she saw. With so many of the people she met 'faced towards her' – opening the conversation with remarks like 'I hope you don't mind my telling you that I have enjoyed your books' – she was forgetting what other people were like; it was easy, she thought, to see how someone like Shaw 'who lives in an atmosphere of one-faceted people all his days, loses touch with what the other facets of human beings are like'.

It was good to renew her friendship with Winifred Holtby, and Stella felt admiration for her bearing – 'so cool and reasonable and serene' – in face of the imminent threat of death from 'hyper-high blood pressure' (Winifred was in fact to survive until September 1935). Stella thought she knew her well enough to take a liberty – besides, Lady Rhondda, Winifred's friend and colleague on *Time and Tide*, and the artist Claire Leighton were urging her to it. So she waited her time and tackled Winifred about 'her bloodsucking friend Vera Brittain'. (Winifred was sharing a house with Vera and her husband as she had done since within a year or so of their marriage, and spectators of this unusual arrangement and of their close, mutually depen-dent relationship not infrequently felt the urge to interfere on Winifred's behalf.) But, as Stella expected, her words had no effect: 'I gathered . . . that Winifred really likes having her blood sucked.'

Meanwhile there was her publishing future to think about. With 'silly old Count de Savine's stories' nearly ready, and $\nabla\triangle$ well on the way, she was anxious to secure definite undertakings, and delighted when Curtis Brown told her that he had 'quite a big offer (for me) from Macmillan for both of them; over lunch at the Savoy grill (Winston Churchill and 'his handsome son' were at the next table) he informed her that she was 'just on the edge, and in doubt whether to flop over into real success (by which he means financial success) and by financial success he means American success'. By her own more modest standards financial success was hers already, for *Tobit* had left her with a comfortable thousand pounds in the bank, part of which she intended to invest in a small London house. Shaemas was still considering early retirement on a part pension (something that the process of sinocisation was making increasingly possible) and even if he were not able to disengage himself from China as soon as they hoped, the house would be a useful refuge for her if for any reason she wished to come home; meanwhile it could be let.

Kensington was to be the place – of all London it was the area with the strongest associations for her – and on 21 April she looked over 6 Pembroke Villas, and believed that she had found the very thing. It was 'a most enchanting little house' just off Pembroke Square, close to Kensington High Street, and less than a mile from her mother at Drayton Court. A demure, entirely unassuming semi-detached property of three storeys, one a half-basement, 6 Pembroke Villas was graced with a downstairs bay window, a short flight of steps to the front door, a small walled back garden and a minimal front one (so close was the bay to the street that Stella was to have her handbag snatched by a passing thief as she sat typing with her back to the window, losing a pound in cash, a gold cigarette case (the one that A. J. Welch had given her in 1920?), her latch and garage keys, her engagement and note books and 'my little 18th century patch box which I use as a hairpin case'). For three hundred and fifty pounds she secured the lease, and with the enthusiasm of inexperience, jumped gaily into the game of furniture and fabric hunting. Harrods and Maples yielded sofas, chairs and beds, Hoxton more utilitarian items, such as kitchen tables.

Preparations were still at an early stage when Phyllis Bottome the novelist came to view the house with an idea of renting it: 'I shall always remember Stella, with a slight colour in her cheeks, a heavy bunch of keys in her small hand, stepping with eager joy between mysterious buckets and telling me where things would be – as if they were already there' (one room was already earmarked as Shaemas's workroom). Stella spoke of her husband, Phyllis Bottome thought, 'though with reticence', with 'an understanding confidence only possible to the well-mated';[6] and she took away with her an impression of Stella at forty as a 'very grave, restrained, unerring person . . . neither cordial nor exuberant in social contacts' – which sounds a little grim, until she adds: 'Humour lifted her face into positive beauty. She *was* the perspicacious, elusive, gallant elf who lurks in every page of her work.'[7]

On 18 June Stella moved in, often – since the weather was hot – chosing to sleep out of doors; she gave a series of house-warming parties, 'binjes' for her noisier friends, professedly quieter ones for the others; at both she sang to her guitar, at both the then fashionable game of 'Murder' was played: 'It really is a very interesting game.' On the day that a man came to prepare an inventory preparatory to letting, she realised with a shock what a large part play had in her whole joyous domestic enterprise: 'I looked on in surprise at the man making the mistake of looking on my possessions as real things.'

On 15 July she was dining with the Woolfs, this time alone. Virginia was 'very much more human and demonstrative than ever before', and Stella found that at last she could be 'easy' with her – though as aware as ever of their points of unalikeness:

> She is far more intelligent than I am, but not so accepting of life. She doesn't know what it is to take each day as a thing by itself and ready made – not to coerce even the hours with hatred or censorship. She is very fascinating because she is, intellectually, completely integritous [*sic*] – and extremely beautiful too. She doesn't let her beauty comfort her at all – she is tense and seems out of place at all times. Leonard Woolf pulls the square peg back into its fated round hole, and pads the corners of the peg a little – he is a very charming, understanding and generous man.

Too few of her contemporaries have left word portraits of Stella, and we are very fortunate that one of them was Virginia Woolf: in her diary next day she gives generous space to her impressions of her guest. Clearly Stella had been relaxed, expansive, enjoying herself, though at the same time she must have been on her mettle with a couple whom she regarded as so much more intelligent and 'civilised' than she.

And indeed, had she known it, she moved fastidious Virginia to faint disdain, certainly to a sense of otherness, by her robust attitude to the money-making function of writing. One is reminded of that earlier dinner party – 'dreadfully sticky' Stella had called it – when the two crossed swords over the desirability or otherwise of winning literary prizes, which had caused Virginia in her letter to her sister to trounce her as 'a suburban lodging house keeper's scullery maid', than which, one inferred, nothing could possibly be more vulgar. This time Stella gets off more lightly. She is simply 'working class':

> Stella Benson last night: as quiet, as controlled, white, drawn as usual, also deaf: with steady, honest eyes; said she had been to a great many parties. 'I just say nothing. I feel none of these people matters. They say how much they liked my book. . . . I was given a medal. The old gentleman could not remember what for. He pinned it on. Both my dogs are dead. I liked one for bounding. But that was only a sign of Stannard's disease. I go back in August – to Lonlon (or some such name) a mud island. I hated Hong Kong. They play games. At Government House they give you a slip of paper with names of games on it: you have to put a cross next the one you play. Sitting out is one. James and I chose that. So we sit

out together.' That was her style in a very weak persistent voice; she coughs; and then goes on with a mild persistent patience. She is bleached, even her blue eyes are bleached. But at the same time she's practical; realistic: talked, of course, of 'Pearnie'[8] doesn't like her – and making money by stories; and *Harpers* and so on; in a sensible matter-of-fact way, like a working class woman. Then smiles with her charming steady eyes. The light faded in the drawing room, and she sat there lying back telling us in a very low voice, which went on steadily about the slave trade in Hong Kong; about James and his little Chinese destroyer, manned by ex-officers from England; how they steam out after sailing ships: the ships can't escape; they throw out bales of cotton and flannel: which float; man cried out 'That little parcel's for my father. Let me have that.' Then all the other men say that the cement is a present for an aunt. There's always fighting [we are now back at Nanning]. Chinese planes come over very low down. Shoot with revolvers. She sits in her kitchen. All the inhabitants crowd round, thinking the English safe, pretend they're selling eggs. Chinese generals come to dine and stand rifles on each side of their chairs: send soldiers into the kitchen to see that the food isn't poisoned. She goes back for another two years. Writes and writes. Must buzz home in her little Morris Cowley to write 8 pages of her monthly notes for *Time and Tide*.[9] I ask why? Oh it's good pay. Has bought a house in Kensington. Will come back for two years with James, who will be The O'Gorman. All this serious, weary, intent. I like her and was glad to sign her *Waves*.[10]

A final, sad echo of the evening comes in Virginia's diary on the day she heard of Stella's death:

I did not know her, but have a sense of those fine patient eyes: the weak voice; the cough; the sense of oppression. She sat on the terrace with me at Rodmell [staying once again at Sussex, Stella had slipped over to lunch with the Woolfs on 2 August, when Virginia had been 'startlingly affectionate' to her]. And now, so quickly it is gone, what might have been a friendship. Trusty and patient and very sincere – I think of her; trying to cut through, in one of those difficult evenings, to some deeper layer – certainly we would have reached it, given the chance. I'm glad I stopped her at the door as she got into her little car and asked her to call me Virginia – to write to me. And she said There's nothing I should like better.[11]

In thanking Virginia for the dinner, Stella sent her a copy of *Tobit*. Acknowledging receipt of it, Virginia mentioned that already she had peeped at a page or two (she was ill in bed), and liked what she had seen. It was a cordial letter that she wrote: after the dinner, she said, she had wanted to talk to Stella longer, about Stella's work, and to ask her what she thought of *The Waves*, 'whether it is on the right tack', but there had been no time: 'if on your island you would ever write me a line about this or anything else it would be a great pleasure'.[12]

Stella did not wait to reach her island before replying; she posted her letter at Marseilles. Humbly she said that she did not 'dare to discuss *The Waves*': 'You are so very much more civilised than I am, you write so much more from what you know – instead of, like me, from what you guess – that I should feel it as impertinent to challenge anything in your work as I should feel if I challenged Einstein.'[13]

But she claimed to have read *The Waves* four times in succession:

While I was living my ordinary life in China, I found I couldn't spare enough of my mind really to give it even a tenth of the understanding it needed, but when I left China last spring and crossed the Pacific – hung in a void, so to speak, alone with my bones – I read it with my whole mind, and, finishing it each time, turned back and began again. I think the phase of me that happens to be most alive just now, is perhaps the wrong phase that would enable me spontaneously to understand a book like *The Waves*; to read it, I have to dismiss my present pre-occupation with hard bones, with things you can tap and measure and compare – one bone with another. Something in my life, these last ten years, has warped me away from rarity – I suppose it is the fact of living so much among very common people, whose only appeal (as it seems to me) is the reality of the bone.[14]

Virginia took four and a half months to reply, by which time she had read *Tobit*:

I like it immensely. You're quite right – you are getting to the bones of things, and I love the bareness, the whiteness the hardness of your bones. But I don't think that when you say you are dealing with what is common . . . you mean what is cheap, nasty, commonplace, trivial, silly, affected. Not at all, I should say what you have done in *Tobit* is precisely the opposite – You've eaten away the soft mash and laid bare the bone. And I admit I envy you. I expect that in some way it is easier for you, living on an island in the China Sea, to shed the relics of the coat of mush that collects round one in London. I meet somebody who says 'You're this or that', and I don't want to be anything when I'm writing. Now in the China Sea you only meet people like my sister-in-law, who is kind and good, but as for seeing you, you might be a zebra or an elephant for all she sees of you. And so when you sit down to write you haven't a mist in front of your eyes and that I think is a healthy state, though horribly painful in the obtaining. I should be driven desperate if I lived in a wilderness of Bellas – she sends home photographs of herself opening golf clubs from which I get my only idea of English life in China; but no doubt I should write much better if I did.

She ended in a particularly warm, informal way:

Leonard, who is about to wash his head, asks me to send you his regards and to say – what I say too – please come back soon and pay us another, and a longer visit.
    Yours ever
      Virginia Woolf.[15]

Stella was to have one more interesting encounter before she sailed. It was with a man with an extraordinary reputation for pugnacity, the avant-garde painter and writer Percy Wyndham Lewis, sometime creator of a new movement in English art, Vorticism, and editor of its strident mouthpiece *Blast*. All that excitement had happened eighteen years ago, but he was not greatly changed. In 1930, in *The Apes of God*, he had turned his celebrated 'Lewis gun' upon the Bloomsburys, the Sitwells and the Schiffs, among others in the literary landscape, and raised a dust of potential libel suits and threats to his life. More recently a book in praise of Hitler had further darkened his reputation, and called a halt to portrait commissions from wealthy English patrons. Lewis was always poor, but the early 1930s were the most poverty-stricken years of his life.

In June 1932 he published two potboilers, *Filibusters in Barbary*, an account of his travels in Morocco (withdrawn from circulation in 1934 after a libel action), and *The Doom of Youth*, the title parodying that of Alec Waugh's best-selling *exposé* of public-school life *The Loom of Youth*, in which he aimed the Lewis gun at Godfrey Winn, calling him a 'hack' and a 'salaried revolutionary agent' and accusing him of asinine writing, and also at Waugh, strongly implying that he was a homosexual (copies were withdrawn from sale and pulped in 1933 for fear of damages for libel).

It happened that *Time and Tide* asked Stella to review both these books, together with a reprint of his dramatic fantasy *The Enemy of the Stars*. She was severe on *The Doom of Youth*, but called *Filibusters* 'a good guide book', and thought that 'with reservations' *The Enemy of the Stars* was 'a fundamentally interesting and noble piece of work'. Lewis, used to much rougher treatment than this, seems to have been well enough pleased with Stella, for he came to dine with her at 6 Pembroke Villas on 8 July, when he astonished and repelled her with his talk, his 'absolute conviction about everything – especially about the absolute rightness of his own oughts'. He wanted to draw her (he was preparing a series of drawings of well-known people, published in 1933 as *Thirty Personalities and a Self-Portrait*), and they arranged a date for a sitting. When he phoned to cancel it, Stella was sufficiently struck by the tenor of his remarks to jot them down verbatim:

'I can't meet you to-day – I must get away – I must get right away at once.'

'What on earth has happened?'

'There is diphtheria in my house – I am terribly afraid – I am quite sure I shall catch it if I stay. It is a fearful disease. Outrageous that I should be turned out of my house by a disease. Absolutely outrageous. But it is no use – if I stay in this house I shall catch it and *die* – I have had three libel cases on my hands this week – and it has been terrible – terrible – I am so nervously weakened that I shall certainly *die* if I catch diphtheria – and in this nervous weak state I am really almost *certain* to catch it, am I not' etc., etc.

What particularly impressed Stella was his deadly seriousness; she thought it 'very odd in these days of understatement and indifference – to meet a man who is really so important to himself – and is not afraid to say so – cannot conceive of being laughed at'.

Evidently he succeeded in evading diphtheria, for a fortnight later Stella found her way to his 'filthy back room (only by courtesy a studio) off the Tottenham Court Road', and sat while this agonised being produced a drawing of her that is austere, controlled, and makes her look like a cold, stern goddess.

All the time he was drawing me he wore his hat and sat crouched over a swivelling easel; I had to keep my eyes fixed on a point just above his head, but I could see his teeth gleaming in his writhing mouth, as he talked of all his cruel experience of men and women . . . there really is something rather wistful in the look of this stout glowering snub-nosed man – sitting hunched on a too small camp stool, describing without the slightest smile or irony, his position as the cynosure of all wickedness.

'He lives a curiously darkened life,' she decided, 'continually assuring both others and himself that he is naturally a simple, gentle and pacific man, forced into the atmosphere of battle by other people. All his friends turn on him, he says – all business men try to cheat him. . . . he is obsessed with the wickedness – active wickedness – of everyone except himself – surely an unlikely state of things.'

She was booked to sail five days later. It was August, and Ellis and Harriet Roberts were her only close friends left in London. Ellis writes:

That last week . . . had the strangest air of unreality. I had never known Stella so depressed about a decision as she was about this one to return to China. . . . I knew she felt that if she went on the 26th of August, she would not see England again. That she made plain, as plain as could be without direct statement. . . . she wished, deep down in her very being, to be stopped from doing what she had decided to do. . . . The little house was a symbol of New Life for her. . . .[16]

Chapter Twenty-Four

On 25 August 'I came out of my safe, bad-luck-proof little house and started for China . . . and now I am in danger again'; it was not a good omen when a porter at Liverpool Street Station dropped her typewriter and smashed it. 'However,' she assured Eileen, 'it will only be about eighteen months, I hope, before James and I are back in the safe, lucky little house. May 15 1934 is the next Poker Party, please note.'[1]

She put the finishing touches to *Pull Devil–Pull Baker* on the voyage, so as to have it ready for posting at Hong Kong. She was dreading Hong Kong. Ever since May she had been worrying about an article on the colony that she had sent to the *Radio Times*. Too late it struck her how very indiscreet it was – certain, she feared, to get Shaemas sacked: 'I have never dreamed that there was any danger in laughing at English people, so safe was I in the knowledge that I *am* English, and that fundamentally I love Englishness.'

Not one of her best, the piece gives the impression of having been tossed off in a fit of pique, and she was quite right in thinking that it would be obnoxious to the colonial mind. It begins with a heresy, 'I have lived for the greater part of two years in Hong Kong, and for the first time in my life have been obliged to doubt whether English is really and truly the best thing to be'; proceeds to a rather cheeky paradox, 'English men and women . . . do not exist at all in Hong Kong; there are only Gentlemen and Ladies there'; and ends with a downright impertinence, 'Hong Kong gentlemen and ladies never say anything at all except "Forty Love – three No Trumps – One up and two to play – I'll raise you fifty cents – Faîtes Vos Jeux, Messieurs, Mesdames – Snap – Tally ho . . .". It seems to me disappointing to set forth upon a journey that may involve changing from car to rickisha [*sic*] – rickisha to funicular – funicular to sedan chair – sedan chair to ferry – ferry to taxi – merely to play Poker Patience with an Oil Magnate, or Snap with a Puisne judge. . . .'[2]

When news of Stella's treachery reached Hong Kong, harsh things were said of her in places where the white man met, and one woman wrote to the

Radio Times to point out that since 'Miss Benson was as much a bird of passage in the colony as any naval or military wife, and during her short stay among us took little or no part in our lives', she had no conceivable right to her views. The sting was in the tail of the letter: Miss Benson was 'a delicate little woman – her brains are too much for her physique'.[3] If this was rather disagreeable, worse was to come: three days before she sailed, Stella heard that the Inspector-General of Customs was 'very angry' about the article.

In the end, she and Shaemas got off rather lightly, more lightly, Stella meekly thought, than they deserved. Instead of receiving a rebuke from the Inspector-General on account of his wife's misdemeanour, Shaemas was officially praised for his work in Hong Kong, and promoted; and she herself was at least left alone – she suspected for fear of what she might write next. Nor were they stretched upon the rack socially. As 'Acting Governess', Bella Southorn was senior lady now, and though she plainly thought Stella a traitress, she was moved to forgive, contenting herself with 'heaping coals of rather *réchauffée* fire on the heads of James and me by asking us to luncheon'.

As for the puisne judge, to her horror Stella came nose to nose with him, swimming in the sea. 'I have only one word to say to you,' he said, 'and after that I will not speak to you again.' Instantly Stella submerged. When she came up, she saw him making triumphantly away. 'I didn't hear the word,' she called out boldly. It was 'Snap!'

They reached Hoi-how on 1 October. The place was hot, airless. She disliked their house – dank, 'scabby', and permeated with the noise of their Chinese neighbours' gramophone. Everywhere lizards stood upside down, 'saying unknown words in strong unexpected baritone voices'. But none of this really mattered, as they were to transfer to Pakhoi, a nearby mainland port, in a few weeks' time.

On the second day Stella went for a swim and emerged very tired. On the third day she was tired and felt 'suffocated'. On the fourth day she went for a short walk. There is no diary entry for the fifth day, nor for the next ten, because she could remember nothing about them.

Stella was desperately ill at Hoi-how, so ill that she thought that she was going to die. Afterwards she recalled a point when 'bogglingly' she tried to tell Shaemas how she wanted her affairs settled, and that he got so flustered and cried so much that she could not explain properly. And she remembered her fever dreams: they were of lizards, loathsome lizards that stood all over her and could not be shaken off. 'I suppose I was in my enfeebled state frightened by luv (lizards being a phallic symbol, I now remember).'

There was a good French doctor at Hoi-how, and he pulled her through. She had had a severe bronchial *crise*, he said, and in a new place. There was also 'a miracle in the way of a neighbour', a Chinese ex-concubine – 'not

James's', Stella hastened to assure Eileen – who nursed her with efficiency
and devotion night and day:

> She did not do it for mere gain for she is richer than we are, and she didn't
> do the pretty-pretty kind of nursing – laying a rosebud on the pillow and
> what not – by any means, but the real rough stuff – really skilled – a very
> light touch with the bed-pan etc. I can't think what should induce a
> Chinese concubine sparkling with diamonds to be so kind, she said it was
> because her heart was hurt by hearing of people in trouble.[4]

As soon as she was strong enough, they put her to lie on a long chair on
the verandah. French Catholic nuns visited and were 'kind and loving'. She
dipped into Pepys: 'I don't think there is in the world a more enchanting
book than the diary. . . . I wish this diary could inherit a ¹⁄₁₀₀₀th part of the
perfection of its great-great. . . . uncle's diary [the dots are Stella's]'. She
thought about ∇△.

The doctor advised her, as soon as she was fit to travel, to go to hospital
in Hong Kong or Hanoi, but she would not even consider it. She was
determined to go with Shaemas to Pakhoi 'and just be quiet. . . . China will
be the death of me anyway.' Her death would mean that ∇△ would not
be finished, and that was sad, 'but it doesn't matter really, there must be
a great many better ideas than that by far rotting in dead skulls in the
earth'.

On 25 October they moved. Shaemas had acquired a fair amount of
miscellaneous property in Hoi-how, so that as well as themselves there were
a motor-car, two ponies, twelve chickens, one dog, one turkey, seven
pigeons, a servant, the servant's wife and two babies, and forty crates to
transport by junk across four miles of rough sea to be hoisted aboard a
waiting ship, and a similar but reverse procedure to go through at the little
port of Pakhoi at the other end. The Russian harbourmaster there, pitying
Stella's enfeebled condition said, '"Will you pardon me if I carry you as I
would a little child?", so I leapt into his arms on which, together, we fell
down the steep gangway practically into the sea – but were caught in mid air,
luckily, by some Customs sailors.'[5]

Pakhoi was a far more charming destination than Hoi-how. Their house
was calm, white and spacious, set in a huge, shady compound that kept all
'Chinese noises' out of earshot: 'It feels safe, like a fortress to me,' Stella was
to tell Virginia Woolf in a letter of 3 February 1933, 'safe in the same way as
my little new 6 Pembroke Villas did in London.'[6] Though there was no fresh
milk or cream to help a convalescent gain weight, and though the neighbours were not exhilarating (a handful of businessmen and minor officials,
and a few missionaries, 'three English and one German – the English ones
are O so roguish, the Germans represent the triumph of matter over mind'),

all in all it was no bad place in which to rest quietly and think about picking up the threads of her novel.

It comes as no surprise, however, to learn that in under a month she was off with Shaemas on an inspectorial tour which for a start involved driving for seven hours over 'the roughest possible of roads and the brokenest of bridges' to Fort Bayard in the tiny French colony of Kwong-tchow-wan; from which every day for a week they sallied forth 'hundreds of miles over the practically trackless waste – our sit-upons are a mass of bruises', coming back at night to put on their 'best dresses and dine with French officials, smiling uneasy Nordic smiles'. This jaunt was followed in January 1933 by a week's visit to Tonkin, and Stella suffered a bronchial asthma attack on the return voyage.

As the year went on the weather grew increasingly trying – hot, and suffocating. 'I never set foot outside the compound,' Stella told Virginia, 'though I set *hoof*, when we ride our ponies over grassy plains patched with pine forest.'[7] Virginia had sent Stella her volume of essays, *The Common Reader*: 'I gobbled it up. . . . To me it is really inconceivable being able to write like that . . . able to know so much, and know it so serenely and dispassionately. It must be wonderful to know exactly what you are doing, as you do. Indeed, that is what it is, to be educated and civilised.'[8]

Her own work went on, steadily and intensely, but not always easily or smoothly. 'I have written four chapters,' she told Virginia, 'but I have suddenly forgotten what I was doing it for. . . . It's like when I try to mend the electric light; I do it all most carefully and accurately . . . and then I switch it on and the light doesn't come. Everything seems exactly right – except that the light doesn't come.' As a postscript she added: 'I shan't send you my just-to-be-published book, *Pull Devil–Pull Baker*, because it is just a folly – but I will send you ▽△ if it ever gets finished.'[9]

An English woman, Hilda Trefusis, a painter, had been staying with them, but she had left now and on most days Stella was alone: 'through being so much alone', she put in her diary, 'I crave to be more and more alone. When James is gone, and the compound gate shuts behind him, I feel a glow of looking forward to hours of silence.' Till such time as he returned, three-quarters of the words she spoke were addressed to Ostapenko – 'Penko' for short – her house dog of pure Airedale descent, most of the rest to Chippie, the base-born yard dog.

At the end of February, as professing pagans Stella and Shaemas were genuinely taken aback at being asked to put up the local Anglican bishop. Rather in the manner of St Paul, he was coming to settle a quarrel which was dividing the Christians of Pakhoi, his sensible notion being that by staying with them – neutrals, so to speak – he would not seem to be taking sides. 'The missionaries say we shall find him Such a Jolly Fellow,' Stella told Eileen, 'always Sees the Funny Side, or rather I think they said the

Ludicrous side of things . . . very discouraging, we think.'[10] He signed himself Ronald Hong Kong.

While to claim that the Bishop in any sense made a convert of Stella would be going altogether too far, he did make her think again about the reasonableness or otherwise of moral imperatives – and even about bishops. Ronald Hall was an intelligent, broadminded cleric, and his views on such problems as prostitution ran unexpectedly close to the Andersons'. He even accepted as reasonable their suggestion of 'temporary marriage', and the countenance of 'semi-respectable' girl friends: 'I was much impressed . . . now that I have seen this rather nice Bishop, I would perhaps admit that in certain circumstances, the words ought and ought not might reasonably be used by the wise to the unwise.'

The weather continued malign: for Stella it was the most oppressive China weather yet. The days were hot and damp, the nights clammy and cold, and she had difficulty in sleeping. Often she felt exhausted, sometimes faint; she was still very thin indeed, and not regaining weight. Bad as her health had always been, she was accustomed to the feeling of getting better. But since Hoi-how, she had to admit that she seemed to have 'got upon a downward slope': 'This is a slow getting worse . . . and I am wondering now if I have not come to the end.'

She entertained the thought calmly: 'I do not really mind. I have come to my full stature, I suppose, such as it is, and do not feel that anything very valuable would be cut off *untried*, by my death.' There was no desperate regret, no panic possessiveness for what she would be leaving behind; increasingly the things that gave her most pleasure were 'the things that do *not* concern me *intensely* – more and more every day – the feeling of dogs, rabbits, grass, everything being itself . . .'. Least of all was she bitter about the course that her life had taken: 'I think that I have been extraordinarily fortunate – as measured by my bones' desserts – for there is no doubt they were rather jejeune and biologically useless bones.' Early in February she wrote to Cambridge offering her diaries, after her death, to the Fitzwilliam Museum. In mid-March she and Shaemas were wondering whether she should go to a sanatorium in the Java mountains, in a bid to recover her lost strength.

The world went on. In March an American book club, the Literary Guild, made *Pull Devil–Pull Baker* one of its monthly choices. Financially it was good news – '£600 down and of course large sales' – but from the artistic point of view Stella was appalled: 'so like the darling Americans to choose this trivial and tenth rate piece of work – and to ignore *Tobit*, which, with all its faults, was a creation of a kind. I know why they chose it – *because* it is a stunt.'

She wrote a long letter to Virginia on 6 June, and the entire first page

consists of embarrassed squirmings over the (shameful) fact of its success –
'it makes me quite uneasy to see that it has had quite portentously kind
reviews in England' – and breast-beatings about her shortcomings as an
artist. The nub of her embarrassment about *Pull Devil* (felt especially
pinkly, of course, in relation to Virginia) was that it seemed to her to be an
example of her 'lack of civilisation, which I called your attention to before':

> I am not, myself, civilised enough to be fastidious: I don't really know
> what's what. The only time I met Michael Arlen he said to me 'I must tell
> you right away that I am a cad; I should be kicked out of any club in
> London – and rightly so, for I am a born cad.' I said, 'Well, if you know it
> and don't enjoy it, why don't you stop being one?' He said 'I can't. All this
> time I have been writing cad's books for money, but now that I have got
> money, I thought I would begin to write books from my heart. But I find I
> have only a cad's heart to write from!'
>
> The poor lamb was, of course, a little binjed at the time, but I have often
> felt that, even sober, I ought to make a similar confession. I have the same
> sense of not knowing what's what. [11]

The kind reviews of *Pull Devil*, she decided, were a sign that 'by mistake' she
had reached a point in her writing career where she could get away with
what wasn't what with impunity: 'a point midway between being big
enough to be challenged, and being small enough to be snubbed'. [12]

And there was another worry. Now that he stood to reap a considerable
sum of money from the book, the old Count would be sure to be causing
trouble, and she called in a Hong Kong lawyer to deal with him, predictably
without success. Though her conscience was clear – he had had his full share
of the royalty – still, she told Vita in June, it was 'dreadfully trying to have
him starving all over the place – at one moment to hear that he is penniless
and threatened with imprisonment in Macao, and feel obliged to send
money there, and at the next moment hear from him (giving no definite
address) in Colombo, saying that he is starving there, and calling me a
loo-born svindler and a genuain kitsen-made for not answering his last
appeal'. [13]

From Cambridge word came that while the Fitzwilliam Museum declined,
the Syndics of the University Library welcomed the donation of her diaries;
and immediately she began 'guiltily' to wonder if they were worth it: 'it is a
trivial diary on the whole, I now think, and only honest – truly honest – in
patches (I am more honest under stress of great emotion, emergency makes
me free myself and defy my vanity – my indirect vanity is irrepressible in
small matters, e.g. I expect I show in my diary as a nicer person than I
am)'. Would it perhaps have been wiser to direct that a space not of fifty
but five hundred years pass before it was read? 'That would allow time

for triviality to mature,' she thought – but happily did not alter her instructions.

As the hot summer progressed, there were launch parties with swimming, as in Hong Kong. Ships called, they entertained the officers. Stella had no illusions about the figure she must cut in their eyes, 'a withered British matron'. Rather to her surprise, she made a friend of one of the missionaries: Marguerite Bradley's evangelistic fervour she could tolerate for the sake of her 'fresh and solid' charm, and her social ease and competence – few missionaries had her advantage, a rich Thames Valley background; when at the end of July she and Shaemas began a six-week tour of the Dutch East Indies, they took Marguerite with them.

As always, Stella's spirits rose to the excitement of new places and new people and – especially at Garoet in the mountains of Java – she felt almost well again. She went on excursions, made voluminous travel notes, swam in the hotel pool. While Shaemas and Marguerite played tennis, she got on with $\nabla\triangle$, and on the five-day return voyage to Hong Kong was busy typing it out. Probably what she was typing was her final draft of the chapters written so far, for as Shaemas explained in a preface when the unfinished novel was published in 1935, her procedure with this book was at variance with her custom in writing her later novels. Normally, he tells us, she would write a chapter and make a first revision of it, and do the same with each succeeding chapter. Not until the book was finished did she apply her final revision, and retype. In the case of *Mundos*, she made the final revision before the book was finished – and because she did so, at her death thirteen out of a projected seventeen or eighteen chapters were in a condition to be published. Shaemas offers no explanation for her change of method, but it seems likely that she did it because by the autumn of 1933 she had come to feel that her tenure of life was uncertain, more uncertain than it had ever been.

After the airy coolness of the Java mountains, the damp September heat of Pakhoi was hard to bear, and within a week she was feeling 'rather ill'. Their wedding anniversary came, and Shaemas forgot. He always did, but this time it set her to thinking how little generally she was valued in her life in China. It was different for Shaemas, for he had the satisfaction of knowing that he was doing well there; *her* vanity could be pleased, *her* confidence built up, only in England. Earlier she had written, 'my very presence here is a giving up of my own ego – a resigning of myself to be away from my natural place, my own friends, and the possibility of attending to my own job'; now she complained, 'sometimes I get a sort of doubt whether I have died – or am I still here? . . . I like imagining myself into other people, but can't life *wholly* without a me.'

As it happened, that very day there stepped ashore from a ship in the harbour someone full of enthusiasm for meeting her, not as any sickly Mrs

Anderson, but as Stella Benson the author. It was a young Frenchman named Teissier, and he had read and enjoyed *Tobit* in both the French and English versions. His work, for a shipping line, brought him regularly in their direction, and in less than a week he was with them again, impressing Stella as a great charmer, staying the night, and promising them luncheon aboard his ship when next he passed through.

Alas, when the day came it was too rough to take a boat out – or so they thought until M. Teissier appeared triumphantly on the doorstep, *aioli* in a dish in one hand, *bouillabaisse* in a basin in the other, a bottle of champagne in his bosom. To have her company sought by an intelligent, attractive young man was a thing that, at forty-one, and badly shaken in her confidence by the Bickerton affair, she could scarcely believe was happening:

> My first thought [more than half seriously, she told Laura] is that he is cynically pretending and watching to see if I am deceived; my second thought is, well, but men nowadays – especially Frenchmen – have all kinds of perversities and abnormalities! – loving corpses, tigresses and so on, they tell me, so even if his kindness is genuine it isn't so surprising . . . and then, my third thought is 'Golly! is it possible that someone can be feeling simply and normally friendly and glad to be with me?' This sounds exaggerated; but you don't know what China is. You don't know what it is to live exclusively among people whose faces freeze the instant you say something spontaneous or home-made.[14]

With Teissier she could talk openly. She told him what she thought of the colonial French (he was from Paris), and he was able to assure her that in metropolitan France there were quite a number of people who thought of things other than food, money and sex. But one has the impression that not even his word was enough, and that only a period of residence in France would convince her. And this was a distinct possibility. She was thinking of spending the early months of 1934 in Paris, and inviting her mother, who was not well, to come over and stay with her for some of the time. The house in Pembroke Villas was let to the end of April, and also there was a tax advantage to be gained by remaining out of England until the middle of that month; besides, she was under the (erroneous) impression that Paris in winter was warmer than London: 'I don't want to die of pneumonia in cold London,' she told Eileen.[15]

But for the more immediate future she and Shaemas had an inspection-trip-cum-jaunt to Tonkin planned. In fact they were packed and all ready to leave on 7 November, but rough weather prevented the sailing, and a fortnight passed before finally they got away. During the period of waiting

Stella felt particularly unwell – 'strangely tired and numb-brained', 'strangely flattened', 'terribly tired'. She could not get on with ▽△, 'though I have it all clear in my mind now. . . . You have to have vitality to *spare* to write – and just now I haven't even enough for my own everyday life.' On 18 November, when again their ship was expected and again did not appear, she felt so ill that she had strong doubts whether she should go. But two days later, with the vessel riding at anchor before her very eyes and Shaemas committed to going, the temptation was too strong: it would have been against her nature to have stayed behind.

As they drew out of Pakhoi 'a newish moon in a plum-coloured sky in the light of the sunset over pink China and pink fishing boats was almost "sugarily" picturesque'. It was her last sight of China.

Next morning Teissier met them on the wharf at Haiphong and drove them to Hanoi, where he had a flat, and where they foregathered with the Lapicques, friends from their Mengtsz days, *monsieur* a middle-aged man on fire with projects and plans – a kind of middle-aged Gallic George Benson. He drove them to his seaside retreat at Vachai, near Hongay, where he had some holiday bungalows under construction, one of which he assigned to Stella and Shaemas, one to Teissier.

But they were not to sleep there that night. Dinner over, the three of them, with M. Lapicque, boarded the Lapicque motor yacht, and after an hour and a half's chugging across the Baie d'Along ('the fantastic crooked pinnacle rocks of the bay rose up like lions round us. It *was* so lovely,' Stella told her mother, in what was to be her last letter to her),[16] they stopped at midnight beside a Chinese *junque*, which the Lapicques had fitted out as a holiday home. For Stella the whole experience was enchanting – midnight drinks, moonlight, the sea, what could be more magical? Even the WC was charming, she noted in her diary – 'an ordinary seat – but the hole looks straight down into luminous water – coral branches – little fishes'. Next day they swam, read, ate oysters pulled from the rocks. Teissier was at his most delightful, and 'anyone could imagine anything she wanted from his beautiful, amiable manners'. The weather was balmy – yet, most unusually for the time of year, coming back from a sail in the yacht it rained. They all got wet, and this may well be how the trouble for Stella began. In the afternoon they returned to Hongay, and Shaemas went away on his inspection trip.

An eruption of anti-Gallic feeling shook Stella that evening. She dined with Teissier and two middle-aged Frenchwomen, who talked exclusively of family life and food: 'My only remark was that there was no food whatever at Pakhoi, which shook both housewives profoundly: "On ne mange pas bien en Chine alors," they pleaded. "On ne mange pas de tout,"' she insisted naughtily (Teissier did what he could to save Pakhoi's gastronomic reputation by praising the Andersons' partridges). In the margin of her diary, apropos one of the said housewives, Stella wrote viciously, 'she had a hole between her thighs, however, and that is all that is required by the PRACTICAL French of women'. Later, alone in her bungalow, she was wishing – timidly, wistfully – that she were twenty years younger, and that it had occurred to Teissier to come along from his: 'I have had so little life in that way, that I think there's no harm in enjoying such pretence thoughts.'

Next day he drove her to Hanoi, and she put up at a hotel. They went shopping together, and she bought some lace. He tried on a mandarin coat, and she persuaded him to buy it because he was 'so overjoyed to see himself looking so lovely'. But she did not feel well, and by the time Teissier delivered her to her hotel she was almost at her last gasp. She went dinnerless to bed, and had 'a wretched night of pains and shivering and diarrhoea. A hurrying heart was almost more trying than the other trials. It bumped and hurried so.' During the two subsequent days she went out shopping, but felt unwell and was twice sick – 'What a waste of good French food!'

On 26 November Shaemas arrived. She explained how ill she had been, but refused to see a doctor, saying that she was nearly all right again. They had planned to return together to Pakhoi, but she was so much taken with the Lapicque *junque*, so keen to go there alone and work on $\nabla\triangle$, that it was decided that she would stay behind. She promised not to overdo it. On the afternoon of 28 November, Stella, Teissier and the Lapicques waved Shaemas goodbye at Haiphong. Stella stayed with the Lapicques for the rest of the day, and in the evening they drove to Vachai, the Lapicques talking volubly all the way about preparations that they were making to entertain the King of Annam to dinner on the *junque*. Stella was too ill and weary to pay attention: 'We got to Vachai at midnight. I fell exhausted into bed.' It was her last diary entry.

For what happened in the next few days, one turns to a letter that Stella wrote Shaemas from her hospital bed – her last letter – and to Shaemas's account in two letters that he addressed to Stephen in London, to be read out at his discretion to Mrs Benson. Evidently Stella went to the Lapicques' *junque* and spent a night there, but, falling ill on the second day, sent a message to the Lapicques and was brought back to Hongay, where she was taken straight to hospital. The doctor who examined her diagnosed pneumonia; since she had the use of only one lung he realised that her condition was grave, but he was not unduly pessimistic.

By this time she was in a high fever, and had lost her sense of time; thus her letter to Shaemas is dated 'January 3rd anyway Saturday', but was actually written either on Saturday 3 or Sunday 4 December. It is a little confused in dates, facts and spelling, but clear:

Dearest James,

You were quite right, I am sorry to say, I did become ill on my second day on the junk, the doctor says it is pneumonia but in fact it is exactly the same as last year at Hoiow – not quite as much pain but much more hemmorhage. I am hoping to get back in the next 'Tonkin' – though the Dr does not seem to think it very certain.

I shall be better soon, at present very wonky. A really first rate little hospital at Hancay, good attentive young doctor, I am very well installed, probably rather expensive. Lapiciques are being very kind. Don't be too much annoyed with me, I didn't even have time to do anything stupid on the *junque* – didn't swim or anything. I think I have been working up to this for some time.

Blessings on you. Don't worry, I will wire if I have anything to say, and in any case will wire when I know about the ship.

Blessings again
Stella.[17]

She wrote this letter and suddenly Shaemas was at her side. She supposed that the doctor or their friends had sent for him. He held her hand and they talked of plans. He had a plan: why not, before they returned to the pleasures and pressures of London, spend the first six months of their leave in Algeria, say, or some other place where it was dry and sunny? Somewhere where she could recapture the sense of well-being that she had experienced in Java? As he spoke, the happiness of it swept over her, and she murmured, 'Thank you, thank you a hundred thousand times.' That was on 5 December.

On the night of the same day, as Shaemas sat and they talked, she felt sure that she would live. 'I am not going to die this time,' she whispered. Only once was she uncertain. At two o'clock in the morning she murmured, 'If they can't do something for my heart, I don't know if I shall be able to hold out.' But the doubt passed, and towards four o'clock she said she could sleep, and urged Shaemas to leave her and get some sorely needed sleep himself. So Shaemas, assured by the doctor that no change was now likely before noon next day, lay down on a mattress just outside the door. When she died, Stella was alone with the Annamite nurse.

Later that morning Shaemas saw her placed in a very plain wooden coffin. Next day, 7 December, at seven o'clock in the morning, she was buried in the small French cemetery in the Île de Charbon, a little island near Hongay and close to the Baie d'Along. On the island there were no buildings, no human habitations, only a few trees to guard the buried bones.

Already Shaemas had telegraphed the news to George at Lutwyche. On 8 and 9 December he composed his mind to writing the two letters to Stephen, in which he gave a full, factual account of the events leading up to Stella's death, the immediate cause of which was heart failure. Above all else, the letters speak his desire that her family should know that all that could possibly have been done for her in her final illness had been done. Only towards the end of the second letter does he speak of himself:

> Of course I have hundreds of regrets. But by and large, I wasn't such a bad husband to her, though I didn't take enough care of her. . . . I feel now that I have had twelve years of undeserved luck, living with so magnanimous, gentle and noble a creature. Her courage has been wonderful. If she had been a man, she would have gone an enormously long way. Being a woman was a great handicap, but I believe that when – fifty years after this – her diary is published, she will become a great legend.
>
> I see that what I have just said reads pompously, when I am trying hard to be truthful and simple. But it is difficult to put on paper the secret pride I have always had in her, even when we were angry with each other (which was not, I think, often).[18]

On 10 December, the Sunday after her death, a memorial service for Stella was held in the little parish church of Lutwyche at Easthope. A large number of local Benson cousins attended (George told Shaemas in a letter), as well as some family friends and the tenants and workpeople, many of whom had known her since she was a child. 'The Rector gave a very good address,' George went on, 'which as a matter of fact I wrote for him, and the whole little country service was, I thought, very good and comforting.'[19]

On 15 December Stella's family and friends and a number of her fellow writers met for a much grander memorial service at St Mary Abbot's, Kensington, the church where twelve years ago she had been married, and where, as she came down the aisle on her husband's arm, Mrs Oneleg had stumped out of her pew to give her three white roses. Mrs Oneleg was there again, to pay her last tribute of love and gratitude.

It had been George who in the first instance insisted that a London service should be held, 'whatever our Stella might have thought about Church services',[20] but in the event he was rather disappointed. It was somehow almost too formal, and too many of the people had come, he felt, 'as in duty bound'. Somehow – and from some individuals – reverence escaped; Cuthbert Orde was observed, long before the congregation had risen from their knees, to be standing up, apparently taking notes on his shirt cuff of who was there.

Postscript

Stella's mother died of cancer in 1934. George died in 1961, having sold the Lutwyche Hall estate in 1952. Stephen married and had two sons; he continued as a lawyer on the Oxford Circuit, and he too died in 1961.

After Stella's death Shaemas remained at Pakhoi for another nine months, in great sadness and loneliness. On his next home leave he carried Stella's diaries to Cambridge and handed them over personally to the Librarian. At the end of Stella's manuscript he added a penned note, which reads as follows:

4 December 1934
1. She died on 6 December 1933 in hospital in the Baie d'Along, near Haiphong.
2. This was a *magnificent* woman.
3. Handing on these diaries is like burying her again. I can hardly bear it.
4. I have not changed one word in the diaries. It is possible that this will not be believed when the diaries are opened and read. But I think the diaries themselves confirm my statement.

At the end of his leave Shaemas remarried, and took his new wife back with him to China; they were to have two sons and a daughter. He died in 1946, of kidney disease, having spent most of the Second World War in the United States engaged in broadcasting British propaganda to the Far East.

Books by Stella Benson

1915   *I Pose* (Macmillan, London)

1917   *This is the End* (Macmillan, London)

1918   *Twenty* (Macmillan, London)

1919   *Living Alone* (Macmillan, London)

1922   *Kwan-Yin* (verse drama) (privately printed, San Francisco)

1922   *The Poor Man* (Macmillan, London). The text of *Kwan-Yin* is repeated here as Prologue.

1924   *Pipers and a Dancer* (Macmillan, London)

1925   *The Little World* (Macmillan, London)

1925   *The Awakening* (privately printed, San Francisco)

1926   *Goodbye, Stranger* (Macmillan, London)

1928   *Worlds Within Worlds* (Macmillan, London)

1928   *The Man Who Missed the Bus* (Elkin Mathews & Marrot, London)

1930   *The Far-Away Bride* (Harper, New York and London); republished 1931 as *Tobit Transplanted* (Macmillan, London)

1931   *Hope Against Hope and Other Stories* (Macmillan, London)

1932   *Christmas Formula and Other Stories* (Jackson, London)

1933   *Pull Devil–Pull Baker* (Macmillan, London)

Posthumous

1935   *Mundos* (Macmillan, London)

1935   *Poems* (Macmillan, London)

1936   *Collected Short Stories* (Macmillan, London)

Notes and Sources

The main source for this book was the Diary of Stella Benson in the University of Cambridge Library. To provide separate references for each of the many quotations from this source would add an air of pedantry to its pages and vastly extend the notes to little advantage. Virtually all the diary quotations can in fact be dated, if not by day then by month and year, from the context. Where quotation is made from letters interleaved with the diary, however, a reference is supplied, and the location given as University of Cambridge.

The Stella Benson Correspondence in the British Library was an important source. Accumulated by R. Ellis Roberts in the course of writing *Portrait of Stella Benson*, it comprises autograph letters of Stella Benson, mostly to himself and his wife Harriet, and to Winifred Holtby, and typed copies of her letters to a variety of other correspondents. The collection of Letters to Sydney Schiff, also at the British Library, includes twenty-seven autograph letters from Stella Benson. *Some Letters of Stella Benson 1928–1933*, edited by Cecil Clarabut (Hong Kong, 1978), contains letters, discovered by a happy chance at an English country-house sale, from Stella Benson and her husband James Anderson to Lady Eileen Orde. Georgina Berkeley, Stella's literary executor, owns letters from her to Florence Cholmondeley. References are given for all letters, whether published or unpublished, and for quotations from printed books.

The quotation which forms the epigraph of this book is taken from *The Diaries and Letters of Marie Belloc Lowndes*, ed. Susan Lowndes (Chatto & Windus, London, 1971), p. 126 (23 January 1934).

Preface

1. *The Diary of Virginia Woolf*, vol. iv, ed. Anne Olivier Bell (Hogarth Press, London, 1982), p. 192.
2. *The Letters of Virginia Woolf*, vol. iv, ed. Nigel Nicolson (Hogarth Press, London, 1978), p. 316 (20 April 1931).
3. W. H. Mellers, 'Fairies in Bloomsbohemia', *Scrutiny*, September 1939.

4. 'Neglected Fictions', *Times Literary Supplement*, 18 October 1985.
5. 'Reputations Revisited', *Times Literary Supplement*, 21 January 1977.
6. James Lees-Milne, *Prophesying Peace* (Chatto & Windus, London, 1977), p. vii.

Chapter One

1. Nikolaus Pevsner, *The Buildings of England: Shropshire* (Penguin Books, Harmondsworth, Middlesex, 1958), p. 190.
2. Mary Cholmondeley, *Under One Roof* (Macmillan, London, 1918), p. 112.
3. R. Ellis Roberts, *Portrait of Stella Benson* (Macmillan, London, 1939), p. 22.
4. Interleaved with Stella Benson's diary for 1911; no date.
5. Ibid.

Chapter Two

1. Lady Emily Lutyens, 1874–1964, wife of the architect Sir Edwin Lutyens, and daughter of Lord Lytton, a Viceroy of India. She was a leading light in the Theosophical Society.
2. The Guild of the Brave Poor Things was the charity that the Benson children supported by means of their *Holiday Magazine*. Founded in 1894, the Guild described itself as 'a band of men, women and children, of any creed or none, who are disabled for the battle of life, and at the same time determined to make a good fight'. Anyone who was physically disabled could join, and meet for 'craft lessons, amusements and music'.
3. John Fothergill, licensee extraordinary of the Spread Eagle inn at Thame in Oxfordshire, took the opportunity of Stella's visit to mark her height on the space eighteen inches square to which he delighted in manoeuvring such of his customers as were (in his words) 'distinguished for their altitude and, or, charm'. See his *An Innkeeper's Diary* (Chatto & Windus, London, 1931), p. 227.
4. Barrie & Rockliff, London, 1960.
5. *Twenty* (Macmillan, London, 1918).
6. E. B. White, *Essays* (Harper & Row, New York and London, 1977), p. 225.

Chapter Four

1. The Culebra Cut (in 1915 renamed the Gaillard Cut in honour of the American engineer who brought it to completion) was a nightmare, one of many, for the canal builders; driven through mountainous country, its progress was impeded by landslides.

Chapter Five

1. The Women Writers' Suffrage League, founded in 1908, besides publishing writings related to the cause, held public meetings, staged pageants and put on plays written by its members and acted by a sister body, the Actresses' Franchise League.
2. Philippa Jessie Benson, the younger of Stella's two paternal aunts and her god-mother; unmarried, she lived in London and engaged in voluntary social work.
3. On release from Holloway Prison, she was set down outside the House of Commons, where she proposed to continue her fast. Prime Minister Herbert Asquith consented to receive a deputation and told its members that he was in complete agreement with their aims. It was his first public acknowledgement of sympathy with the cause.
4. In the church of St Leonard, Shoreditch, can still be seen the drums and standard that later in 1914 accompanied to France the 20th (Shoreditch) Battalion, the Middlesex Regiment, a volunteer battalion of Kitchener's army; 'most of the men who went into action made the great sacrifice', the inscription reads.
5. The Charity Organisation Society, founded in 1869, survived the Second World War to become the Family Welfare Association.
6. A. S. Jasper, *A Hoxton Childhood* (Centerprise Publications, London, 1969), p. 73.
7. *Portrait of Stella Benson*, p. 42.
8. In the Ethical Church's handsomely produced service book, *Social Worship*, the 'substitute Creed' opens: 'Thou Law hid in our spirit, / That bidst us die to save others, / Unto Thee we commit ourselves! / In Thee is our liberty. / Like Thee, they who follow Thee. . . . Good men are blessed, they are true deity. / Goodness is God, the Good are God's sons.' Stella attended the church fairly regularly during 1915 and occasionally in 1916.

Chapter Six

1. Letter from Laura Hutton to R. Ellis Roberts, *Portrait of Stella Benson*, p. 344 (no date given).
2. May Sinclair, 1863–1946, novelist and journalist, was one of the first English writers to show the influence of Freud and Jung. *The Three Sisters* echoes the Brontë story; *Mary Olivier* (1919), partly autobiographical in content, is about a girl's escape from the damaging effects of a repressive upbringing. Until her books were reissued by Virago in the 1980s, May Sinclair was largely forgotten.
3. *The Three Sisters* (Virago Press, London, 1984), p. ix.
4. Letter from Laura Hutton to R. Ellis Roberts (see note 1).
5. *The Buildings of England: London*, vol. ii (1952), p. 387.
6. Quoted in *Portrait of Stella Benson*, pp. 35–7.
7. Letter from Laura Hutton to R. Ellis Roberts (see note 1).
8. University of Cambridge.

Chapter Seven

1. 'The Little Back Room', *Dial*, Chicago, October 1919.
2. Ibid.
3. Stella Benson Correspondence, 4 July 1916.
4. Harold Monro, 1879–1932, poet, publisher, bookseller. He published *Georgian Poetry*, edited by Edward Marsh. The Poetry Bookshop opened in 1913.
5. Thomas Sturge Moore, 1870–1944, poet and wood engraver. His verse, in the classical tradition and on classical themes, was unlikely to appeal to Stella.

Chapter Eight

1. 'Bags and Barrows', *Dial*, July 1919.

Chapter Nine

1. Gaby Deslys, 1884–1920, star of revue. The lavish gifts of jewels bestowed upon her by King Manuel II aroused popular indignation in Portugal, and were said to have contributed to the fall of the monarchy.
2. Stella Benson Correspondence, 14 February 1918 (wrongly dated 1915 in typed copy).
3. Ibid., 8 July 1918 (wrongly dated 18 July in typed copy).

Chapter Ten

1. The comment was repeated to Stella, to her mortification, by Ellis Roberts in June 1929.
2. Winston Churchill, 1871–1947. Most of his fiction is based on heroic episodes in US history, or deals with contemporary political issues, though his later works, which were far less successful, are on religious themes.
3. Ridgely Torrence, 1874–1950, poet and playwright; in 1917 his series of plays about blacks and played by blacks had been a 'turning point in Negro theatre history'.

Chapter Eleven

1. Stella Benson Correspondence, 25 February 1919. The initials are Stella's.
2. Ibid., 15 March 1919.
3. Ibid.
4. Ibid., 10 April 1919.
5. Ibid., 17 April 1919.

6. Harold Witter Bynner, 1881–1968, poet, playwright, critic and essayist. From 1922 he lived in Santa Fé, New Mexico, where he met and became friends with D. H. and Frieda Lawrence; *Journey with Genius* (1951) describes the relationship.
7. Stella Benson Correspondence, 31 January 1919.
8. In the possession of Riou Benson, 27 August 1919.
9. Katherine Mansfield, *Novels and Novelists*, ed. J. Middleton Murry (Constable, London, 1930), p. 107.
10. Stella Benson Correspondence, 26 August 1919.
11. The 1919 ban on alcohol put into effect wartime legislation of 1918; not to be confused with the 'Volstead Act' (the Eighteenth Amendment to the Constitution), which followed in 1920 and remained in force until 1933.

Chapter Twelve

1. Stella Benson Correspondence, to Doris Estcourt, 26 December 1919.
2. Ibid., 1 February 1920.
3. Ibid., 4 March [1920].
4. Ibid., to Doris Estcourt, 2 May 1920.
5. Ibid.
6. Ibid., to Laura Hutton, 17 May 1920.
7. In the possession of Georgina Berkeley, 18 June 1920.
8. Ibid.
9. Ibid.
10. The standard work on the subject is Stanley F. Wright, *Hart and the Chinese Customs* (Mullen, Belfast, 1950).
11. Quoted in *Portrait of Stella Benson*, p. 364 (25 October 1920).
12. University of Cambridge, 1 November 1920.
13. Ibid., 8 December 1920.
14. Ibid., 16 December 1920.
15. Ibid.
16. Ibid., 30 November 1920.
17. Ibid., 5 January 1921.

Chapter Fourteen

1. University of Cambridge, 13 July 1921.
2. Ibid., 22 July 1921.
3. Ibid., 29 July 1921.
4. Ibid., 9 August 1921.
5. Ibid., August 1921.
6. Ibid., 21 September 1921.
7. Ibid., 12 September 1921.

Chapter Fifteen

1. 'The States Again – I', *The Little World*, pp. 128–9.
2. Ibid., p. 150.
3. Denton Welch, 1915–48, trained as an artist but, as a result of a road accident when he was twenty-one, turned to writing, and during the 1940s (thanks to some extent to the help of Edith Sitwell) enjoyed considerable success with his autobiographical novels *Maiden Voyage* and *In Youth is Pleasure*; his *Voice from a Cloud* was posthumously published, as were his journals.

Chapter Sixteen

1. Stella Benson Correspondence, 11 November [1924].
2. Letters to Sydney Schiff, 12 March 1925.
3. In the possession of Georgina Berkeley, 7 November [1933].
4. Letters to Sydney Schiff, 12 March 1925.
5. University of Cambridge, 3 September 1923.
6. *Portrait of Stella Benson*, pp. 116–17.
7. Stella Benson Correspondence, to Laura Hutton, 9 January 1924.
8. Ibid., 19 February [1925].
9. With one stated exception, all Stella's comments on the Indo-China trip are from her *Star* articles, as reprinted in *The Little World*.
10. In the possession of Georgina Berkeley, 27 December 1923.
11. Doris Estcourt, 'Stella Benson', *The Bookman*, May 1932.
12. Stella Benson Correspondence, to Naomi Mitchison, 26 November 1924.
13. Letters to Sydney Schiff, 15 December 1924.
14. Ibid.
15. Ibid., 2 March 1925.
16. In the possession of Georgina Berkeley, 26 May 1924.

Chapter Seventeen

1. Letters to Sydney Schiff, 15 December 1924.
2. Naomi Mitchison, *You May Well Ask* (Gollancz, London, 1979), p. 127.
3. Stella Benson Correspondence, 26 November 1924.
4. Dominick and Margery Spring Rice. Dominick, 1888–1952, was a journalist, economist and company director.
5. Naomi Mitchison, 'Stella Benson', *The Laburnum Branch* (Cape, London, 1926), p. 27.
6. Original in the possession of Naomi Mitchison; not previously published.
7. Winifred Holtby, *Letters to a Friend*, ed. Alice Holtby and Jean McWilliam (Collins, London, 1937), p. 345. To Jean McWilliam (as are all the letters), 17 June [1925].
8. Ibid., p. 366 (1 September 1925).

9. Vera Brittain, *Testament of Friendship* (Macmillan, London, 1940), p. 146.
10. Stella Benson Correspondence, 10 August 1924.
11. Herbert Giles, 1845–1935, author of monumental works of scholarship; he had been Professor of Chinese at Cambridge since 1897, and was to retire in 1932 aged eighty-seven.
12. 'Good-bye, Manchuria', *Worlds Within Worlds*, p. 249.
13. Quoted in *Portrait of Stella Benson*, p. 165 (no date given).
14. 'Russian Christmas', *Worlds Within Worlds*, pp. 120–1.
15. 'The Barber's Wife', *Worlds Within Worlds*, p. 190.
16. In the possession of Georgina Berkeley, 30 August [1926].
17. Ibid.
18. Ibid.

Chapter Eighteen

1. University of Cambridge, 10 December 1929.
2. 'Storm in a Manchurian Teacup', *Nation and Athenaeum*, 27 August 1927.
3. 'Good-bye, Manchuria', *Worlds Within Worlds*, pp. 248–9.

Chapter Nineteen

1. William Gerhardi, 1895–1977, novelist. Of English parentage, he was born and educated in St Petersburg. During the First World War he served in the British embassy in Petrograd and with the British military mission in Siberia. His *Futility* (1920), published with assistance from Katherine Mansfield, dealt with contemporary Russia, as did *The Polyglots* (1925). His name was spelt 'Gerhardie' for the first time on the revised collected edition of his works in the early 1970s.
2. Rose Macaulay, 1881–1958, novelist, travel writer and critic. Her career as novelist opened in 1920 with *Potterism*, an amusing satire on vulgarity and humbug.
3. Storm Jameson, *b.* 1891, prolific Yorkshire novelist.
4. Captain Cuthbert 'Turps' Orde, 1888–1968, served in the Royal Flying Corps during the First World War. As artist, he is perhaps best remembered for a series of 150 portrait drawings, commissioned by the Air Council, of Battle of Britain pilots. Some of them hang in the officers' mess of RAF Biggin Hill; others are in the RAF museum at Hendon, north London.
5. Lance Sieveking, 1896–1972, author, playwright and BBC producer, especially associated with his work for radio drama.
6. Stuart Hibberd, 1893–1983, employed in the BBC from 1924–51. For some years he was Chief Announcer.
7. Francis Howard Bickerton, 1889–1954. After the First World War he was involved in exploration in Africa and North America; on his death he left a widow and a small daughter.

8. *The Letters of Virginia Woolf*, vol. iii, p. 489 (29 April [1928]).

9. *Siegfried Sassoon Diaries, 1920–22*, ed. Rupert Hart-Davis (Faber & Faber, London, 1985), p. 131.

10. Stella Benson Correspondence, Stella Benson to Winifred Holtby, 2 July [1928].

11. *Letters to a Friend*, p. 454 (21 June 1928).

Chapter Twenty

1. C. R. W. Nevinson, 1889–1946, during the First World War was among the painters nominated as official war artists and was the first of them to go to France.

2. *Some Letters of Stella Benson 1928–1933*, ed. Cecil Clarabut (Libra Press, Hong Kong, 1978), p. 4 (29 November [1928]).

3. *Recollections of Virginia Woolf*, ed. Joan Russell Noble (Peter Owen, London, 1972), p. 124.

4. *Some Letters of Stella Benson*, p. 5 (no date, but written on 29 December).

5. *Portrait of Stella Benson*, p. 201.

6. Ibid., p. 210.

7. W. B. D. Henderson, *The New Argonautica* (Cape, London, 1928).

8. 'Unsatisfactory Conversation on Soft-Boiled Eggs', *Worlds Within Worlds*.

9. Quoted in *Portrait of Stella Benson*, p. 215 (date given as 'August').

Chapter Twenty-One

1. *Some Letters of Stella Benson*, pp. 57–8 (14 July 1929).

2. Stella Benson Correspondence, no date.

3. *Some Letters of Stella Benson*, p. 18 (10 March 1930).

4. Stella Benson Correspondence, 24 March 1930.

5. Ibid., 21 April 1930.

6. Somerset Maugham, *The Painted Veil* (Heinemann, London, 1925), pp. 18–19.

7. *Some Letters of Stella Benson*, p. 68 (22 June 1930).

8. Ibid., p. 69 (17 July 1930).

9. Stella Benson Correspondence, 27 August 1930.

10. Ibid.

11. A. E. Housman, *Complete Poems* (Jonathan Cape, London, 1960), p. 47.

12. 'Reflections in a Mirror', *New Statesman and Nation*, 13 June 1931.

13. *Some Letters of Stella Benson*, p. 30 (25 September 1931).

14. Stella Benson Correspondence, to Winifred Holtby, 26 December 1931.

15. *Some Letters of Stella Benson*, p. 71 (1 February 1931).

16. Ibid., p. 70 (6 December 1930).

17. Ibid., p. 70.

18. Ibid., p. 30 (25 September [1931]).

19. In the possession of Nigel Nicolson, 28 June 1933.
20. Stella Benson, *Pull Devil—Pull Baker*, pp. 9–10.
21. Ibid., p. 15.
22. 'The Old Prince', *English Review*, April 1933.

Chapter Twenty-Two

1. Stella Benson Correspondence, 27 June 1931.
2. Quoted in *Portrait of Stella Benson*, p. 272.
3. Ibid.
4. For this definition – and in my discussion of *Mundos* – I am indebted to Hugh I'Anson Fausset's review, which appeared in the *London Mercury*, May 1935.
5. Phyllis Bottome, *Stella Benson* (essay) (privately printed, San Francisco, 1934), p. 3.

Chapter Twenty-Three

1. *Some Letters of Stella Benson*, pp. 80–1 (no date).
2. In 1932 Kate O'Brien carried off the two most prestigious literary prizes of the day – the Hawthornden and the James Tait Black Memorial – with *Without My Cloak*, but she was not in London that summer to steal any of Stella's thunder.
3. The PEN Club, founded in 1921 by Amy Dawson Scott, encouraged friendship and co-operation between writers (Poets, Essayists, Novelists) of different nations.
4. G. B. Stern, 1890–1973, prolific popular novelist.
5. Amabel Williams-Ellis, 1895–1984, novelist, biographer, writer of children's books. A cousin of Lytton Strachey, she was married to the architect Clough Williams-Ellis.
6. Phyllis Bottome, *Stella Benson*, p. 7.
7. Ibid, p. 12.
8. Nancy Pearn was a literary agent, at this time with Curtis Brown.
9. Since 1925 Stella had been an occasional contributor to *Time and Tide*, the periodical founded in 1920 by Lady Rhondda to foster pacifist and feminist ideals, and of which from 1926 Winifred Holtby was a director. During the summer of 1932 Stella contributed to the series 'Notes on the Way'.
10. *The Diary of Virginia Woolf*, vol. iv, p. 117 (16 July 1932).
11. Ibid., p. 192.
12. University of Cambridge, 14 August 1932.
13. Berg Collection, New York Public Library, 1 September 1932.
14. Ibid.
15. University of Cambridge, 12 January 1933.
16. *Portrait of Stella Benson*, pp. 283–4.

Chapter Twenty-Four

1. *Some Letters of Stella Benson*, p. 37 (28 August 1932).
2. *Radio Times*, 6 May 1932.
3. Ibid., 3 June 1932.
4. *Some Letters of Stella Benson*, p. 38 (22 November [1932]).
5. Ibid., p. 39.
6. Berg Collection.
7. Ibid.
8. Ibid.
9. Ibid.
10. *Some Letters of Stella Benson*, p. 41 (12 February [1933]).
11. Berg Collection.
12. Ibid.
13. In the possession of Nigel Nicolson, 28 June 1933.
14. Quoted in *Portrait of Stella Benson*, p. 297 (no date).
15. *Some Letters of Stella Benson*, p. 45 (19 October [1933]).
16. Quoted in full in *Portrait of Stella Benson*, p. 414 (no date, but posted 27 November 1933).
17. Ibid., pp. 299–300.
18. In the possession of Riou Benson, 9 December 1933.
19. Ibid., 6 January 1934.
20. Ibid.

Index